D1621970

Some Potentialities of

EXPERIMENTAL JURISPRUDENCE

as a New Branch of Social Science

FREDERICK K. BEUTEL

☆

UNIVERSITY OF NEBRASKA PRESS * LINCOLN

To

two Chancellors and The Board of Regents
of the University of Nebraska.
Without their action this book might
never have been written.

PREFACE

It is customary in writing a book on jurisprudence or social science to review the works of all the learned authors on the subject, giving the writer's criticism of each. At the end of the review there may be added a paragraph or chapter setting out his own theories. Thus the author is enabled to show his erudition and the relation of his ideas to the world of learning on the subject.

In that sense Part I of this book is only a last chapter or paragraph in such a treatise, supplemented in Part II by a laboratory demonstration of the theory. Insofar as the writings of Bentham, James, Dewey, Jhering, Pound, Lundberg and many others may have furnished an inspiration for this short summary, one will have to assume that the masters have been read and to some extent understood. To the degree that it may be desirable to place the theories advanced here in a context of the current literature of law, jurisprudence or social science, the reader is left to his own devices. Materials which have been cited in the footnotes are not offered either as conclusive proof of the arguments set forth in the text or as evidences of exhaustive research, which is, of course, impossible in a subject as broad as this. While the writings cited may offer some corroboration, they are set out largely as hints for those who may desire to pursue the subject further.

The laboratory demonstration offered in Part II is, of course, meager and incomplete, but it tends to show the complicated nature of the subject matter. The suggested procedures of Experimental Jurisprudence must be recognized merely as brief and tentative hypotheses subject to broader development and radical change. As the impact of their adoption in practice upon government, law, education and current theories of science becomes better understood, the ultimate outlines of methods and aims of social science will, of course, undergo sweeping revision. This, then, must be taken for what it really is, just a primitive beginning.

I am deeply indebted to many persons for direct aid and suggestions: to Alexander Goldfarb of the Connecticut Bar and Herbert Hochberg, my assistants during the formative years of this work; to Professor John E. Behnke, Jr., who did the bulk of the interviewing of businessmen, the results of which appear in the Bad-Check Study; to Margaret A. Cooper, the statistician who compiled the tables and graphs therein; and to Dr. Ira Cohen, who aided in the formulation of the jural laws and helped see the manuscript through the press. There were also numerous students, now members of the Bar, from whose work and reports I have quoted liberally, many others of my classes in jurisprudence too numerous to name, members of the state police and peace officers who have taken an essential part in the research and experiments which have furnished the information or basic material for some of the following chapters. Then a word of thanks should also be said to the judges, county attorneys, bankers and businessmen who gave so liberally of their time to make available the basic information on bad checks which forms the illustrative portion of this text.

Experimental Jurisprudence is indeed a cooperative venture wherein all must share.

FREDERICK K. BEUTEL

CONTENTS

PART I

THE THEORY AND SOME OF ITS PRESENT APPLICATIONS

PART II

ILLUSTRATIONS OF EXPERIMENTAL METHODS AS APPLIED TO NEW LEGAL PROBLEMS

TABLES

PART I

PART II

xiii

FIGURES

PART I

PART II

PART I

The Theory and Some of Its Present Applications

CHAPTER I

Can the Scientific Method Be Used in Jurisprudence?*

THE LAG IN SOCIAL SCIENCE AND GOVERNMENT

For some time there has been a realization among philosophers and others interested in the course of social development that social science and government were failing to inspire practical social changes comparable to those made in the application of physical sciences and engineering. Although the last century alone has witnessed phenomenal technical and scientific progress on the material side, the general science and art of lawmaking, law enforcement and government seems to have developed practically nothing new since the days of the Roman Empire. In fact, so striking has been the failure of the philosophy of social control and the machinery of government to keep pace with the revolutionary developments of physical science that the resulting mental, political and social maladjustments have persuaded at least one leading sociologist to classify the present age as that of the decay of modern culture.[1]

This failure of man to govern himself as adequately as he has been able to achieve control over nature was dramatically illustrated at Hiroshima and Nagasaki where highly advanced mastery over nature was graphically displayed against anarchy in human relations. Since that time even the physical scientists, who have long proclaimed their neutrality in matters of law and government, have begun to fear lest they have placed God-like destructive powers in the hands of a political animal who, due to his absence of control over the passions and frictions of the society in which he lives, might be so stupid as to destroy not only that society but even humanity itself.[2]

In the light of this obvious disproportion between man's power over himself and over the elements about him, it might be wise to

---

* Reprinted in part by permission from 51 Columbia Law Review.
[1] Sorokin, The Crisis of Our Age (1946).
[2] Waddington, The Scientific Attitude (Penguin ed. 1941).

direct attention to the question of whether or not the techniques and knowledge so successfully developed in the physical sciences could be transferred into the field of social control; or, putting it another way, whether or not jurisprudence and the political and social sciences could be placed on a footing and subjected to methods of study and control similar to those which prevail in physical, biological and medical sciences. If this transition could be made, what would be the nature of the science thus developed, the techniques employed and the changes that might be expected in the theory and practice of government under law?

THE NATURE OF SCIENTIFIC METHODS AND DISCOVERIES

Before attempting an answer to these questions, it might be worth while to re-examine briefly the nature of the scientific method which has produced such spectacular results in other fields.

Concisely speaking, the scientific method, as perhaps distinguished from the many other senses in which the term "science" is used, is one of the means of satisfying human curiosity and attempting to explain various sensations that come to the human brain. Water seems to run downhill, fire to burn wood, and stones apparently can be collected and counted. These and others of our numerous sensations can be better understood if classified and explained. It should be quite clear, however, that the scientific method affords only one of many explanations which curious human beings have attempted to offer for their various feelings and sensations. There are others such as religion or mysticism,[3] but the scientific method is the one tool which has produced, in addition to an explanation, astounding progress in obtaining control over physical nature.

This method has been characterized as consisting of varying numbers of steps, depending upon the particular person using it, but for convenience it might be said to contain the following series of activities:[4]

1. Observation, and identification of the sensations.

2. An attempt to explain the activity apparent in the sensations. Such an explanation is commonly called a hypothesis.

3. Further observations to check the accuracy of the hypothesis; in attempting these observations, scientists have invented many mechan-

---

[3] Huxley, A., The Perennial Philosophy (1945); Huxley, A., Science, Liberty and Peace (1946); Maritain, Christianity and Democracy (1944).

[4] See Otto, Science and the Moral Life 155 (Mentor ed. 1949); Davis, The Reasonableness of Science in Readings in the Physical Sciences 18 (Shapley, Wright & Rapport ed. 1948).

ical means to increase the accuracy and the penetration of sensory perception, for example, the telescope, the microscope, the camera, the X-ray, and myriad other gadgets and processes, all of which permit observation and checking to an extent far beyond that of the unassisted human senses.

4. When a series of observations offers a vertification or check of the hypothesis, it is taken to be a statement of tentative scientific fact.

5. This statement is then enlarged to include other phenomena similar to the one tested, and if it works there, we sometimes speak of the explanation as a scientific law.

6. Usually when the hypothesis is so extended it soon encounters a situation which it no longer explains. The hypothesis is then remodeled in an attempt to explain this new phenomenon, and the process of observation, checking and verification is again repeated.

In this manner science has developed thousands of working hypotheses which have been sufficiently accurate in their explanation of the reactions of the thing studied so that engineers, using these principles, have been able to devise instruments which have afforded a substantial degree of control over various aspects of nature. This added power has so increased our productive capacity, extended our areas of travel and thinking, and generally so changed the face of the world that civilized man today, using these hypotheses and the machinery which we have been able to invent because of them, has completely revolutionized his method of living.

In this entire process the role of the hypothesis and the attitude of the scientist toward the "knowledge" thereby stated have been the central features. For it should be noted that whenever a true scientist develops a new hypothesis he immediately throws it out in an entirely open-minded attitude to be checked by his fellow scientists. If the hypothesis can be verified by checking, it is adopted and enlarged. If it cannot, it is immediately discarded, and the scientist, working alone or with his fellows, attempts to develop another. Indeed, one might say that the progress of science has been marked by the wrecks of hypotheses; far more have been disproved than verified, and none has yet been created which will stand up against all tests and conditions.

Mathematics is often spoken of as the true experimental science in which verification is always possible; but an examination of the facts well known to all mathematicians will show that there are many mathematical systems which cannot be verified, and none which go very far in explaining the world about us. For example, it seems perfectly clear that one and one make two, and this can be verified easily with almost any objects which one cares to pick up. For instance, one glass of water and one glass of water make two glasses, but if an attempt is made to extend the rule to unlike things, it is equally clear that one glass of water and one glass of sugar put together do not fill two glasses. So also, one cubic yard of sand, one cubic yard of gravel and one cubic yard of cement when mixed do not make three cubic yards of concrete. The scientist will at once recognize that the law "one and one make two" when removed from the abstract is a mere hypothesis, and when he encounters these new obstacles, he invents the molecular theory, which is capable of explaining the phenomena of solutions and chemical combinations; but when he experiments further with chemistry, he soon must create a hypothesis which subdivides the molecule and creates the atom. More advanced chemical experiments reach the law of indestructibility of matter, which has proved very useful in engineering, chemistry and many other fields; but recently, due to the discovery of uranium and other radioactive elements, we have now found that the laws of conservation of energy and indestructibility of matter no longer afford a sufficient explanation of such phenomena as the atomic bomb and radioactivity. So new sets of hypotheses, all of which will have to be checked and verified, are now appearing on the scientific scene.[5]

In fact, so numerous have been the special hypotheses and laws developed in the field of sciences underlying medicine that one writer,[6] at least, is complaining that medicine is not a science at all but a conglomeration of many hypotheses wherein no fundamental truths are known.[7] The physicists and astronomers are also beginning to reach the conclusion that man cannot truly encounter the facts of matter; that he sees mere shadows of shadows[8] and derives nothing more from his scientific study than a tentative verification of the hypothetical reasoning which he has brought to bear upon it.[9] If the sole end of science were the discovery of ultimate truths, these con-

[5] For a detailed discussion of this process as it has been applied throughout the history of science, see Sullivan, Limitations of Science c. 3 (Mentor ed. 1949).

[6] Stevenson, Why Medicine Is Not A Science, 198 Harpers 24 (Apr. 1949).

[7] Conant, On Understanding Science (1947); Lewis, The Scientific Meaning of Chance in Readings in the Physical Sciences 381 (Shapley, Wright & Rapport ed. 1948).

[8] Bridgman, The Logic of Modern Physics 33 (1927); Planck, The Universe in the Light of Modern Physics 14, 40 (Johnston's transl. 1931). The psychologists concur. See the report of Dr. Pieron's address before the American Association for the Advancement of Science, 116 Literary Digest 19 (Jan. 1933).

[9] Oppenheimer, Physics in the Contemporary World, 50 Technology Rev. 201 (Feb. 1948).

6

clusions would be disturbing indeed, and man might as well give up his quest for knowledge; but although many scientists and teachers lay great emphasis upon the theoretical knowledge obtained by the scientific method, knowledge as such is not the really significant product.

The paramount value of the scientific method lies in the open-minded attitude it engenders, which makes possible an immediate discarding of obsolescent practices and the consequent creation of new and useful devices for the control of nature and satisfaction of human wants. The gadgets developed by engineers based upon these admittedly tentative hypotheses have become the instruments of a technical organization which, by any test of values the philosopher cares to ascribe to it, produces more of the tangible and intangible goods of life than any system the world has ever known. Even discredited or superseded scientific laws have left behind them means of solving practical problems. Thus Euclidean geometry is still useful for measuring floors, buildings and small land areas, but it falls down when it attempts to measure the universe. In similar fashion Newton's laws can be employed to explain many of the phenomena of the solar system, but only Einstein's theory of relativity explains other aspects of the universe.[10] Although our scientific laws have been merely tentative, the useful machinery and information that have come as by-products of these various theories and the engineering achievements constructed thereon have given us a new world.[11]

It should be noted in this respect that the sciences can be divided into two general classes, one descriptive and one experimental. Where the subject matter is beyond the power of interference by the observer to any material extent, the science is considered purely descriptive. Geology is such a science; likewise meteorology and astronomy. Here, despite lack of any control over the subject matter, the scientist is able to formulate hypotheses which will offer useful predictions upon which man can base many activities, such as navigation, flying, and the collection of vast amounts of useful data. The second type of science is characterized by the use of controlled experiments; the observer is able to test his hypotheses by removing certain elements from or adding them to the phenomena observed. Physics, chemistry, biology, medicine, agronomy and even psychology are a few of the many examples

---

[10] Sullivan, op. cit. supra note 5, at 59 et seq.

[11] Dewey, Philosophy's Future in Our Scientific Age, 8 Commentary 388 (Oct. 1949); Edman, Science and the Dream of Happiness in Readings in the Physical Sciences 56 (Shapley, Wright & Rapport ed. 1948).

of this type. The controlled experiment has greatly accelerated the processes of creating and verifying hypotheses, accumulating useful "knowledge," and developing machinery of production. Both of these types of science, however, offer fruitful sources of analogy for the student of jurisprudence and much information which indicates that many of their methods and techniques can be adopted in the field of social science.

THEORETICAL OBJECTIONS TO THE TRANSFER OF THE SCIENTIFIC METHOD FROM THE PHYSICAL TO THE SOCIAL SCIENCES

Ever since the infancy of physical science there have been suggestions that its methodology could be transferred to the field of social science. In fact Roger Bacon is credited with suggesting an experimental social science in the thirteenth century long before the elements of physical science had been devised.[12] These proposals have met with many and varied objections, which at one time were thought insuperable, but which, as the nature of science has become better understood, have gradually lost their potency. Indeed, there are many philosophers and scientists today who confidently assert that there is no longer any line separating physical and social science.[13]

[12] Thomas, Living Biographies of Great Scientists 20 (1941) quotes Roger Bacon as follows:

"I believe that humanity shall accept as an axiom for its conduct the principle for which I have laid down my life—the right to investigate. It is the credo of free men—this opportunity to try, this privilege to err, this courage to experiment anew. We scientists of the human spirit shall experiment, experiment, ever experiment. Through centuries of trial and error, through agonies of research . . . let us experiment with laws and customs, with money systems and governments, until we chart the one true course—until we find the majesty of our proper orbit as the planets above have found theirs."

[13] Chase, The Proper Study of Mankind (1948); Huxley, J., Man in the Modern World (Mentor ed. 1948); Lundberg, Can Science Save Us? (1947); Northrop, Physical Science and Human Values 98 (Wigner ed. 1947); Otto, op. cit. supra note 4, at 122-26 (Mentor ed. 1949); Robinson, The Humanizing of Knowledge (1924); Sullivan, op. cit. supra note 5; Leighton, Human Relations in a Changing World (1949); Chapin, Social Obstacles to the Acceptance of Existing Social Science Knowledge, 26 Social Forces 7-12 (Oct. 1947); Conant, The Role of Science in Our Unique Society, 107 Science 77 (Jan. 1948); Condon, Science and National Welfare, 107 Science 6 (Jan. 1948); Oppenheimer, op. cit. supra note 9; Sears, Integration at the Community Level, 37 American Scientist 235 (Apr. 1949); Stewart, Challenge to Social Science, 110 Science 179 (Aug. 1949); Stewart, Concerning Social Physics, 180 Scientific American 21 (May 1948); Stone, Science and Statecraft, 105 Science 509 (May 1947); Williams, Natural Science and Social Problems, 36 American Scientist 116 (Jan. 1948); Young, Limiting Factors in the Development of the Social Sciences, 92 Proceedings Am. Philo. Soc'y 325 (1948).

The difference is considered one only of degree and not of kind. The objection that man's mind is separate from nature and exists in a different universe from that of physical phenomena and animals[14] is no longer taken too seriously. Most advanced thinkers have now come to the conclusion that man in his most intricate aspects is as much a part of the universe as is an animal or a stone, and that his actions and reactions are as capable of study as are those of the objects that surround him.[15] The familiar assumption that man has free will, whereas other things in the universe act with mechanical uniformity, has been dissipated by the quantum theory[16] and by Heisenberg's Uncertainty Principle,[17] as they operate even in the field where physical science examines inanimate matter. The old argument that if man is subject to scientific laws he is reduced to a mere mechanical robot overlooks the new awareness of the vastly complicated nature of physical matter; while the corollary belief that sequences of cause and effect are much more certain in the physical than in the human area has been proved so illusory even in physics and chemistry that scientists in these fields, previously classified as "exact," often use examples of people's movements on the corner of Forty-second Street and Broadway to illustrate the gyrations of atoms, electrons and protons.[18] These hypotheses, in short, have thrown much doubt on the general theory that the forces of social science are so much more complex and various than are those of physical science that we can never hope to master or arrange them in ordered explanations.

It has also been seriously advocated by some that man cannot ob-

[14] Otto, op. cit. supra note 4, passim; Sullivan, op. cit. supra note 5, at 100; cf. Harlow & Harlow, Learning to Think, 181 Scientific American 36 (Aug. 1949).

[15] Beadle, The Genes of Men and Molds, 180 Scientific American 30 (Sept. 1948); Conklin & Groff, Cancer and Environment, 181 Scientific American 11 (Jan. 1949); Jacobs, The Application of Sociometry to Industry, 8 Sociometry 181 (1945); Mills, Temperature Dominance Over Human Life, 110 Science 267 (Aug. 1949); Ruderfer & Martin, The Concept of Action as a Measure of Living Phenomena, 110 Science 245 (Sept. 1949); Reusch & Bateson, Structure and Process in Social Relations, 12 Psychiatry 105 (May 1949); Sears, Integration at the Community Level, 37 American Scientist 235 (Apr. 1949); Stern, Selection and Eugenics, 110 Science 201 (Aug. 1949); Stouffer, A Study of Attitudes, 181 Scientific American 11 (May 1949).

[16] Planck, A Survey of Physics 159 (Jones & Williams transl. 1925). For the use of the quantum theory in biology, see Schrodinger, What Is Life? c. 14 (1945).

[17] Jeans, Exploring the Atom in Readings in the Physical Sciences 337 (Shapley, Wright & Rapport ed. 1948); see also Sullivan, op. cit. supra note 5, at 72.

[18] Lewis, op. cit. supra note 7, at 383; cf. Eddington, The Philosophy of Physical Science (1939); Einstein & Infield, The Evolution of Physics 299 ff. (1938).

serve himself,[19] presumably on the ground that his own prejudices toward human activities will prevent him from obtaining an accurate perspective of his own reactions. The anthropologists, psychologists and psychiatrists, however, have amply demonstrated that some men can observe and classify the actions of other men and that if they will be open-minded about it, they can create plenty of useful hypotheses about these actions. On the other hand, this subjective relationship of man to himself may be a great advantage in that it opens up the possibility of viewing human reactions both from within and without. One need only consider the rapid advances now being made in organic chemistry and biological science by the use of radioactive particles to trace the movement of atoms through organisms to see an example of the great latent advantages which the social scientist has over his brothers in the physical sciences.

The ancient contention between the materialists and idealists as to whether or not man operates mechanically as do machines and other physical matter appears rather pointless in the light of modern surgery, which can induce dreams, sensory impressions and memories in the human brain by means of electric currents.[20] Moreover, there now exist calculating machines which can perform certain functions beyond the powers of any human brain[21] and, indeed, which offer perhaps as good an explanation of the thinking process itself as has yet been devised.[22] Even the ancient mechanistic explanation of physical matter has taken a pretty bad beating under the influence of relativity and Heisenberg's Uncertainty Principle. If all of this is hard on the human ego, which insists that man is different from matter and that social science is concerned only with ultimate values and fundamental immutable truths, it still should not keep scientists from attempting to find some working hypotheses which will help explain the reaction of man to man and of men to laws and controls put upon them by other men or which they themselves have devised.

The specter of impracticability has also been raised by those who object to the transfer of the scientific method to the field of juris-

---

[19] Huxley, J., op. cit. supra note 13, at 115. Contra: Otto, op. cit. supra note 4, at 153 et seq.

[20] Gray, The Great Ravelled Knot, 180 Scientific American 27 (Oct. 1948); Silverman, Now They're Exploring the Brain, Sat. Eve. Post 26 (Oct. 8, 1948).

[21] Machines Without Men, 34 Fortune 165 (Nov. 1946); A Key to the Automatic Factory, 39 Fortune 139 (Nov. 1949); Ashby, The Electronic Brain, Radio Science 77 (Mar. 1949); Ridenour, The Roll of the Computer, 187 Sci. American 116, 130 (Sept. 1952).

[22] Wiener, Cybernetics 32, cc. 5, 7 (1948).

prudence. To be sure, problems of observation, recording of data, and control of experiments are far more complicated but hardly insurmountable. We are told, however, that the methods of experimental science cannot be applied to jurisprudence,[23] that human actions are beyond observation, control, and predictability,[24] that the science of law must depend upon rationalization,[25] ethics,[26] politics,[27] sociology,[28] psychology, religion, the judicial hunch,[29] the traditions of a trained bar[30] and the like. It is submitted that these and similar discouraging statements are mere excuses given for the jurists' failure to come to grips with the real problems of legal science.

One of the tragedies of modern government lies in the fact that its so-called "social leaders" and lawyers are still relying upon ancient theories, institutions and dogmas about the nature of man fomented by clerics and philosophers in that simple state of society just antedating the emergence of the scientific method. Among the great sources of the art of social control and law still influential in the field today are the Bible, Aristotle, Plato, Adam Smith, Rousseau, Kant, Hegel, Montesquieu, Bentham, Blackstone and Marx. At the time when these and other "great books" in law, government and philosophy were being written, infant science was barely tolerated as an associate in "learning" with the humanities on the ground that it was quasi-respectable and on the condition that it should stay in its own field. Galileo escaped excommunication only by agreeing to recant and keep

[23] See Lauterpacht, Kelsen's Pure Science of Law in Modern Theories of Law 105 (1933); Pound, Law and the Science of Law in Recent Theories, 43 Yale L.J. 525, 532 (1934).

[24] Beard, Method in the Study of Political Science as an Aspect of Social Science in Essays on Research in the Social Science 51, 59 (1931); Oliphant, Facts, Opinions, and Value-Judgments, 10 Tex. L. Rev. 127 (1932); Spengler, Social Science Becomes Exact, 20 Am. Mercury 202 (June 1930).

[25] Cf. Yntema, The Rational Basis of Legal Science, 31 Columbia L. Rev. 925 (1931).

[26] Cf. Cohen, F., The Ethical Basis of Legal Criticism, 41 Yale L.J. 201 (1931); Cohen, M., Philosophy and Legal Science, 32 Columbia L. Rev. 1103 (1932).

[27] Hutchins, The Autobiography of an Ex-Law Student, 7 Am. L. School Rev. 1051, 1055 (1934).

[28] See Angell, The Value of Sociology to Law, 31 Mich. L. Rev. 512 (1933); cf. Greenwood, Experimental Sociology (1945).

[29] Hutcheson, Lawyer's Law and the Little, Small Dice, 7 Tulane L. Rev. 1 (1932); Hutcheson, The Judgment Intuitive: The Functions of the "Hunch" in Judicial Decision, 14 Corn. L. Q. 274 (1929).

[30] Harno, Theory, Experience, Experimentation and the Logical Method, 17 A.B.A.J. 659, 663 (1931).

still.[31] Luckily, neither he nor his successors kept the promise but rather proceeded by means of the scientific method so to revolutionize the world that today it can be asserted that "the future of our civilization depends upon the widening spread and deepening hold of the scientific habit of mind."[32]

The foregoing remarks strongly suggest the need to re-examine the basic postulates of social control in general and of the legal system in particular in the light of what science in all its aspects has to offer. Medieval conceptions should no longer be allowed to govern those who live in a modern scientific era. Jurisprudential science ought to be developed at least along the lines of a descriptive science and, as will be shown later, it contains distinct potentialities of enlargement into a complete experimental science.

The possibility of constructing a descriptive social science of the forces governing man's reaction to men and nature is already highly developed in certain portions of anthropology, social psychology, paleontology and perhaps in history. Here the problem of recording the actions of humans, plotting their course and predicting future events is little more complicated than observing the cosmos or predicting the wind, the weather and the tides. There are hardly more factors involved in forecasting the state of the tides, winds and waves for the landing at Okinawa than there are in determining the conditions of the morale of the Japanese people in relation to surrender. Both of these feats were accomplished during World War II.[33] In like manner there seems to be no reason why the reactions of a city, county or nation to the enactment and enforcement of a particular kind of law are not within the reach of a descriptive social science, jurisprudence.[34]

Experimental science, differing slightly from its descriptive brother, usually fares better under controlled conditions. The experiment under rigidly regulated environment is said to produce the fastest and most accurate results. Detractors of social science love to point out that such controls are impossible when man is studying man. These criticisms wholly overlook the fact that law is one of the chief means of social control and if its manipulators so desire, can be used as an

---

[31] Cohen, I.B., Galileo, 181 Scientific American 40 et seq. (Aug. 1949).
[32] Dewey, quoted in Readings in the Physical Sciences 10 (Shapley, Wright & Rapport ed. 1948).
[33] See Zacharias, Secret Missions 334 (1946); id. Behind Closed Doors 56-57 (1950).
[34] See for example, Esslinger, Politics and Science (1955); Lundberg, Social Research (1929).

intelligent means of varying the factors in a given social situation. But law is not the only control available to man. Propaganda, education, social pressure, brute force and many others may be immediately identified. It should be noted, however, that almost all of these may be made subsidiaries to legal sanctions and, to a certain extent, may be brought within the power of law for manipulative purposes. The totalitarian legal organization is a reality. It is capable of direction for good as well as for evil. The use of laws, therefore, as a means of control of experiments in social science is further developed than a mere dream.

It would appear then that scientific method as described above might be applicable to many of the facets of our social life.

A FEW OF THE OBSTACLES AND AIDS TO THE CREATION OF AN EXPERIMENTAL SOCIAL SCIENCE

The possibility of using law as a control in developing both a descriptive and an experimental science, though conceivable, is subject to many obvious objections. Practically, though descriptive social science has long been a reality, there are now many apparently insuperable obstacles to the development of such an experimental science. Among these are the difficulties of creating a technical theory for such an experimental science dealing with observation and control of the actions of men. Then there is the further obstacle of the effect on social experiments of preconceived notions of individual and social values, morals and group habits. Any such science also would meet opposition in entrenched systems of law, government, education, legal methods and procedures, and the general habits and mental behavior of the public at large.

On the other hand there already exists in some areas, especially where the subject matter is within the field of a highly developed physical science, a technique of experimental lawmaking where the results are within the reach of already highly developed experimental methods within a narrow factual range. In these few limited fields we are already entering an era of experimental social engineering.

A complete discussion of the obstacles and a cataloging of the favorable developments in the areas within the all-inclusive ken of social science is of course impossible; but an attempt will be made in Part I to observe and comment upon some of the theoretical difficulties and the practical developments on the road to an experimental social science. There will also be an attempt to raise the subject of and comment briefly upon the effect of such a science, if it were developed, upon research and governmental organization. In so doing it will be possible to discuss a few sample types of problems which, as far as is now foreseeable, may be expected to arise. A detailed discussion of the impact of each of these fields upon a possible experimental branch of social science must await further developments.

CHAPTER II

The Nature of Experimental Jurisprudence[1]

It was pointed out in Chapter I that, keeping in mind the fact that it is one of the chief but not the only method of social control, law conceivably may be used as a factor in developing a new branch of social science. While the writer is fully conscious of both the theoretical and practical difficulties of creating and practicing such a science, it may be worth while to examine the theoretical structure which it might take. In the material which follows, such a scientific method and its possible application to social phenomena, for convenience, will be called Experimental Jurisprudence. Without further discussion, then, of the possibilities of erecting such a science, but on the hypothesis that it is possible, it will be useful at this point to turn to a direct examination of the first difficulty in such an undertaking, the theoretical means and techniques by which such a science can be created, and the manner in which it might be used in the field of jurisprudence.

LAW AND THE "JURAL LAW"

Before setting out an outline of Experimental Jurisprudence or a science of law based on adherence to the scientific method, it might be well to clarify the term "law." As used in its many senses in the various media of discourse, law is a very ambiguous word indeed. Even in jurisprudence itself it has changing meanings. For the sake of precision, therefore, the meanings of the term should be divided into at least four categories.

1. Law as used in its usual sense refers to a means of social control, a statute, ordinance, court decision, traffic light, etc.; it is in no sense scientific. It may or may not be the result of a scientific process of experimentation, but in essence it is simply a social or governmental phenomenon.

[1] Reprinted in large part from 51 Col. L. Rev. 423 (1951).

2. There is also the so-called "Law Behind the Law" or the ideal "Natural Law." This is believed by some to be a collection of rules which all laws as a means of social control should approximate.[2]

3. Another use of the term can be found in the so-called "Scientific Law," which merely states that under given circumstances there will be a given sequence of events. For example, an unsupported object will fall to the ground, or perhaps a highly unpopular law cannot be enforced against the will of an active majority.

4. A fourth meaning inheres in the expression "Jural Law," which is a statement of a scientific law as it applies to the sequence or pattern of social reactions which actually follow, or which it is predicted will follow, the enactment of a particular law. Jural law might be synonymous with natural law if the latter term were used in a scientific sense to designate those natural reactions which surround or follow the enactment of law. The term "natural law," however, when used in its historical sense by the natural law school of jurisprudence,[3] has a religious or intuitive-idealistic meaning not based in the least upon the nature of real reactions of people in society to laws in operation. In this context it refers to an allegedly perfect system of law, whereas a jural law would state the reactions of society to such a system, in the same manner as in the case of any other system. The historic meaning of natural law will therefore be retained, and jural law will be used to indicate the scientific generalities to be derived from examination of the operation of laws in society. An effort will be made in the material which follows to confine the use of the four terms to the senses indicated.

At the outset of any discussion involving the legal system, one is immediately confronted by the age-long dispute as to the nature of law. Although this question has intrigued scholars for centuries, it is of little immediate interest to the experimental jurist. It needs no argument, however, to show that the law is a social phenomenon and

[2] This theory is ably refuted in Dickinson, The Law Behind Law, 29 Col. L. Rev. 113, 285, 289 et seq. (1929).

[3] Aristotle, Ethics v. 7, Rhetoric i. 13; Justinian, Pandects I, tit. 2; Aquinas, Summa Theologica 1, 2, q. 91, a. 2; q. 95, a. 5; Coke, L.J., in Calvin's Case, 7 Co. Rep. 2a (1609); 1 Grotius, De Jure Belli et Pacis i. 10; Locke, Second Treatise on Civil Government c. 2, § 12; Vattel, Le Droit Des Gens Int. 5; Mansfield, L.J., in Moses v. MacFerlan, 2 Burr. 1005 (1760); 1 Bl. Comm. *38-43; American Declaration of Independence; Chase, J., in Calder v. Bull, 3 Dall. 386, 387, 388 (U.S. 1798); Waite, J., in United States v. Cruickshank, 92 U.S. 542, 551 (1875); McReynolds, J., in Pierce v. Society of Sisters, 268 U.S. 510 (1925); Frank, Law and the Modern Mind 11 (preface) (6th ed. 1949).

that any science of law and the reactions surrounding it must necessarily be a social science. For the purpose of developing such a science, it may be tentatively assumed that law is a man-made instrument of social control devised to accomplish the purpose of the lawmaker. It cannot be exclusively characterized as either the inevitable workings of history,[4] the immutable will of God,[5] the command of the sovereign,[6] the ultimate embodiment of justice,[7] the will of the governed,[8] the result of uncontrollable forces[9] or the proper adjustment of social interests.[10] Under different conditions and circumstances there is probably an element of truth in each of these explanations given by the various schools of jurisprudence, but none of them can be accepted as the whole truth. Furthermore, little is to be gained by a debate as to which if any of them is the dominant explanation of the phenomena of law. It is sufficient to start with the obvious fact that sometimes, as in the case of legislation, it is a conscious creation to solve a particular social problem. In other instances, law is developed by a subtle process of impressionistic settlement of disputes by courts, commissions, lawyers and other mediators. The important thing to note here is that the decision in a particular case is a sort of judicial accident. Habit, morals, precedent and perhaps the visceral impression of justice are all brought to bear in complex patterns on the resolution of the dispute. A succession of official actions or inactions under similar facts slowly crystallizes into a rule for decision which the expert can recognize or predict as a means of reaching judgment in similar cases.

Nevertheless, whether the law is in one form or the other should be of insignificant consequence to the experimental jurist. He takes it simply as a man-made set of rules or controls which can be changed to conform it to the dictates of scientific discoveries. It is a means of achieving an end. He is not so much interested in the nature of the law, but rather concentrates his attention upon how it and the institutions surrounding it function. Just as the physicist cannot define electricity but works constantly to see what it does, so also the experimental jurist pays far more attention to the effect of law than to its

---

[4] Maine, Ancient Law (4th Am. ed. 1906).

[5] Cicero, De Legibus 379-81.

[6] Brown, The Austinian Theory of Law (1906).

[7] Stammler, The Theory of Justice (1925).

[8] 5 Jefferson, Writings 115-24 (Ford ed. 1899).

[9] Carter, Law: Its Origin, Growth and Function (1907).

[10] Cardozo, The Nature of the Judicial Process 112-115 (1921); Jhering, Law as a Means to an End (Husik's transl. 1913); Pound, Social Control Through Law 63-80 (1942).

definition. When the phenomena surrounding it are better understood, the definition will probably take care of itself. A great mass of scientific data and engineering advancement had been achieved on the practical plane before the scientist reached the theory that electricity consisted of the flow of electrons through atoms.[11] Whether this latest theory is the ultimate truth is of little importance when we look back over the progress made in the application of a force which has quite possibly not yet been accurately defined. A scientific study of law along similar lines should reach equally important results long before any accurate definition is needed.

THE ESSENCE OF EXPERIMENTAL JURISPRUDENCE

A science of law based on a rigorous application of the scientific method should be devoted to the study of the phenomena of lawmaking, the effect of law upon society and the efficiency of laws in accomplishing the purposes for which they came into existence. It is immaterial whether Experimental Jurisprudence is a branch of sociology, or whether or not all of political science, part of each of sociology, economics, philosophy and many of the other social sciences are included within its ken. The line between the "sciences," like the definition of law, is little more than a quibble which can be left to the pundits, bureaucrats and administrators; to the scientist, the nature of its subject matter, the methods which it uses and the results which it achieves, rather than its definition, are fundamental.

With these preliminary observations in mind, it might be stated that the steps employed in prosecuting a method of Experimental Jurisprudence should be approximately as follows:

1. The nature of the phenomena which law attempts to regulate should be studied. In particular, the social problem to which a specific law is directed should be carefully isolated and examined.

2. The rule of law or other method used to regulate the phenomena or intended to solve the social problem should be accurately stated.

3. The effect on society of adopting the rule should be observed and measured.

4. There should then be constructed a hypothesis that attempts to explain the reasons for this reaction.

5. This description, when broadened to apply to other analogous situations, might be considered a jural law that describes or predicts

[11] Millikan, Electronics $(+ \ \& \ -)$ Protons, Photons, Neutrons, Mesotrons and Cosmic Rays 66 (1947).

results which would occur on application of a similar regulatory law to similar problems.

6. If analysis shows that the law is inefficient, there could then be suggested new methods of accomplishing the originally desired result.

7. The proposed new law could be enacted and the process repeated.

8. A series of such adoptions of new laws and the study of their results might throw important light upon the usefulness of the underlying purposes behind the enactment, thus effecting a possible alteration in or abandonment of this objective, or in the long run, though this now appears doubtful, even induce a revision of our present scale of social and political ethics.

Each of the steps in this process may require the skillful use of complicated machinery and techniques of observation. Some are now in existence, others will have to be developed. The important thing is that scientific jurisprudence is essentially a problem-solving device.

THE NATURE OF THE PHENOMENA REGULATED

The first step in the methodology of scientific jurisprudence must be a careful isolation of comparatively simple problems. So long as the philosopher-scientists speculated about the nature of the universe or of matter in general, little progress was made; but when Galileo devoted his attention to the swinging pendulum or the speed of falling objects, when Newton sought the reason for a falling apple, or medical sciences began to concentrate upon the cause and cure of a specific disease such as smallpox, the glorious development of natural science was on its way. We may expect similar progress when jurisprudence begins the isolation and study of phenomena that follow simple patterns of behavior. This involves a careful examination of the factual elements of the phenomena toward which a particular law is directed. There are available for such study numerous undesirable conditions with which laws have attempted to deal. For example, a dangerous intersection of two roads results in traffic snarls and accidents; the youths of a city steal merchandise from the stores and destroy property; a large number of bad checks are being cashed; landlords charge unconscionably high rent; the indigent aged persons in the community do not receive proper care. The solution of these and myriads of other concrete social problems are the tasks which the officers of society have attempted to solve by one or another device. If jurisprudence is to follow the scientific method, it would seem wise and relatively easy for the jurist to isolate such a problem for investigation. Indeed, many

19

such studies have already been completed,[12] and more have been initiated.[13]

When the problem has been thus isolated for study, the determination of its nature as a social phenomenon will often involve the use of other sciences. It is obvious that a traffic study involves mechanical knowledge and some psychology, while a juvenile delinquency problem calls for the help of doctors, psychiatrists and psychologists. Similarly, studies of bad checks and rent control will use economic data. In fact, an adequate analysis of any problem will require aid from many of the modern sciences to expose the implications of its basic facts.

The choice of one particular subject to be studied rather than another, as illustrated in Part II, will depend upon such factors as convenience, urgency of the problem, resources of finance, personnel available, scientific data, technical tools existing or to be created capable of exposing the pertinent details, time, organization and many other considerations. Each problem will develop its own requirements for solution which will have to follow the experimental design most appropriate to its needs. This will be touched upon briefly in later chapters.

IDENTIFYING THE LAW AND REGULATORY DEVICES

Once the problem is isolated, it may then be easy to discover what legal devices have actually been created for its solution. In the case of a dangerous corner, many are available. To name only a few, there are city ordinances creating stop lights and stop signs, assigning traffic officers for busy hours, designating one-way streets, prohibiting right or left turns or both, and ordering the construction of overhead crossings and by-passes. To solve the juvenile delinquency problems, laws have been devised punishing particular acts, setting up children's courts, building reformatories and even instituting preventive measures, such as the creation of youth centers.

Sometimes the procedure may profitably be reversed and an attempt made to discover the phenomena toward which a law is directed.

[12] Glueck & Glueck, Five Hundred Criminal Careers (1930), Criminal Careers in Retrospect (1943); Pound & Frankfurter, Criminal Justice in Cleveland (1922); Tappan, Delinquent Girls in Court (1947); Moore & Callahan, Law and Learning Theory: A Study in Legal Control, 53 Yale L.J. 1 (1943).

[13] The Hoover Commission Report on Organization of the Executive Branch of the Government (1949); Fine, Connecticut Studies Schools: Everyone's Opinion Asked, N.Y. Times, Nov. 14, 1949, p. 1, col. 3; cf. Chase, The Proper Study of Mankind 50 (1948).

There are many laws in connection with which it is difficult to identify the problem or problems attempted to be solved. For example, one investigating enactments against divorce or for the licensing of saloons or public bus lines may find that they exist for multiple purposes. Other laws may remain on the books long after the purposes for which they were created have ceased to exist; for example, the celebrated Louisiana statute limiting the length of ladies' hat pins.[14] The important thing at this stage of the inquiry, however, is to identify the rules of law with the social problems they are supposed to solve. Whether the approach is from the law to the problem or from the problem to the law is immaterial. Although this second step is particularly easy in the case of statutes, it can present an imposing research problem when the so-called common law is involved. Here a rule of law is often identified only after an extended search by expert counsel, as was generally the case with the Restatements of the law promulgated by the American Law Institute, and particularly with many of the rules of torts and property.

Logically there is a third situation where there may be a pressing social problem for the solution of which there is no existing "law." Theoretically, from the point of view of the lawyer, no such condition is possible, since all such cases are supposed to fall into the great residue called the common law. Here when a problem gets to court, or other legal machinery is set in motion, it becomes necessary for the judge or official to improvise a decision. The reason he gives for his results becomes the basis of determining the common law for the future. Actually, as in the case of settling the legal rights of children conceived by the new medical process of artificial insemination, even the legal experts may be faced with so many conflicting analogies and so many possible solutions that for all practical purposes it may be said that there is no rule of "law," or that the legal analogies are in complete confusion.

In such a case it might be argued that facts of this sort fall outside the ken of jurisprudence and into the field of other social sciences; or it could be suggested that in such a situation Steps Three to Five as outlined above should be omitted and the jurist should proceed at once under Step Six to recommend desirable changes in the law to meet the social data which have been collected on the actual facts resulting from the absence of or confusion in the "law." It makes little

[14] La. Laws 1914, No. 64, p. 156; see La. Laws 1896, No. 62, p. 95; (illegal for women to wear hats in theatres); cf. also Palmer, Vestigial Remnants in the Law, 35 A.B.A.J. 905 (1949).

difference which approach is adopted. In either case it is possible to construct on the basis of knowable facts, either proceeding from the confused "law" or existing in the absence of it, a determination of the desirability for legal change, if any. If such a law were enacted, the process of Experimental Jurisprudence could then proceed as suggested beginning with Step Seven.

Again on critical examination, however, it may appear that a particular law exists for no other social purpose than to provide a rule for settling lawsuits. Whereas laws on negligence may in some instances accomplish social regulation, the "last clear chance" doctrine clearly serves no purpose other than that of reaching a judgment in a litigated case. Nevertheless, even here careful inquiry into the purpose of the law in conjunction with other steps in the methodology of scientific jurisprudence would prove extremely fruitful and might throw great light on its ultimate utility.

On the other hand, the search for the underlying social problem may reveal that the law in its present form was devised to correspond with a theory concerning the nature of the problem toward which it is directed which is entirely at odds with later discoveries regarding the same problem. For example, the current laws governing crime, the treatment of the insane and the weighing of evidence were crystallized long before the scientific method shed new light on the nature of man. Psychiatry and psychology indicate that the tests of *mens rea*, criminal intent and knowledge of right and wrong, presently applied as basic concepts in criminal law, bear no relation to the real state of mind of criminals,[15] while modern methods of proof of scientific facts have rendered many aspects of the jury system not only obsolete but an actual impediment to fact-finding.[16] In these fields the necessary reconstruction of the problem toward which the law is oriented will require the aid of many other scientists cooperating with the research lawyer. When the reports of such a team are in, many of our present laws will be found to rest upon theories as to the nature of man and the world about him which have been shown by modern science to be inaccurate. Considerations such as these may force the abandonment of many of the basic postulates of criminal law and evidence and will point the way to revisions in the laws themselves.

[15] Wertham, The Show of Violence 86, 149, 152 (1949); Zilboorg, Mind, Medicine and Man c. 8 (1943).

[16] See Berry v. Chaplin, 74 Cal. App. 2d 652, 169 P.2d 442 (1946), 34 Corn. L. Q. 78-80 (1948).

Just as legal theories on the nature of the problem which the law is attempting to solve may be out of line with scientific discoveries, so also methods or tools sanctioned by the legal system to reach the desired result may not be efficient. As indicated more in detail in Chapter V, our legal system has been woefully slow to adopt the products of physical and social science to modernize its procedures. The discovery and application of current scientific knowledge for the use of legal and government agencies provides one of the most fruitful and neglected fields for current social research. Here again, as indicated more in detail in subsequent chapters, there is a growing demand for cooperative research between jurists and other scientists, both social and physical.

THE REACTION OF SOCIETY TO A LAW

The third step—the collection of data to gauge the efficiency of the law in accomplishing its purpose—is far more difficult than either of the previous steps. Here the effect of the administration of law on the actions of people in society must be observed. Patterns of mass action and not individual reactions are the important consideration.[17] Such patterns are similar to physical, statistical or mass reactions, such as the molecular action when two colored liquids coalesce in solution, and are made up of the sum total of what appear to be indiscriminate individual reactions. To obtain the information desired here, statistical studies of many individual reactions, both physical and mental, are necessary to make up the picture of group responses and attitudes.[18] Other sciences must again be called upon to produce data, and experts will have to work in teams and pool their results.

In the case of a single-purpose statute like a traffic law, observation of a particular fact on a particular corner is comparatively easy. The patterns of social action caused by the impact of the legal device on the comparatively simple phenomenon of the movement of vehicular and pedestrian traffic at the corner is readily observable. Here mechanical counters, statistics, moving picture cameras and the like are useful in assembling the pattern of traffic before and after the change in the law.

---

[17] Cooley, Case Study of Small Institutions as a Method of Research in Personality and the Social Group 182 (Burgess ed. 1929); see also Ohlin, Selection for Parole (1951) and authorities there cited 131 ff.

[18] See for example, Stewart, Empirical Methematical Rules Concerning the Distribution and Equilibrium of Population, 37 Geographical Rev. 461 (1947).

Where the multiple-purpose statute is involved, the social picture is more complicated. A study might be attempted to determine either the efficiency of the statute in accomplishing only one of its alleged purposes or its success in relation to two or more or all of the postulated purposes. The analyses of sociologists, economists, criminologists, psychiatrists, poll-takers and many other specialists should be employed in assembling the data. To insure accuracy, the elements of the program will have to be isolated and the area selected for study made statistically large enough to eliminate individual variations. Thus the reactions of traffic on one corner will not be enough; behavior patterns at many intersections will have to be observed and compared. So also the study of one juvenile court might be enlightening, but it should be extended to include others over a long period of time in order to eliminate chance factors. This process is similar to the creation of a complicated experimental design in other scientific fields.

On the other hand, the problem of checking a law suspected of obsolescence may be relatively simple. For example, if a preliminary study discloses that ladies have discontinued wearing long hat pins, that there have been no instances of prosecution under the statute regulating them for years, and that the women are neither afraid of the law nor in fact know anything about it, the inference is obvious.[19] Nevertheless, the possibility should not be overlooked that a law which no longer serves the purpose for which it was originally enacted may yet be useful in regulating new phenomena.

THE REASONS FOR REACTIONS TO A LAW

Although the discovery, in the absence of well documented legislative sources, of the purposes for which laws are created may cause some speculation and perhaps difficult problems of proof, so far in the process of Experimental Jurisprudence there has been little else suggested than the descriptive scientific technique. In the fourth step, however, scientific imagination, speculation and intuition begin to assert themselves. The formulation of a hypothesis to explain the pattern of group or individual actions revealed by the research may be a simple or complex but not impossible task. Where mere traffic regulations are involved, the results before and after the change in the law are easily and quickly understandable, for when the effect of the law has been identified and described, one can readily infer why congestion has been increased or decreased. If a one-way street or an

---

[19] The Hatpin Act was repealed by La. Crim. Code § 21, No. 43 (1942).

overhead crossing is established, the results are obvious, and the re-action of society to the rule of law can be explained with little diffi-culty. On the other hand, where multiple-purpose statutes, such as those creating juvenile courts or probation officers or providing for licensing procedures, are involved, the observation of the effect of the statute on society requires that all of the techniques of descriptive social study be brought to bear on the problem. With their contribu-tion, a hypothesis explaining the effect of the law may be successfully constructed.

THE PERFECTION OF A JURAL LAW

After a hypothesis concerning the effect of the law on a single situation has been constructed, it may be capable of enlargement into a proper jural law. By examination of similar situations where the same law has been applied, the statement of social reactions in single instances may be generalized. Thus it may be determined that under certain conditions traffic lights eliminate a percentage of accidents on busy crossings, while it is certain that an overhead pass will entirely eliminate traffic accidents caused by collisions at intersections. Again, in the case of the juvenile court, if careful studies of the functioning of a single court are expanded to take like institutions into account, it may be possible to state jural laws regarding the effect of this par-ticular type of organization on juvenile delinquency in general.

Such a comparison is readily available in the United States, where a central government, forty-eight state governments, thousands of county governments, and over one hundred thousand independent governmental units, many of which perform identical functions, exist side by side.[20] By proper statistical study, individual variations can be eliminated, and the jural law governing the institution itself can be clarified. Our uniform commercial statutes, uniform codes of court procedure and almost identical organizations for law enforcement all offer a mine of raw material upon which, after the collection and assimilation of sufficient data, jural laws of social reaction can be con-structed. When such studies are made, the results should minimize the basic controversies about the usefulness of the institution or law studied.

A striking illustration of this principle was shown by a recent study of progressive education.[21] Prior to this investigation, emotions ran

---

[20] Anderson, The Units of Government in the United States (Pub. Adm. Serv. Monograph 83, 1942).
[21] Aikin, The Story of the Eight-Year Study (1942).

high among secondary educators as to the value of "tried and true" conservative methods of teaching "the three R's"; progressive education with its haphazard and unorganized methods was roundly denounced all over the country. But when a careful study was made of the success in college of well sampled students from the various progressive and non-progressive institutions under a pattern which eliminated most of the chance variations, the results showed that the students from progressive schools fared slightly better than did those from the orthodox institutions.[22] One striking result of this study which should give pause to any dogmatist in the field of social or legal regulation indicated that students from progressive schools with no previous training in science made better grades in college science courses than did their fellows well drilled in secondary school sciences by the conservative methods.[23] It is clear that success in college is not the sole purpose of secondary education, but it is certainly one. Since this study, much of the heat has gone out of the recurrent controversies in this area, and educators are at least one step further toward finding what is the "best" method of secondary education.

Techniques that are applicable to the study of regulations made by educators are equally applicable to laws passed by legislatures or devised through generalizations upon decisions of judges. The pattern of human reactions in both instances is now within the grasp of our methods of social scrutiny. One leading scientist has summarized the situation as follows:

> There is no longer excuse for anyone to ignore the fact that human beings, on the average and at least in certain circumstances, obey mathematical rules resembling in a general way some of the primitive "laws" of physics. "Social physics" lies within the grasp of scholarship that is truly modern. When we have found it, people will wonder at the blind opposition its proponents first encountered.[24]

Up to this point, a scientific jurisprudence has attempted only the descriptive technique of social physics, but, due to variations in the laws of various jurisdictions having similar social structure, jurists can reap many of the benefits of controlled experiments by simply comparing results of studies in existing societies without the necessity of making any changes in the law. Moreover, where societies differ markedly in their legal structure, as is the case when comparing the

---

[22] Time, Feb. 16, 1942, p. 53.
[23] Thirty Schools Tell Their Story 668 (1943).
[24] Stewart, supra note 18 at 485.

United States, Spain and Soviet Russia, jural laws can be further verified by comparing the results of social physics as applied to similar phenomena but under totally different legal conditions.

SUGGESTIONS FOR CHANGE IN THE LAW

When the sixth step in the methods of Experimental Jurisprudence is reached, however, social science or "social physics" may become as truly experimental a science as is physics or chemistry. After observations of the reaction of people to a particular law or class of laws have been collected and formalized, it is possible for the jurist to point out inefficiencies in both the administration of the law and in its technical structure. At this stage most of these defects will appear in terms of failure to accomplish the purposes of the enactment. He can then suggest to statesmen or to other policy-makers changes in the law which might better effectuate the policy for which it was created.

In the past the objection has always been raised at this stage that whether one rule of law or another is adopted poses a question of social values which science alone is unable to answer. Furthermore, it is claimed no change in the law should be undertaken without a value judgment, since people do not like to consider themselves experimental guinea pigs. This argument, however, wholly overlooks the fact that an overwhelming majority of the laws now on the books and most current policy judgments are made on an impressionistic basis to solve a specific problem. Often they are the product of impassioned emotions rather than systematic study. Whether we like it or not, therefore, these laws are all in a sense experimental, but they are experiments that have not been subjected to any systematic check as to their results. As a result of this haphazard practice, most current laws are carried along by the force of inertia until they either become obsolete or are repealed due to further pressures based not upon scientific investigation but upon public clamor which often arises from the effectiveness of the law itself. In fact, it is, perhaps, a jural law of our representative democracy that the more effectively a law limits the actions of particular groups, the more it is subject to pressure from these groups for change. It is thus an interesting paradox that governmental agencies created by law to regulate certain "anti-social activity" are often in turn captured by the forces which they are set up to control. The police are occasionally dominated by the underworld,[25] the Interstate Commerce Commission by the railroads,[26] and the labor

[25] Frank Costello, 54 Time Magazine 15 (Nov. 28, 1949) (cover story).
[26] Georgia v. Pennsylvania Ry., 324 U.S. 439, 458 (1945).

boards by the unions or the employers, depending upon which is the socially stronger at the moment.[27] This haphazard governmental experimentation might be brought to an end under a regime of scientific jurisprudential study.

In addition, there is no reason to suppose that there would be any immediate necessity for the experimental jurist to make determinations of value. He should study the law to find out its effectiveness in accomplishing the purpose for which the statesmen or judge allegedly created it and be able to advise what changes would further that purpose.

> The only value judgments which any properly trained scientist makes about his data are judgments regarding their relevance to his problem, the weight to be assigned to each aspect, and the general interpretation to be made of the observed events. These are problems which no scientist can escape, and they are not at all unique or insuperable in the social sciences.
>
> Have scientists, then, no special function or obligation in determining the ends for which scientific knowledge is to be used? As scientists, it is their business to determine reliably the immediate and remote costs and consequences of alternate possible courses of action, and to make these known to the public.[28]

It should be the function of the scientific jurist to state these "natural consequences" in the form of jural laws. Thus in the beginning he is necessarily the servant of the lawmaker.

If the experimental jurist will start his work by solving simple problems by an impartial process based upon facts and social reactions while entirely free from preconceived ideas concerning the good or evil of the ultimate results in the same manner in which a medical researcher studies syphilis, it will not be long until he will become the most important colleague of any lawmaker. Thus "the services of real social scientists would be as indispensable to Fascists as to Communists and Democrats, just as are the services of physicists and physicians."[29]

In any event, when the facts of the social reaction to law are known and the jural laws properly determined, much of the argument concerning ultimate values will cease to exist. For example, it was at one time believed that it was a "good" thing to suppress liquor traffic by prohibition laws, but experimentation, haphazard as it was, has shown

---

[27] Cohen & Cohen, The National Labor Relations Board in Retrospect, 1 Indus. & Lab. Rel. Rev. 648 (1948).

[28] Lundberg, Can Science Save Us 28 (1947).

[29] Id. 48; cf. Lynd, The Implications of Economic Planning of Sociology, 9 Am. Sociol. Rev. 14, 17 (1944).

us that by almost any test the results of prohibition are "worse" than the liquor traffic. If the lawmakers had employed the methods of Experimental Jurisprudence, this jural law would have been known sooner, there would have been less emotionalism, and we would have been far more sophisticated in our attempts to regulate the "evil" in the liquor traffic. In fact, it is not too much to hope that the application of careful scientific methods of study to such problems of social control could lead to means of entirely eliminating many of the "evils" with which we are plagued.[30]

THE ENACTMENT OF SUGGESTED LAWS

It is apparent that the seventh step, if Experimental Jurisprudence is to reach maximum effectiveness, must consist in the actual enactment of the changes in the law suggested by the jurist after his studies. But in the present state of lawmaking, the governmental machinery is an only partially adequate device for this process. Thus the objector can easily point out that legislatures are independent bodies in no way obligated to the jurist, and that he will be lucky indeed if he ever gets his new reforms enacted. This is certainly a difficulty, but in actual practice it should be far from insurmountable.

There are three practical ways of overcoming this legislative lag. (1) The first is delegation by the legislature of rule-making power to officials with authority to change current rules of law. (2) The variation in rules of law now in evidence governing the same or similar phenomena are so great that after a study of the operation of law in a few jurisdictions a little further research may disclose that most of the theoretical legal and administrative variations which an experimental jurist might desire to use as controls to check the working of a law have already been enacted in legal units of similar structure. (3) Third and last, the legislatures, even as now constituted, may themselves be persuaded to change the law.

(1) *Delegation of power* is a current governmental practice in all fields of administrative activity. Its constitutionality with slight checks in the form of standards is recognized in almost every field of legal administration, and as indicated in Chapters VI and VII it is already beginning to achieve important results in the current development of Experimental Jurisprudence. Where the lawmaking power is thus delegated to an official, he is able to experiment with the sub-

---

[30] For a more complete discussion of the possible effects of Experimental Jurisprudence on problems of value, see Ch. III.

ject matter under his jurisdiction in a manner similar to that used by the physical scientist in his laboratory. Chapter VI contains numerous examples of how the scientific knowledge about traffic law and its jural laws has been developed by forward-looking officials through experiments controlled by changing laws and regulations to perfect their direction of the flow of traffic and to increase their knowledge of the practicable use of legal devices.

(2) *The variations in rules of law* in the various jurisdictions in the United States alone is a phenomenon known to all lawyers and many social scientists. As indicated elsewhere, there are in this country over one hundred fifty thousand units of government with lawmaking power running across the entire hierarchy from the federal government with its various territorial subdivisions through states, counties, school districts, improvement units and various other authorities. Hundreds of these units serve similar functions. Seldom, if ever, do they have identical rules of law or methods of enforcement.

A recent study of the laws and health regulations governing vaccination for smallpox[31] shows that there are at least eight general categories of enforcement in this field scattered among the forty-eight states, varying all the way from compulsory requirement of vaccination for everybody to prohibition of compulsory vaccination in three states. The eight categories in turn can be broken down into numerous variations in the practical rule or method of enforcement. By a careful study of the statistics of the instances of smallpox in the various areas covered by similar regulations, it has been possible to show the effectiveness in general of the eight major categories, and in addition, by comparing variations within categories it has been pointed out that it is now possible to determine the strength and weakness of almost every known type of legal control of smallpox vaccination. Where local laws fail to yield the particular control desired, it is possible to extend the study to foreign nations. Here is a field where existing variations in the type of law and administration supply to the jural scientist, if he is willing to travel a bit through his available governmental laboratory, almost every type of experimental control that the physicist can apply in his laboratory. As indicated in later chapters, similar controls are available in hundreds of other fields of legal activity.

(3) *Legislative lawmaking bodies* are not beyond the reach of the experimental scientist. Once a legislature or other rule-making body

[31] Ravenscroft & Solomon, An Experiment in Scientific Jurisprudence, **32 Neb. L.** Rev. 547 (1953).

has initiated a course of action based upon a chosen conclusion of desirability, however derived, experience will show that it is not too difficult to persuade it to adopt changes in the law better calculated to effectuate the original policy. Many of the most fertile fields of initial study for the experimental jurist lie in such areas as traffic control, procedural reform, criminal administration, city government and area planning, where there are few if any violent political prejudices.

Should careful scientific studies indicate a change in direction or policy, they are likely to be the most persuasive argument to all but an emotionally blinded lawmaker. Even where deep-seated emotions that impinge upon individual interests like property ownership, religion or morals are involved, a carefully executed study supporting the suggested changes may be able to win over all but the most prejudiced. Except in cases where these unreasoning positions are held by major political forces, the scientific jurist can expect progress along the lines suggested by his studies. If this result is reached, a new instrument of statesmanship will have been erected which will make possible continued progress in the field of law and government. Legal machinery will be enabled to adopt a technique of orderly social change which will keep abreast of scientific and industrial development. There is no reason why violent revolution must continue to be the chief means of accomplishing permanent social reform.

Where blind prejudiced emotionalism, selfishness or ignorance on the part of the controlling political forces stand in the way of ordered change, the studies of impartial jurists may still be of great aid in shifting the balance of power. Progress temporarily halted may again be resumed, regardless of the means by which the change in political power was accomplished.

> Meanwhile let "social planners" beware! Water must be pumped to flow up hill, natural tendencies in human relations cannot be combated and controlled by singing to them. The architect must accept and understand the law of gravity and the limitation of materials. The city or national planner must likewise adapt his studies to natural principles.[32]

It is interesting to note that in the past, whatever may have been the manner in which revolutions have been brought about, whether political or by the force of arms, the leaders of the following reconstruction have often adopted schemes of government already at hand.[33]

[32] Stewart, supra note 18 at 485.
[33] Lasswell, Power and Personality 164 (1948).

The transplantation of the theories of Montesquieu into the Constitution of the United States, the adoption of the Civil Code by Napoleon, the use of *Das Kapital* and other works of Marx and Engels by the Russian Politburo and the implementation of *Mein Kampf* by the Nazis all followed revolutions. Historians can offer many other examples of this tendency. Would it not be safer, therefore, when inevitable political upsets occur for the new leaders to have at hand enlightened theories of law and government carefully worked out by rational experimental processes rather than be left to rely on the speculation of cloistered philosophers or the mad dreams of imprisoned fanatics?

Whatever may be the form of government or lack of it, there is strong likelihood that the suggested legal devices built upon carefully studied jural laws will have a chance of enactment. Thus the science of jurisprudence may become fully experimental.

AN EXPERIMENTAL SYSTEM OF ETHICS

A system of Experimental Jurisprudence in its complete workings would not necessarily be limited to studying the efficiency of various legal devices in accomplishing their purpose. It could also throw considerable light on the value of the purposes themselves. Philosophers, clerics and students of ethics have devoted much attention to what they call the basic values or purposes for which law and other social regulations exist. These values have been postulated in the form of hedonism, the greatest happiness for the greatest number; materialism, the largest pile of tangible assets; idealism, the development of the things of the spirit; and in other ways too numerous to mention. Or, to state it another way, these lovers of generality may say that the purpose of law is race power, national aggrandizement, spiritual or intellectual advancement, the preservation of freedom, the development of the state, the rule of the proletariat, the perpetuation of the nobility and so on. Legal philosophers like to think that when the lawmaker comes to his ultimate decision, he consciously turns to these ethical sources or else relies on intuition based upon his early conditioning in morals.

In the past there may have been some truth in this theory. Any realist, however, can see that, even without a system of Experimental Jurisprudence which would place the facts at issue before the lawmaker, statements of these ultimate values are often rationalizations which come after decisions which have already been made on much more practical grounds.[34] Thus Hitler's doctrine of race purity and Nordic supremacy was offered as the reason for exterminating the German Jews, but any realist would recognize that this was simply an excuse for prolonging in an even more barbarous form a persecution of these people which had gone on long before Hitler advanced his hypothesis of race supremacy and which continues as a reality despite the fact that this theory has now been entirely discredited.[35] Another example of the manner in which the ideals follow rather than precede the decision will be found in the American Revolution, which we now know was actually motivated by resentment of unfair taxes, trade barriers and colonial exploitation long before Jefferson wrote the Declaration of Independence or Patrick Henry issued his immortal "Give me liberty or give me death." In fact, the great Virginia patriots thought so little of liberty and equality of man in the abstract that freeing the slaves was not seriously attempted.

In like fashion it should be observed that many of our modern policy problems are grounded to no greater extent on these ultimate ideals or ethical standards. A realistic study will show clashes of interest on much simpler and more measurable levels. The rich want to avoid taxes and obtain security by means of high, unearned incomes and the ability to bequeath their advantages to their children. The poor want security in the form of pensions, unearned incomes and confiscation of wealth in order to give their own children equality of opportunity. The actual pressure of these and many other interests can be measured in terms of number, volume and power and the lawmaker can settle them on that basis. With the aid of the experimental jurist, in co-operation with other scientists, the facts could be exposed and suggestions for changes in law and government administration could be offered which might go a long way toward permanently resolving these conflicts without ever having to come to grips with ultimate questions of ethical value. Occasionally, of course, the lawmaker may be forced to fall back on generalities, but he is more likely to think in immediate terms.

It should also be noted that there exists as a basis for decision a second level of less vague ideals that are currently propounded, such as sovereignty and power of local governments, private ownership of public utilities, or the opposite, and preservation of the family and support of the morals of the community, whose values can be scien-

---

[34] Robinson, The Mind in the Making (1921).
[35] Montagu, Man's Most Dangerous Myth: The Fallacy of Race 178 (1942).

tifically weighed and tested. Thus the absolute necessity for preservation of local government may seem to be overstated in light of the
fact that there are now over 150,000 separate units of local government
operating in the United States[36] at great cost and low efficiency. It
might be possible to show that many of them are historical anachronisms and that their tasks, in view of changed conditions of transportation and communication, could be accomplished at much less cost
by a fraction of their number. Some of these facts have already been
developed by impartial research,[37] and proof of the rest is certainly
within the grasp of modern social science and Experimental Jurisprudence.

On the other hand, a comparative study might show that a local
regional government in the nature of the TVA is much more efficient
than a national administration of the same problems. Again it might
not, but these facts too are now within our comprehension if we will
take the trouble to go after them. Experimentation or even careful
examination of the problems to be solved by impartial experts would
not be long in disclosing whether economic government of a river
valley can be better accomplished by a single unit extending to the
borders of the watershed or by a number of cooperating states or local
bodies, none of which covers the entire area. Such comparison is now
available in the Pick-Sloan plan for the Missouri Valley as distinguished from the Tennessee Valley Authority. When the facts of
such studies are made available, the blind love of local government
as such will disappear from all but the most stubbornly prejudiced
minds. In its place there will be useful information to show where
local government is best fitted to operate and where a wider system
is preferable.

Material is also available for a complete study of all of the factors
bearing on the question of public versus private ownership of electric
power companies, which should remove this vexing question from its
present state of hot controversy. If experts, including economists,
lawyers, engineers and sociological investigators, were to make a comparative study of the various factors involved in the operation of public and private utilities, such as cost of service, excellence of service,
cost of capital construction, rates to the consumer, dividends to stock-
holders, expense of state supervision, presence or absence of political
corruption, wages to workmen and executives, employees' morale and

[36] Anderson, op. cit. supra note 20.
[37] Anderson, op. cit. supra note 20; County Gov't. & Admin. in Tenn. Valley
States, T.V.A. Doc. No. 120 (1940), and authorities there cited.

initiative shown in making improvements and such other pertinent factors as economic experts might agree were pertinent, the comparison of results ought to show conclusively which is the better system without the necessity of speculation in the confused area of ultimate values. In case the study did not show a preponderance of efficiency, all factors considered, then intermediate ideals of public or private ownership and ultimate values of human happiness would be unimportant, and it might be well to continue to offer public utility service under both systems. However, it is highly unlikely that this would be the case. In either event the lawmaker and the jurist could dispense with ultimate values.

The Federal Trade Commission's report on public utilities[38] went a long way in this direction, but unfortunately it was not set up as a test of efficiency of operation to meet the various factors involved in such problems, but rather as a journalistic report of what was going on. But even as such, its findings have proved very useful in policy determinations by enlightened officials in this field.

It should be noted here that experimental studies into the facts underlying even such comparatively simple problems as those just discussed are only theoretically possible. The complete failure of the Second Commission on the Organization of the Executive Branch of the Government, discussed in Chapter VII, to come to grips with the underlying facts of government control versus private ownership show that such problems for a long time to come will continue to be resolved on the basis of prejudice excused by an underlying so-called system of values. But can such current failure to use available tools of research into pertinent facts be said to preclude forever their utilization when the tools of social research and fact-finding are later developed?

Finally, in those situations where law touches more closely upon matters of personal morality, the recent Kinsey Report on sex activities of the American male[39] and the second report on similar activities of the female indicate that a dosage of experimental ethics might well be applied under the guidance of scientific jurists. It has already been noted that if the present laws on sex were enforced as written, approximately five per cent of the American males would be policing the other ninety-five per cent found guilty of sex crimes.[40] A team of

---

[38] Ann. Reps. F.T.C. 1929-1934.

[39] Kinsey, Pomeroy & Martin, Sexual Behavior in the Human Male (1948).

[40] MacIver, Sex and Social Attitudes in, About the Kinsey Report 85 (Geddes & Curie ed. 1948); cf. Chisholm, The Reestablishment of Peacetime Society: the Responsibility of Psychiatry, 9 Psychiatry 1, 3, 7 et seq. (1946).

psychologists, medical men, experimental jurists, anthropologists and other researchers working on the legal problems involved might conceivably be able to set up experimental social groups, which would indicate a way out of our present dilemma caused, among others, by the fact that medical discoveries have rendered unnecessary many of the social taboos which have been enacted into law. The results developed by such experimental groups, for which many volunteers could be found, operating under new laws suggested by experts, might go a long way toward preventing the ultimate breakdown of our present morals and the tremendous human wreckage in the form of mental traumas, broken homes and emotional upsets consequent upon the strains preceding and following such a collapse, which is likely to come if we go on with our present mores and laws based upon the beliefs and superstitions of a pre-scientific era.[41] There is reason to believe that here, and in many other fields, scientific jurisprudence could become the instrument of experimental ethics in developing a new and finer civilization.

Nobody should be prepared to argue that the solution of all moral, social and international problems are presently possible by the technique of Experimental Jurisprudence, but can it not be said that it is foreseeable that the ultimate projection of procedures here suggested may lead to a possible means of resolution of clashes of opinion which in the past have been settled only by brute force? If one starts, as all experimental sciences have, with simple problems and moves forward to the more complex, larger social adjustments, both national and international,[41] may come into focus much more quickly than now seems possible.

The place of the so-called human values in this process will be discussed at length in **Chapter III.**

---

[41] Cf. Chisholm, The Psychiatry of Enduring Peace, 9 Psychiatry 7 ff. (1946).

Value and Interests in the Legal System

In the following discussion, it should be kept continually in mind that various fields of social science such as economics, sociology, political science and certain branches of psychology are flooded with writings concerning value and theories of value. These considerations may be useful when one attempts to speculate as to the underlying drives which bring individuals or groups to a choice. Jurisprudence deals with law which is a mass regulation of society, so it may well be that such a science can be built primarily upon the factual existence of both individual and group choices and preferences. The so-called "values" which lead persons or groups to make decisions may be of only secondary importance. Nevertheless it may still be enlightening to examine the term "value" and its derivatives "values" and "valuation" to see if they can be used in the vocabulary of Experimental Jurisprudence.

THE USEFULNESS OF THE TERM "VALUE"

The process of evaluation in its usual sense is basically one of making a choice between two or more objects. When a person says "*A* is more valuable than *B*," he is normally announcing that if he had to make a choice, he would choose *A* rather than *B*. Value is thus a sort of shorthand term for stating the results of a myriad of impulses which cause him to prefer one object, idea, law or ideal over another. In dealing with the problems of why individuals chose, the social scientist, if he is to be accurate, may desire to develop a terminology for describing what takes place when this process of choosing or evaluating occurs. Viewed objectively, the statement that a thing, *A*, is valuable is simply a shorthand expression for summarizing the fact that *A* evokes clusters of emotions or desires which are more powerful than those which *B* stimulates. But value is also used in a number of other senses. Among the adjectives used to describe it are such terms as "inherent," "subjective," "objective," "moral," "instrumental" and "valuation for the purpose of measuring." Critical examination of these concepts will go a long way toward placing the term in its true perspective as a device of Experimental Jurisprudence.

Inherent value seems to be a concept which regards an object, an idea, a law or any other thing as having a quality attached to it or part of it which is its value.

This concept often appears in its most complete form in writings on economics which speak of things having a value in the market, or better, that they command a price on the exchange. A closer look at this concept shows that it really amounts to a measuring of the interest which people have in buying a thing on one hand, and the desire of the sellers to keep it, on the other, or the extent to which both groups would exchange money or other objects for it. But the concept necessarily requires the presence of people who demand it and are willing to pay for it. Thus the expression "value" is really a measure of the relationship between the thing and the humans: but value comes from the human desire and not from the thing itself. It is only an expression of the sum total of the human's demand for or interest in the thing at the moment as it is diluted by available supply. The term "price" is all that one needs to express this concept.

That there is no value inherent in the thing itself, but that such value as it has is determined by the attitude of the humans toward it, can very easily be seen if we contemplate the question of the iron ore in Minnesota. For years the Indians traversing this area regarded it merely as red dirt which had no "value," but when the whites with a civilization using iron and steel came along, the red dirt acquired tremendous "value" and has been the basis for creating great fortunes. Thus it is clearly the human attitude toward the ore which gave the iron ore "value," which, if it exists at all, is wholly on the human side of the relationship.

Sometimes the term "inherent value" is used as a quality in the thing which is discoverable. Thus it is often said that a piece of art has beauty or value within itself which can be discovered only by people who appreciate such inherent values. In these circumstances some people can see the value (beauty), others can't. Those who can see it are said to have discovered its inherent value. But here again the "value" lies in the state of mind on the human side and not in the thing itself.

There is a third type of inherent value which is sometimes postulated by philosophers. On this theory it is suggested that each object, considering all possible demands, has one most effective use which is its value. Thus iron ore might be most valuable for making tungsten steel. This position is theoretically conceivable but is actually not possible to reach because such an estimate of value would require a cataloging and testing of all possible uses for an object. Such a cataloging would be almost impossible in a static society but is wholly inconceivable in a dynamic society in which the uses for the object would change even before the cataloging could be accomplished. For example, it might be said that there is one most valuable use for a forty-mile-an-hour speed limit; but in a horse-and-buggy society or on a rough country road it would have no value at all, whereas on a super-highway it would be too slow. Thus it is the conditions to which the law is applied that give it its "value," and these conditions are capable of infinite change; so the best possible use or value is impossible to determine. All that can be said for inherent value is that under some conditions people find the article being valued useful. Here again value is simply a shorthand phrase for human desires which might be directed toward the object under any given conditions, and the conditions are subject to infinite variations. The one most useful value can never inhere in the article.

Thus in all instances any attempt to discover inherent value in a thing must lead to the state of mind of the human or other volitional beings who are brought into contact with it.

Subjective value is said to be the value which an individual in his own mind places upon a thing. When he is able to choose *A* rather than *B*, or would in his secret soul prefer *A* over *B*, it is often said that *A* is subjectively more valuable than *B*. This again is shorthand for saying that for reasons known only to himself, considering all his emotions, judgments and other psychological drives, he is more interested at the moment in having *A* than *B*. If any use is to be made out of this theory, it is in studying the interest and emotional drives which cause the choice; here analysis is needed.

Whether or not an individual's multiple drives, such as habits, emotions, needs for nourishment, tastes, impulses and the like, when directed toward a choice between two things, flow together along neuronic or other lines of impulses into an evaluating switchbox where they are weighed and eventually combined by the evaluating mechanism into a decision or whether the preponderant impulses toward one object simply automatically overcome the less potent impulses toward the other is primarily a problem for the psychologist. So far as the jurist is concerned, all he needs to know is the fact of choice, or, stated another way, the fact that people *de facto* are interested in or just choose certain things over others. Why or how the choice comes to be made within the nervous system is not of major importance. When such interests are divided into their various components of interests, demands, wants, needs, etc., there is no process left where value or valuation is needed. It is simply a conscious or unconscious choice between conflicting drives within the individual, the study of which is best left to psychology.

When law as a matter of regular practice enters the field of thought control, as is already the case in some totalitarian states, then the findings of the psychologists as to the working of the mind in reaching subjective choices will be of great use to the jurists. But this development lies far in the future. For the purpose of current legal science, all that is necessary to be known is the objective result of the subjective choice. That is, for reasons of their own, people want certain things in preference to others. When these wants are made known, the task of legal science will be to state the jural laws which result from giving them recognition by passing laws for the purpose of implementing the objectively expressed choices.

It is not necessary at the outset for the jurist to enter into the current quarrel of the psychologists over the questions of behaviorism. Since law deals with the regulation of the activity of a large number of people, their objective behavior or expressed statements of inner desires are a sound basis for initiating legal science. In the present state of law and social science, subjective value has no function whatsoever. Until the point where law goes in for regular thought control, it can be disposed of by using the term "interests" and its components which will be discussed later.

Objective value. It is sometimes said that things may have an objective value; that is, a sort of total of all the subjective choices which may be attached to it by individuals. This objective value may theoretically be based upon uniform agreement among mankind, i.e., unanimity of subjective choices in similar situations, a statistical average of such choices or a set of choices held by the dominating classes or individuals who rule society. Insofar as these decisions are an aggregate of such called subjective values, they add nothing except multiplicity to the meaning of subjective value discussed above; but as separate concepts, it is possible that they may have different meanings, and it might be well to examine these possibilities.

In the first place, the idea of objective value as uniform choices which all persons would make under similar situations is an interesting theory, but in fact no such objective choices have been shown.

One might say that in any given situation a human being might choose life over death, but hundreds of examples can be offered that in any situation some individuals have been known to prefer death rather than life. If any such unanimity of preference exists on any subject, it would probably fall into the field of anthropology; but currently available evidence has not shown that any such objective value exists.[1]

Statistical results of choices which individuals make or would make under certain conditions are of course possible, but these are simply mechanical statements of a large number of individual preferences or choices. The Gallup Poll is a valid example of a useful statement of such statistical preferences, but it is hardly to be considered as a statement of valuation in any sense. It does not appear, for example, that anybody has suggested that because more people wanted him that Eisenhower is a more valuable man for President than was Stevenson. All we know is that he was the choice of the majority of people for that office. To state this in terms of value is to add nothing to the statistical enumeration of preferences. Such statistical enumeration of preferences is a useful tool in social science, but it should be described as such rather than using a vague collective term like "objective value."

Objective values or social values are sometimes spoken of as separate from individual values, or, put in more understandable terms, a society as a whole might choose *A* rather than *B* when the individuals would prefer *B*. If there is such a social choice as distinguished from the aggregate of individual choices by members of society, there is no evidence to support it. We like to talk about social interests as contrary to individual interests, but social values as some kind of unanimity choice probably mean nothing more than the statistical combinations indicated above, or they represent situations where certain individuals make decisions or choices on behalf of the entire social unit. Careful examination will show that these choices made by individuals or groups stand upon the same pattern upon which individuals make their own choices. The process of valuation or choice, if it be other than a statistical one, is the same except that the presence of others aiding in a group choice may have some further psychological weight; but the choice is made in the name of the group or society rather than the individuals. If there is a social interest or value wholly apart from the interests of individuals in society, nobody has yet demonstrated it;[2] and if it were postulated, it is hard to see that

[1] See for example, Benedict, Patterns of Culture (1934).

[2] See Duguit, The Law and the State, (de Sloovere's transl.) 31 Har. L. Rev. 1, 8 (1917).

it would amount to other than mysticism. Objective social value then is a collective concept which either wholly disappears or is based upon some kind of mathematical formula describing the aggregate of individual choices where the individual is influenced by considerations of the effect of his choice upon others as well as upon himself. It would be very difficult to prove that such considerations are not also present in all subjective individual choices.

Moral value is another term which constantly appears in the literature. This seems to mean that when a person is influenced by moral, ethical, intellectual, or social urges, he has a set of values or choices which would be different from those cases in which he makes his choice when not under the influence of such drives. About all this term does is to indicate that individuals have drives or impulses toward choices which are influenced by their state of mind toward certain moral concepts. It is simply an attempt to describe the choice in terms of one of his drives. In the same sense one might speak of hunger values, anger values, love values and all of those other impulses which may be dominant at the time a man makes a choice. It would be better therefore instead of using the term "moral value" to speak of choices as influenced by morals. The drives of religion, hunger, love, etc., are in the same class. These things are mere factors in making a choice and so are no more necessary to be considered than any of the other psychological urges behind choice.

Instrumental value is another sense in which the term appears. This seems to mean that the thing evalued is good to accomplish a particular purpose, as, for example, a two-inch coupling is instrumentally valuable to fasten two pieces of two-inch pipe together, while a three-inch coupling has no value for that purpose. Value in this sense simply means that it can be predicted that the object will be engineeringly useful to solve particular problems. In fact the term "useful" is much more accurate to describe this particular quality of value. When one speaks of a good (or valuable) law in this sense, he means that it is useful under certain conditions for solving a particular problem. Thus a youth-correction legal setup may be more useful for preventing juvenile delinquency in a given city than is a juvenile court.

It may be argued that in the nature of the universes there is but one best law for the governing of each situation, and that, even speaking pragmatically, the time will come when the lawmaker has to call upon his values to decide which of the two laws will be best for application in such a situation, so he is ultimately driven back to values. This is a logical but not a real difficulty. As a practical matter all that the lawmaker will ever have to decide is which of two or more possible courses of action or proposed laws will serve best to solve the problem before him. If he uses methods of Experimental Jurisprudence, he will choose the law which promises solution with the least disturbing results in the form of further predictable dislocation of the desires of the body politic or with the minimum of further clashes of interest between its members. Using the information and jural laws available to him, he can make the prediction in the same manner in which an engineer predicts how much power will be necessary to move a given mountain. Having made such a prediction on the available data, he must choose the law or course of action which he believes will be the most useful to accomplish the purpose of keeping the peace or satisfying the interests. If after making the choice and watching the results, his guess is confirmed, he has a useful (instrumentally valuable) law; but if subsequent facts do not bear out his prediction or there is a change in the factors, which is likely, he may revise his data for his previous estimate of usefulness and continue the process of working, as the scientist does, toward endless improvement. In such a process if he checks his data, he will develop a large number of jural laws to aid in solving current human problems and to implement his choice of regulatory laws. In such a practice ultimate values need never and can never be reached.

If the lawmaker discards the scientific method and returns to intuitive decisions, making a choice based upon his inner conscious or unconscious momentary psychological drives, one studying the process is reverted to psychology as he is in the case of other subjective choices (values). Whether or not such a choice is good will ultimately have to be tested by its usefulness to the lawmaker or to the public. If the lawmaker is a natural lawyer or idealist who starts from a preconceived ideal or pattern, still the instrumental value of his choice of law will have to be tested by determining its success in conforming society to the idea pattern. Instrumental valuation then is better expressed simply as the choice of useful devices for satisfying the human interests which lie at the basis of all legal problems. The problem of analysis of interests themselves will be discussed below. Instrumental value is simply usefulness to accomplish particular ends.

Valuation or evaluation process is another way in which the term "value" often appears. For example, one speaks of valuation for rate-making purposes or valuation for tax purposes. In this process the equipment of a company or an object owned by a taxpayer is compared with other equipment and objects for the purpose of determining whether the rates or taxes shall be higher or lower. This is simply a measuring device. The purpose for it is measurement and no more. The problems involved are simply those of measurement which are common to all sciences.

It appears then that the term "value" serves no purpose in Experimental Jurisprudence. Its continued use in the language makes it very much like the term "phlogiston" which all physicists once used to describe an element which they believed was necessary for explaining the phenomenon of fire; but, as has been suggested, just as physics now gets along without phlogiston, a descriptive and experimental social science can do without the term "value."[3] All that is necessary is to discover the actual condition of the interests or demands of people in society to expose the need for granting the demands which they make, and to choose the legal devices which will be useful for making possible the fulfillment of the desires represented by the choices, with the least social friction.

THE NATURE OF INTERESTS

It is obvious in any scheme involving choosing legal devices to protect or satisfy the interests of people and society that it will be necessary to isolate and examine the things called interests. The term has been variously used by philosophers and jurists to describe many concepts from theoretical rights to an analysis of the results achieved by various rules of law.[4] To an experimental jurist the term has little meaning unless it is actually identified with the real wants of individuals or of society as they come into play or ought to come into play in the creation of rules of law. When examined in this light it will be seen that the interests or wants of an individual or of groups of individuals break down into three classifications involving their objective interests or the discoverability thereof. These three categories or degrees of intensity as they affect the law might be expressed by the terms "demands," "desires" and "needs."

Demands may be classified as wants which are expressed in such a manner that they may be objectively stated. Demands are the stuff involved in most legal operations. In the case of litigation they take the form of claims, as of right or simply baldly asserted. Where legislation is involved, demands are commonly expressed through the lobbies, the hearings and at the polls. It is commonly believed that where

---

[3] Cf. Lundberg, Foundations of Sociology, 10 ff. (1939); Wild, Plato's Modern Enemies and the Theory of Natural Law, 204 ff. (1953).

[4] See the remarks and collected bibliography on this subject, Pound, Outline of Lectures on Jurisprudence, 60 ff. (4th ed. 1928).

unheeded demands pile up, they may result in breaches of the peace or other dislocation of the legal system. Most legal problems operate in the field of making decisions which will reconcile these demands by granting some and refusing others with an eye to keeping the peace, but interests or wants also have deeper and more subtle meanings which any student of law must consider.

Desires may be classified as human interests in things which may or may not be expressed but which the individual or group subjectively wants, craves or would if encouraged claim. It is of course entirely possible that an individual or group may desire something but not demand it. Also it is possible to have demands which are not based on desires but are asserted for strategical, political or other reasons. Unexpressed desires seem important to the legal scientist only insofar as they may be the basis for later demands or because suppression of them stores up forces, either rational or irrational, which may cause social upheaval or interfere with law enforcement. They need to be taken into account by the experimental jurist if he can reach, observe and measure them.

Needs are a third class of interests or wants which play an important part. They might be said to be those conditions or things in the current state of society which, if present and effective, would cause the individual or society to function with the least friction and more in accordance with the natural order of his or its universe at that moment. Needs clearly change with changing conditions in society. Primitive man needs no automobiles, airplanes, telephones, machine tools or universities, but modern American society could not exist without them. The creation of laws to meet current needs in turn develops new ones. Social security laws, for example, create a need for social workers, universal military training, a need for officers, and the United Nations, a whole legion of new needs. It also seems clear that needs may or may not correspond with desires and demands; if man were perfectly rational there might be a one-to-one correspondence between the three, but in the present state of affairs it is quite common to see demands for what one does not need, or what experience may show is bad for one, like a child demanding too much candy. Needs also may or may not correspond with desires. Demands or desires not complied with or recognized may cause social upheaval. Needs not provided for may be the basis of the failure of a whole civilization. For example, according to one theory it seems that the ancient Mayans cultivated corn by burning off the jungle and planting with a pointed stick. When the strong grasses and weeds invaded the clearings and choked out their corn, burning did no good. The Mayans were never able to invent anything like a plow to cut the grass, so it encroached upon the corn fields, and the numerous and advanced society apparently ran out of jungles and food.[5] The failure to enact laws to meet the needs of society can have a like effect.

Too often the leaders of the legal system overlook needs of the people. Unrequited demands may cause revolution or other change but the traditional legal system may go right on after the change failing to meet the needs, simply because the leaders of the revolution or other political change, having overthrown the symbols of the law which was oppressing them, have neither the knowledge nor the ability to make the proper legal adjustments to put the system in line with the needs which were the basis of the trouble. When this is the case, the legal system may go through a series of further revolutionary upheavals, as has been the case in Central and South America; or the civilization, having restored order, as has been the case with many ancient cultures, simply withers and dies due to failure of the lawmakers to meet the needs of the society which they govern.

In the modern world where great technical advances have made revolution more and more difficult and where the complication of the governmental machinery impedes orderly change, the legal system must devise new ways for finding the true needs of the people, or internal decay begins. The art of government reconciles demands and discovers some desires. Science should disclose the needs by determining the effectiveness of laws to accomplish their purposes. It can also predict that meeting certain present needs will cause other future needs to arise. For the purpose of Experimental Jurisprudence or an objective social science, it would probably be better to dispense with the term "interests" and in its place use its three components, demands, desires and needs. Experimental Jurisprudence offers the means of discovering and measuring demands, desires and needs, provides a means for determining which ones should be satisfied, and can create a technique for choosing the devices best calculated to make the needed change. Careful checking of this process will yield many jural laws which will prevent wrong decisions by future lawmakers and will also point out the mistake of yielding to insistent demands for unnecessary things.

[5] Morley, The Ancient Maya 71 (1946). The Maya tribes still do it that way. Higbee, Agriculture in the Maya Homeland, 38 Geographical Review 457 (1948), Gann, Maya Cities 156 (1928).

The levels of demands, desires and needs may fall into at least two classifications. There are wants for immediate things like food, clothing, amusement, books, education and the like, which might be called primary. There are also secondary or instrumental wants; that is, individuals or groups may demand or desire a rule of law, a public official or a commission to get something else. This is often expressed in the cliche, "There ought to be a law." Thus the W.C.T.U. demanded a prohibition law to cut down or abolish the consumption of liquor, and later other citizens demanded repeal to get cheaper liquor or to get rid of gangsters. As it turned out, all were largely mistaken. The secondary instruments which they demanded did not produce the desired primary results. Sometimes a secondary want may seem primary. A city, for example, may and often does demand a city manager form of government, or a state a unicameral legislature, as an end in itself rather than as a means of meeting certain needs. Many of the so-called social interests fall into this classification.

It seems clear that wants in all three categories may be either primary or secondary. Experimental Jurisprudence is a scientific method for predicting usefulness especially of the secondary wants, also for pointing out that what appears at the moment to be a primary want is really secondary. It should also be in a position to indicate what may be the predicted effects of granting a primary or a secondary demand or desire.

DRIVES BEHIND DEMANDS, DESIRES AND NEEDS

It must always be kept in mind that in dealing with desires, demands and needs, a social scientist or experimental jurist is working with real human feelings, wants and claims which are subject to discovery, measurement and classification in a manner similar to the measurement of height, weight, race, patterns of culture and the like. From the purely objective point of view, the existence of the demand or need might be enough for a working basis of a purely objective science of law. But man is a rational being; he gives reasons for his wants. When these reasons are expressed with his demands, they become a symbol behind the enactment of laws or the judgments of courts. Very often the reasons given are purely hypocritical, but an examination of the expressed purposes for which laws are created and their success in accomplishing the purposes, Step Three in Experimental Jurisprudence, will go a long way toward exposing hypocritical demands and discovering real or fanciful needs.

There are many unique motivations which may combine to create a demand for laws and legal devices. These can be roughly gathered into three classes: (1) the purely selfish desires of man as an individual for food, clothing, riches, power, self-assertion and the like; (2) narrow altruistic desires of man as a member of a kinship, family or other small group; and (3) broader altruistic desires, whereby man demands things as a member of a larger entity where group feeling plays an important part. Expressions of such larger group solidarity are found in racial hatred, patriotism, political parties, loyalty to college, lodge, church and the like.

The fact of existence of these drives is important, and their effects upon law, the process of lawmaking, and law enforcement may all fall within the ken of Experimental Jurisprudence. Here the jurist will need the aid of the psychologist, psychiatrist, criminologist, sociologist, economist, anthropologist and other social scientists. Information obtainable from these disciplines would seem to indicate that man is born with few if any of these demands or needs as inherent instincts in the same fashion in which a bird is born with the ability to build a complicated nest. Apparently basic needs arising from these drives are created by environment, and thus are subject to the force of law.

Law recognizes and aids many institutions which are important means for creating the drives behind the wants which men express through their demands, desires and needs. These may be roughly classified into five groups: family, religious, ethical, patriotic and commercial. The family group, although the one closest to the biological requirements, is heavily sanctioned, protected and encouraged by many laws. Among the religious institutions protected and fostered which play an important part in creating the wants of men are churches and their subsidiary and kindred organizations such as church schools, lodges like the Masons, the Knights of Columbus, Boy Scouts, and others with close church and emotional connections. On the ethical or intellectual side are institutions such as schools, universities, professional associations and the like. Patriotic orders like veterans' organization, sons of veterans, college alumni and local improvement societies also receive much legal sanction and support. Commercial institutions such as corporations, chambers of commerce, business associations and the like also play their part.

All of these are sanctioned by law and in turn bring pressure to bear for change in the legal system through direct demands and the creation of indirect drives which appear to influence the law and the social structure through desires and needs. It is well known that corporations and other legal devices for the purpose of supporting institutions of the type just mentioned are numbered in the millions.

These legal entities with a further sanction of the law have combined into trade, business, professional, educational, religious and other associations busily engaged in expressing demands for legal change to meet their real or fancied desires or needs and in creating others. A recent summary shows that there are over 4,000 such legally constituted organizations of institutions,[6] most of which are active in making secondary demands in the form of requests for changes in the law.

Although these institutions and organized pressure groups contain among their numbers representatives which foster the strongest aspirations of man, aspirations which are usually designated by noblest, highest, dearest and similar laudatory adjectives, they also include others just as strong which may be classified by selfish, base and other derogatory expressions. When one is faced with the problem of lawmaking by choosing between the demands of certain pressure groups, he cannot help but be struck by the fact that even though their desires and demands may be diametrically opposed, all groups are pretty well living up to their own integrated or rationalized moral codes. Thus the Bartenders Union in advocating the sale of liquor is no less true to its morals than is the W.C.T.U. in opposing it. Who is there to say that the tobacco companies in spending millions to advertise their products are less honestly advancing their interests than were the lobbyists on behalf of religious groups having laws passed prohibiting the sale of cigarettes? Most of the attitudes of professional moralists or some social scientists toward these organizations and institutions constitute an expression of predetermined beliefs, ideals and values, which were probably implanted in their minds by institutions fostered and protected by law in the form of churches, schools, religious and moral propaganda, educational and pressure groups, constantly pushing for their own moral precepts. Those opposed likewise have their minds filled with education and propaganda sent out by legally protected agencies on their side. Each set of succeeding minds is in danger of traveling in a constantly closing spiral of thought revolving about a central core or "moral" code. The advocates of each position in their own minds test the validity of their contending positions by reference to a set of "principles" previously set up to justify those very positions. So society is split by contending factions relying for their moral support upon the output of legally sanctioned institutions busily engaged in feeding upon their own contending moral concepts. Who is to say which is right? But it is significant that all of these entities serve the same purpose, satisfying human wants. It might therefore be wise to

---

[6] Judkins, National Associations of the United States (1949).

approach a study of their effect upon the legal system with a realization that they serve an important function in expressing *de facto* human demands and desires which may point the way toward discovering basic needs.

On the opposite side of the picture, there are powerful forces working against change in the law. Among these are habitual ways of doing things, folkways, some of the institutions just mentioned and just plain inertia, all of which exert terrific force upon individual and group beliefs expressed through customs, ideas of right and wrong, desires to protect vested interests and other demands and needs. These are forces with which traditional legal systems have been required to contend.

As the numbers of people increase and the legally supported institutions continue to multiply and to use mass communications, even the orthodox legal systems must take into account all of these drives for stability and change or they will lose control over society. Experimental Jurisprudence must be put into effect to measure the forces here involved, to state the jural laws which they develop, and to suggest regulation, formalization and direction of these forces.

LAW AND THOUGHT CONTROL

But legal devices in the hands of many rulers of totalitarian countries and of powerful forces within the democracies are already moving into the area formerly occupied by voluntary but legally supported institutions which create wants and direct choices. With the advent and use of mass communication media like the press, radio and television, it takes no trained social scientist to observe that these legally supported efforts at thought control are producing concrete results. The so-called public relation branches of the Army, Navy and other American governmental departments are examples of the success of this effort in democratic countries, and the advances of the rulers of totalitarian states along these lines are well known to all. If people wielding these legally sanctioned powers are motivated by selfishness, prejudice or preconceived arbitrary ideals or ends, there may be unleashed vicious forces in the form of impassioned and warped demands followed by demonic national and international actions. The resulting damage to the body politic and even to the whole world may be catastrophic. One has only to observe the actions of Hitler Germany and Fascist Italy to see the results of such legally sanctioned thought control when directed by skillful and fanatical lawmakers. The menace of Communist Russia and China, now beginning to use these legal devices even on a wider scale, is truly frightening.

Denouncing such activities, even attacking them with a force of arms, does not seem to be the solution. Now that such powers have been shown to be capable of human control for whatever ends the lawmaker wants to use them, it is time that the jurists begin to consider subjecting the processes of thought control to careful observation and scientific analysis. This will involve a study of public reaction to various kinds of official and unofficial propaganda, devising hypotheses to explain the reasons for such actions and stating jural laws to describe the effectiveness of public and private efforts to lead the people to adopt certain conclusions and attitudes.

The results of efforts of psychologists to explore the workings of the individual mind in reaching subjective choices will offer useful material upon which to construct hypotheses as to mass reactions. Social psychology should also be helpful, but the jurists cooperating with psychologists need not wait for them to produce conclusive results. Here again the statistically collected objective reactions of people will be a useful tool in measuring the effectiveness of the various devices of thought control. In addition to the methods of psychology, consumer-demand surveys, radio-listener polls and numerous studies of the effectiveness of various advertising methods are suggestive of the possibilities of observation in this field.

Looking far into the future, it may be predicted that the methods of legally directed thought control may eventually take over the direction and control of what some now call human values and that this power may be turned to scientific purposes. If this is to be accomplished, it should be along the lines of Experimental Jurisprudence. When this is done, there will no longer be any basis for the belief that social science is impossible because it contains no elements of control such as those found in physical sciences. The means of social control by law are now developing and increasing all about us. Mankind may soon be required to make the choice whether these powers are to be exercised for greed, lust and caprice of individuals or are to be used in the scientific advancement of the race.

DECISIONS, THE OPEN MIND, OR THE SCIENTIFIC POINT OF VIEW

No enlightened person today will deny that what he is, what he believes, his express demands, his innermost desires and needs, are shaped and to a large extent controlled by the myriad of social and legal forces about him. Whether or not they make up all of his personality or character or whether something is left to innate structure and heredity are problems for the psychologist, the psychiatrist, ethnologist and similar scientists. But even before it examines the force of legal institutions in creating these psychological drives, Experimental Jurisprudence can start with the existing demands, desires, needs and with the problems of reconciling and choosing between them. It cannot avoid preconceived motivation toward evaluating, especially as it exists in current lawmakers, but the jurist need not be dominated by them. In approaching inanimate matter, a physical scientist, being human, is to a certain extent influenced by his religion, habits and preconceived notions, but it is easier for him to achieve an impartial position than it is for a social scientist.

Preconceived idealistic notions of the good, the beautiful, the right, the fair, etc., are ground into all humans from birth. Willingness to fight and die for these beliefs, which are rationalizations of wants, whatever they may be, is considered one of the noblest traits of human nature. In the past, social science has been intrigued by the attempt to discover the ultimate truth, good, values and the like. A careful examination of the facts of life will show that this effort viewed in scientific terms is merely the pursuit of a mirage. In the past, these ultimates have been dogmatically asserted with no attempt at proof or efforts to determine their usefulness in society. Leaders and followers alike have been accustomed to assert their belief in their own particular ultimate truths and then stick to them doggedly. This is probably an excellent quality in an individual subject of the law, but there is grave doubt whether it is a useful characteristic in a lawmaker, and it is clear that it has no place in the makeup of a jurist. As our knowledge of anthropology and of the various ideals held throughout the world is broadened, it becomes apparent that this alleged virtue in the latter two may possibly be self-defeating. Since the ideal positions held by various nations and races of people throughout the world have proven to be in direct conflict, as, for example, the aims and purposes of communism and capitalism, the territorial aspirations of the Poles, the Germans and the Czechs in Eastern Europe, the trait of fighting to the death for one's own position, if taken and held by lawmakers, assures immediate war and chaos. In the present state of the development of modern science, continued action of this kind is pointing toward eventual annihilation of the race. Even complete victory by one ideal over another by the use of force does not guarantee its validity. A society dominated by the victor is assured of survival only if it is able to meet the needs of the situation which follows. If it is not able to satisfy these needs, history has shown that there may follow the death or frustration of the individuals and of the society. Failure of the rulers of society to conform to the needs of the people in light of the conditions in which they live has been one of the causes of the decay of every civilization in history. The capable leader in society is the one who is able to adjust to its environment by changing its fixed laws to meet the requirements of the universe in which it lives. In the nature of things, the best laws are the ones which succeed in making the most useful adjustment. Failure to do so means that, to the extent of the failure, there follows either the breakdown of the sanctions of law or the crippling or death of society. In modern society, where organizations and armaments make revolution much harder, the danger of inner collapse is greatly accentuated.

Experimental Jurisprudence will ultimately stand ready on behalf of the jurist to undertake the task of recording how legal phenomena develop, run their courses and meet the needs of the society which they govern. Thus the lawmaker should approach his problems with as open a mind as possible so that he can consider the demands and desires of the society. As a lawmaker, he is called upon to make decisions between conflicting demands. Whether he approaches these decisions with an open mind or merely relies upon his own prejudices or selfish desires, the exigencies of the moment require that he act.

The jurist should take the law which has thus been created and answer at least three questions. (1) To what extent does it satisfy the demands which brought it into existence? (2) Does it accomplish the express purposes for which the lawmaker enacted it? (3) How does it affect the needs of the people whom it governs? Since the jurist likewise must examine the facts with an open mind willing to reconsider, on the basis of observable data, the usefulness of laws in operation, to him there can be no absolutes, but the usefulness of each law must be judged on the facts of the human reaction to it. While it is important even in an experimental system that ideals and beliefs of the lawmaker as well as the citizen be firmly held and bravely acted upon, the jurist should always keep in mind the principle that any ideal or plan of lawmaking is like a scientific hypothesis to be followed faithfully until a more workable one appears. Preconceived absolutes in human conduct which do not work out in practice if held to the bitter end can only result in certain conflict and eventual tragedy. After a law has had a fair trial and failed to achieve its purpose, it should be discarded like an unworkable hypothesis. In making these decisions, both the lawmaker and the jurist must take disclosed desires, demands and needs as they find them and work with them toward a proper reconcilation of all. Preconceived ideals of usefulness, ends, purposes and the like necessarily have some effect on the lawmaker, but the jurist need only look at results.

For the present it seems that in weighing or measuring wants, each demand or desire should have a one-to-one ratio with every other desire and demand. Thus the unit for consideration would seem to be the single want of each person and not the person himself. Intensity of the desires and demands and the numbers of people having them, of course, must also be considered. For the present, the numerical or statistical basis seems useful. When needs are discovered, they should, of course, be given preference ahead of both demands and desires, but these latter two cannot be entirely ignored because there is probably a human need for satisfying demands and desires even though the things demanded are not needed and may not even be useful to the persons making the demands.

This is not the test of utilitarianism where the happiness of each person counts for one.[7] Here the demands, desires and needs are the units that should be considered. The laws to be enacted or recommended should be those which lead to the greatest sum total of satisfaction of needs, demands and desires, in that order of rank. Thus a more complicated person is certain to have greater wants than a simple individual, and his combined interests as a whole will therefore weigh heavier in the scientific scale than those of a less complicated (less intelligent, if you will) individual. Thus a scientist needs and demands very expensive and intricate materials to do his work while the simple (less intelligent) individual may need only food and clothing, which the scientist also needs. If all the needs and demands are considered in making the social adjustments by regulations or laws, the more complicated (intelligent) person receives greater consideration, and thus insofar as a complicated person is the product of advanced civilization (which seems to be the case), such civilization can and will be encouraged by law.

Experimentation may develop jural laws which will eventually discard this formula, but it seems a good starting point for the creation of laws to reconcile clashing human wants. Further experience will eventually determine its validity, perhaps in a manner similar to that in which science first verified the law of conservation of energy and then disproved it. It must be realized that there is less possibility of a social scientist discovering the ultimate good than there is a physicist determining the final construction of matter, but this need not lead to despair. If man will adopt the experimental method in government, it seems possible that he can, working stage by stage, create jural

---

[7] Hall, Readings in Jurisprudence c. 4, 177 (1938) and authorities there cited.

laws which will eventually offer a workable description of the effect of various aspects of the legal system upon society. With properly developed jural laws offering predictions of the effect of particular laws whose operation is subject to further experimental check and verification, ideas of the ultimate good and the like will be replaced with a pragmatic set of working hypotheses which will enable man to approach his maximum controlled development within the limitations of the universe in which he finds himself. If this open-minded experimental method be seriously adopted in lawmaking and government, there is no reason why it should be necessary to witness the rise, fall and decay of civilizations. Steady progress toward a society better integrated with the natural requirements of the universe is thus possible. If lawmakers and jurists will give up their preconceived notions of ultimate truth, good, value and the like, they can work steadily to create an apparatus of Experimental Jurisprudence. This, of course, will demand an extensive change in our attitude toward what may now be regarded by some as fundamental values. It may eventually require an extensive reorganization of the present forms of government, but such problems are too far in the future to require present discussion.

CONCLUSION

In short, Experimental Jurisprudence, when properly applied, can now be expected only to test the efficiency of a law in attaining the particular ends for which it was adopted and in turn can state the results which will follow various attempts to reach such ends. The data thus accumulated may throw great light on the ultimate usefulness of the objectives and the effectiveness of the means used to attain them. The ethical problem of what, in the abstract, is the ultimate good is not likely ever to come within the ken of Experimental Jurisprudence; it is today too far removed to require consideration.

Jurisprudence as a science of ethical values, norms and the like can have no function, in light of the present state of research techniques, other than that of philosophical speculation. Such speculation may be exceedingly interesting and may result in highly suggestive working hypotheses, but it can never have any true scientific usefulness until it is put to the acid test of practical application by means of social control applied under the careful observation of scientists. In this way pragmatic ethics may become a living reality through the development of the technique of Experimental Jurisprudence.

When a so-called value judgment is approached, the question should be: "Value for the solution of what social problem?"; if the problem is then carefully identified, its factual basis studied and the scientific and jural laws surrounding its phenomena developed, the question of value as a philosophical speculation or political issue will usually be found to have vanished.

CHAPTER IV

Purposes of Law and Government; Relationship of Experimental Jurisprudence to Government, Lawmaking and Policy Decisions

In discussing the theoretical nature of Experimental Jurisprudence, one immediately impinges upon the questions of the relationship of law to government and the purposes which they serve; one encounters such terms as "the state," "sovereignity," "the sovereign" and the concept of the lawmaker or the law-giver. Some of these are real and some of them are fictional. It is imperative for clear thinking to separate the real from the fictional and to note how they bear upon the theories of jurisprudence.

RELATIONSHIP OF LAW, GOVERNMENT, STATE AND SOVEREIGN

The phenomena of lawmaking and law enforcement involve two real things: organization of human beings and the rules which they make to control their own organization, its members and others. In this process, the human organization gathered together working or cooperating toward a common end may be called the government. This group makes rules and enforces them. These rules are found in various publications and are called laws.

Sometimes, however, so-called rules of law may also be fictions. This often happens, as, for example, where a court is called upon to decide a case which is not covered by any written statute, by an administrative rule or by any clearly identifiable precedent. In such a case accuracy would require the statement that the rule of law (usually written) authorizes the court to decide the case and no more; but in common-law countries at least when the court decides such a case, it states its reasons for so deciding, and in giving its opinion, it adopts the fiction that the rule of law stated in the decision existed all the time. The fact is, of course, that the court is indulging in fiction to make its decision the more plausible. When a series of such decisions is sufficient to create a recognizable rule of common law, it is obvious that at some stage in the process the fiction has become a reality. The exact point at which the fiction becomes a real rule of law is one of the chief preoccupations of the practicing lawyer and of the law teacher but it is of little consequence to the experimental jurist. As civilization advances, the courts seem to indulge less and less in this lawmaking function and are increasingly called upon to interpret and apply rules made by other bodies.

It is interesting to note that there are many organizations which gather together either as principals or as representatives of others to make rules. In ancient times these organizations were families, clans, religions, orders, cities and the like; today some of these bodies still make rules or laws, but they have been largely replaced by voluntary associations. So far as their behavior in conclave assembly is concerned, a man from Mars could not distinguish between a meeting of a legislature, the House of Delegates of the American Bar Association or the American Medical Association, the American Law Institute, the Assembly of the United Nations, the National Convention of the American Legion or of the Masonic Lodge. These and any one of a thousand trade or professional associations seem to behave in about the same manner. All of these bodies hold debates under similar procedures and make rules to govern their actions; all have governing bodies and representatives who contact members and carry on the business of the organization.

One difference between these organizations and the government is that the so-called private bodies do not usually try to make rules to control persons outside of their membership. Legal government makes rules that are supposed to be binding upon the members of the lawmaking group and upon outsiders.

The state is a term often used to designate the ultimate power to control outsiders within a given territory. This power of the state to make rules binding upon all its subjects may be delegated to existing non-state organizations, after which they are called agents or arms of the state and their rules are enforced against the organization itself and against non-members.

In other cases, as in that of the Uniform Laws Commission, the American Law Institute, the Chamber of Commerce and many others, the private organization makes rules like the new Uniform Commercial Code to govern outsiders, which they expect to receive the official sanction of the government, after which they become laws.

It should be noted that the term "state," in its modern sense, is a creation of the writers on philosophy and political science, sometimes used, as is the case in the United States, to designate a geographical portion of a larger federal government, again as a synonym for the ultimate power or sovereignity of a particular government. In its older sense, it was the military power distinguished from the jurisdiction of the civil government.[1] Again it is used, perhaps, as a collective noun to represent the powers and interests of the body politic as a unit distinguished from the powers and interests of the individual subjects of the government. Although the origin of the concept seems to be lost in antiquity,[2] it is a fiction about which much real loyalty has been built. The doctrine of states' rights, the theories of the all-prevailing power, might and interest of the state and the claims for the state as an agent of local government are some of many fictions which have created real emotional responses and political issues of all kinds, some of which have led to the justification of contention, violence and bloodshed.

While philosophers and political theorists may and have argued *ad nauseam* as to the proper use of the concept, the experimental jurist is chiefly interested, among others, in such things as the extent to which it is used as a symbol to mask demands of certain local groups, as a facade to protect big business against law enforcement by big government, as a means for weakening the power and effectiveness of a central government, as a device for getting government closer to the people, or, conversely, as an excuse for strengthening the power of a central bureaucracy at the expense of the liberties of individuals. These and many other examples which can be given of the use of the term "state" indicate the power of the concept when used as an emotional focus like God, homeland, mother, and the like to direct the actions of men.

The extent of the real power and the results of the use of the term "state" must be studied, but as a lawmaking unit it should be recognized for what it really is, largely a fiction used to justify or denote lawmaking power. When an organization or group not previously designated as the government purports to act for or on behalf of this fiction or is enabled to enforce its will upon others, it is termed a *de facto* government. It should be noted that a *de facto* government in

---

[1] Ehrlich, Fundamental Principles of The Sociology of Law c. 7 ff. (Moll's transl. 1936).

[2] For the confusion of the terms "state" and "sovereignty" see XIV Encyclopedia of the Social Sciences 265, 328 (1934) and authorities there cited.

fact has all the attributes of a state. The only element lacking is the willingness of other states to "officially" admit the existence of this fact, and to receive "official" representatives of the government, but it is not at all uncommon for the other established governments to negotiate with it in the same manner as with others. The relation of the United States to Communist China in the Korean War and in the following negotiations is a case in point. In the field of international law, if other governmental organizations do "recognize" its power to enforce its will upon others, its subjects, it becomes a *"de jure government"* which is said to have "sovereignty."

Sovereignty, like the state, is also a fiction revived in the sixteenth century as a rationalization of emerging nationalism. It is sometimes used to describe the power of a person or group to change the rules or laws without any restraint or interference by others and without suffering any sanction for so doing.[3] In the past this irresponsible lawmaking power was said to be one of the attributes of the state; but as the interrelation of nations has grown, the fiction of this irresponsible sovereign state, the ideal of the eighteenth century, is gradually vanishing. Modern national and international governments are beginning, however slowly, to recognize their mutual *de facto* and *de jure* obligations to each other.

The Communist philosophy which has argued for the ultimate disappearance of the state is not a mere attack upon a fiction. It might really be better classed as a move to abolish national governments as such; but the practical results of this attempt to dispose of the concept of the sovereign state has brought into more vivid reality the existence and necessity of a rule-making and enforcing agency against all persons by an organization which we commonly call the government. In no place is this overriding governmental organization more in evidence than in the Russian Communist party and the bureaucracy which it controls.

The lawmaker or *the law-giver* is a combination of fact and fiction which usually designates that part of the governmental organization which enacts and creates laws. In simple governments the lawmaker is the man, the council or the legislating body which acts to make laws. And in modern complicated governments like the United States, the British Empire or Soviet Russia, the law-giving or lawmaking function has been delegated to so many agencies that the term as a unit has be-

---

[3] See Krable, The Modern Idea of the State, p. xviii. (Transl. by Sabine and Shephard, 1922).

come a mere fiction. Rules having the force and effect of law are now made by a myriad of agencies operating under constitutional or delegated power. *De facto* and *de jure* the lawmaker may be an individual, a court, a commission, a legislature, a body, an executive, a private organization, a pressure group or combinations of two or more of these and others. Today "the lawmaking function" and "lawmaker" are simply symbolic expressions to cover the entire process of making laws. Thus law, government and the lawmaking function are the realities about which men build up many persuasive fictions in addition to the state and the sovereign.

THE PURPOSES OF LAW AND GOVERNMENT

One of the most profitable fields for the creation of fictions about government and the law is in the area of attempting to determine the purpose for which governments exist. Here the actual purposes seem to intermingle with the pretended, ostensible, theoretical and fictional to such an extent that a casual observer may doubt whether real purposes can be distinguished from the fictional ones. However, it is apparent that the one underlying necessity of law and government must be to keep the internal peace. Without this, any regime of law or government is impossible.

Beyond the elemental requirements of keeping the peace, the general reasons offered for the existence of government and the real purposes of particular rules of law are legion. Once peace is established and the regime of law enforcement begins, the powers of government may be directed toward whatever ends the ruling class or classes of individuals desire and the particular rules of law which they enact, create, decree or demand may be oriented toward a myriad of conscious or unconscious purposes.

Philosophers and so-called political theorists have loved to speculate about the fictional and real ends for which government exists. Literature is full of erudite discussions as to which is the best, the real or the preferable purpose of government and the lawmaking power. Much of this is rationalization of existing powers, and much more is speculation about what the general purpose or direction of the power ought to be. To review all of these theories on governmental policy would require a learned treatise which would add little to the literature already published. It will be necessary here to mention as examples only a few, not pausing to separate fiction from fact, as if that really could be done, to raise the background for the discussion of the relationship of Experimental Jurisprudence to government and lawmaking.

The postulated ends for which government and the law may be used are legion, and the resulting policies, both real and fictional, run in all directions. Among some of the most ancient and widely held are those which cluster about the concepts of absolute monarchy. In this group are the theories that government exists for the purpose of carrying out the will of the sovereign, which in turn may be an existing absolute monarch, as was recently the case with King Saiud of Arabia, or the abstract fictional ruler expounded as sovereign in Austinian Jurisprudence. Closely related are the theories that government must perpetuate the interests of a nobility or a ruling class of some sort or other. This concept may be tinged with reality in more modern governments than the rulers care to admit.

Advancing toward the realm of fiction, one immediately encounters the theocracy where the force behind the policy of the law is said to be the will of God. This theory finds various expressions in the ancient doctrine of divine right of kings, in such modern states as the Papal State and in the recently overthrown government of Tibet.

Still further advanced in the realm of fiction are the theories of the Declaration of Independence, that the government was instituted to preserve natural rights like those set out in the first ten Amendments to the United States Constitution. Partially related to these are the expressions of Jefferson, Lincoln and other great democratic leaders that government exists to express the will of the governed. A probable offshoot of this concept is the teaching of Marx that the purpose of government is to carry out the will of the proletariat, with its corollary that one of the ends of government is to achieve the disappearance of the state. This in turn seems to be some sort of fictional rationalization of government itself. The antithesis of the Marxian doctrine is that man exists for the state and that governmental policies should be guided accordingly. Closely approaching this is another tenet, the Nazi's doctrine that government exists to create a super-race of men.

These are but a few of the general theories which appear in various forms to justify governmental actions or policies. Some of them may accidentally describe the real purposes behind lawmaking, but it should be recognized that in the main they are largely fictional, produced as the occasion may demand to rationalize the acts of lawmakers, to pacify subjects of the law or to persuade legislators, judges or other officials to adopt a new course of action or to continue the one they are presently following. Past attempts to compare or evaluate the general theories on the purpose of law and government with or against any others have led only to fruitless philosophizing, bickering, argument or even to the justification of bloodshed.

If one desires to adopt the tentative theories advanced in Chapter III, one may assume that government exists to meet the demands, desires and needs of its subjects. Using this approach, the question immediately arises as to what in fact are these wants and how, in truth, are they being promoted, recognized or satisfied by the legal system. From this angle, one must be struck immediately by the fact that an inventory of all such wants and an attempt to determine the extent to which a particular legal system or government properly evaluates and satisfies them all is a task requiring an apparatus of social observation and measurement perhaps not theoretically impossible but certainly far beyond any yet conceived.

On the other hand, it is entirely possible to apply such tests to particular discoverable rules of law, whatever their form may be. By isolating such a rule one may ask and expect to find the answers to the questions of how far it meets the demands, desires and needs which brought it into being. Here again the real must be separated from the ostensible and the fictional. While it is possible and fruitful for the scientist to determine the extent to which a law actually succeeds in accomplishing an ostensible or fictional purpose, and though many hypotheses and some proof can be developed in this area, the real purpose for the enactment of particular laws lies below the surface and can be disclosed only by social research which probes into the motives touching upon the wants, expressed and hidden, which brought it into existence. Here the scientist may find good use for his talents.

THE RELATION OF THE EXPERIMENTAL JURIST TO THE GOVERNMENT

The experimental jurist as such has little interest in the general theories advanced to explain the purposes of government as a whole or to justify certain lines of policy. As a scientist he must recognize that these expressions are largely fictional. While he might possibly desire to examine the factual effectiveness of various devices used to disseminate these fictions in persuading the public to submit to the general policies of a particular government, his immediate attention preferably would be directed toward the effect of a particular law in accomplishing the real purpose for which it was created. As indicated in Chapter II, this would involve examining the reasons given for enacting a particular law to determine which were real and which were fictional and proceding through Steps Two to Six to determine the effectiveness of the law and the reason for the social reactions to it. Having made these determinations as to a particular rule of law, he would then be in a position to recommend changes.

In this process the relationship of the experimental jurist to the government might take four forms: (1) that of an independent organization; (2) part of the government itself as an advisor or subordinate to the lawmaker and policy-maker; (3) the experimental jurist himself might be in control of the lawmaking process; (4) there might be a combination or mixture in varying degrees of the three pure forms just mentioned. It seems that the experimental jurist has a particularly important function in lawmaking no matter which of the three or more positions in government he might take. The advisability of one or the other of the forms would depend upon the state of the government at the time of instituting the activity.

The independent organization has certain advantages and disadvantages. In the state of the law where independent criticism of the government is allowed, as in the United States today, the experimental jurist could function as an organization independent of the government, like a foundation or educational institution. It would be free to investigate and to criticize, but it might be denied access to government offices and government papers. Being wholly independent, it might or might not get cooperation of the bureaucracy, the courts, the legislature and the like. There is also the grave danger that, without the coercive power of government in the form of subpoena and the like, the independent organization could not command the necessary information and attention from private citizens. Having no control over legislatures, as pointed out in Chapter II, there might also be great difficulty in getting suggestions adopted, but this would not be an impossibility. The adoption of independently suggested laws or policies would depend upon the vigor and persuasion with which they were advocated. The time-lag between the formulation of a hypothesis or a jural law and the opportunity to test it by the adoption of a new law and the observation of its effects might be discouraging indeed. In a totalitarian government, of course, activities of this type would probably not be tolerated. As indicated in later chapters, some work of this nature is going on today in the United States in cooperation with the government.

As an arm of the government itself the experimental jurist would have certain advantages. Among these would be the power to compel access to all sorts of information denied to a private agency. When the facts were gathered, there would be available easier cooperation with the bureaucracy, larger appropriations and possible continuity together with the chance to advise policy-makers and perhaps to get suggestions more readily put into the force of law. As indicated in later chapters, a lot of this type of research has become part of the routine of the government of the United States. But, being part of the government, the experimental jurist might be subject to control of the policy-makers who would interfere with scientific conclusions. This danger is even greater in a dictatorship where the party line might not tolerate deviation in the form of scientific findings; but even there the experimental jurist could and even now does serve an important function of advising the lawmaker of the success of his laws in operation. Likewise in democracies, popular prejudices, emotions of elected officials and waves of swinging sentiment might and do interfere with scientific findings. As indicated in later chapters, this happened to the Hoover Law Enforcement Commission investigating prohibition and is occurring in the case of the Tariff Commission and many quasi-scientific agencies of the United States government. On the other hand, there is a steady growth of the use of scientific data, and more and more research branches of the government both in totalitarian and democratic countries are determining policy.

Scientific control of lawmaking policy is both a present reality and a growing future possibility. As shown in later chapters, in the field of traffic laws, public health, the conservation of natural resources and many others where data from advanced experimental sciences are available, already policy-making in drafting and enforcement of laws is being delegated to scientific bodies applying the techniques of Experimental Jurisprudence. In the areas of government control over city planning, economic developments, criminal administration and the like, increasingly lawmakers are becoming accustomed to relying upon the advice of experts who can appraise the effect of old laws and predict the course of enforcement of new ones. Here one finds the most efficient organs of law enforcement and the greatest flexibility of the legal system to adopt innovations necessary to meet the needs of a dynamic civilization. As Experimental Jurisprudence develops more data, as the social effects of laws are studied, as jural laws postulating the results of enactments are created and tested, the area in which the policy-maker remains at large to choose from alternate proposed laws in any field on other considerations than facts and scientific data will be constantly narrowed. The experimental scientist will more easily take over the policy-making function, but the rate of progress will be correspondingly accelerated.

The fourth or mixed relationship of the experimental jurist to lawmakers and administrators is likely to be found in all advanced types of government existing today. It is also certain to appear in the evolutionary stages as the form of the government changes to adopt more and more scientific methods. This will involve a change in the functions of various departments; it will also affect relationship of lawmaking units, state, national, city, etc., to each other and should encourage new cooperation between governmental and non-governmental bodies to conduct research and to determine policies.

The nature of this development on the federal level will be discussed in more detail in Chapter VII. One example that may be pertinent here, showing the cooperation of all divisions of the government and private agencies, is in the field of public health as it affects milk purity. There the federal government's Public Health Service has done much research on the effect of various laws specifying means of purifying milk. It has drafted model statutes and ordinances which have been adopted by states, counties and municipalities. The progress of these laws in improving healthful milk supplies has been checked by both state and federal agencies, while, with the aid of the federal Department of Agriculture, the effectiveness of the entire program has been studied by the National Academy of Sciences, National Research Council[4] and a private foundation, aided by a number of milk trade associations.[5] Here one finds a good example of how a mixed group of government and private organizations is advancing the methods of Experimental Jurisprudence.

PRESENT AND FUTURE DEVELOPMENTS

If one will let his imagination go, he may see that if the techniques of Experimental Jurisprudence develop and enlarge, their use may impinge upon the present organizations and methods of government. Conceivably there might be considerable change in both the theory and practice of government as it adopts the research methods outlined here. Lawmaking based upon experimental science might, by the sheer force of its usefulness, find a place in governmental technique, just as automatic machine production is replacing handicraft on the economic front. Whether fostered by private foundations and educational institutions, by governmental advisors or by a combination of both, the influence on policy determination of experimental scientists may parallel the growth of engineering in charting the course of industry. Whether or not this will occur is at present too speculative to be worthy of serious comment; but as indicated in Chapter V, progress along these lines faces more opposition than one at first glance might expect.

[4] See their report—Dahlberg, Adams and Held, Sanitary Milk Control and its relation to Sanitary, Nutritive, and other Qualities of Milk (1953).

[5] The governing committee actually included representatives of the American Dairy Science Assn., International Assn. of Milk Sanitarians, Am. Public Health Assn., Int. Assn. of Milk Dealers and Nat. Cooperative Milk Producers Federation. See report, supra note 4, at v.

CHAPTER V

The Lag Between Scientific Discoveries and Legal Procedures*

Steps Seven and Eight of the process of Experimental Jurisprudence set out in Chapter II show that if it is to achieve its greatest efficiency, the products of scientific theory should be enacted into law, and the effects of that law on the body politic will need to be studied. In this respect it may be noted that the suggested techniques of Experimental Jurisprudence are similar to those used in the development and practice of medicine. There, after cures are devised as far as possible by means of laboratory technique in the manipulation of the underlying scientific theories and experiments, the final test is the application of the new remedy to the public. The recent mass inoculations to establish the efficiency of the Salk vaccine are the most spectacular example of the success of the practice of medicine as an applied science where human beings become, so to speak, the laboratory material.

Since law, like medicine, is a device to control people, it too must stand the ultimate test of application to the public. Experimental Jurisprudence, like medicine, must necessarily become an applied science partaking of the qualities of both pure science and engineering. The ultimate success of the theories will depend upon the willingness of the public and lawmaking agencies to pick up the developments of scientific jurisprudence and turn them into law where the theories will meet the final laboratory test of public reaction. Here also it would seem helpful in the progress of the law if developments in other scientific fields could be used as an aid in law enforcement and administration. Both of these efforts can properly be said to fall into the ken of Experimental Jurisprudence, and both for optimum results require that the legal machinery be so geared that it can immediately utilize and test scientific developments.

---

* This chapter is, to a large extent, reprinted with permission from 33 Neb. Law Rev. 1 (1953).

Unfortunately the actual conditions of the legal structure of society leave much to be desired in this area.

FACTORS ENCOURAGING THE LAG BETWEEN SCIENCE AND LEGAL PROCEDURE

It is a generally recognized fact that law and legal procedures lag far behind any type of social change. This is true even in matters of change in social custom, religion and habits of the people. But it seems to be far more marked when one approaches the problem of picking up scientific developments and transposing them to be used as tools in legal and governmental procedures. The reasons for the failure of the legal system immediately to adopt scientific innovations are numerous. Many of them are found in the nature of the legal system itself. Its ancient origins, written statutes and constitutions, judicial reliance upon precedent, the doctrine of *stare decisis* and the habit of a free legal profession to be largely occupied in the profitable business of defending the status quo all constitute brakes on any sudden change. The machinery for change which is provided by most governments, the system of legislative law, is also not very well calculated to pick up innovations from the field of science. In America, at least, the legislature is not provided with facilities for acting on change in the law such as ministers of justice or research organizations. It depends for its information on interested pressure groups and donated time of public-spirited citizens or do-gooders.

The separation of governmental functions, which is supposed to be one of the basic tenets of government in this country, also stands in the way of progress. Our separation of powers in the national government plus our division into states, cities, counties and myriads of local units all are likely to retard the bringing of new information into the law. When there is added to all of this the complete reliance on the democratic process which assumes that desired change will arise from an informed public and when considered in the light of the fact that scientific data is known only to a few people and is so complicated as to be beyond the reach of the masses at large, it might be expected that it is not only difficult but almost impossible to bring the information from the new and rapidly growing scientific revolution back into our conservative forms of government and law.

THE ANCIENT ORGINS OF THE LEGAL SYSTEM

All of our legal and major governmental devices were established before the industrial and scientific revolution to govern a type of society now almost extinct. Our legal forms, customs and methods of procedure are much older than any known science, and many of them have existed almost without change through the centuries. Wigmore in his panorama of the world's legal systems sets out a negotiable promissory note which meets the requirements of our modern legal system, a note which was in current use in 2100 B.C.[1] Like many of our commercial forms, the court system goes back beyond history or the discoveries of archeology.[2] Our own American type of procedure can be traced directly and in continuous line to the thirteenth-century British courts.[3] The present American system in most of its details was completely crystalized at the founding of the American colonies,[4] and before great inventions like the steam engine,[5] the power loom[6] and the cotton gin[7] could have had any social effect—to say nothing of the automatic factories, electrical and atomic energy and all the products of modern science which have appeared in the last one hundred years. The English legislative system, often called the mother of parliaments although it is a mere infant among the popular and representative legislatures of the world,[8] was maturing in most of its details as it now appears in the American constitutions and statutes early in the seventeenth century[9] and during the lifetime of Sir Francis Bacon,[10] who is often called the forerunner of modern science.

WRITTEN STATUTES AND CONSTITUTION

The American system of government and law, based on written statutes and constitutions, is also of ancient origin. Mankind from the dawn of history has believed that fundamental legal rules could be written down for all times. The Babylonian code of Hammurabi, 2100 B.C., the Hebrew Ten Commandments, about 1200 B.C., and the Roman Twelve Tables, 400 B.C.,[11] are all early examples of the world

---

[1] Wigmore, A Panorama of the World's Legal Systems 69 (1928).

[2] Id. at 12, 73, 177, 289, 406 et seq.; see also Gluckman, The Judicial Process of the Barotse of Northern Rhodesia, 357 ff. (1955) where the author points out that the court system of these savages closely resembles our own.

[3] 1 Holdsworth, History of English Law 54 et seq. (3d ed. 1922).

[4] See Harlow, Legislative Methods Before 1828, c. 1 (1884); Atkins, Lex Parliamentaria (1748).

[5] Patented in 1769, 28 Encyc. Brit. 415 (1926).

[6] Patented in 1785, 5 Encyc. Brit. 435 (1926).

[7] Patented in 1794, 28 Encyc. Brit. 611 (1926).

[8] See 1 Wigmore, op. cit. supra note 1, at 343; Buckland and McNair, Roman Law and Common Law 1 et seq. (1936).

[9] Atkins, op. cit. supra note 4.

[10] Bacon died in 1621.

[11] 1 Wigmore, op. cit. supra note 1, at 86, 104, 374.

habit of reducing current legal concepts to writing, endowing them with supernatural sanctions and setting them up as guides for future generations. Our own constitutions and statutes are directly descended from this age-old device of freezing social control to prevent change. True, we no longer rely upon the supernatural, and our founding fathers wisely provided machinery for amendment and interpretation to take care of change, but it should be kept in mind that the federal Constitution crystalized a form of government which grew out of the pre-scientific age, and that the Constitution itself was reduced to its present form long before scientific discoveries had created any appreciable change in society.[12] It should also be remembered that in practice the means provided by the fathers for change have not been particularly effective in picking up new ideas.

If there is one thing which science has demonstrated, it is that there is no correlation between the age of an idea and its validity for any purpose.

JUDICIAL INTERPRETATION AND STARE DECISIS

One of the methods for change upon which most reliance has been placed in the history of our country has been the interpretative devices developed in the court system; but it should be noted that the nature of the judicial system is such that change by the process of accretion and interpretation cannot be very great. All over the world, courts feel themselves bound to follow the written law, and in the Anglo-American system they suffer under a further brake upon the process of change in the doctrine of *stare decisis,* the great Anglo-American rule which provides that once a court has decided an issue it becomes a basic rule of law that is not be changed except in the most unusual situations. This had its origin in the English system where, by historical accident, the fundamental rules of law had not been reduced to writing, so the court decision was the only evidence of the law. But through professional custom it has been applied to interpretation of both legislation and constitutions and has been one of the greatest stumbling blocks in the way of change of the law even by legislative process.

In many situations where an ancient rule of law has been specifically abolished in plain words by legislative action, the doctrine of *stare decisis* has again and again prevented the courts from following the clear intention of the legislature. A few examples of this tendency

[12] See Lynd and Lynd, Middletown c. 2 (1929); cf. Seagle, Law, The Science of Inefficiency (1952).

will suffice. In the field of commercial law, the Negotiable Instruments Act adopted almost uniformly in England and in all states of the United States provided in plain terms that credit should be value for the purpose of giving a transferee the special rights of a holder in due course,[13] but to this day the majority of the courts, in spite of the clear meaning of the Negotiable Instruments Act, following pre-statutory decisions, refuse to treat bank credit as value.[14] In the field of constitutional law, in like manner the doctrine of *stare decisis* has been used to cut down the growth of civil rights under the Constitution of the United States. The courts first put a narrow interpretation upon the Bill of Rights, holding, in spite of much plain language to the contrary, that it only limited the federal government.[15] Then after the Civil War when the Fourteenth Amendment provided that "no state shall make or enforce any law which shall abridge the privileges and immunities of citizens of the United States," obviously referring to the first ten amendments, the courts, following the older decisions, continued to hold that the many rights set up in the first ten amendments applied only against the federal government,[16] and even limited federal enforcement of civil rights,[17] which was specifically authorized by the Thirteenth, Fourteenth and Fifteenth Amendments. Today they are still quibbling over the question of whether freedom of speech, freedom of press, freedom of religion, the right to trial by jury and the protection against unreasonable search and seizure, among some of the "privileges and immunities of citizens of the United States," are all beyond the power of restriction by the laws of the several states.[18] These are only two examples of the common tendency of courts to refuse to give effect to legislative change in the rules of law.

The habit of *stare decisis* is so strong that it can be said almost without danger of contradiction that judicial decisions lag from thirty to

[13] British Bills of Exchange Act § 27; Uniform Negotiable Instruments Law §§ 25, 191.

[14] See Beutel's Brannan, Negotiable Instruments Law 498 (1948), and authorities there cited.

[15] See, e.g., 2 Crosskey, Politics and the Constitution 1058 et seq. (1953); Rottschaeffer, Constitutional Law 781, 782, 785, 800, 812, 817 (1939).

[16] Rottschaeffer, op. cit. supra note 15, at 446 et seq. For the true meaning of the Fourteenth Amendment and its history, see 2 Crosskey, op. cit. supra note 15, at 1083 et seq.

[17] See Edgerton, The Incidence of Judicial Control Over Congress, 22 Cornell L. Q. 299, 320 et seq. (1937).

[18] See a prize-winning attempt to rationalize this confusion, Kauper, The First Ten Amendments, 37 A.B.A.J. 717 (1951).

one hundred years behind the intention of legislatures in adopting new statutes and rules of law. It took forty years and the affirmative vote of nineteen state legislatures[19] before the federal courts would recognize that the enactments of maximum hours of labor were reasonable exercises of the state police power. The same process for minimum wages took over twenty-five years more of enactments[20] and a similar fight. In all, it required over seventy years from the adoption of the eight-hour-day-for-women statute in Wisconsin in 1867[21] until the Supreme Court finally admitted that regulation of hours and pay of labor was within due process of law.[22] It makes little difference whether these innovations are in the field of significant social reforms like minimum wages and hours or, as will be shown later, whether they are in non-controversial fields; where there has been an attempt to adopt scientific techniques, the courts in either case usually have stood as a road block against legislatively adopted progress.[23]

LEGISLATIVE CHANGES

Legislative change itself is not geared to the immediate adoption of new ideas. Anglo-American legislatures as such have little continuity, depending almost entirely upon the whim of public election. Constituted as they were in England at the begining of the eighteenth century,[24] our American legislatures have no independent research equipment. They depend for their factual material almost entirely upon public pressure which makes its appearance at the legislative hearing and in various forms of lobbying. This pressure is usually from people who want something; these people fall into two main categories: those who are so pinched by social conditions that they are

[19] See Brandeis' brief, Muller v. Oregon, 208 U.S. 412 (1908); cf. Lochner v. New York, 198 U.S. 45 (1905); Frankfurter, Hours of Labor and Realism in Constitutional Law, 29 Harv. L. Rev. 352 (1916).

[20] See Stephens and Frankfurter, losing brief, Adkins v. Children's Hospital, 261 U.S. 525, 544-652 (1923); cf. West Coast Hotel v. Parrish, 300 U.S. 379 (1937); Morehead v. People, 298 U.S. 587 (1936). See Powell, The Judiciality of Minimum Wage Laws, 37 Harv. L. Rev. 545 (1924).

[21] Wis. Gen. Laws c. 83 (1867).

[22] United States v. Darby Lumber Co., 312 U.S. 100 (1941).

[23] The whole doctrine of substantive due process of law is now almost dead since the case of Nebbia v. New York, 291 U.S. 502 (1934). These cases were simply a rationalization of the Court's opposition to reading progress into the Fifth and Fourteenth Amendments. See Holmes' dissents in Baldwin v. Missouri, 281 U.S. 586, 595 (1930), and Lochner v. New York, 198 U.S. 45, 75 (1905); Black's dissent, Connecticut General Ins. Co. v. Johnson, 303 U.S. 77, 85 (1938).

[24] Cf. Harlow, op. cit. supra note 4; Atkins, op. cit. supra note 4.

forced to demand change, mostly for selfish ends, and those who are already adversely affected by current legal regulations.[25] As the old saying goes, it's the wheel that squeaks which gets the grease. Often this results in anti-social forces, such as that exerted by gamblers, criminal elements, predatory big business and big labor, gaining control of the legislative and administrative machinery which has been set up to regulate them.

There is no ministry of justice such as exists in European governments,[26] chiefly interested in perfecting the legal system. The Congressional investigating committee which is supposed to take its place is more interested in politics and sensationalism than it is in pursuit of the truth. Most of the demand for change, even before the investigating committee, takes some sort of popular pressure which because of its nature is always far behind those innovations which would be dictated by the discoveries of science. But even when this change is slowly accomplished, it must be piecemeal.

The endless separation of government functions is a further impediment to change. The founding fathers had reason to be afraid of centralized government because it could be used as an instrument of irresponsible class tyranny. So they carefully prevented the centralization of power. The separation of powers within our governments and our multiple governmental system with its more than one hundred and fifty thousand units with lawmaking power[27] is an effective check on the adoption of new ideas. New laws of whatever nature must be put through thousands of legislative bodies before they can become effective. This requires tremendous public sentiment, all of which eventually leads us to consider the effectiveness of the so-called democratic process.

DEMOCRACY

The democratic process which is supposed to control our present form of government, whatever its good features may be, is not adapted to social change involving the adoption and use of scientific ideas. The reasons are legion; only a few need to be discussed here.

[25] See Beutel, Pressure of Organized Interests on Legislation, 3 So. Calif. L. Rev. 10 (1929).

[26] See Cardozo, A Ministry of Justice, 35 Harv. L. Rev. 113 (1921). Even to this day little has been done to implement the suggestions of this great jurist. The so-called legislative research agencies connected with many state legislatures should not be confused with a Ministry of Justice. Most of them are mere drafting bureaus or devices for continuous committee hearings during recess.

[27] Anderson, The Units of Government, Pub. Ad. Serv. 11 et seq. (1934).

The people as a whole who do the voting and form the core of the democratic power are not in direct contact with legal administration and machinery. They are only conscious of its existence at election time, when it interferes with their activities or provides them a means of getting something which they cannot otherwise attain. Therefore, most of the ideas concerning the administration of justice and the operation of the law come to the voters in a second-hand or in a roundabout manner from public servants and lawyers who are in direct control of the legal machinery.

Both of these groups have a very important interest in maintaining the status quo. They are in direct control of the legal machinery and in a sense have a monopoly upon its operation. Their stock-in-trade is their knowledge of the current machinery and their ability to manipulate it to serve the purpose of their clients. Changes in methods and rules upset the tranquillity of their control and make them learn new techniques and sometimes even result in their displacement by others. Failures in the operation of the legal and governmental machinery reflect directly upon lawyers and public servants, so it is in their interest to see that the status quo appears in the best light to the voters. In the case of the lawyers, this has become such an obsession that even a casual visitor to a bar association meeting cannot help being impressed by the amount of oratory devoted to the glory of the legal system, the honesty of the judges and the uprightness of the profession.

The lawyer by the very nature of his training has his ideas deeply rooted in the past. Precedent is his most important weapon, and most of the leading lawyers represent clients who have succeeded under the present system and whose main purpose, therefore, is to preserve the status quo. It is not surprising, then, that most bar associations will be found in the forefront of the leadership of conservatism or reaction. Such information and influence as they may have on public sentiment will scarcely ever be found to move in the direction of the adoption of new ideas, especially those coming from members of other professions, like scientists.

Public interest at large in the adoption of changes indicated by scientific developments is very hard to develop. This is partly due to the fact that the complicated nature of our society has created many divisions of labor and interests. The average citizen is lucky if he can understand the ramifications of his own business without ever expecting to absorb the new developments of science in other fields. The nature of scientific information is so highly technical that it requires years of study to grasp its implications even in those fields which it directly affects. It is very difficult for anyone, to say nothing of the average voter, to comprehend the social result of scientific change and to foresee the usefulness of adopting scientific methods and inventions to aid in the law enforcement machinery.

Recent intelligence tests and census figures in 1950 show that of the adult population of America, eighty-seven per cent have only a high school education, or less. A further six per cent have completed college, and of the total population only forty per cent are capable of advanced scientific study. Of this latter group only one-sixth, or six per cent of the entire population, have actually received sufficient advanced scientific training to qualify for a bachelor's degree.[28] This last group of potential scholars is the only one that can hope to comprehend the implications of scientific developments or to construct means whereby they can be adapted to the use of the legal and governmental machinery. If, therefore, sufficient public interest is to be developed in adopting new scientific methods, it will be necessary for this small nucleus from which come the able scientists[29] to convince the great majority to agree to types of governmental and legal devices which the overwhelming mass of people cannot even understand. Under the circumstances, the development of popular pressure for adoption of scientific discoveries into the legal and governmental field sufficient to overcome the inertia of those in control of the machinery is difficult, if not impossible, to achieve.

SPEED OF SCIENTIFIC DEVELOPMENT

The newness, speed and complications of scientific developments is the last and most important factor in the lag between science and law. As measured by the age of legal institutions and procedures, the scientific method is a mere infant. With the exception of a very few administrative agencies initiated in the twentieth century, all of our legal agencies, procedures and governmental devices were started and had reached full maturity before science had any impact whatsoever upon social control. This is more graphically illustrated in the introduction to *Middletown,* an anthropoligical study of a midwest American city published in 1929. There is described an old man living in Middletown who was born in a civilization nearer in its essentials to the year 1 A.D. than to the year 1929. During the life of this one doctor,

---

[28] Wolfe, Intellectual Resources, 185 Sci. Am. 42, 45 (Sept., 1951).

[29] The number of people granted Ph.D.'s in science totaled less than 4,000 in 1950, less than 6/1000 of one per cent of the population over their age. Wolfe, Intellectual Resources, 185 Sci. Am. 46 (Sept., 1951).

scientific developments had completely changed the nature of life and the ways of living:[30]

> Within the lifetime of this one man local transportation has changed from virtually the 'hoof and sail' methods in use in the time of Homer; grain has ceased to be cut in the state by thrusting the sickle into the ripened grain as in the days of Ruth and threshing done by trampling out by horses on the threshing floor or by flail; getting a living and making a home have ceased to be conducted under one roof by the majority of the American people; education has ceased to be a luxury accessible only to the few; in his own field of medicine the X-ray, anaesthetics, asepsis, and other developments have tended to make the healing art a science; electricity, the telephone, telegraph, and radio have appeared; and the theory of evolution has shaken the theological cosmogony that had reigned for centuries.

Today scientific advancements are being carried on at an even more accelerated pace. Figures from the patent office show that there have been twice as many inventions registered since 1907 as in the whole history of the patent office from the founding of the republic down to that time.[31] These inventions and discoveries are being turned back into the scientific process where each innovation breeds a myriad of other changes in scientific methods and devices. New and magic gadgets, elixirs for the cure of disease and marvelous changes in production, distribution and transportation coupled with corresponding changes in methods of living are appearing at an ever accelerated pace. Vast research organizations, both private and public, are operating to spend billions of dollars to accentuate this scientific change.

THE LAG IN THE ADOPTION OF SCIENTIFIC METHODS BY THE LEGAL SYSTEM

In contrast to the many institutions and organizations set up to accelerate scientific change in the economic and social life of man, there are few if any bodies or organized efforts to place this vast accumulation of scientific data at the disposal of the legal system to be used for the benefit of the body politic. With all of its handicaps, it is to be expected therefore that our legal system would be slow to adapt to its uses the developments of science. Although this should be obvious from the nature of its organization, few people seem to

---

[30] Lynd and Lynd. op. cit. supra note 12, at 10.

[31] One of the railroad block signal patents issued to Bliss in 1907 was No. 861,015. As of June, 1952, the number of issued patents had passed 2,600,000. See Annual Rep. of Comm. of Patents 6 (1951).

realize the extent to which law has failed to pick up the scientific information which could be used to accomplish its purpose. A complete catalog of all the instances of this lag is impossible because it would require a collection of all scientific developments, a task beyond the grasp of any group of men or institutions. A few examples of this general tendency, however, will be sufficient to show the grossness of this shocking lag and to indicate its dangerous implications to the public welfare.

The most spectacular developments in government control and in the use of scientific information, as shown in Chapters VI and VII, are in the areas where lawmaking power and sanctions, including authority to experiment, are delegated to agencies with great research potentials supported by large appropriations; but it might be interesting to examine the slowness of science in penetrating even into these fields.

PUBLIC HEALTH LAWS

One of the foremost of these advances, further discussed in Chapter VII, is in the field of public health. Here there are well organized educational and research institutions for the development of scientific data and numerous governmental bodies for promoting the adoption of scientific data for the use of the legal system. Almost every governmental unit of any general jurisdiction in this country has some kind of public health official whose duty it is to apply medical information to the maintenance of the health of the community. Most medical colleges have courses in the subject, and there are even a few schools devoted entirely to the discipline of public health. But in spite of this, the instances of the lag between medical knowledge and its use in legal devices or sanctions to protect the public health are revealing and shocking. A few examples chosen from those areas where science has made great progress toward infiltrating the legal machinery will be enlightening.

Vaccination to prevent smallpox is one of the oldest, most effective and widely adopted means of preserving public health. Prior to the perfection of vaccination, smallpox was one of the most deadly scourges of mankind, killing about sixty per cent of its victims, and few people escaped it.[32]

Although the first European scientific discovery and publication on vaccination was nine years after the adoption of the American

---

[32] Rehberger, Lippincott's Reference Book of Medical Science 512 (11th ed. 1940); Stedman, Reference Book of Medical Science 782 (3d ed. 1947).

Constitution,[33] the effect of the disease was so deadly that there was immediate demand for any kind of relief. Statutes authorizing vaccination at public expense appeared in Massachusetts in 1810,[34] only twelve years after Jenner's publication of his paper on the subject in England and ten years after the first experiments in the United States.[35] There followed almost immediately a federal statute[36] encouraging vaccination in cooperation with state governments desiring to use it.[37] Vaccination was made mandatory in Massachusetts in 1855,[38] but was not finally held constitutional by the Supreme Court of the United States until after the turn of the twentieth century,[39] at which time many states had adopted regulations similar to those of Massachusetts.[40]

Today, although the efficiency of vaccination is proved beyond a shadow of a doubt, though every state in the Union has some method of providing the public with protection against smallpox, and while the scientific means exist for wiping the disease off the face of the earth, largely through the use of quarantine and vaccination, the law lags far behind the science. There are still six states where there are statutory provisions against compulsory vaccination, some even in the face of epidemics.[41] It would require a treatise to give even a rough summary of the laws and regulations of states and local governments bearing on the subject of smallpox control and vaccination. The laws of the several states vary all the way from those requiring compulsory vaccination of all citizens or as a prerequisite for school attendance, through various stages of administrative discretion in different fields, to those which prohibit compulsory vaccination,[42] and three of the

---

[33] Jenner, An Inquiry into the Causes and Effects of the Varioulae Vaccurae (1798); Clendening, A Source Book of Medical History 291 (1942).

[34] Mass. Laws c. 116, p. 204 (1808-1812).

[35] See Clendening, op. cit. supra note 33, at 301-305.

[36] 2 Stat. 806 (1813).

[37] See, e.g., Va. Laws c. 14, p. 43 (1813-1814).

[38] Mass. Laws c. 414, p. 812 (1854-1855).

[39] Jacobson v. Massachusetts, 197 U.S. 11 (1905).

[40] See Note, 25 L.R.A. 152 (1894); Note, 17 L.R.A. (n.s.) 709 (1909).

[41] Ariz. Code Ann. § 68-307 (1939); Minn. Stat. Ann. § 144.12 (9) (West, 1947); N.D. Rev. Code § 23-0717 (1943); S.D. Code § 27.2201 (1939); Utah Code Ann. § 26-5-10 (1953); Wash. Rev. Stat. Ann. § 4805 thirteenth (1932).

[42] See Fowler, Principal Provisions of Small-pox Vaccination Laws and Regulations in the United States, 56 U.S. Pub. Health Rep. 167 (1941); cf. Fowler, Small-pox Vaccination Laws, Regulations and Court Decisions, U.S. Pub. Health Rep. Supp. No. 60 (1927); Ravenscroft and Solomon, Vaccinations, Small-pox and the Law—An Experment in Scientific Jurisprudence, 32 Neb. L. Rev. 547, 552 et seq. (1953).

states which seem to have no important law on the subject.[43] The statistical studies have been legion proving that the incidence of the disease decreases in direct proportion to the strictness of the laws or regulations requiring vaccination.[44] In Germany, where compulsory vaccination for the army was adopted in 1845 and for civilians in 1875, the disease has practically disappeared.[45]

Yet in spite of all this scientific proof, there remains much active opposition to vaccination, not only among the Christian Scientists and other religious sects, but by many others, some of whom even masquerade under the banner of science. A recent carefully conducted public opinion poll[46] showed that eighteen per cent of mothers regarded vaccination as "worse than the disease itself," twenty-four per cent of the people did not know or did not believe that vaccination could prevent smallpox. Even though doctors advise infant vaccination, thirty-five per cent of the mothers refused to have their children vaccinated before going to school and sixty per cent of the population said vaccination could not prevent smallpox but thought it might lessen the disease.

Although there is an encouraging tendency to delegate the regulation and enforcement of vaccination and other contagious disease controls to competent scientific bodies, this adverse public opinion, spurred by a hard core of fanatics, is resulting in the weakening of the enforcement of compulsory vaccination laws. In the six states where there are limitations on the power of the authorities to enforce vaccination, it has actually caused the repeal or watering down of the statutes. In Arizona, for example, the compulsory vaccination law was repealed by popular initiative.[47] In Utah such repeal was passed over the veto of the governor,[48] and in the remaining four states the previous power of the authorities to enforce vaccination was taken away by ordinary

---

[43] Delaware, Nevada, Oklahoma; Ravenscroft and Solomon, Vaccination, Smallpox and the Law—An Experiment in Scientific Jurisprudence, 32 Neb. L. Rev. 547, 555 (1953).

[44] See, e.g., Ravenscroft and Solomon, op. cit. supra note 43, at 547; Force and Leak, Small-pox in Twenty States 1915-1920, 36 Pub. Health Rep. 1979 (1921); Hampton, State Vaccination Laws and Regulations, 58 Pub. Health Rep. 1771 (1943); Steadman, Reference Handbook of Medical Sciences 371 (3d ed. 1917).

[45] Steadman, op. cit. supra note 44.

[46] See Byrd, Health Instruction Yearbook 106 (1943).

[47] Ariz. Laws (Referendum and Initiative) p. 21 (1919).

[48] Utah Laws c. 18, p. 15 (1901); cf. State v. Bd. of Ed. of Salt Lake City, 21 Utah 401, 60 Pac. 1013 (1900).

legislative action.[49] It would take a much wider survey than is possible here to determine whether or not vaccination laws and their enforcement as a whole are being relaxed throughout the country. But these specific instances show that popular opposition and ignorance of the scientific facts could easily reach alarming proportions.

That this situation could exist in the United States where smallpox still continues in spite of the fact that there are scientific methods for completely eradicating it calls for serious thought. Although public health authorities have been making steady progress in eliminating the disease through quarantine, compulsory statutes and persuasion, there are still many places in this country where the disease is being preserved and where the latent possibilities of epidemics are present. In Idaho and Nevada, in which there are no compulsory vaccination statutes, between the years 1945 and 1950 there was one case per 100,000 of population every year.[50] In the state of Pennsylvania as recently as 1943 there was an outbreak of the disease, brought in from outside the state, which when studied showed that all but five of the cases were among non-vaccinated persons, and of the five all of the vaccinations were over thirty years old.[51]

In spite of the fact that science undoubtedly has the means of completely eradicating smallpox, and although this has been one of the most successful fields of the operation of public health administration, the laws of the several states are still in such a state as to preserve this deadly scourge of mankind for possible future epidemics. There is considerable evidence that the lawmakers, administrators and the public, no longer driven by the lash of the fear of epidemics, are becoming more lax, thus falling farther and farther behind the scientific developments.

Fluoridation of water to prevent dental caries is one of the recent discoveries of science and also a good example of what can be done with Experimental Jurisprudence.

Dentists and research scientists first began to notice the relation of mottling on the enamel of children's teeth to dental caries about 1928. Further study of this phenomenon revealed that children with mottling on their teeth showed a marked absence of decay. About 1939 there was developed an hypothesis that fluorine in solution in the water

[49] See Minn. Laws c. 299 (1903); cf. Note, 8 Minn. L. Rev. 453 (1924). See N.D. Laws c. 236 (1919); S.D. Laws c. 223 (1903); Wash. Laws c. 90, § 9 (1919). For this same tendency, see Mass. Laws c. 337 (1908), repealing in part compulsory vaccination laws.

[50] Ravenscroft & Solomon, op. cit. supra note 43, at 547, 563.

[51] 58 U.S. Pub. Health Rep. 359 (1943).

supply was responsible both for mottling of teeth and reduction of dental caries.[52] A further examination of this theory showed that there were approximately fourteen hundred communities in the United States where the public water supply contains more than a trace of fluorine compounds in solution. The percentage of such solution varies from five-tenths up to five parts of fluoride compounds to a million parts of water. As shown by Table One, a study of tooth decay in these

TABLE 1

Relationship of Dental Health to Fluoride in Drinking Water

Cities	* No. of Children Examined	** No. D.M.F. Permanent Teeth Per 100 Children	Incidence of Mottled Enamel	Fluorine Content of Water p.p.m. ***
Colorado Springs, Colo.	404	246	Slight	2.6
Galesburg, Ill.	273	236	Slight	1.9
Elmhurst, Ill.	170	252	....	1.8
Joliet, Ill.	447	323	....	1.3
East Moline, Ill.	152	303	Borderline	1.2
Aurora, Ill.	635	281	....	1.2
Maywood, Ill.	171	258	....	1.2
Kewanee, Ill.	123	343	....	0.9
Pueblo, Colo.	614	412	Negative	0.6
Elgin, Ill.	403	444	....	0.5
Marion, Ohio	263	556	....	0.4
Lima, Ohio	454	652	....	0.3
Middletown, Ohio	370	703	....	0.2
Zanesville, Ohio	459	733	Negative	0.2
Quincy, Ill.	330	706	....	0.1
Portsmouth, Ohio	469	772	....	0.1
Elkhart, Ind.	278	823	....	0.1
Michigan City, Ind.	236	1037	....	0.1
Evanston, Ill.	256	673	....	0.0
Oak Park, Ill.	329	772	....	0.0
Waukegan, Ill.	423	810	....	0.0

* The children examined were of the 12 to 14 year age group all of whom had lived in that particular locality all of the time.
** D.M.F. per 100 means the number of decayed, missing or filled permanent teeth per 100 children examined.
*** p.p.m. means parts of fluoride to million parts of water.

Nebraska State Department of Health
Division of Dental Health

areas proved that noticeable mottling occurred only when there were more than two parts of fluoride compounds to a million parts of water but was almost entirely absent when the percentage of solution was

[52] Dean, Epidemological Studies in the United States in Dental Caries and Fluorine 5 et seq. (1946).

TABLE 2

Comparative Loss of Teeth and Dental Decay Experience

3358 Observed Cases

Colorado Springs, Colorado	Madison, Wisconsin
2.6 Fluorine P.P.M.	0.05 Fluorine P.P.M.
and other *High Fluoride* districts	and other *Low Fluoride* districts

Ages		Number Examined	Number with No decay	Decayed and Filled Teeth	Extracted Teeth	Average Number Decayed, Missing & Filled Permanent Teeth Per Person	Average Number of Extracted Teeth Per Person
Ages 10-14	High Fluoride	479	294	481	45	1.10	0.09
	Low Fluoride	848	34	5600	389	7.07	0.46
	Six times as much decay experienced per person						
	Five times as many extracted teeth per person						
Ages 15-19	High Fluoride	372	161	690	73	2.05	0.20
	Low Fluoride	310	4	3604	415	12.97	1.34
	Six times as much decay experienced per person						
	Seven times as many teeth extracted per person						
Ages 20-24	High Fluoride	108	36	259	13	2.51	0.12
	Low Fluoride	265	0	4698	746	17.69	2.82
	Seven times as much decay experienced per person						
	Twenty-three times as many extracted teeth per person						
Ages 25-29	High Fluoride	95	20	367	19	4.01	0.20
	Low Fluoride	174	0	2308	867	18.29	4.92
	Four times as much decay experienced per person						
	Twenty-four times as many extracted teeth per person						
Ages 30-34	High Fluoride	54	11	204	21	4.16	0.39
	Low Fluoride	117	0	1698	654	20.09	5.58
	Five times as much decay experienced per person						
	Fourteen times as many extracted teeth per person						
Ages 35-39	High Fluoride	43	8	162	17	4.17	0.39
	Low Fluoride	115	0	1446	846	19.93	7.36
	Five times as much decay experienced per person						
	Nineteen times as many extracted teeth per person						
Ages 40 & over	High Fluoride	78	10	452	54	6.49	0.70
	Low Fluoride	300	0	2710	3679	21.29	12.26
	Three times as much decay experienced per person						
	Seventeen times as many extracted teeth per person						

(Third Molars Excluded)		* All Causes.
Frederick S. McKay, D.D.S.		John G. Frisch, D.D.S.
Colorado Springs, Colorado	October 1949	Madison, Wisconsin

Nebraska State Department of Health
Division of Dental Health

TABLE 3

Comparison of the Resistance to Dental Caries Between Colorado
Springs, Colorado, with Fluorine of 2.6 p.p.m., and Madison,
Wisconsin, with Less than 0.05 p.p.m. of Fluorine.

Ages	Average *DMF Permanent Teeth Per Person		Average Number of Permanent Teeth Extracted Per Person	
	Madison	Colorado Springs	Madison	Colorado Springs
10-14	7.1	1.1	0.46	0.09
15-19	12.9	2.1	1.34	0.20
20-24	17.6	2.5	2.82	0.12
25-29	18.3	4.0	4.92	0.20
30-34	20.1	4.2	5.58	0.39
35-39	19.9	4.2	7.36	0.39
40 and over	21.3	6.4	12.26	0.70

* D.M.F. means Decayed, Missing or Filled Permanent teeth per person.

Nebraska State Department of Health
Division of Dental Health

below that amount.[53] An actual study of the decay of children's teeth set out in Table One in the various cities where there was a water supply containing natural fluorides showed that where there were about 1.2 parts of fluoride compound in solution in a million parts of water there was no mottling on teeth, and that the number of decayed teeth was at the lowest in these areas.[54] A comparison of the cities of Madison, Wisconsin, and Colorado Springs, Colorado, set out in Tables Two and Three, shows that the advantage of fluorine content extends to all age groups. There was over six times as much damage from decay per person in Madison where fluorides were absent from the water as in Colorado Springs which contained more than the optimum amount. After these discoveries in 1943, there was a suggestion by Dean, one of the principal research scientists in the field, to the American Water Works Association that fluoride compounds be added to the water of certain cities for the purpose of improving the structure of the teeth of the population.[55]

Controlled experiments, as suggested by Dean, by adding fluorides to the water supply have been made in a number of widely scattered

[53] For the geographic distribution of these areas see Am. Dent. Ass'n Infor. Bull. 2 (May, 1952).

[54] Cf. Carr, Dentistry, An Agency of Health Service 157 et seq. (1946), and authorities there cited.

[55] Wolman, Fluorine and Public Water Supply, Fluoride Ingestion 108, 110 (1946).

states, among others in Wisconsin, New York, Michigan, Texas and Idaho. Before-and-after studies of the condition of children's teeth and comparison of decay, both in the cities where the experiments were conducted and in control cities operating under like circumstances except for the addition of fluorides to the water, show that the per-

FIGURE 1*

PERCENTAGE OF FIRST PERMANENT MOLARS FREE OF DECAY AMONG CHILDREN RESIDING IN CITY AFTER WATER SUPPLIES WERE FLUORIDATED AND THOSE LIVING IN NEARBY CITY WITH FLUORIDE-FREE WATER.

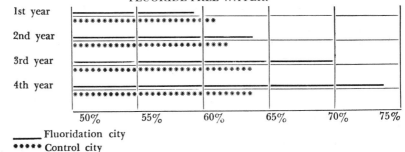

_____ Fluoridation city
***** Control city

FIGURE 2*

DECAYED, MISSING AND FILLED TEETH PER CHILD IN TYPICAL CITY WITH WATER SUPPLY CONTAINING 1.2 PARTS PER MILLION FLUORIDE AND A CITY WITH FLUORIDE-FREE WATER.

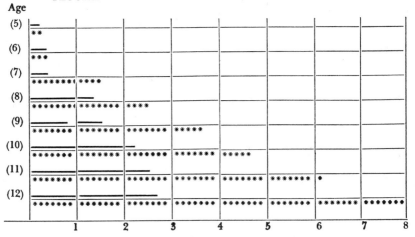

Fluoride City ——
Non-Fluoride City *****

* A.D.A. Information Bull. (May 1952).

centage of caries-free teeth in children increased from fifty to three hundred per cent and the number of decayed or missing teeth dropped from twenty-three to sixty-five per cent due to the addition of fluorine compounds to the water.[56] The charts set out in Figures 1 and 2 indicate graphically a rough summary of all these experiments compiled by the American Dental Association.[57]

As a result of these operations combining dental research with experiments in the laws governing the operation of water works by authorizing the addition of fluoride compounds to the water, it has been determined that the best procedure to reduce decay in teeth is to create a percentage of approximately one and two-tenths parts of fluorides to a million parts of water. This program is now unqualifiedly recommended by the American Dental Association and by numerous scientific societies, not only in the field of dentistry, but in medicine, nursing and many allied professions.[58] There is now proof that proper fluoridation of public water supplies ultimately will decrease dental caries about sixty-five per cent, and the scientific literature supporting this conclusion is legion.[59]

The opposition to fluoridation comes, as in the case of smallpox, from religious sects, a few doctors who talk about socialized medicine and socialism and from miscellaneous other groups. Many objections have been raised of dangers from fluoridation, including some twenty-five or thirty arguments, among others that it creates brittle bones, increases cancer, heart disease and the like.[60] Each of these allegations has been carefully checked in communities where fluoride compounds exist in the water and has been found to be absolutely baseless. There is no proof that fluoridation of water is harmful in any fashion, and overwhelming evidence exists that it is a tremendous boon to the

[56] Finn and Chase, 42 J. Am. Dent. Ass'n 188 (1952); Cox and Ast, Water Fluoridation, 43 Am. Water Works Ass'n J. 642 (1951); Dean, Arnold and Knutson, Studies on Mass Control of Dental Caries, 65 U.S. Pub. Health Rep. 1403 (1950).

[57] Am. Dent. Ass'n Infor. Bull. (May 1952).

[58] Among these are: Am. Dent. Ass'n; Am. Medical Ass'n; Am. Water Works Ass'n; Am. Pub. Health Ass'n; National Research Council; United States Pub. Health Serv.; State and Territorial Health Officers Ass'n; Am. Ass'n of Pub. Health Dentists and the Inter-Ass'n Comm. on Health of the Am. Dental Ass'n; Am. Hospital Ass'n; Am. Nurses Ass'n; and the Am. Pub. Welfare Ass'n., Am. Dent. Ass'n Infor. Bull. (May 1952).

[59] See, e.g., Am. Dent. Ass'n, Fluoridation in the Prevention of Dental Caries (1951), and the Index of Dental Periodical Literature 1949-51, under "Fluorides." Also see Rhyne and Mullin, Fluoridation of Municipal Water Supply (1952), and authorities there cited.

[60] Am. Dent. Ass'n Infor. Bull. (May 1952).

health of the teeth of both children and adults in the areas where it is now in use.

The cost of fluoridation is very low. The annual experience of a number of cities shows that the cost of installing and maintaining a proper fluoridation system runs from three to twelve cents a year per capita.[61] Thus, the expense of a lifetime of fluoridation of water, which would produce an expected reduction of about two-thirds in the dental caries of the citizens drinking the water, would be less than the average cost to each person of one visit to a dentist. Fluoridation can accomplish an immense improvement in individual health and a tremendous savings in dental bills. The supply of soluble fluorides to be used in water is adequate. Foolproof machinery for creating proper solutions has been invented.[62] So there seems to be every reason why public water works should be subjected to a fluoridation treatment.

The legal machinery for adopting fluoridation, like that for controlling smallpox, is in widely divergent conditions. Laws providing for public water works were passed long before modern chemistry devised means for artificial purification either by fluoridation, chlorination or any other similar process. In fact the process of creating a community water supply goes back as far as the time when people began to live together in cities and towns.

The control of public water supply in America today is vested by law in a number of various governing bodies. In some instances public water supply is provided by private corporations under the control of public service commissions or private corporations holding franchises with municipal authorities or both.[63] In other instances the water supply is created and managed directly by municipal authorities set up by state law which provides for different governmental units of control in cities of different classifications throughout the state.[64] Power to add chemicals to the water may rest with the city councils, water commissioners or local health officers, but in almost all instances approval of the state board of health is necessary before final action

[61] Maier, Fluoridation of Water Supplies, 42 Am. Water Works Ass'n J. 1120 (1950); Blayney and Tucker, Evanston Dental Caries Study, 27 J. Dent. Research 279, 286 (1948); Zufelt, Sheboygan Experience with Fluoridation of Drinking Water, 42 Am. Water Works Ass'n J. 839 (1950); Am. Dent. Ass'n Infor. Bull. (May 1952).

[62] Smith, Fluoridation as Practiced at Madison, Wisconsin, 96 Water and Sewage Works 125 (1949).

[63] See, e.g., N.Y. Pub. Serv. Law § 89-c (McKinney, 1939).

[64] See Wis. Stat. § 66.071 et seq. (1947).

can be taken.[65] Thus, the initiation of such a program may rest with appointed officials or city councils, or in some instances it must be determined by popular referendum subject to approval of the state board of health.

Boards of health themselves are also a recent phenomenon found on national, state and local levels. Most of them came into the law after the Civil War.[66] The National Board of Health,[67] now the Public Health Service, was started in 1879 and offers valuable advice in the field both of purification and fluoridation of water. Most states have some centralized public health authority which makes rules and regulations for the water supply of the entire state, but many have statutes providing that city councils and health bodies are more or less independent of the state centralized authority.[68]

A distinction must be drawn between purification of water, such as chlorination, and the addition of certain valuable solids to the water, of which fluoridation is an excellent example.

Chlorination of public water supplies started in about 1910,[69] and many statutes passed since that time specifically provide for purification processes.[70] But since fluoridation is not a purification process, a number of legal technicalities stand in the way of any movement for adding fluorides to the water. There are questions of legal authority to add chemicals to water for other purposes than purification. Also there is the difficulty of divided authority. The problem of initiating fluoridation thus may involve convincing public health authorities, city councils, appointed officials, the electorate or a combination of two or more of these groups. Where the public health authorities have the power to initiate the decision, which seems to be normal in Ontario[71] but which is an exception in the United States, the movement for fluoridation has been quick and easy because the scientific value of the process has been completely established, and the average public health official is well versed in the science of his trade.

The problem of convincing city councils and the electorate is much more difficult. Progress along these lines over the last nine years seems

[65] N.Y. Pub. Health Law § 70 (McKinney, 1943); N.J. Stat. Ann. § 58: 11-13 (West, 1940); Pa. Stat. Ann. tit. 53, §§ 8732, 9673 (Purdon, 1938); Wis. Stat. §§ 140.05 (3), 140.05 (7), 162.03 (b) (1947).

[66] See, e.g., N.Y. Laws c. 534 (1885). See 22 Encyc. Brit. 628 (13th ed. 1926), and authorities there cited.

[67] 20 Stat. 484 (1879).

[68] See N.Y. Pub. Health Law § 70 (McKinney, 1943).

[69] 31 Encyc. Brit. 994 (13th ed. 1926).

[70] See statutes cited supra note 65.

[71] See, e.g., 3 Ont. Rev. Stat. c. 306, § 111 (1950).

to have been fairly rapid. According to the American Dental Association, which is actively pushing the movement for fluoridation in cooperation with United States and state public health officials, four hundred twenty-three communities covering thirty-five million people have instituted, or are about to institute, fluoridation.[72] This seems like a sizable number; but when there is added to it the two and one-half million people who drink water fluoridated by nature,[73] the total still represents less than fifty-three per cent of the population being supplied by public water systems[74] and only eleven per cent of the cities and towns which will have to give approval before a fluoridation program is uniformly adopted,[75] as science clearly shows it should be. Thus it will be seen that a tremendous amount of propaganda is necessary to overcome public inertia and opposition in this field.

A recent Gallup poll[76] shows that only fifty-six per cent of the public have even heard of fluoridation and that three-fifths of these, or only thirty-five per cent of the whole, favor it, that four per cent of the population oppose it and that the rest have no opinion on the subject. Therefore those desiring action where public sentiment is required face an inertia of ignorance in about sixty per cent of the population. The extent of this obstacle has been shown by the fact that fifty-seven out of one hundred and four of the communities where there have been popular referenda have voted down fluoridation of the water supply. A striking example of this difficulty occurred in the city of Seattle. Due to the fact that its water supply is almost pure snow and rain water, it has one of the worst instances of dental caries in the United States.[77] But in spite of this condition, the public voted

---

[72] Am. Dent. Ass'n Infor. Bull. (May 1952); see 45 J. Am. Dent. Ass'n 555 (1952). for later and smaller figures.

[73] Fluoridation, Am. Dent. Ass'n Pamp. 1 (1951); 45 J. Am. Dent. Ass'n 555 (1952).

[74] In 1933 over eighty-five per cent of the urban population was supplied with purified water systems. Am. Water Works Ass'n, Census of Municipal Water Plants 26 (1933). The urban population of the United States is now about eighty-eight million, U.S. Census, Prelim. Count (1950).

[75] In 1933 there were 3,015 purification systems in the United States. Am. Water Works Census, supra note 74, at 28. The number today is much larger. The American Dental Association estimates that there are 16,747 public water supplies in America, 45 J. Am. Dent. Ass'n 556 (1952). There are 6,300 communities with public water supply, of which over 5,000 have less than the optimum of fluorides, Am. Dent. Ass'n, Fluoridation in the Prevention of Dental Caries (1951). If these figures be used, then the percentage drops to eight per cent, but if the later figure of 16,747 public water systems given by the Journal be used, the percentage is only three.

[76] Reported, 44 J. Am. Dent. Ass'n 350 (1952).

[77] Life, 42 (Mar. 24, 1952).

two to one against fluoridation in a recent referendum.[78] The governing bodies of seventeen cities have also voted against fluoridation. This makes the total population of communities where there have been rejections over two million four hundred thousand, including such other great cities as New Orleans, Minneapolis and Memphis.[79] Many of the others are refusing to act simply due to inertia. In spite of the fact that both science and Experimental Jurisprudence have demonstrated the value of fluoridation, and even though it is supported by practically all the organized scientific bodies in the country, this inertia remains a block to progress. Here again, the adoption of scientific protective measures for the benefit of the health of the entire community is being hampered by the fact that our legal system has placed the initial decisions in the hands of the people in the community who are least qualified to resolve the issue. Again legal action lags far behind the results of science.

Milk purification is another field in which Experimental Jurisprudence has made great progress.

As indicated in Chapter VII, the United States Public Health Service, since the turn of the century, has been studying the science of pasteurization and sanitation of milk, its relation to disease and the effect of statutes and ordinances upon the incidence of milk-borne epidemics. As part of this study, in cooperation with local governments, they have developed a standard milk ordinance and code. The latest figures show that as of 1950 it had been adopted in fifty-five cities with a population over one hundred thousand, in thirty-eight with a population between fifty and one hundred thousand, and in fourteen hundred municipalities. It covers over eight hundred and eighty counties scattered throughout thirty-eight states. There are also thirty-two states which have adopted statutes on the subject with partial coverage and thirteen which are completely covered. In all, fifty-nine million people are receiving the benefit of the law.[80]

This is a very impressive showing; but as indicated by Table Four there are approximately ninety-one million, or sixty per cent of the population, who are not receiving this benefit. While it is doubtful if all the population could ever be covered, there still remains much to be desired. Table Four shows that a third of the urban population,

---

[78] Life, 42 (Mar. 24, 1952); Time, 17 (Mar. 24, 1952).

[79] The figures on acceptances and rejections are from Phair and Driscol, The Status of Fluoridation Programs, 45 J. Am. Dent. Ass'n 555 (1952); see also Bernard and Judith Manser, A Study of the Anti-Scientific Attitude 192 Sci. Am. 35 (Feb. 1955); note, 194 id. 58 (Feb. 1956).

[80] F.S.A. Pub. Health Serv., Div. of San. Release (Nov. 1950).

TABLE 4

Adoption of United States Public Health Milk Ordinance,
Progress Chart

	Adopted or Covered [1]	Total	Per cent not Covered
Total Population	59,000,000	150,000,000	60
Urban Population	59,000,000	88,000,000	33
Cities over 100,000	55	106[2]	48
Cities 50,000-100,000	38	125[2]	61
Counties	887	3,050[3]	70

[1] Taken from F.S.A., Pub. Health Serv. Release (Nov. 1950).
[2] U.S. Census, Preliminary Report (1950).
[3] Anderson, Units of Government, Pub. Ad. Service, No. 83, 17 (1942).

forty-eight per cent of the cities over one hundred thousand and sixty-one per cent of those between fifty and one hundred thousand, and the population of seventy per cent of the counties of the country are not subject to the law. There are over seventy-six cities in the United States without any requirement of pasteurization, and it should be noted that in the first nine months of 1950, six counties and twenty-three municipalities with a population of over two hundred thousand people repealed the ordinance. This is the greatest number that have dropped it in any one year since its original adoption.[81]

Disregarding the quality of enforcement, in spite of a half century of experimental scientific work and over twenty-five years of experimental study behind the statute, this unquestionably excellent and scientifically sound law is still only about fifty per cent enacted. According to the last figures, it is just slightly better than holding its own with the local legislative bodies.

PUBLIC SAFETY

The enforcement of public safety stands on middle ground insofar as research and institutions are available for collecting scientific material and transferring it into the legal system. In areas of traffic control, discussed at length in Chapter VI, the technique, research, education and government experimentation have reached a degree of perfection. The apprehension, punishment and control of the criminal population in some areas is on its way to much scientific exploitation; in others it has scarcely progressed beyond the middle ages. There has been some government action but little thorough experimentation. In all, the lag between scientific knowledge and its use in the legal system is apparent.

[81] F.S.A. Release, supra note 80.

Traffic control is a field where the methods of Experimental Jurisprudence have made startling advances.[82] Here there has emerged a complete experimental social science in which the institutionally trained traffic engineer becomes the person to whom lawmaking power is most effectively delegated. Under such a system the progress of traffic control and safety measures have been phenomenal. Twenty-five per cent of the cities of over one hundred thousand population have delegated the lawmaking power to experts,[83] but it is significant that the remaining seventy-five per cent have not. On the state level there is no unified legal control. In approximately half of the states the department of highway control or its equivalent has power to conduct research and make statistical studies and recommendations,[84] but in the other half such a department is little more than a police unit with some additional record-keeping duties. In almost all the states the power to change the law remains with the state legislatures or local bodies, and except for one-fourth of the larger cities noted above, there is little delegation to experts, who normally serve only in an "advisory" capacity.

The net result of the traffic system as a whole shows a shocking failure to live up to the potentialities of modern scientific knowledge. Traffic deaths and injuries in the United States during the first two years of the Korean war were much greater than the American casualties at the front. There have been over three times as many deaths and twenty-five times as many injuries in traffic as there were on the battlefield.[85] The accumulation of accidental deaths during little more than fifty years of use of automobiles has been over a million, which is greater than all the deaths from war in this country since 1776.[86] But in spite of these appalling facts which are being spectacularly exposed by the federal government through the National Safety Council, over three-fourths of our legal system as it

[82] Beutel, Traffic Control as Experimental Jurisprudence in Action, 31 Neb. L. Rev. 349 (1952). See also Chapter VI infra.

[83] Smith and LeCraw, Speed Laws and Enforcement, Traffic Q. 117, 121 (April 1947).

[84] See Report of Comm. on Laws and Ordinances, The President's Highway Safety Conference 19 et seq. (1949); Art. v. Uniform Vehicle Code, Pub. Rds. Adm. (1945).

[85] Deaths from traffic accidents in two years have run over 76,000 and injuries over 2,300,000; Accident Facts, Nat'l Safety Council F.S.A. (1950-51); Econ. Almanac 30 (1951-52). The casualty figures from Korea at the end of two years' fighting were approximately 110,000, of whom less than 20,000 were killed; see 112 Facts on File 149 (1952).

[86] The Millionth Man, 59 Scholastic 10 (1951).

affects traffic still limps along, failing to adopt the proven measures which the science of traffic control offers to reduce this slaughter.

The problem of crime control easily breaks down into three areas: crime detection, the law and methods of punishment, and crime prevention.

In crime detection there has been considerable progress in bringing science to bear upon the problem of identifying criminals. Due to pioneering work at the University of California, Northwestern University and in the laboratory of the Federal Bureau of Investigation, the apprehension of individual criminals has now taken on many of the aspects of an applied science. Most of this development, however, is quite recent.

Crime detection methods which use scientific information are well publicized. Knowledge of fingerprint identification and some other similar scientific devices appeared far back in the nineteenth century.[87] But serious and widespread official adoption of these and other scientific methods for crime detection date from the creation of the Federal Bureau of Investigation's laboratory in 1932.[88] At that time the federal government, building upon the pioneering work of some universities and a few city police departments, began the central laboratory which has grown until it now employs over three hundred scientists in many fields to aid in the detection of crime.[89] This central bureau now offers national services to police departments to identify criminals, soil, fabrics, paint, auto headlights, tire tracks and thousands of other clues. Over twelve thousand local police departments have called upon this service in a single year, and as many as seven thousand criminal suspects have been apprehended yearly[90] through the central fingerprint office, which now contains nearly one hundred million individual prints classified so that any one may be identified from a sample in a few minutes.

The laboratory is limited to the application of scientific technique for the solution of crimes and identifying criminals. There is no direct research into the success of the methods themselves as is the case in traffic studies, and there are no scientific tests of the social effect of criminal law. There is a section which collects criminal statistics, but these are used largely for propaganda effect upon Congress and others

[87] The Federal Bureau of Criminal Identification was started in 1904. Lowenthal, The Federal Bureau of Investigation 360 et seq. (1950).

[88] Lowenthal, op. cit. supra note 87, at 388; Floherty, Inside the F.B.I. 47 et seq. (1943).

[89] Floherty, op. cit. supra note 88, at 49.

[90] Floherty, op. cit. supra note 88, at 88.

to sustain the large appropriation necessary to operate the whole bureau.[91] The validity of the figures so produced for scientific purposes is subject to serious question.[92]

The National Police Academy,[93] which is also a branch of the F.B.I., is devoted primarily to training police officers and not to scientific research. The phenomenal progress of the laboratory and the Police Academy together with the work of universities like Northwestern, which trains police officers and prosecuters, has raised the art of the law enforcement officer to the status of a profession.[94]

There is still a tremendous lag between the applied science so developed and the level of knowledge of police forces generally. Although there is considerable doubt about it,[95] the F.B.I. itself is generally recognized as a highly trained professional organization, but it constitutes less than eight per cent of the national police force.[96] Some of the large cities like New York, Philadelphia, Chicago and Cincinnati have excellent scientific identification laboratories and police schools, as do many of the states.[97] But the local sheriffs, city, town and county police forces are still elected or dependent upon politics for their positions. Although crime detection is adopting scientific gadgets and methods, the majority of enforcement officers are still non-professional, and there is no experimental science in the field beyond that produced in the crime-detection laboratories. Even this information has not yet become a tool of the majority of law enforcement officers.

Conduct of the coroner's office is an example of the almost complete failure of modern scientific methods to penetrate our legal institutions. Since the twelfth century it has been the duty of the coroner to hold inquests into unexpected deaths and otherwise to assist the sheriff in the execution of the criminal law. Originally the coroner, who was a layman, impaneled a jury, also of laymen, to aid him in finding the facts surrounding unexpected or unexplained deaths, to bring in verdicts and to initiate criminal charges or in-

[91] For an example of this sort of propaganda see Collins, The F.B.I. in Peace and War (1943).

[92] Lowenthal, op. cit. supra note 87, at 395 et seq.

[93] Floherty, op. cit. supra note 88, at 187.

[94] Cf. O'Hara and Osterberg, An Introduction to Criminalistics (1949).

[95] This controversy is discussed at length by Lowenthal, op. cit. supra note 87.

[96] Figures are hard to get, and this estimate is probably too large. Cf. Lowenthal, op. cit. supra note 87, at 1, 397; 6 Floherty, op. cit. supra note 88, at 18.

[97] Soderman and O'Connell, Modern Criminal Investigations (1945).

vestigations.⁹⁸ In the absence of medical knowledge characteristic of those times, this method was as good as any for getting at the facts. But since the development of the science and art of pathology, it is foolish to charge either a single layman or a jury of laymen with such duties.

The books are full of startling cases where crimes have been missed or innocent people convicted by failure of untrained officials properly to examine into the cause of death.⁹⁹ It is now common knowledge that pathological examinations are the only sure and scientific method of uncovering all of the causes or nature of unexplained deaths.

In light of these well known facts, one might expect that the duties and procedures of the coroner would have been revised to keep up with the development of modern medicine. Unfortunately the state of the law is just the opposite. In thirty-nine of the forty-eight states,¹⁰⁰ the coroner is still a layman, usually elected, but sometimes appointed. He continues to hold inquests over the dead much as he did in the

---

⁹⁸ 1 Holdsworth, History of English Law 82 et seq. (3d ed. 1922) (The coroner originally had many other duties; but many of these have gradually disappeared.)

⁹⁹ A few of these are: The Coroner's Office, Efficiency Series, Rep. No. 2. Municipal Ass'n of Cleveland (1912); Adler, Medical Science and Criminal Justice, Part V, Cleveland Survey of Criminal Justice in Cleveland (1921); Wickersham, Should the Coroner's Office be Abolished, 1 Minn. L. Rev. 197 (1917); Breyfogle, The Laws of Missouri, Relating to Inquests and Coroners, 10 Mo. L. Rev. 34 (1945); Jordan, North Carolina's Archaic Coroner System, 26 N.C.L. Rev. 96 (1947).

¹⁰⁰ Ala. Code Ann. tit. 12, § 54 (1941); Ariz. Code Ann. § 17-1103 (1940); Ark. Const. Art. VII, § 46 (1947); Cal. Gov. Codes §§ 24000, 24001, 27531 (Deering, 1951); Colo. Stat. Ann. c. 45, §§ 116 et seq. (1936); Del. Rev. Code §§ 1519 et seq. (1935); Fla. Stat. Ann. §§ 936.01 et seq. (1944); Ga. Code Ann. tit. 21 (Supp. 1951); Idaho Code Ann. § 34-202 (1948); Ill. Ann. Stat. c. 46, § 2-14 (Smith-Hurd, Supp. 1952); Ill. Const. Art. X, § 8; Ind. Ann. Stat. §§ 49-2901 et seq. (Burns, 1951); Iowa Code Ann. § 39.17 (1949); Kan. Gen. Stat. Ann. §§ 19-1001 et seq. (1935); Ky. Const. §§ 99, 100; Mich. Stat. Ann. § 6.264 (Henderson, 1936); Minn. Stat. Ann. § 382.01 (West, 1947); Miss. Const. Art. V, § 138; Mo. Const. Art. IX, § 10; Mo. Rev. Stat. § 11459 (West, 1943); Mont. Const. Art. XVI, § 5; Neb. Rev. Stat. § 23-1210 (1943); N.C. Gen. Stat. Ann. § 152-1 (1952); N.D. Rev. Code §§ 11-0927, 11-1002, 11-1919 (1943); Nev. Comp. Laws Ann. §§ 11426 et seq. (1930); N.J. Stat. Ann. §§ 40:40-1 et seq. (Supp. 1952); N.M. Stat. Ann. §§ 38-1701 to 38-1704 (1942); N.Y. County Law § 400 (McKinney, Supp. 1953); Okla. Stat. Ann. tit. 19, §§ 461 et seq. (1937); Ore. Comp. Laws Ann. §§ 87-101, 87-102 (Supp. 1943); Pa. Stat. Ann. tit. 16, § 51 (Supp. 1952); S.C. Code Ann. § 17-51 (1952); S.C. Const. Art. V, § 30; S.D. Const. Art. IX, § 5; Tenn. Code Ann. § 712 et seq. (Williams, 1943); Tex. Code Crim. Proc. art. 968 et seq. (1950); Utah Code §§ 77-58-1 et seq. (1953); Vt. Rev. Stat. § 4142 (1947); Wash. Rev. Code §§ 36.16.030, 36.24.010 et seq. (1952); W. Va. Const. Art. IX, § 2; Wisc. Stat. §§ 59.34 et seq. (1951); Wyo. Comp. Stat. Ann. § 31-103 (1945). It should be noted that many of these provisions are embodied in the state constitutions.

twelfth century and to impanel juries to determine the cause of deaths as he did then.[101] In only nine states is there any statewide requirement that the coroner or an official performing his duties have any medical training or assistance.[102] In two of these[103] the medical man is merely an aid to a layman; in one the coroner is required to be a professional man only if a physician is available for the purpose,[104] in five he must be a licensed physician,[105] but in only two is there any mandatory provision for the services of a trained pathologist.[106] Maryland is the lone state requiring, as it should, that such procedures be under the direction of a board headed by a competent pathologist.[107]

Thus there exists the unjustifiable condition that in the overwhelming majority of cases untrained laymen are determining the causes of violent and unexplained deaths, often under conditions where even a doctor who is not a pathologist would not be competent to solve the problem. Criminals are daily escaping detection and innocent men are charged with crimes where trained pathologists would reveal the true state of facts. Mortality statistics are also being contaminated by laymen's judgment as to the causes of many reported deaths. Here again the dead hand of the middle ages operates one of the important divisions of our legal system, ignoring the enlightened and easily available scientific methods.

The substantive criminal law and administration of the penal systems are areas into which scientific methods have almost completely failed to penetrate.

It has been nearly a half century since former President and Chief Justice Taft, not a noted radical or reformer, said,[108] "I grieve for my country to say that the administration of the criminal law in all the states of the union is a disgrace to our civilization." Little has happened

---

[101] In twenty-seven of the states cited supra note 100 there seems to be clear authority to hire medical assistance or witnesses; see Jackson, The Law of Cadavers 171 (1950).

[102] Conn. Gen. Stat. § 470 et seq. (1949); La. Const. Art. VII, § 70; Me. Rev. Stat. c. 79, § 258 et seq. (1944); Mass. Ann. Laws c. 38 (Supp. 1952); Md. Ann. Code Gen. Laws art. 22 (1951); N.H. Rev. Laws c. 436 (1942); R.I. Gen. Laws c. 11 (1938); Va. Code Ann. § 19-21 et seq. (1950). In a number of states there are statutory requirements for local medical examiners in populous cities or counties. See, e.g., N.Y. County Law § 400; Wis. Stat. c. 366.15 et seq. (1947).

[103] Connecticut and Rhode Island statutes, supra note 102.

[104] Louisiana statute, supra note 102.

[105] Maine, Maryland, Massachusetts, New Hampshire and Virginia statutes, supra note 102.

[106] Maryland and Virginia.

[107] Maryland statute, supra note 102.

[108] Taft, The Administration of Criminal Law, 15 Yale L.J. 1, 11 (1905).

to render this indictment any less true than it was then. The substance as well as the procedure of the criminal law is a direct survival of the pre-scientific era. Our rules of criminal intent and the other basic concepts of responsibility and punishment are based upon ancient theological concepts that have no place in modern psychology and psychiatry. The field of insanity as a defense is a good example of the condition of the entire criminal law. In a recent murder case where the defense of insanity was offered, there was the familiar spectacle of experts testifying for both sides; but upon inquiry it developed that the five experts, though differing widely in their conclusion as to the effect of legal rules on the defendant, all agreed completely on the psychiatric diagnosis. The trouble was, of course, that the substantive legal rules had no meaning to the modern medical practitioner.

In like manner ideas of responsibility, punishment and reform are also untouched by science. There have been statutory attempts at reform by do-gooders and scientists which have been pushed through the legislatures with little regard for further study and often with insufficient financial support for proper administration.[109] Weihofen, in his excellent discussion of insanity as a defense, summarizes the situation as follows:[110]

> Our criminal jurisprudence today presents a patchwork pattern of these competing theories. Specific reforms have been enacted into law, but the underlying conception which inspired these reforms has not usually been given much thought, and has certainly not been accepted as the basis of our methods of dealing with offenders. "All theories on the subject of punishment," said Sir Henry Maine in 1864, "have more or less broken down; and we are at sea as to first principles." In 1925, Lord Oxford, quoting these words, added, "Nothing has since been said or written that has brought us any nearer to these principles."

In other areas of the criminal law there has been even less research, reform or effort to bring the criminal law in line with modern science. Much has been written about theories of penology, psychology and psychiatry as applied to crime, but with rare exception[111] there has been little cooperative research or experimentation in this field. The modern prison remains substantially a medieval dungeon with plumb-

---

[109] For example, see the discussion of the "Briggs Law," Weihofen, Insanity as a Defense in Criminal Law 401 et seq. (1933).

[110] Weihofen, op. cit. supra note 109, at 441; see also Wechsler, The Challenge of a Model Penal Code, 65 Harv. L. Rev. 1097 (1952), and authorities there cited.

[111] One example of good scientific work is Ohlin, Selection for Parole (1951).

ing, electric lights, a machine shop and a few modern gadgets for opening gates or sounding alarms. It is a pity, in this field where, by the force of law, the criminal loses his liberty and where experimentation is therefore easiest, that there has been little application of applied experimental science.

Crime prevention as a science is still in the realm of speculation. The formation of juvenile courts is one attempt to implement some theories, but the statistics and studies on the subject are still inconclusive[112] or entirely missing.

SCIENCE IN THE JUDICIAL AND LEGISLATIVE SYSTEMS

When one approaches what is generally regarded as the heart of the lawmaking and enforcement machinery, the legislatures and the courts, the absence of scientific progress, machinery to support it or institutions devoted to research is shocking.

The judicial system has failed completely to pick up any of the available scientific advances to improve its procedure. This was graphically illustrated in a recent case. According to radio reports, Senator McCarthy, in defending himself against a libel suit, wanted to use a wire recorder to take a record of the testimony. Although no possible harm could be done by the introduction of such a device and much time could be saved, the court summarily denied the request.

Similar unreasonable refusal to adopt scientific advances appears throughout the entire system. The determination of the facts underlying litigation is archaic. The jury which remains the chief fact-finding device of courts has come down from the days of the Carlovigian kings.[113] In its inception it was, of course, an advancement because it replaced trial by battle, oath and ordeal. Although it was originally made up from a group of neighbors who knew all of the facts, it has gradually become a body of twelve men who are entirely ignorant of the subject matter of the litigation. By the end of the fourteenth century the English jury had developed all the principal characteristics which it still retains. Although the average American lawyer today would be shocked by the statement, the modern jury as an institution is almost as antiquated as was trial by battle and oath and ordeal, which it replaced. Since the seventeenth century, in the principal European countries, experts have been designated by the parties or by the court from approved lists finally to determine scientific or com-

---

[112] A good beginning is Tappan, Delinquent Girls in Court (1947).
[113] 1 Holdsworth, History of English Law 312 et seq. (3d ed. 1922) (setting out this history).

plicated contrivances within the field of their special knowledge.[114] Nevertheless, the jury remains the principal method of fact-finding used by the American courts, which have strenuously resisted any infringement upon their ultimate power, by other than the judge himself, to find the facts.

Illustrations are legion of this dogged and unreasonable refusal to replace the jury with modern devices for finding the facts. Only a few need be set out here. Sometimes the judges use the Constitution as an excuse for refusing to allow change in areas that the clause which was applied was never intended to cover. Some of the most complicated and technical problems of fact-finding to come before the legal tribunals are those surrounding valuation of electric and other utilities for rate-making purposes. Early in this procedure the courts held that placing the final determination of the fact of value in the power of an expert commission was a denial of due process of law and therefore unconstitutional[115] but giving an inexpert jury of twelve good and true men this final power was proper.[116] The mess which followed in the regulation of private utilities is current history.[117]

In like manner blood tests to aid in the determination of parentage have now been developed by medical science to a point where it may be possible to prove conclusively by comparing blood samples that a certain man is not the father of a certain child. These tests have been adopted all over Europe as conclusive in cases of disputed paternity[118] but not in the United States. Matters of this sort are still submitted to juries in all the states, and they have been authorized by statute in only eight[119] to determine that a man is not the father of an illegitimate child in cases where the blood tests showed conclusively that this was an impossibility. In spite of the fact that in the city of New York alone blood tests have shown conclusively that thirty per cent of the examined men accused in paternity cases and who denied it were

[114] The European procedures are summarized briefly in Engelman, History of Continental Civil Procedure (Millar's transl. 1927); 7 Continental Legal History Series 557, 563 (Germany), 762 (France), 789, 816 (Italy).

[115] Ohio Valley Water Co. v. Ben Avon Burough, 253 U.S. 287 (1920); Chicago, M. & St.P. Ry. v. Minnesota, 134 U.S. 418 (1889); see Buchanan, The Ohio Valley Water Case and The Valuation of Railroads, 40 Harv. L. Rev. 1033 (1927), and authorities there cited.

[116] United Gas Pub. Serv. Co. v. Texas, 303 U.S. 123 (1938).

[117] Beutel, Due Process in Valuation of Local Utilities, 13 Minn. L. Rev. 409 (1929); Mr. Justice Black's dissent, McCart v. Indianapolis Water Co., 302 U.S. 419, 423 (1938).

[118] Schatkin, Disputed Paternity Proceedings 211 et seq. (2d ed. 1947).

[119] Schatkin, op. cit. supra note 118, at 183.

actually not the fathers, only a few courts in this country even rely upon such evidence.[120] In many cases the juries have been allowed to hold men as fathers where the blood tests showed this to be impossible. [121]

Another example is the use of scientific methods to determine the truth of statements made by witnesses and suspects. Mechanical lie detectors have been developed which have been proved to be accurate in over seventy-five per cent of the cases,[122] but no such proof is available for the accuracy of verdicts of juries in judging the veracity of witnesses. In a recent test under controlled conditions where a mock crime was staged by the writer and investigated by the standard devices, out of five guilty persons only one was apprehended by ordinary criminal invesigation. He was tried and found not guilty. Afterwards a lie detector operator, by testing the suspects and a number of innocent parties, reproduced the crime in most of its details, identifying three principals and one accomplice. The fifth guilty party was able to beat the lie detector by taking an overdose of aspirin, but the operator also discovered this fact, and on re-test after the effects of the drug had worn off, he could undoubtedly have found the fifth principal guilty. So far as the writer knows, this is the only situation in which the lie detector has been used in competition with criminal investigations, judge and jury. Further experiments of this nature are, of course, possible and ought to be conducted at once.

As things stand, the lie detector is rapidly becoming one of the most important means of crime detection but it is not yet tolerated in the courts even to be introduced as evidence to a jury, to say nothing of standing on its own merits to replace the jury as a fact-finding device, and there seems to be little research in progress to develop it further as an evidentiary device.[123]

There are thousands of other scientific means in physics, chemistry and other sciences for determining basic facts in litigation which are far more efficient, but none of these devices are used by the courts, which still follow the plan of submitting expert testimony to inexpert jurors without any qualifications for distinguishing between the scientist and the charlatan. What is worse, there are apparently no institutions in this country devoting any objective social research to the

---

[120] Ploscowe, Sex and the Law 124 et seq. (1951); Schatkin, op. cit. supra note 118.

[121] Numerous cases are collected by the authorities cited supra notes 118 and 120.

[122] Inbau, Lie Detection and Criminal Interrogation 77 (1948).

[123] See Inbau, op. cit. supra note 122, at 86 et seq.

problem of correcting and improving this antiquated court procedure.

Professor Smith at the University of Texas[124] has begun some work along this line, but at present he is devoting most of his attention to enlightening the legal and medical professions on the means of using the present obsolete court fact-finding machinery. It is hoped that his work may soon be the beginning of a procedural reform in the courts themselves.

The legislatures, as indicated above, have no continuing research organization and therefore no machinery for bringing scientific discoveries into the legal system. Like the courts, they have little inclination or equipment to take on new procedures. These facts stand as a direct block to the adoption of scientific methods by law.

The examples listed here are a mere drop in the bucket to the number of instances where the legislative system is behind or unconscious of scientific development. To the items discussed there could easily be added such subjects as tests for intoxication; the use of truth serums; the revision of sex, marriage and divorce laws; sterilization and artificial insemination; the adoption of intelligence tests in the education process—in fact, the overhaul of the entire educational system to conform to the known dictates of science; economic valuations for tax purposes and thousands of others, many of which the reader can name himself, in which scientific information is developed and waiting to be adopted into our legal system.

AMERICAN LAW INSTITUTE

No discussion of the lag between science and law would be complete without noting the work of the American Law Institute. Although there are other organizations and foundations of considerable size devoted to the problem of modernizing the legal system,[125] the American Law Institute[126] is the principal one devoted to this task, and has probably turned out more concrete work in this direction than all the others put together. Founded in 1923 as the blue-ribbon organization for the legal profession for the purpose of modernizing the law, it is made up of leaders of the organized bar, the judges of the federal and state supreme courts and outstanding law professors. The judges and deans of law schools are ex officio members, and the

[124] Bull. Law-Science Short Course (1953).

[125] Among these are: Am. Bar Ass'n, Commissioners on Uniform Laws, Am. Institute of Crim. Law and Criminology, Louisiana Law Institute, Council of State Governments, and Survey of the Legal Profession.

[126] See Goodrich, The Story of the American Law Institute, Wash. U.L.Q. 283 (1951), which contains the facts about the Institute not otherwise documented here.

leaders of the bar and professors are elected on the basis of their scholarly and professional achievements. In all, its membership consists of about fourteen hundred prominent lawyers, judges and professors from all over the country.[127] According to its charter, it is organized ". . . to promote the clarification and simplification of the law and its better adaptation to social needs, to secure better administration of justice and to encourage and carry on scholarly and scientific legal work."

During the thirty-three years of its existence, it has spent, in addition to the dues of its members and other miscellaneous accounts, over three million dollars granted to it by a number of large foundations in its effort at improvement of the law. Great progress should be expected from the efforts of so prominent a group of men and the expenditure of such a large amount, and considerable progress has been made.

Over three-fourths of the funds expended and energy of the organization has gone into the Restatement of the Common Law. This corresponds roughly to Step Two in the methods of Experimental Jurisprudence explained elsewhere,[128] except that it is not an accurate statement of the law as applied to social problems of a particular jurisdiction but rather a synthetic creation of a law common to all. The project was not an attempt to codify the complete law but only to restate the common law as it appeared in decided cases in Anglo-American jurisdictions. The Restatement is not a code because it is not for official adoption and ignores the statutes, merely attempting to survey and state the holdings of thousands upon thousands of court decisions. The technique of compiling the law resembles very closely that used by Justinian in formulating the Digest and the Corpus Juris of the Roman law in the sixth century.[129] The work was done largely by paid law professors called Reporters working in their spare time with the aid of volunteer committees of lawyers acting as advisors. The drafts were then discussed and approved by the members of the Institute in convention assembled. There was no attempt to get the social facts and no use of the technique of any other science. The completed Restatement makes up a library of over twenty-two volumes

[127] The list of members is set out in the programs of the annual meetings. See A.L.I., Twenty-ninth Annual Meeting 9-28 (1952).

[128] Beutel, An Outline of the Nature and Methods of Experimental Jurisprudence, 51 Col. L. Rev. 415, 425 et seq. (1951). Also see Beutel, Traffic Control as Experimental Jurisprudence in Action, 31 Neb. L. Rev. 349 (1952). See Ch. II.

[129] See 1 Wigmore, A Panorama of the World's Legal System 444 (1928). The difference is that the Digest compiled legal writings; the Restatement, cases.

covering more than sixteen thousand pages together with a lot of smaller miscellaneous publications, annotations, indices and the like. Although it does no more than attempt to state unofficially the result of court decisions, it has secured wide recognition as the authoritative statement of the law in the fields which it covers and has done much to reduce the confusion in the court decisions. Without attempting to improve, reform or modernize, it crystallizes the common law and no more.

Efforts at law reform have occupied less than one-fourth of the energy of the Institute, but now that the Restatement is out of the way it is hoped that this aspect of the work may receive major emphasis. Outside of the educational program, which is no more than technical training for lawyers in the use of the present legal machinery, the Institute has undertaken the drafting of five statutes which are a frank attempt at improving the law, corresponding roughly to Step Six in the process of Experimental Jurisprudence, but without the trouble of doing the research and thinking involved in Steps Three through Five. These proposed laws are the Code of Criminal Procedure, the Youth Correction Authority Act, the Model Code of Evidence, the Uniform Commercial Code and the Federal Income Tax Statute. In attempting to create these codes, the Institute unfortunately adopted the same sort of procedure which proved so successful in the Restatement of the Common Law. The work on each project was under the direction of a group of law professor Reporters surrounded by committees from the bar who relied upon the Reporters' knowledge to draft the new statutes. There was practically no social research nor cooperation with other sciences or groups of scientists. So these statutes are primarily ex cathedra pronunciamentos by great authorities in the law-teaching profession, but little attention has been paid to problems of science or social science.

In the compilation of the Youth Correction Code, there was some ex cathedra advice from social scientists in other fields but little effort at research beyond the determination of the state of the law.

The drafting of the Commercial Code was done on the same pattern[130] as the Restatement but in cooperation with the Uniform Laws Commission of the American Bar Association, which is a voluntary organization of lawyers closely resembling in its deliberations the

---

[130] For a more detailed criticism of this technique see Beutel, The Proposal Uniform Commercial Code as a Problem in Codification, 16 Law & Contemp. Prob. 141 et seq. (1951); Beutel, The Proposed Uniform Commercial Code Should Not Be Adopted, 61 Yale L.J. 334, 358 et seq. (1952).

procedures of a legislative body. In the drafting of the Commercial Code, the aid and advice of various business associations was sought and received, much in the way in which lobbyists appear before legislative committees; and as indicated elsewhere,[131] in one instance, that of Article 4, Bank Deposits and Collections, the control of the project was taken away from the Institute and the Commissioners on Uniform Laws by the bank lobby.

The work of the Institute has had little effect in changing the law. The Restatement of course intended no such result, and the model codes have had little influence. By 1951, after twenty-eight years of work by the Institute, the Code of Criminal Procedure, which attempted no more than to remove some of the anachronisms from the criminal practice, was adopted almost completely in only five states and in some of its detail in the others. The Model Youth Correction Authority Act, which attempts some inconsequential reform in the handling of young criminals, had been adopted with a number of changes in only five states. The Model Code of Evidence, which was an ex cathedra authoritative compilation built upon the present rules of court procedures with only a few minor changes, had not been adopted any place. The Uniform Commercial Code, which is a huge undertaking but not a particularly satisfactory one, has been completed five years but has received the approval of the legislature of only one state.[132] The Federal Income Tax Statute, which, as its title indicates, is an attempt at recodification of parts of the Internal Revenue Code, is not yet finished, but it is being compiled by the same procedure as the Restatement.

The creation of a Model Penal Code, which has been under discussion for twenty years, is now being attempted with funds donated by the Rockefeller Foundation. From the statement by the Reporter[133] of the problems involved, there is hope that some real scientific research into the social problems and the results of the present criminal law may go into this work. The group is of approximately the same type as that used for the Commercial Code, and it is doubtful whether any Model Penal Code could ever be drafted before there has been far-reaching research into the new scientific discoveries surrounding

---

[131] Beutel, The Proposed Uniform Commercial Code Should Not Be Adopted, 61 Yale L.J. 334, 358 et seq. (1952).

[132] Pennsylvania, to become effective July, 1954, Pa. Stat. Ann. tit. 12A (Purdon, 1954). At the present writing it has been introduced in the New York, Massachusetts, and Georgia legislatures, but the New York Law Revision Commission has rejected it, N.Y. Leg. Dec., 65A (1956).

[133] Wechsler, The Challenge of a Model Penal Code, 65 Harv. L. Rev. 1097 (1952).

the field of penology and into the comparative effects of various statutes now in existence.

As shown by the results of the work on the Commercial Code,[134] the domination of the American Law Institute by a group of blue-stocking lawyers makes it subject to the pressure of the interests of their clients. But the compilation of a penal code does not include a direct infringement upon these interests, as was the case in the Commercial Code. It may be that the Reporters, who realize the difficulties involved in the application of the law which they are attempting to codify, will be able to obtain real scientific aid from other fields. The Institute as now organized is not likely to push this effort; but since there is little direct financial interest among the members of the bar in this field, they may not be unwilling to accept from help outside scientists.

Thus there is still a chance that the Institute may go on to the adoption of truly scientific and experimental methods after it has done the necessary job of fighting its way through the confusions in the law. Already there is a projected study of the effects of adoption of the Model Youth Correction Authority Act[135] in the various states. When this is undertaken, the Institute will be embarking on the last step in the process of Experimental Jurisprudence, the re-study of the effect of a reform. If this work is successful, it should encourage further application of complete experimental method by the Institute.

If the codes serve no other purpose than to present methods of formulating a statement of the law as it applies to various problems discussed in the long commentaries attached to the various sections, they will, to some extent, result in the completion of Step Two in the procedure of Experimental Jurisprudence. From that, the American Law Institute may move on to the discoveries of the social needs and the creation and real area of scientific legislation or the intelligent use of the fruits of science in other fields; but as the Institute is now constituted, it partakes more of the nature of a social gathering and an unofficial but skilled legislature than it does of a scientific organization. It still has a long way to go before it even begins to cut down on the lag between the developments of science and the condition of the law; but there are indications that its continued efforts at law reform may eventually drive it to significant developments in this

[134] See material cited supra note 130.
[135] Wechsler, The Challenge of a Model Penal Code, op. cit. supra note 133, at 1121.

direction. At the present writing it represents an important institutionalized hope for bringing scientific developments into the law.

THE JOHNS HOPKINS INSTITUTE OF LAW

Probably the most important of all attempts by legally trained personnel to develop significant social research on the operation and functioning of law occurred at Johns Hopkins University under the direction of its Institute of Law. This was the first major effort to institutionalize social research into the operation of law. The Johns Hopkins Institute was established in June, 1928[136] and suspended a little over four years later.[137]

The original plan was to create a scientific institute to study law as an instrument of social regulation and to serve as an initial research and development center, much as Johns Hopkins had pioneered in the development of the science of medicine. There are two major purposes behind the Institute: (1) to study the social effect of the operation of laws and legal institutions such as courts; (2) to train young people as experts in the development of this new science.[138]

The research program envisaged studies of various types of institutions for the administration of justice through reporting on the results of their operations in situations where different legal systems used various devices to accomplish the same purposes. It was thought that comparison of the statistical facts about the operation of government units such as the courts, public utility commissions and similar administrative agencies would reveal the strength and defects of their structure and suggest significant reforms to increase their efficency. The plans of the Institute also suggested that it might be possible to conduct experiments in the administration of law based on the results of the studies.[139]

The prospectus also contemplated cooperation of members of various branches of the social sciences in developing the work of the Institute.[140]

The original plans contemplated a very substantial outlay. The projected annual budget called for approximately $300,000 a year to be spent mostly on research, but the actual expenditures at their height reached less than half this amount. There were also hopes for con-

---

[136] Johns Hopkins University Circular No. 7, p. 7 (1929-30).
[137] Marshall & May, The Divorce Court in Ohio 8 (1933).
[138] Goodnow & Griswold, The Institute for the Study of Law 31 ff. (1929).
[139] Id. 60.
[140] Id. 66.

struction of an ample building costing about a half-million dollars.[141] The building never got under way, but there was created a personnel nucleus of from six to ten permanent experts. The plan also called for three visiting experts to work with the permanent staff on an annual basis and for about twenty younger scholars and clerical workers.[142]

The Institute as actually organized had a permanent staff of five lawyers and one economist.[143] Of the five lawyers on the staff, Walter Wheeler Cook, who was the chief promoter of the entire plan, was also trained in physics.

The staff of assistants, like the top personnel, although it varied from time to time during the life of the project, was predominately law-trained, and the few research associates who were visiting authorities also turned out to be lawyers.[144]

The fact that its staff consisted so predominately of persons with legal background and training probably had a very marked influence upon the subjects chosen for the original research. Since legal education was completely dominated by the case method and study of the functions of the judiciary, it was only natural that under the guidance of lawyers the main research efforts of the Institute should have been directed almost entirely toward the judicial aspect of the legal administration. The shortage of funds and the element of time may also have played a part in the failure to examine other social results of legal activity.

SURVEYS OF LITIGATION

During its life the Institute undertook three major research tasks. These were a survey of litigation in New York City, including the Supreme Court of New York, the County Court, the Municipal Court and some of the work of the federal courts in that area,[145] a study of

---

[141] Id. 83 ff.

[142] Johns Hopkins University Circular No. 7 (1929-30), also sets out the entire program.

[143] Walter W. Cook, Leon C. Marshall, Herman Oliphant, W. W. Willoughby, Hessel E. Yntema, J.V.A. MacMurray, Johns Hopkins University Circular No. 7 (1931-32). Willoughby and MacMurray served largely in the capacity of consultants.

[144] The details on this personnel can be found in the annual Johns Hopkins University Circulars Nos. 6 and 7 (1929-30) to (1932-33).

[145] Descriptions of these studies can be found in the university circulars cited in note 144 supra. Results of the New York study as here reported are taken from Study of Civil Justice in New York, a confidential Institute document found in the papers of Walter W. Cook; see also, J. H. Survey of Litigation in New York, Bulletins Nos. 1-3 (1931-32).

the judicial administration of the state of Ohio[146] and the similar study of judicial administration in the state of Maryland.[147] These latter two projects were carried on in cooperation with the judicial councils of the two states.

In addition to its three major studies, the Johns Hopkins Institute also cooperated in many minor research efforts on the part of individual scholars conducted under the general direction of the Institute or the almost unguided hand of individual scholars. It is quite impossible at the present time even to note all of these studies. However, its 1931-1932 circular[148] lists twenty-six such projects that were being carried on to some extent in cooperation with the Institute at the same time it was making its major examination of judicial administration. Of these twenty-six, all but three were attempts to study some form of judicial activity. Of the remaining three, two were inquiries into the functioning of public utility commissions[149] and one an examination of criminal statistics.

There was also undertaken the task of cataloging all current research projects in law.[150]

This short summary indicates that although the Institute was formed to make a scientific study of the social effect of laws in hope of developing experiments and improvements, as a matter of fact it made no major examination into more than one branch of the legal machinery, namely, the judiciary itself.

THE RESULTS OF THE STUDIES OF JUDICIAL ADMINISTRATION

The three chief projects in judicial administration were all similar in nature and may be roughly said to have had the following purposes:[151]

"1. To study the trends of litigation and to ascertain its human causes and effects.

---

[146] J. H. Judicial System of Ohio, Bulletin Nos. 1-6 gives the plans and their progress; Marshall & May, The Divorce Court in Ohio (1933); Martin, Waiver of Jury Trial in Criminal Cases in Ohio (1933); Marshall, Comparative Judicial Criminal Statistics: Ohio and Maryland (1932) among others are partial results of this study.

[147] Marshall & May, The Divorce Court in Maryland (1932) is a partial fruit of this study; see also J. H. Judicial System of Maryland, Bulletins Nos. 1-5 (1930-32).

[148] P. 12 ff.

[149] One of these is Burke, The Public Service Commission of Maryland (1932), an excellent statistical study with some suggestions for reform.

[150] See Harron, Current Research in Law (1928-29); Iddings, id. (1928-30).

[151] Bond & Cook, Preface to The Divorce Court in Maryland 7 (1932); see also Marshall, Outline of Statement Concerning State Wide Judicial Administration (1932.)

107

"2. To study the machinery and the functioning of the various agencies and offices which directly and indirectly have to do with the administration of law.

"3. To learn reasons for delays, expense, and uncertainty in litigation.

"4. To institute a permanent system of judicial records and statistics which will automatically provide information now secured after great labor.

"5. To detect points at which changes in substantive law would contribute markedly to social justice."

The studies proceeded by no means far enough to reach the ambitious goals which were set for them by the directing committee. There was an effort to collect and develop judicial statistics. A large staff of workers was given data sheets to fill in details of the operation of courts to produce an analysis of various litigated cases. The analysis contemplated by each of these sheets goes into such items as personal data about the parties in divorce cases, the origin of the case, the jurisdiction, the relief, the parties, amounts of money involved, mode of disposition of the cases, types of judgments and over a hundred details of miscellaneous information about a particular lawsuit in trial courts and on appeal.[152] Over a dozen different forms of data sheets, each containing approximately one hundred individual items, seem to have been used in each of the studies in Ohio and Maryland. After one or more data sheets were completed for each of a set of chosen cases, the notes were assembled and the resulting statistics analyzed by hand and machine much as is the fashion for work in the Census Bureau. The material then was collected and classified in the form of statistical reports. Some idea of the immensity of this task may be gleaned from the statistics contained in the final reports. The New York study, for example, covered approximately 10,000 judgments in the supreme court, a similar number in the county court, 18,000 in the city court and 28,000 in the municipal court. In addition to this, there was an attempt to collect statistically some data on over 300,000 cases in these three courts.[153]

Although the analysis of cases was a partial sample of the total number decided in the year 1930, together with a sampling from other

---

[152] Some of the data sheets themselves have been collected and preserved in two pamphlets, Sample of Data Sheets Used in Analysis of Current Litigation, Studies of Maryland and Ohio, see also J.H. Judicial System of Ohio, Bulletin No. 5, pp. 18-47 (1931) and J. H. Judicial System of Maryland Bulletin No. 2, pp. 18-47 (1930) where data sheets are set out in full.

[153] See Tables 1 to 3, Study of Civil Justice in New York supra note 145.

years in the studies in Ohio and Maryland, where the data sheets mentioned above were used, there was an analysis of data sheets of over 135,000 cases chosen from the dockets of the various courts. Among these were 9,000 divorce actions in the Ohio courts in the first six months of 1930, a similar number of criminal actions in the same time, 40,000 civil cases and many others. A smaller number of divorces, common-law actions, equity and criminal cases were studied and analyzed in the state of Maryland.[154]

It will be seen at once that this formidable mass of judicial statistics should have yielded a tremendous amount of information about the judicial machinery of the three states which were chosen for the initial investigation; and although the work was never completed due to absence of funds, caused largely by the fact that the project was unfortunately started and operated during the bottom of the worst financial depression this country has even seen, it did accumulate a mountain of judicial statistics and miscellaneous information about the courts of the three states. Just what use the Institute might have made of this material had it continued in its operation must be left wholly to speculation. Of the five goals which the directors of the studies set for themselves, only the first and second were partly accomplished. Data were collected which give the statistical information upon samples of every level of the court system of Ohio and practical information on Maryland and New York. Among others, nine statistical monographs were published, analyzing the work and expenses of operating Ohio courts, including the justice of the peace courts[155] and mayor's courts[156] of Hamilton County, criminal actions in the common pleas courts,[157] receiverships in Franklin County,[158] the divorce court,[159] appellate courts and appellate procedure,[160] administration of criminal justice in Franklin County,[161] expenditure for the administration of justice for one year[162] and criminal statistics for another.[163] These publications, like others of the Institute, were largely detailed factual

---

[154] Johns Hopkins University Circular (1931-32) No. 7 pp. 11 ff; J. H. Judicial System of Maryland, Bulletin No. 2, pp. 4 ff.

[155] Douglas, Justice of the Peace Courts of Hamilton County, Ohio (1932).

[156] Douglas, The Mayor Courts of Hamilton County, Ohio (1933).

[157] Gehlke, Criminal Actions in the Common Pleas Courts of Ohio (1936).

[158] Billig (1932).

[159] Marshall and May, The Divorce Court in Ohio (1933).

[160] Harris (1933).

[161] Blackburn (1935).

[162] Reticker and Marshall, Expenditures of Public Money for the Administration of Justice in Ohio, 1930 (1933).

[163] Bettman, Jamison, Marshall and Miles, Ohio Criminal Statutes, 1931 (1932).

109

descriptions of one unit of the court system with a few suggestions for improvement in the particular court studied. The trends of litigation and the grist of the judicial mills are exposed in detail and with great accuracy.

Insofar as masses of data will do it, parts of the third heading (delays, expense and uncertainty in litigation) are developed, but the task of gathering and ordering facts was so large as to consume almost all the initial efforts of the staff.

The Institute itself suggested as its fourth objective that the results of its work in this field should be used as a basis for creating a permanent system of collecting judicial statistics not only for the states of Maryland and Ohio but for the entire country.[164] In fact among its published studies there is a comparison of the criminal statistics of the two states of Maryland and Ohio.[165] There is also a circular suggesting a uniform classification for judicial criminal statistics.[166] However, an examination of the latter publication itself indicates that it is little more than a preliminary study, and most of the conclusions seemed to be ex cathedra rather than based on practical experimental operation of any particular system. The tentative conclusions of this report were followed by further suggestions;[167] but is it unfortunate that they could not have been tested against the results of the later and larger studies.

It should be noted here that at the start of the project, judicial statistics throughout the country were in a deplorable state, and there is no doubt that the work of the Institute gave much encouragement along the lines of creating better basic provisions for collecting data in this field. However, its recommendations seem to have left no trace on the system of collecting judicial statistics in either Maryland or Ohio.

The fifth objective, which envisaged changes in the substantive law as a result of the studies, seems to have been reached in one instance, at least. The Institute, in cooperation with the judicial council of Ohio, did draft model statutes for municipal courts[168] and methods of appellate review.[169] The former does not seem to have been enacted,

---

[164] Johns Hopkins University Circular 9 ff. (1930-31).

[165] Marshall, Comparative Judicial Criminal Statistics: Ohio and Maryland (1932).

[166] Hotchkiss and Gehlke, Uniform Classification for Judicial Criminal Statistics (1931).

[167] J. H. Judicial System of Ohio, Bulletins Nos. 11 & 12 (1932 and 1933).

[168] Yntema, Draft of Uniform Municipal Court Act for the State of Ohio, J. H. Bulletin No. 7 (1932).

[169] Harris, Study of Judicial Administration in Ohio, J. H. Bulletin No. 9 (1932); id. Appellate Courts and Appellate Procedure in Ohio 165 ff. (1933).

but the latter was passed by the Ohio legislature in 1935[170] and made a number of changes in the appellate procedure in the state. While the new law does not establish any radical changes in the procedure of the appellate court and is not based entirely upon the results of research by the Institute, it does mark a step forward in the cooperation between legislatures and professional bodies on one side and scientific research on the other. Here, in a small way, is an instance of the seventh step in the process of Experimental Jurisprudence discussed in Chapter II. It is unfortunate that the Institute was disbanded before the law was enacted, thus making it impossible to carry on a further study of the effect of the amendment.

RESULTS OF THE WORK OF THE INSTITUTE

It is a tragedy that the Institute went out of existence before it had completed the cycle of its attempted research. The early plans and its stated objectives, if they had been carried to a conclusion, gave promise of developing a true science of law. It is clear from the preliminary statements quoted above and the purposes as outlined in prospectuses and circulars[171] that the founders had ideas that might, under better auspices, in cooperation with other sciences, have borne much more fruit for experimental juridical method. Due to the fact that it was so predominately dominated by legally trained men, it undertook the problem of studying as a whole the judicial systems, which was really too large a problem to yield any significant preliminary results. The choice of the states to be compared, namely, New York, Ohio and Maryland, was probably a poor one because these judicial systems as a whole were too much alike. Had there been much more collaboration by other scientists not so over-impressed with the place and importance of the judiciary in the total scheme of social control, this disproportionate emphasis on the courts might have been avoided, and attention might have been devoted to smaller and more significant units of the administration of the law.

Such studies of individual parts of the systems which emerge from the mass of statistics where differences exist seem to have yielded the most fruit. For example, the statistics in the divorce courts of Ohio and Maryland where the legal grounds for divorce differ radically

---

[170] H.B. 42, Acts 116 Ohio Laws 1935, now §§ 12223-1 to 12223-49 and changes in other sections there listed of Ohio Gen. Code (Page, 1938).

[171] Law as a Social Instrument, Johns Hopkins Publication; Goodnow & Griswold, Institute for the Study of Law (1929); Johns Hopkins University Circular 28 ff. (1929-30).

seem to have exposed some important facts on the nature and grounds for divorce. In Maryland, where the legal grounds for divorce are few, the rate of divorces is only 1.25 per thousand population,[172] while in Ohio, where they are many and relatively easy of proof, the rate is 2.15 per thousand population.[173] On the other hand, in Maryland about one-third of the cases are on the legal grounds of adultery,[174] while in Ohio adultery is alleged in less than two per cent of the cases.[175] Now it is inconceivable that the morals of married people or connubial bliss differ to this extent in the two states. The excuses given in the formulation of the legal remedies in the two states are probably mere subterfuges used to break undesirable wedlocks. These figures might have been taken for a beginning of further and pertinent study into the real causes of divorce and the actual state of marital happiness which were probably the same in Ohio and Maryland, but unfortunately the work of the Institute in this area never got beyond the gathering of judicial statistics.

Because the initial research was an attempt to study facts about the complicated and far-flung judicial machinery of three states, little or no attention was paid to the problem of determining the usefulness of individual legal devices in solving specific social problems. This type of research was clearly within the contemplation of the founders, and this stage of the development of legal science might have been reached had the Institute gone on with its work. Unfortunately, the preoccupation with mass statistics prevented pertinent research of this nature. Masses of facts are important only in light of social problems to which they are related. Since the Institute never reached the stage of isolating particular social problems, the masses of facts collected are informative but not particularly significant. It might be said that the scientific work of the Institute reached approximately the same stage as botany would, had its efforts been devoted wholly to counting leaves on trees. However, the results do show that facts about our courts can be gathered in volume sufficient to entirely eliminate personal variations and, in such form, can serve as criticism for the activities of the courts themselves. These criticisms are much better and more useful than the classification of written decisions, and in one instance at least resulted in changes in the rules governing the court procedure.

[172] 1 Marshall & May, The Divorce Court 24 ff. (1932).
[173] 2 id. 28 (1933).
[174] 1 id. 169 (1932).
[175] 2 id. 315 (1933).

This constituted an immediate step forward in developing a true science of jurisprudence, but it was only an incomplete one. Judicial statistics, like other statistics, are impressive, but their gathering is too tedious and expensive to be scientifically fruitful if the only purpose in their collection is assembling facts. Legal institutions are so complicated that they will yield a myriad of factual information for statistical study which has no particular significance unless correllated to a problem-solving technique. The work of the Institute shows that unless fact-gathering is carefully directed to problem-solving, it can be a quagmire into which endless labor can be sunk without appreciable results.

The monographs also show that statistics are a useful part but not the end of Experimental Jurisprudence. But the very necessity of their use to obtain facts precludes quick solutions to scientific jural problems. The process is long and expensive, but no more so than in many other experimental sciences. The whole cost of the Johns Hopkins Institute of Law over its entire life of about four years was less than half the initial expenditure for one cyclotron, and who is there to say that it might not have been much more fruitful if given an equal chance?[176]

RECENT NEW RESEARCH PROGRAMS

In the interim following the demise of the Johns Hopkins Institute and the completion of World War II, there was practically no cooperative objective social research of any sizable proportions in the law schools. There were, of course, many noted bits of individual research by persons connected with law schools, such as the work of Moore,[177] Hall,[178] the Gluecks,[179] Tappan[180] and others discussed elsewhere; but in the last few years institutional activities are beginning to reappear. Recently the Ford Foundation and other large charitable trusts have begun to look about and to make grants for sociological research on the effect of laws. Some of this money has gone to the

[176] For a complete list of these publications including all cited supra see Gehlke, Criminal Actions in the Common Pleas Courts of Ohio back flyleaf (1936).

[177] Moore and Callahan, Law and Learning Theory, A Study in Legal Control, 53 Yale L.J. 1 (1943) discussed more in detail in Chapter VI.

[178] Theft, Law and Society (1935).

[179] For example see, Glueck and Glueck, 500 Criminal Careers (1930); Glueck and Glueck, One Thousand Juvenile Delinquents (1934); Glueck and Glueck, Unraveling Juvenile Delinquency (1950).

[180] Delinquent Girls in Court (1947).

newly created research division of the Harvard Law School,[181] and to others.

One of the most promising of these current studies is that being conducted at the University of Chicago Law School in cooperation with social scientists at that institution. The Ford Foundation has recently appropriated a million dollars to be spent by the university over a four-year period on studies in three fields, public attitudes toward federal taxation, commercial arbitration and the functioning of the jury system.[182] It is too early yet to evaluate the results of research of this kind, but it seems to be a continuation of the type of work envisioned by the founders of the Johns Hopkins Institute, and, if carried forward to success as it almost certainly will be, it should have a profound influence upon legal research and may aid in closing the lag between scientific discoveries and legal procedures.

[181] See Dean's Report, The Law School, Harvard University 17 (1951-52).
[182] See Kalvin, How Jurors Think, University of Chicago Magazine 5 (Mar. 1956).

Experimental Jurisprudence in Action[2]

In spite of the difficulties discussed in Chapter V, Experimental Jurisprudence is not merely a theoretical hypothesis that the application of law to society can be so controlled and studied as to develop a science of law which corresponds in its outlines to the sciences in the physical field. As a matter of fact, parts of the processes outlined are now being used in many areas of lawmaking and enforcement. Some of these partial developments of the science will be discussed elsewhere; but there is one place where the manner of evolving the law and the regulations which are a part of it has matured into a full-fledged science following the general outline indicated above. This is in the field of traffic regulation and control. Here there is not only a science, but also a system of engineering built upon it.

TRAFFIC CONTROL AS A COMPLETE DEVELOPMENT OF EXPERIMENTAL JURISPRUDENCE

Although casual observation might indicate that the control of traffic is more nearly mechanical than is generally the case in operation of other laws, a careful analysis will show that the traffic in urban centers and on country roads involves all sorts of human reactions. Though automobiles are machines, they are driven by human beings who are capable, as drivers and pedestrians, of the same varied reactions as are humans in any other field. It is true that the movement of people both as drivers and pedestrians is somewhat canalized by the exist-

---

[1] This is in large part reprinted by permission from 31 Nebraska Law Review 349 (1952).

[2] The writer is deeply indebted to Mr. J. E. Johnson, Traffic Engineer, and to the Department of Roads and Irrigation of the State of Nebraska for suggestions and for permission to use the illustrations set out in this chapter. Acknowledgment should also be given to Alexander Goldfarb of the Connecticut Bar for aid in research. The following notes do not purport to be exhaustive; they are merely illustrative of some of the available materials.

ence of streets, sidewalks, roads, buildings and the like, but a careful examination will show that the construction of these objects which tend to confine the human movements is itself rapidly taking a form dictated by an experimental science.

The variation in the nature of objects regulated in traffic is extremely intricate. Actions of streetcars, trackless buses, trucks, horse-drawn vehicles, automobiles, motorcycles, push carts, all guided by people, and pedestrians meandering among the vehicles in response to a myriad of purposes and going in many directions can be as complicated as other patterns of human reactions. Nevertheless these activities are now controlled by laws, ordinances, design of streets, highways, lights and other devices, all of which are sanctioned by law and enforced and constructed by police and other legally directed officials. Thousands of criminal acts and multifarious civil rights, duties and liabilities arise daily from the conflicting actions and desires of this maze we call traffic.

Superficial investigation might indicate that this is as good an example as can be found of human activities believed by some to be beyond the control of science. But a review of the growth of traffic regulation in the last forty years will show the emergence of a coherent and developing juridical science involving all the steps listed above.

Since the turn of the century, there has been a rapidly expanding science of traffic engineering research both in this country and abroad. Traffic studies were made in London, England, as early as 1904 by a royal commission.[3] Similar work was done by Eno, one of the earliest traffic engineers, in this country, in France and Japan during the first two decades of the century.[4] As early as 1925 a bureau of street and traffic research was established at Harvard University. The history of this development has been set out elsewhere[5] and need not be discussed further here. But it should be emphasized that we now have in actual operation a science and art of traffic engineering which covers all of the steps in Experimental Jurisprudence.

THE SOCIAL PROBLEM TO BE STUDIED AND ISOLATED

The procedures involved in the modern regulation of traffic require precision studies of each and every phenomenon having to do with its activities in various localities. As traffic control is now progressing, responsible persons in charge insist upon intensive studies

---

[3] Morrison, Research in Traffic Engineering, Traffic Q. 119, 121 (April 1948).
[4] Eno, The Story of Highway Traffic Control (1939).
[5] Morrison, op. cit. supra note 3; Eno, op. cit. supra note 4.

involving individual streets,[6] crossings,[7] highways,[8] traffic signals[9] and road constructions.[10] The movements of pedestrians[11] and vehicles at each locality are carefully counted, timed and classified. Velocity,[12] direction[13] and distances of stopping, starting,[14] turning and slowing[15] in response to signals and road conditions are recorded, tabulated and averaged. Whole arteries of traffic and the direction and flow thereof are carefully plotted.[16] The movements of vehicles and pedestrians in whole cities are now being studied and reduced to statistical diagrams and charts.[17] Figure 3 shows such a graph of the origin and flow of city traffic in Lincoln, Nebraska. Every aspect of traffic activity and the group and individual actions of persons concerned are carefully recorded and plotted.[18] Patterns of mass movements in whole cities[19] and states[20] are subject to study and description. Under modern direction, before any new action on traffic regulation is taken, this

[6] Note charts, Moore & Callahan, Law and Learning Theory: A Study in Legal Control, 53 Yale L.J. 1, 10-33; Mich. Highway Dept., Street Traffic, City of Detroit 81-97 (1936-37).

[7] W.P.A. Survey of Street Conditions in New Orleans 367-378 (Mimeo 1937); Mich. Highway Dept., op. cit. supra note 6, at 223-237.

[8] See study of Route U.S. 6—Danielson Area, Jorgensen, Priority for Highway Improvement, Traffic Q. 5, 8 ff. (Jan. 1950).

[9] Smith, Road Signs, Signals, and Markings: What Do They Mean?, Traffic Q. 149 (April 1949); Mich. Highway Dept., op. cit. supra note 6, at 153-158.

[10] Lochner & Co., La. Dept. Highways, Highway Plan for Shreveport, La. 6 ff. (1947); Evans, Traffic Planning in San Francisco, Traffic Q. 31 (Jan. 1949).

[11] W.P.A. Survey of Street Conditions in New Orleans, Pedestrian Flow, 160 ff. (Mimeo 1937); Mich. Highway Dept., op. cit. supra note 6, at 138-145; Erskine Bureau, Traffic Control Plan for Kansas City (Mo.) 104-107 (1930).

[12] Erskine Bureau, op. cit. supra note 11, at 88-95; F.E.R.A., No. L.60-E5-220 Atlantic Traffic Survey 21 ff. (Mimeo 1934).

[13] Lochner & Co., op. cit. supra note 10, at 4-5; Mich. Highway Dept. op. cit. supra note 6, at 82.

[14] F.E.R.A., op. cit. supra note 12, at 37-45.

[15] Id. at 43 ff.

[16] Dorsey, The Use of the Off-Center Lane Movement in Los Angeles, Traffic Q. 291 (July 1948); La. Dept. of Highways & U.S. Pub. Rds. Adm., Monroe Traffic Survey 36-39 (1947); F.E.R.A., op. cit. supra note 12, at 12 ff.

[17] All of the traffic surveys herein cited are replete with such charts, e.g., see Mich. Highway Dept., op. cit. supra note 6. Just turn the pages of this or any other similar report.

[18] See, e.g., Conn. Dept. of Motor Vehicles, Traffic Topics, Statistical Summary 1938-39.

[19] La. Dept. of Highways & U.S. Pub. Rds. Adm., Monroe Traffic Survey (1947); Mich. Highway Dept., op. cit. supra note 6, at 126-137.

[20] Willey, Statewide Origin—Destination Survey of Traffic in Arizona, Traffic Q. 189 (April 1949).

FIGURE 3

ORIGIN OF TRAFFIC DESTINED TO CENTRAL BUSINESS DISTRICT, LIN-
COLN, NEBRASKA, FOR AVERAGE DAY DURING 1950

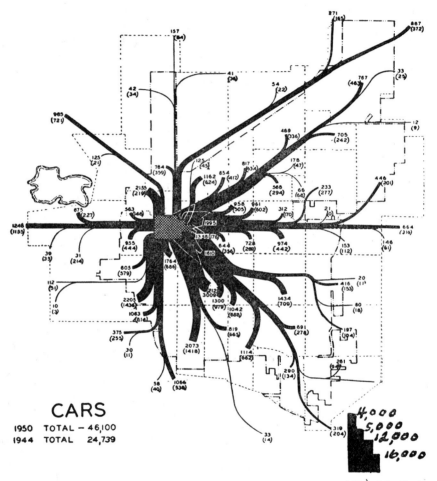

CARS

1950 TOTAL — 46,100
1944 TOTAL   24,739

Graphic Scale

NUMBERS IN PAREN. (177) INDICATE AVERAGE
DAY DURING 1944

City Planning Commission, Lincoln, Nebr.
Data for Figure Prepared by Division of
Highway Planning, Nebr. Dept. of Roads.

Cooperating Agencies
U. S. Bureau of Pub. Roads
Harland Bartholomew
St. Louis, Missouri

118

FIGURE 4

HASTINGS TRAFFIC ENGINEERING SURVEY
TRAFFIC ACCIDENTS, LOCATION AND FREQUENCY, CENTRAL BUSINESS
DISTRICT AND VICINITY, JANUARY 1, 1946–NOVEMBER 30, 1949

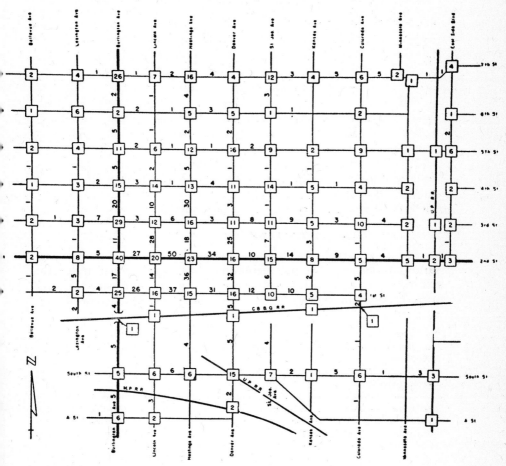

TOTAL ACCIDENTS IN AREA SHOWN – 1409

material is made available to the responsible lawmaking officers.[21]
Here the scientist will recognize immediately a description of the
phenomena involved which corresponds with the scientific study of
facts in other fields and which has a highly developed technique of
its own.[22]

FINDING THE LAW INVOLVED

The second step in the science of traffic regulation, that of identifying the law involved, is comparatively simple. In most instances little
research is required to discover the law or regulation which controls
traffic at a given intersection or on a road. Due to the antiquated
condition of files of laws and ordinances, a complete picture of the
traffic laws of the city or state may be a little more complex, and many
studies have been published indicating the rules that are applied to
particular phenomena.[23] However, in most of the scientific examinations of ordinary traffic conditions, this step has been so obvious as
to require little research. But on the question of uniformity of state
and city laws, a vast research exists, showing in detail an analysis of
the laws of each state on every set of facts subject to regulation.[24]

THE SOCIAL RESULTS OF THE LAWS

The social results of the laws and ordinances as they affect the
various problems in traffic regulation have been studied at length.
For example, the reactions of drivers to parking ordinances,[25] stop
signs,[26] speed law systems,[27] street markings,[28] the interaction of stop

[21] Jorgensen, Priority for Highway Improvement, Traffic Q. 5 (Jan. 1950); Johnson, Factual Studies Needed in Solving Urban Traffic Problems, Traffic Q. 78 (Jan.
1950).

[22] See Aust and Janda, Method of Making Short Traffic Counts and Estimating
Traffic Circulation, U. of Wis. Bull. (1931).

[23] The Legal Responsibilities of Traffic Agencies, Eno Foundation Bulletin
(1948); Levin, An Analysis of General State Enabling Legislation Dealing with Automobile Parking Facilities, Bull. No. 2, Highway Research Board (1946); Report of
Committee on Laws and Ordinances, The President's Highway Safety Conference,
54 ff. (1949); Motor Vehicle Inspection, Traffic Q. 174 (April 1949).

[24] National Highway Users Conference, Uniform Laws. 1 Law Bull. (1947); Owen,
Automotive Transportation 102-103 (1949); Report of Committee on Law and
Ordinances, op. cit. supra note 23.

[25] Moore and Callahan, supra note 6, at 1, 5, 88 ff.; Erskine Bureau, op. cit. supra
note 11, at 139 ff., 244, 245.

[26] F.E.R.A., op. cit. supra note 12, at 35-42; Raff, A New Study of Urban Stop
Signs: A Volume Warrant, Traffic Q. 48 (Jan. 1950); Allport, The J-Curve Hypothesis of Conforming Behavior in Newcomb, Hartley, et al., Readings in Social Psychology 57-58 (1947).

and go signals[29] and revocation of licenses[30] have been scrupulously examined and statistically tabulated. Figure 4 is such a tabulation of accidents in the business district of Hastings, Nebraska. The figures in the small squares represent those which occurred at intersections, the ones on the lines, accidents between corners, mostly parking difficulties.

Another study showed that of people in New Haven, Connecticut, in certain places twenty-four per cent obeyed and seventy-six per cent violated a two-minute parking limit, fifty-five per cent obeyed and forty-five per cent violated a fifteen-minute limit, seventy per cent obeyed and thirty per cent violated a thirty-minute limit, while fifty-two per cent obeyed and forty-eight per cent violated an hour limit; but ten minutes after each limit had expired the following percentages of the total parkers had left: two minutes, eighty-two per cent; fifteen minutes, sixty-nine per cent; thirty minutes, seventy-eight per cent; one hour, sixty-four per cent. Each amount of time is set out in detail in exhaustive tables.[31] Other studies indicated that urban drivers on the average drove at speeds about ten miles an hour above posted speed limits, but where the limits were unreasonable, as for example a fifteen-mile limit on an open road, the drivers habitually ignored the posted signs.[32] Figure 5 shows the result of a statewide study of actual speeds in urban areas across Nebraska on U. S. Highway 30. At the time the study[33] was made, the posted speed limits in the various towns were mostly from twenty to twenty-five miles per hour. The eighty-five per cent speed is the speed below which eighty-five per cent of the drivers operated their cars. Since the study, the majority of these limits as indicated below have been raised. It should be noted that speed limits provided by law had little effect.

A fourth investigation showed that the effect of the authorization of additional intersecting roads, gas stations and cut-offs along main highways was to cut down the safe speed on the Boston Post Road fifty per cent, as compared with the parallel Merritt Parkway, where

[27] F.E.R.A., op. cit. supra note 12, at 20-22, app. 23 ff.; W.P.A. Survey of Street Conditions in New Orleans 154 (Mimeo 1937); Smith & LeCraw, Speed Laws and Enforcement, Traffic Q. 117 (April 1947); Smith & LeCraw, Travel Speeds and Posted Speeds in Three States, Traffic Q. 101 (Jan. 1948).

[28] Mich. Highway Dept., op. cit. supra note 6, at 119-125.

[29] F.E.R.A., op. cit. supra note 12, at 23-34.

[30] Transeau, Suspending and Revoking Drivers Licenses, Traffic Q. 228-230 (July 1947).

[31] Moore & Callahan, supra note 6, at 1, 95 ff.

[32] Smith and LeCraw, op. cit. supra note 27 at 101, 107 (Jan. 1948; cf. W.P.A. Survey of Street Conditions in New Orleans, 143 (Mimeo 1937).

[33] Johnson, How About Vehicle Speeds?, 5 Traffic Q. 325, 329 (1951).

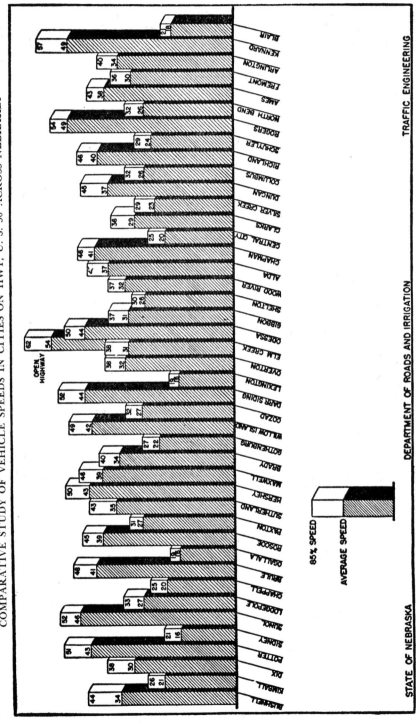

FIGURE 5

COMPARATIVE STUDY OF VEHICLE SPEEDS IN CITIES ON HWY, U. S. 30 ACROSS NEBRASKA

such obstacles were not authorized. Similar changes were found to exist on the highways of Los Angeles, Chicago and New York.[34]

THE CONSTRUCTION OF HYPOTHESES

The construction of hypotheses explaining group reactions to a single law has been developed to a high degree in this field. There are now published results of countless studies on the reaction to signs,[35] the influence of lettering of various heights,[36] the use of marks on the street,[37] the purpose of traffic islands,[38] the reactions to one-way streets in particular places,[39] the efficiency of stop and go signs,[40] the enforcement of speed laws[41] and the effect of all of the other host of gadgets for regulating traffic. The use of each device has been examined in detail, and all have been the subject of carefully gathered data. The unpublished studies to solve hundreds of everyday problems far outnumber those available in libraries. The New York State Traffic Commission alone in 1948 made one thousand twenty-seven traffic surveys and studies.[42] Any person familiar with traffic control in metropolitan areas can cite many examples where scientific procedure achieved more effective regulation of drivers. One instance of this sort occurred in the metropolitan district of New York where the records showed that an unusually large number of accidents occurred on one of the parkways due to drivers' falling asleep at the wheel. On careful examination it was discovered that posts along the right of way were set at such monotonous regularity that a driver passing them was lulled to sleep by the continuous regularity of the sound of the car as it moved along. Respacing of the poles at irregular intervals removed the difficulty and

[34] Owen, op. cit. supra note 24; Winter, Development of a Freeway System in Los Angeles Metropolitan Area, Traffic Q. 105, 114, 115 (April 1949).

[35] Smith, op. cit. supra note 9 at 149; Raff, supra note 26, at 48.

[36] Wright, Highway Speed-zoning and Control as Practiced in State of Utah, Traffic Q. 119, 123-124 (April 1949); Forbes & Holmes, Legibility Distances of Highway Destination Signs, Proc. Highway Research Bd. 19, 321-325 (1939); Mitchell & Forbes, Design of Sign Letter Sizes, Proc. Am. Soc. Civil Engineers 68, 95-104 (1942); Hammond & Sorenson, Traffic Engineering Handbook 104 (1941).

[37] Smith, op. cit. supra note 9, at 152; Hammond & Sorenson, op. cit. supra note 36, at 88.

[38] Hammond & Sorenson, op. cit. supra note 36, at 202 ff.

[39] Smith & Hart, A Case Study of One-Way Streets, Traffic Q. 378 (Oct. 1949); Hammond & Sorenson, op. cit. supra note 36 at 173 ff.

[40] McEachern, A Four-Way Stop-Sign System at Urban Intersections, Traffic Q. 128 (April 1949); Erskine Bureau, op. cit. supra note 11, at 211.

[41] Smith & LeCraw, Speed Laws and Enforcement, Traffic Q. 117 (April 1947); also Traffic Speed Enforcement Policies, Eno Found. Pub. (1948).

[42] Georger, New York State Traffic Commission, Traffic Q. 252, 257 (July 1949).

the accident rate immediately dropped. Other studies are available showing accident locations on specially constructed maps for cities, counties and states,[43] such as the one in Figure 4 and that used in New York in the instance cited, which, with all the other material, form a mass of data for constructing scientific rules as to the reactions caused by these regulatory devices.

JURAL LAWS DEVELOPED

As the result of hundreds of individual studies of the use of each type of traffic regulation in various places, there has been developed a series of jural laws which explain the necessity, efficiency and advantage of a particular device in a particular situation. These jural laws based on experimental data will usually be called warrants in the terminology of the traffic engineer.[44] For example, a traffic engineering handbook states, "Total vehicular volume entering the intersections from all directions must average at least one thousand vehicles per hour for 8 hours" to warrant the use of a stop light at a corner; and, "When the total vehicular volume entering an intersection having fixed-time signals falls below five hundred vehicles per hour for a period of two or more consecutive hours, the fixed-time signals shall be operated as caution or stop signals, or a combination thereof."[45] Although some of these warrants are still in the estimate stage[46] and may be expected to become much more accurate as the science develops, traffic engineering manuals today contain, among others, accurate statements of warrants for the place and location of signs in relation to roads, the amount of traffic per hour which justifies the use of a particular type of signal, stop sign, left and right turn and through street.[47] Accident hazards can be predicted in advance for roads of a specific structure and volume of traffic.[48]

---

[43] F.E.R.A., op. cit. supra note 12, at 1-8; W.P.A. Survey of Street Conditions in New Orleans, 19 ff., (Mimeo 1937); Mich. Highway Dept., op. cit. supra note 6, at 238 ff.; Conn. Dept. of Motor Vehicles, op. cit. supra note 18; Hammond & Sorenson, op. cit. supra note 36, at 61.

[44] Hammond & Sorenson, op. cit. supra note 36, c. IX.

[45] Id. at 117.

[46] Smith, op. cit. supra note 9, at 149, 155; Morrison, op. cit. supra note 3, at 119, 125; McEachern, op. cit. supra note 40, at 128, 129.

[47] Smith, op. cit. supra note 9, at 149; Raff, op. cit. supra note 26, at 48; Neal. Uniformity in Traffic Markings, Traffic Q. 389 (Oct. 1947); Manual of Uniform Traffic Control Devices, U.S. Pub. Rds. Adm. (1948).

[48] Mich. Highway Dept., op. cit. supra note 6, at 238 ff.; Hammond & Sorenson. op. cit. supra note 36, at 77; Owen, op. cit. supra note 24, at 120 ff.

The installation of traffic-actuated, as distinguished from automatic, signal systems under certain traffic conditions also has its warrant depending upon the nature of the traffic load for a particular thoroughfare.[49] A whole science of conducting such studies to create new warrants and the statistical devices for tabulating and reporting them has been developed, and textbooks indicating various techniques in these fields are available.[50]

SUGGESTED CHANGES IN THE LAW

Suggested changes in the law as a result of the jural laws, or the so-called warrants, have become commonplace in the art of controlling urban and rural traffic. Hundreds of changes are made in individual regulations every month to correspond with the results of studies.[51] Stop signs, traffic lights, one-way streets, parking areas and right and left turns are constantly being altered to bring the control of traffic into better correspondence with jural laws involved and to improve control where warrants indicate a more effective operation.[52]

Figure 6 illustrates the results of such technique. At the crossing of U. S. 30 and the state highway pictured, because of a number of accidents, the city installed a set of automatic traffic lights where the traffic was far below the warranted volume. As a result, accidents actually increased. The state highway department made a study and suggested that the stop lights be replaced by a "Stop Ahead" and a "Stop" sign on the state highway on each side of U. S. 30. The result was a decrease in accidents from fourteen to one over similar periods

[49] Hammond & Sorenson, op. cit. supra note 36, at 118-119.

[50] For an example of the type of study involved here see Hammond & Sorenson, op. cit. supra note 36, at 86; Engineering Manual for Traffic Surveys, F.E.R.A., §§ 7-11 (1934); Halsey, Traffic Accidents and Congestion 62 (1941); Malcher, Steady Flow Traffic System (1935); Pub. Rds. Adm. Highway Practice (1949).

[51] Halsey, op. cit. supra note 50; Eno, The Science of Highway Traffic Regulation 1899-1920 (1920); One thousand twenty-seven such studies were made by the New York State Traffic Commission in 1948 alone, Traffic Q. 252, 257 (July 1949).

[52] Leroy, Signal Time to Meet Peak Loads of Traffic Demands, Traffic Q. 23, 24 ff. (Jan. 1949); Halsey, op. cit. supra note 50; McEachern, op. cit. supra note 40, at 128, 133; Smith & Hart, op. cit. supra note 39, at 378, 379 ff.; Raff, op. cit. supra note 26, at 48; Hurd, The Designing of Intersection Channelization, Traffic Q. 89 (Jan. 1950); Zannettos, Two-way, Non-stop Cross-Traffic, Traffic Q. 128, 137 (April 1948); Ricker, The Traffic Design of Parking Garages (Eno Found. 1948); Hart, Right Turns at Urban Intersections, Traffic Q. 74 (Jan. 1949); Owen, op. cit. supra note 24, at 94, 106; Eno, op. cit. supra note 4; Caplow, Express Transit Streets to Speed Traffic, American City 123 (May 1948).

FIGURE 6

THE EFFECT OF AN UNWARRANTED TRAFFIC "STOP & GO" SIGNAL*
ACCIDENT EXPERIENCE TWO YEARS BEFORE AND AFTER
REMOVAL OF SIGNAL

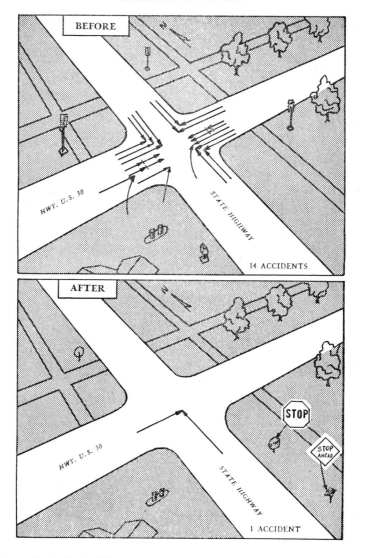

* An actual situation in Nebraska.

before and after the change. The converging arrows on the illustration indicate the position and direction of the cars involved in the accidents.

Traffic patterns of whole cities are now studied, and recommendations for the change of laws and methods of traffic regulations are based upon the resulting reports.[53] Among many others there are published studies of the whole traffic systems of cities such as Detroit,[54] New Orleans,[55] Kansas City,[56] Shreveport[57] and Los Angeles.[58] The first three of the published studies indicated above contain complete traffic codes in detail, worked out on the basis of the facts and jural laws involved.[59] In addition to these, there are model uniform traffic codes available for use which can be changed to meet the individual requirements of various cities[60] and states.[61]

Such studies are not isolated or unusual instances. During the early nineteen-thirties the Work's Progress Administration made hundreds of such surveys of various cities and The Federal Emergency Relief Administration even developed an extensive manual on the details of how such material should be compiled.[62] The United States Bureau of Public Roads, following this direction, has aided in over eighty detailed studies such as those indicated.[63] The Erskine Foundation at Harvard, now moved to Yale, as the Bureau of Highway Traffic, supervised or cooperated in many more surveys of state and urban highway systems.[64] In addition, state highway administration and city departments and private foundations are constantly engaged in studies

[53] Elder, Houston's Urban Expressways, Traffic Q. 166 (April 1949); Johnson, op. cit. supra note 21, at 78, 82 ff.

[54] Mich. Highway Dept., op. cit. supra note 6.

[55] W.P.A. Survey of Street Conditions in New Orleans (Mimeo 1937).

[56] Erskine Bureau, op. cit. supra note 11.

[57] Lochner & Co., op. cit. supra note 10; Andrews, Shreveport's Traffic Runs More Easily, The American City 171 (Sept. 1949).

[58] Winter, op. cit. supra note 34, at 105.

[59] Mich. Highway Dept., op. cit. supra note 6, at 263-302; Erskine Bureau, op. cit. supra note 11, at 7 ff.; W.P.A. Survey of Street Conditions in New Orleans, 231 ff. (Mimeo 1937).

[60] Model Traffic Ordinances, U.S. Dept. of Agri., Bureau of Pub. Rds., Parts I, II (1936). Compare this especially with the Kansas City ordinances.

[61] Uniform Act Regulating Traffic on Highways, Uniform Vehicle Code (Acts I & III), Pub. Rds. Adm. (1945), (Acts II, IV and V) Bureau of Pub. Rds. (1952); Report of Committee on Laws and Ordinances, op.cit. supra note 23, at 15-45.

[62] Engineering Manual for Traffic Surveys, F.E.R.A. (1934); cf. Aust & Janda, op. cit. supra note 22.

[63] Barnett, Progress in the National Status of Urban Arterial Routes, Traffic Q. 80, 84 (Jan. 1948).

[64] E.g., Erskine Bureau, op. cit. supra note 11.

and restudies of the operation of the traffic laws.[65] In fact in the year 1948 alone there were over one hundred and eighty such systematic surveys in the process of being planned or enacted in as many cities and towns.[66]

ADOPTION OF NEW LAWS

The suggested new laws are being constantly adopted. The present traffic code of Kansas City was enacted in 1930 almost completely as recommended by the scientific study of traffic and traffic-law operation in that city.[67] Los Angeles[68] and even the whole state of California[69] are other examples of places where a system of laws has been adopted or altered, based on careful scientific investigation.

In some instances laws have been adopted as a result of only a cursory or shallow study such as is usually carried on by a hearing in a legislative committee or council, but more and more the new traffic regulations are the result of exhaustive scientific scrutiny, by impartial and non-political bodies, of the operation of traffic laws and regulations. The surveys of New Orleans, Detroit and Kansas City mentioned above run into reports of four hundred, three hundred, and two hundred and fifty pages respectively, containing numerous maps, graphs and charts based on volumes of carefully collected statistics, showing the patterns of reactions to the current laws on individual street corners, in regions and over the city at large. Items recommended for change in the law when adopted are predicated on these carefully tabulated factual studies.

ADOPTION OF NEW LAWS AND STUDIES OF THEIR RESULTS

Throughout the country, hundreds of laws and systems of traffic regulation have been revised or newly adopted as a result of these

---

[65] Wright, op. cit. supra note 36, at 119; McConaughy, Safety Commission Procedures in Conn., Traffic Q. 5 (Jan. 1948); see also Erskine Bureau, op. cit. supra note 11.

[66] Barnett, op. cit. supra note 63, at 92-93.

[67] Traffic Code of Kansas City, Mo. Ordinance Nos. 2031, 2260, 2310, 2340, effective Jan. 1, 1931.

[68] Winter, op. cit. supra note 34, at 105.

[69] California's Highway Problem, A Report by the Joint Fact-Finding Committee on Highways, Streets and Bridges to the Fifty-Seventh Session of the Calif. Legislature (Jan. 13, 1947); Collier, California's Highway Problem, Traffic Q. 202 (July 1947); Warren, A Governor's Message on Highways, Traffic Q. 103 (April 1947); Davis, Development of the Institute of Transportation and Traffic Engineering at the University of California, U. of Calif. Institute of Transportation and Traffic Engineering Report (May 1949); California Highway Act of 1947, Extra Sess., cc. 11-16, p. 3788 ff. (Collier-Burns, 1947).

scientific studies. The enactments of many cities and the statutes of states following uniform ordinances and statutes recommended by national bodies of experts provide that the highway departments shall continue to examine the results achieved by their traffic regulations and recommend changes in the law based upon such studies.[70] In California, for example, the state department of highway patrol is required to make complete investigation and to publish annually statistical information based upon the analysis and detailed research into the operation of the traffic laws.[71] Similar provisions are in effect in twenty-three other states.[72] And in Kansas City the director of public works is authorized upon the basis of traffic studies to change parking regulations, regulate through streets, change signs and signals and generally to improve traffic conditions;[73] and for this work he has at his disposal a special division of traffic engineering directed by a trained traffic expert.[74]

California and Kansas City are in no wise unique in this respect, for similar work is authorized in many other governmental units.[75] The result has been the development of a new profession of traffic engineers able and willing to advise changes and improvements in the laws and regulations based upon scientifically gleaned data. Thus there is being accumulated rapidly a prolific scientific literature delineating and supporting an engineering technique[76] which gives

[70] Model Traffic Ordinances, op. cit. supra note 60, Part II, § 3, pp. 12-13; Uniform Act Regulating Traffic on Highways, Uniform Vehicle Code (Act V), Pub. Rds. Adm. §§ 28, 57-59, 60b, 161, 163 (1945). For the adoption of the model traffic ordinances and the uniform state statutes, see Report of Committee on Laws and Ordinances, op. cit. supra note 23, at 17 ff., 45-47.

[71] Cal. Vehicle Code Ann. § 139.35 (Deering, 1948).

[72] See Report of Committee on Laws and Ordinances, op. cit. supra note 23, at 19 showing the states that have adopted Act V of the Uniform Vehicle Code which contains provisions for study and recommendations as cited, supra note 61.

[73] Traffic Code of Kansas City, Mo., §§ 4, 8, 31, 47 (d), 59, effective Jan. 1, 1931; for similar provisions in Detroit, see Ordinance 61-D (1938).

[74] Traffic Code of Kansas City, Mo., §§ 113, 114 and 115, effective Jan. 1, 1931; Administrative Code of Kansas City § 31; for a similar provision in Detroit see Ordinance 61-D (1938).

[75] Booker, Proposed Additional San Francisco Bay Crossing, Traffic Q. 224. (July 1949); Georger, op. cit. supra note 42, at 252, 256; Dorsey, op. cit. supra note 16, at 291; Lawrence, Pittsburgh's Traffic Program, Traffic Q. 301, 304 (Oct. 1949); Rutland, The Dallas Cooperative Experience in Achieving Traffic Results, Traffic Q. 31 (Jan. 1950); Johnson, op. cit. supra note 21, at 78, 82 ff.; Bartholomew, Street Plan and Interstate Highway Experience in St. Louis, Traffic Q. 24 (Jan. 1950); Traffic Engineering Functions and Administration, Pub. 100, Pub. Adm. Serv. 122 ff. (1948).

[76] For an indication of the size of such a library and a partial list of materials therein, see Cassidy & Redfield, Library Classification Scheme and Selected Biblio-

FIGURE 7

TYPICAL VEHICLE SPEED DISTRIBUTION NORMAL CURVE, SHOWING
CHARACTERISTICS OF AN OPERATION PATTERN

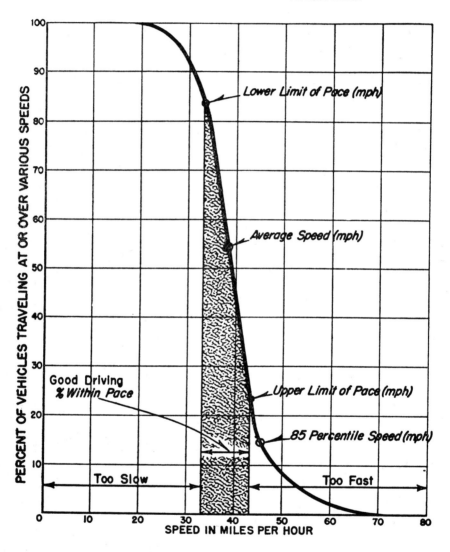

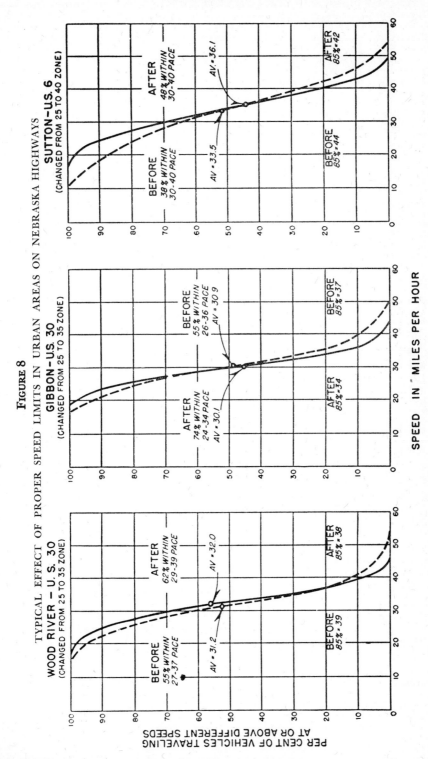

FIGURE 8

TYPICAL EFFECT OF PROPER SPEED LIMITS IN URBAN AREAS ON NEBRASKA HIGHWAYS

traffic engineering a position similar to civil and chemical engineering. The new knowledge being developed as a result of the application of this engineering technique to lawmaking is often startling in its revelations. For example, it has been shown to be a jural law in many instances that raising the speed limit within reasonable bounds will actually cut down high-speed driving and increase safety. Figure 7 shows a normal curve of driving speeds on the open road. Figure 8 shows a number of such curves for urban areas. The dotted line is the curve before the indicated increase in the speed limit, and the solid line, the curve after the limit was raised. It should be noted that the change caused a speeding up of the slow drivers and slowing of the fast ones, thus creating a more uniform pace. The results of a series of such changes were an adjusted eleven per cent decrease in traffic accidents and a decrease of twenty per cent in fatal and sixteen per cent in non-fatal accidents.[77]

SIGNIFICANT ASPECTS OF THE DEVELOPMENT OF SCIENTIFIC TRAFFIC REGULATIONS

This new science in its many aspects indicates significantly the direction and scope which Experimental Jurisprudence should take in other fields. It is first to be noted that we have here research based upon mass patterns of human reactions to laws in one of the simpler but more widespread activities of human conduct, namely, driving vehicles. This method is creating the regulations touching upon the everyday activities of almost the entire population. The development of the science and the engineering devices which have sprung from it would be impossible without recurrent changes in the legal controls. Here has been evolved an experimental science of control of human conduct under situations using legal sanctions to set up pertinent experiments, testing the efficiency of law and human reactions to it.

The solution of comparatively simple problems was the beginning. The studies of regulations of traffic at particular street crossings and zones and in villages, towns and cities came first. Only after data was assembled there did the traffic engineers press on to city planning and state and national developments.

In the growth of this science, court decisions and rationalization of their results are almost entirely missing from the data. Although the reports are so full of appellate cases arising from traffic that large por-

graphy of Traffic Engineering Litterature 69 ff. (Bureau of Highway Traffic, Yale Univ. 1948); Wilson, Bibliography on Highway Safety, U.S. Dept. of Agri., Misc. Pub. No. 296 (1938).

[77] Johnson, op. cit. supra note 33, at 325, 330.

tions of the digest are devoted to this field, and while texts on "automobile law" can be found in any law library, few of either are mentioned in the scientific literature.[78] Lawyers have cooperated, but their efforts seem to be peculiarly absent from the studies used as a basis of legal change. The research has been carried on by teams of workers, police officers, psychologists,[79] economists,[80] statisticians and now traffic engineers. It is significant that lawyers may and actually do cooperate in Steps Two and Six involving the identification of the law and redrafting of ordinances and laws to incorporate the results of the studies, but even here their contribution may be minor.

As can be expected in all sciences, technically expert agencies are emerging to carry on the work in this field. Privately endowed institutions such as the Eno Foundation for Highway Traffic Control, the Yale University Bureau of Highway Traffic and the Northwestern University Traffic Institute, public bodies like the U. S. Bureau of Public Roads and state and city traffic bureaus and state university organizations such as the Institute of Transportation and Engineering at the University of California, to name only a few, are spending millions of dollars in teaching, research and collecting whole libraries of scientific data in this field. Numerous professional periodicals are also appearing.[81] Many of our schools of higher learning have created curricula in traffic engineering and have developed police schools which are actively training enforcement officers, engineers, specialists and directors for public administration.[82]

It is interesting to note that the power to make the laws and regulations governing traffic in the various jurisdictions is being

---

[78] Court decisions appear only in a cursory manner to help in explaining some aspects of the state of the law. See e.g., Belser, The Legal Responsibilities of Traffic Agencies, Eno Foundation Bulletin (1948).

[79] See Forbes, Psychotechnology in Traffic Studies, Traffic Q. 158 (April 1949) and authorities there cited; Allgaier, Some Road-User Characteristics in Traffic Problems, Traffic Q. 59 (Jan. 1950).

[80] Lawton, Evaluation of Highway Improvements on Mileage-and-Time-Cost Basis, Traffic Q. 102 (Jan. 1950).

[81] A few of these are: Traffic Quarterly, Saugatuck, Conn.; Traffic Engineering, New Haven, Conn.; The American City, N.Y. 16, N.Y.; Public Roads; Traffic Business.

[82] See Traffic Services for Public Officials, Northwestern U. Bull.; U. of Calif. Quarterly Bull., Institute of Transportation and Traffic Engineering; Yale University, Bureau of Highway Traffic, Bull., Grad. Training (1950); Id., Annual Report (1948-49); New School for Traffic Judges, The American City 147 (Sept. 1949); see also Holmes, Traffic Engineering as a Profession, Traffic Q. 413, 417 (Oct. 1949).

delegated. In Washington, D. C.,[83] New York State,[84] in fact in more than twenty-five per cent of the cities over one hundred thousand population,[85] the lawmaking power has been transferred in whole or in part to the official in charge of traffic regulation. Sometimes this includes power to change the laws before or after scientific study. In some instances, as in the case of Kansas City, democratically elected bodies like state legislatures and city councils retain the power to veto or approve the regulations of the traffic director.[86] But more often, as is the practice in Washington, D. C., there is a complete delegation to the expert.[87]

It is rapidly being recognized that, after a study of the facts and the body of available scientific knowledge, the expert traffic engineer or director is far better qualified than any elective body to institute laws to regulate drivers and pedestrians.[88] Popular referenda on the advisability of diagonal parking in specific locations, such as was recently held in the city of Lincoln, Nebraska,[89] are silly procedures which will soon become as obsolete as the carrier pigeon. It is not surprising to find that this particular referendum was in part held invalid by the local court because "enforced diagonal parking would constitute an unreasonable and arbitrary interference with property rights of business firms in that area,"[90] simply illustrating that it is impossible for the public or publicly elected bodies to know or master the details of law enforcement where a science has been or can be developed.

Notably, also, precedents in the form of court decisions or previous regulations handed down by administrative bodies carry little or no weight in the development of new laws. These are based directly upon studies of what is going on in society and what is needed to direct traffic in light of previously developed scientific concepts.[91]

---

[83] 43 Stat. 1119, § 6 (a) (1925), D.C. Code § 40-603 (1940).

[84] Georger, op. cit. supra note 42, at 252, 253.

[85] Smith & LeCraw, Speed Laws and Enforcement, Traffic Q. 117, 121 (April 1947).

[86] E.g., see Traffic Code of Kansas City, Mo., §§ 31, 59, effective Jan. 1, 1931.

[87] D.C. Code § 40.603 (1940); delegation sustained in LaForest v. Board of Commissioners, 92 F.2d 547 (D.C. Cir. 1937), cert. denied, 302 U.S. 760 (1937).

[88] McClintock, Street Traffic Control 178 ff. (1925); Holmes, op. cit. supra note 82, at 413, 419-420; Georger, op. cit. supra note 42, at 252, 254.

[89] Lincoln Evening Journal, April 6, 1949, p. 1, col. 1.

[90] Lincoln Evening Journal, October 4, 1949, p. 2, col. 1.

[91] Sells, New York State's Answer to Urban Traffic Problems, American City 72 (July 1948); Johnson, op. cit. supra note 21, at 78, 82 ff.; cf. Williams, Cities Not Courts Should Provide Traffic Solution, American City 127 (May 1945).

Under this new approach to legal science, developments have been phenomenal. Road designs,[92] traffic control mechanisms of all kinds,[93] electric counters,[94] radar speed recorders,[95] stop lights, myriads of automatic signals, scientific recording systems for accident data[96] and complicated mechanisms for calculating and recording have come into such wide use as almost to obscure to casual gaze the law-enacting and law-enforcing problems.

The individual person in this new social science of traffic control occupies much the same position as a particle in quantum theory physics and under Hisenberg's Uncertainty Principle.[97] The scientists and engineers of traffic do not look to or attempt to predict the reactions of individual persons any more than the physicists and engineers operating under those theories try to prophesy the actions of single particles of matter. Both are interested in mass reactions, the traffic engineering scientist of people, the physicist of streams of particles. As the physicist examines the neutrons, electrons and the like, the traffic engineer works with patterns of massed individual reactions, statistical laws and averages from which he produces the jural laws upon which his engineering science is based.

Jural laws and warrants predicting success or failure of particular laws and devices are multiplying almost as rapidly in this field as scientific discoveries in the oldest sciences, and their application has proved equally useful. Corps of experts are now giving us miraculous developments in actually making human laws by a complete technique of experimental science to increase comfortable transportation, build new cities, redesign highways to reduce human wastage, accidents and discomfort and to create great new industries. Although millions of dollars are being spent in research and development of the science

---

[92] Hurd, op. cit. supra note 52, at 89; Hammond & Sorenson, op. cit. supra note 36, c. XIV.

[93] Manual of Uniform Traffic Control Devices, op. cit. supra note 47, see American City 125, 127 (Jan. 1949); Old-Fashioned Traffic Signals in Most Business Districts, The American City, 125 ff. (Feb. 1949); and see the advertisements for all sorts of traffic devices in any issue of Traffic Engineering.

[94] For example, Traficounter, Traffic Engineering 393 (May 1948).

[95] Barker, Radar Measures Vehicle Speed, Traffic Q. 239 (July 1948).

[96] Hammond & Sorenson, op. cit. supra note 36, cc. V & VII; Leroy, op. cit. supra note 52, at 23; Uses of Traffic Accident Records (Eno Found. Manual 1947); Uses of Traffic Accident Records, Groth, The Use of Accident Records in a State Traffic Program, Traffic Q. 183 (April 1948).

[97] Jeaus, Exploring the Atom in Readings in the Physical Sciences (Shapley, Wright & Raport ed., 1948); see also Sullivan, Limitations of Science 72 (Mentor ed., 1949).

of traffic regulation, the returns in better living, saving of life, development of convenient transportation and many other scientific ventures greatly exceed the outlay.

Another extremely pertinent fact is that in all the literature of this new science, one encounters almost no discussion of policy or ultimate and immediate values. Here the art of lawmaking, resting as it does upon the observation and determination of the needs, demands and habits of the motoring public, requires no such speculation. The decision to raise or lower speed limits, to install or remove a particular regulatory device, in each case is based upon known data and jural laws which tend to predict the effect of the change and the extent to which it is likely to meet a calculated and observed demand for change. Under such conditions, the "value" or "policy" considerations are reduced to such an unimporant role as to be scarcely noticeable. The traffic lawmaker really has only to consider the chances that the proposed new rule of law will meet the demands of the situation where the factors are known or fairly predictable. The determination to change the rule becomes one of relevance rather than "value."

It is a sad fact to note that, although this entire science has developed in the field of lawmaking and law enforcement, only in the most isolated instances did any law school or its personnel have any part in it.[98]

This rapidly developing science points out the direction that can be taken to develop other fields of the law. The many scientifically controlled devices here indicate that it is possible for scientific jurisprudence to create a new legal system which will make our present methods of social control look as obsolete as a country road when compared to a modern *Autobahn*.

Lastly, it should be remembered that this is not merely local, but, like other science, is being applied in engineering projects all over the world.[99]

CITY PLANNING—A NEW AND FERTILE FIELD FOR EXPERIMENTAL JURISPRUDENCE

The completely successful methods of Experimental Jurisprudence in the traffic field are rapidly expanding into other activities where law affects human conduct. As part of the traffic problem itself, the

[98] One such exception is Moore's and Callahan's contribution, op. cit. supra note 6.

[99] Europe and Japan: Eno, Simplification of Highway Traffic 181 ff. (1929); Israel: Klein, Solving the Traffic Problem, Traffic Q. 214, 222 (July 1949); Germany: Owen, op. cit. supra note 24, at 117 ff.; Schlums, Correlations Between Road Traffic and Size of Cities, Traffic Q. 219 (1948).

development of parking areas both on the ground and in buildings especially constructed for the purpose,[100] so located as to give the maximum results for shopping, has been subjected to the technique of the traffic engineer.[101] The results are a rapidly growing science from which there is emerging a series of laws and ordinances for planning, arranging and controlling business districts.[102]

New airports, with their accompanying traffic problems and through highways, are opening another field of traffic engineering and city planning of areas adjacent to the fields.[103] In a like manner the completion of express highways and bridges has been found drastically to change the nature of neighborhoods through which they pass. This, in turn, raises the question of business districts at one end of the freeway and residential areas at the other.[104] The technique of the traffic engineer is being expanded into problems of apartment construction and location of huge housing projects,[105] which, in turn, involve zoning and town, city and state area planning.[106]

REGULATION OF AIR TRAFFIC

Another fruitful source of information on the practical operation of Experimental Jurisprudence where engineering necessarily impringes upon lawmaking will emerge in the activities of the federal government in the process of promulgating and enforcing regulations governing air travel. Although the direction of air traffic has been moved about from one administrative unit to another and has been divided,

---

[100] Ricker, op. cit. supra note 52.

[101] E.g., see, LeCraw & Smith, Parking Lot Operation (Eno Found. 1948); Hanna, Factors Affecting Parkers' Choice, Traffic Q. 400 (Oct. 1949).

[102] Nolting and Opperman, The Parking Problem in Central Business Districts, Pub. Adm. Pub. No. 64 (1938).

[103] Malcher, op. cit. supra note 50; Ramspeck, Problems of Ground Transport to Air Terminals, Traffic Q. 251 (July 1948).

[104] Mott and Wehrly, Traffic and Parking in Suburban Shopping Development, Traffic Q. 358 (Oct. 1949); LeCraw, Allentown Saves Its Shopping Area, Traffic Q. 63; Elder, op. cit. supra note 53, at 166.

[105] Norton, Metropolitan Planning, Traffic Q. 367 (Oct. 1949); U.S. Bureau, Labor Stat. Bull. No. 896 (1947).

[106] Halsey, op. cit. supra note 50, at 55 ff.; Kennedy, Planning the Statewide System of Highway Transportation, Traffic Q. 201 (July 1949); Fargo, Local Level Planning in California, Traffic Q. 259 (July 1949); Kennedy, A Ministry for All Town Planning in England and Wales, Traffic Q. 138 (April 1949); and for the great developments in city planning for Washington, D. C., see National Capitol Park Planning Commission, Ann. Repts. (1926-32); id. Plans and Studies of Washington and Vicinity (1928); id. Reports and Plans, Washington Region (1930); Report of National Capitol Housing Authority (1934-44) (Mimeo.); National Capitol Park Planning Commission, Monographs 1-6 (1950) where there is worked out a complete set of data using a technique similar to traffic studies.

the Civil Aeronautics Board is gradually coming into centralized control with power to make the regulations[107] which vitally govern the movement of air commerce. Its Bureaus of Safety Regulation and Safety Investigation are carrying on scientific inquiries into the workings of air transportation, the causes and prevention of accidents and the creation and workings of regulations governing flying.[108] Although the enforcement and operation features of their rules are within the province of the Civil Aeronautics Administration,[109] which has jurisdiction over most of the technical and mechanical developments covering safety and operation where scientific research is constantly in progress,[110] much of its work eventually finds its way into rules promulgated by the Civil Aeronautics Board, with which it closely cooperates. In the traffic investigation and surveys of the CAB, one interested in the development of jural laws will find research reports on air traffic that closely parallel the automobile traffic survey discussed above and which adopt similar techniques.[111] Here the researcher into the methods of social research will find a mine of material on scientific rule-making to govern human conduct, and will probably uncover numerous examples of carefully verified jural laws governing the enforcement of air regulations.

These and probably many other examples of scientific governmental activities which can be uncovered show that the methods of research in the growth of laws and regulations pioneered by the traffic engineer are rapidly being adopted in new fields, and it is fair to say that a complete science of Experimental Jurisprudence will emerge there, in a very short time reaching a point of development as high as we now have in traffic regulation.

[107] But cf. Hoover Comm. Reports on Organization of the Executive Branch of the Government, Regulatory Commission Report No. 13, App. N, c. 7 pp. 19 et seq. (Dept. of Commerce Pub. Mar. 1949).

[108] 3 Air Affairs 71 (Autumn 1949).

[109] 3 Air Affairs 83 (Autumn 1949).

[110] E.g., see Morse, The Correlation of Aircraft Take-Off and Landing Characteristics With Airport Size, Tech. Rep. No. 40, USDC, CAA (April 1944); Field, Edwards, Kangas and Pigman, Measurement of Sound Levels Associated with Aircraft, Highway and Railroad Traffic, Tech. Rep. No. 68, USDC, CAA (July 1947); Hurley, Ultra-High-Frequency Airport Traffic Control, Tech. Rep. No. 44, USDC, CAA (Aug. 1944); McFarland, The Effects of Oxygen Deprivation (High Altitude) on the Human Organism, Tech. Rep. No. 11, USDC, CAA (May 1938); Lee, Measurements of Noise Radiation from High-Voltage Transmission Lines, Tech. Rep. No. 46, USDC, CAA (May 1947); cf. the powers of the National Advisory Committee for Aeronautics, 50 U.S.C.A. § 151 (Supp. 1949); 3 Air Affairs 96 (Autumn 1949).

[111] E.g., see Airline Traffic Survey, CAB (March 1947); Non-Air Carrier Accident Trend Report, CAB (Jan. 24, 1950).

CHAPTER VII

Experimental Jurisprudence in the Federal Government

The manner in which the techniques of Experimental Jurisprudence have been followed in the development of laws to control traffic as discussed in Chapter VI is not typical, but examples of the use of scientific data in the aid of lawmaking may be found in many branches of government. They vary all the way from complete scientific methods, as in the control of some elements of traffic law, to pure intuition sometimes apparent in the legislative halls. Some governmental units may have a modicum of science in their lawmaking procedures; others will be found to have none.

It will be useful to illustrate some of the possibilities of scientific lawmaking to examine some of the methods now in use in light of the possibilities of Experimental Jurisprudence. Such an investigation might be made on any level of government and if thoroughly done would be a monumental work. Since the federal government is the best known, a few illustrations from some of its activities might give some hint of the extent of the use of the methods of Experimental Jurisprudence found there.

The ramifications of federal jurisdiction are so extensive that even a partial survey of the activities of its various bureaus and authorities in light of the methods and purposes of scientific government would run into volumes of reports requiring an army of researchers delving into mountains of files, traversing mazes of organization charts, many of which are unpublished, devising comparative analyses of volumes of statutes and administrative regulations and classifying work-loads of millions of federal employees. Since the theories underlying the organization and functions of the Constitution antedate the rise of the effective application of the scientific method, any experimental or scientific devices for administration existing under its protection are likely to be accidental or unconsciously instituted to meet the demands for a government regulating a civilization dominated by science. There is therefore no simple touchstone by which these processes and methods, if they exist, may be readily revealed. This must be left to more detailed and heavily endowed research. All that can be done in a theoretical discussion of this kind is to indicate the directions which such research might take and the places where it would be most fruitful. A detailed criticism must be reserved to a later time.

RESEARCH IN THE FEDERAL GOVERNMENT

COST OF RESEARCH

With the possible exception of the Soviet Union, the government of the United States contains the largest conglomeration of research organizations in the world. The second Hoover Commission on Organization of the Executive branch of the government put the yearly expenditure for this purpose in 1955 at $1,500,000,000,[1] and another authority says that there are over fifty-two[2] agencies engaged in spending this appropriation. Although the amount is huge, the estimate is probably far too small to even approach the amounts being spent for research today. The federal budget does not easily disclose sums that are appropriated for research, and when it does, it seldom includes the payment of permanent personnel devoting all or part of their time to research activities. There are also many administrative branches of the government, like the Census Bureau, the Weather Bureau, the Bureau of Standards and many others, whose entire activity, in the strict sense, is research, but it is seldom so classified. In the form in which the term "research" would be used by an experimental jurist, the chances are that government resources devoted to this activity reach a total much larger than that indicated in the Hoover Report, and even this would be an extremely doubtful estimate because of the skill with which government administrators hide research from the sharp eye of the supervising Bureau of the Budget. It should also be noted that the $1,500,000,000 estimated above does not include all amounts spent for atomic research and undoubtedly overlooks vast sums spent by the military.

The amount appropriated for the Department of Defense, Research and Development for the fiscal year ending July, 1956 equaled

---

[1] See **Big Government: Can it be managed efficiently?** Fortune Supp. 23 (May 1, 1949); 2d **Hoover Commission, Sub-Comm. Rep. on Research Activities** 1 (1955).
[2] Lambert, The Administration of Federal Research 107 Science 179 (Feb. 20, 1948).

one and one-half billion dollars and is similar in size to that spent during the last three fiscal years.[3] This is probably larger than the combined endowments and annual appropriations for research of all the universities and schools of learning in the entire United States; but an almost equal and independent amount is being spent yearly on the development of atomic energy,[4] the basic share of which also goes to pure and applied research. It should be a cause for consternation to anyone concerned with the purposes of government that the bulk of these huge appropriations is going to support one of the basest, most destructive and useless of all governmental activities, war. If this trend to harness science to emotionally controlled mass destruction is not soon reversed, one may well despair of the future of the race.

TABLE 5

Obligations and Expenditures of Federal Agencies for Scientific Research and Development in Fiscal Years 1952, 1953, and 1954.

(Millions of dollars)

Agency	Obligations			Expenditures		
	Fiscal year 1952	Fiscal year 1953	Fiscal year 1954[1]	Fiscal year 1952	Fiscal year 1953	Fiscal year 1954[1]
Department of Defense	1,705	1,650	1,556	1,315	1,646	1,636
Atomic Energy Commission	229	247	239	250	260	266
National Advisory Committee for Aeronautics	82	79	73	67	79	88
Department of Agriculture	56	57	68	57	58	63
Department of Health, Education and Welfare	53	67	63	65	74	61
Department of the Interior	36	36	32	33	37	33
Department of Commerce	31	23	17	28	24	17
Other agencies	25	28	26	24	26	24
Total, all agencies	2,217	2,187	2,074	1,839	2,205	2,187

[1] Estimate. Revised: August 24, 1953.
Source: National Science Foundation.

A step in the effort at directing governmental scientific research was the creating in 1950 of the National Science Foundation, whose purpose is to encourage the broad development of all sciences both within and outside the governmental organizations.[5] From a small annual appropriation of $225,000, this agency is growing to a commanding position in the development of science in the United States. Its ap-

[3] Budget of the United States Government 1195 (1956).
[4] Id. 90, $1,300,000,000.
[5] 64 Stat. 149 (1950).

propriation in 1956 was estimated at $20,000,000.[6] It is concerned primarily with grants and fellowships, surveying, classifying and encouraging scientific development.[7] The annual reports of the foundation, attempting to state the amounts being spent by the federal government for research, show that the percentage of the entire budget for this purpose has grown from one per cent in the 1940-1943 period to about three per cent in 1952-1954.[8] The estimated total appropriated by the United States government for scientific purposes in 1955 ran well over two billion dollars; but of this amount about ninety per cent went for physical science, seven or eight per cent for life science and only two or three per cent for social sciences; and the military and atomic energy absorbed over eighty-seven per cent of the whole.[9] Table 5 shows the amount the foundation estimated as being spent by the various governmental agencies on research down to 1954.

Bad as the situation is, all is not lost. Some crumbs from the table of the military are falling to research in social science. Even the army, being concerned with governing soldiers and other people, having learned to rely upon research to solve some of its problems, naturally turns to the same process to resolve others. Operation Research,[10] the Committee on Human Resources of the Research and Development Board,[11] the efforts of the Psychological Warfare Division,[12] to name only a few, have turned up material which is a valuable asset to social science and offers important tools for use by the experimental jurist.[13]

---

[6] Budget of the United States 138 (1956).

[7] See Lessing, The National Science Foundation Takes Stock, 190 Scientific American No. 3, 29 (March 1954).

[8] Third An. Rep. Natl. Sci. Foundation 5 (1953). See Table 5. A more complete report appeared while this book was in preparation. See id. Organization of the Federal Government for Scientific Activities (1956).

[9] Id. 3. According to the second Hoover Commission the government appropriated in 1954 $1,416,000,000 for research in the Department of Defense. Of this, forty per cent was expended in the military establishment itself, one per cent in other governmental agencies, forty-nine per cent in private industry, ten per cent in academic and non-profit institutions. Sub-Comm. Rep. on Research 39 (1955).

[10] Morse and Kimball, Methods of Operations Research (1950); Salow, Operations Research, 43 Fortune 105 (April 1951).

[11] See Stouffer and others, Studies on Social Psychology in World War II (1949) in four volumes; 1 Id. 3 ff.

[12] See Lerner, Propaganda in War and Crisis (1951), Margolin, Paper Bullets (1946).

[13] "In the fiscal year 1952, the Federal Government doled out nearly $542 million for research and development in the nation's nonprofit institutions—$44 million more than it spent in 1951 and more than 60% of all the money spent on research

Of smaller research appropriations given to the civil branches, the lion's share, of course, goes to activities in the field of pure and applied science, with much lesser sums covering political and social sciences. The budget of the Department of Agriculture discloses about $85,000,000[14] appropriated to the Agricultural Research Administration.

The Department of the Interior is largely a research organization, with the Bureau of Mines, the Geological Survey and the Bureau of Reclamation spending huge sums. The Department of Commerce, in addition to the Bureau of Census and the others mentioned above, carries on extensive research in the Department of Foreign Commerce and in many of the aspects of business conditions. In the Department of Labor, the Bureau of Labor Statistics and the Children's Bureau are well known for their publications in the field of social science alone, while the Department of Health, Education and Welfare has a vast organization not only in public health but also in the field of checking their own welfare activities. Independent agencies like the Tennessee Valley Authority, Interstate Commerce Commission, Federal Trade Commission, the Federal Reserve Board and many others have a large stake in research in social sciences as distinguished from physical science. The Executive Office of the President, through its Council of Economic Advisors and many of its other far-flung activities both inside the Bureau of the Budget and out, engages in much research, which will be discussed later. So also, the various committees of Congress take part in activities which in many instances can be classified as real governmental and social science research.

It is impossible in a short chapter even to attempt thoroughly to review and classify these activities. It is sufficient to say here that a large amount of the so-called research in the social sciences under the current influence of the prevailing theories in that field amounts to a little more than description. Any file of government documents will yield thousands of publications varying from the eighty-four-volume

and development in the U. S. Last week the National Science Foundation released some preliminary figures to show how the money is being spent.

"More than half the Government's science bill is paid by the Department of Defense, 35% by the AEC, 6% by the Federal Security Agency and 5% by the Department of Agriculture. All other agencies combined paid less than 3% of the total. This year, as usual, the biggest chunk of cash was spent on the physical sciences ($255 million). Second: the biological, medical, and agricultural sciences ($70 million). Social sciences brought up the rear with $17 million." 60 Time 42 (December 1, 1952).

[14] Budget of the U.S. Gov't. 1198 (1956).

report of the Federal Trade Commission on the public utility industry[15] to mimeographed brochures of five or six pages,[16] all busily engaged in describing subjects varying from activities of governmental bureaus to how to feed infants or raise corn. The social science material which comprises a goodly portion of these publications, but a very small amount of the money invested in research, varies from pure description of phenomena that have nothing to do with law to carefully studied and documented materials on nothing but law. In all this vast array of material, it would not be surprising if there were instances of research and publication which meet the standards of some of the steps in Experimental Jurisprudence. Without attempting to classify or discuss in detail more than a small fraction of the material, it might be worth while to look to see to what extent the methods of scientific Experimental Jurisprudence are being developed in these activities.

MISNAMED RESEARCH

Before discussing sources of examples of truly scientific and experimental research, it might be wise to eliminate much of the pseudo-scientific and other activity which carries such labels as "research," "experimental" and "fact-finding" but which on close analysis will be shown to bear no relation to their titles. An instance of this misuse of the term "fact-finding" is found in the so-called Fact-Finding Boards used in labor disputes. In the steel, coal and railway labor troubles, we constantly hear of the authorization under law of fact-finding boards. This, of course, is a misnomer. In actual practice these boards are simply mediators appointed by the President who attempt to settle the dispute. There is little or no fact-finding in the scientific sense. For example, in the 1950 strike of the United Mine Workers the "Fact-Finding Board" had been in session only three days when it reported to the President that an agreement could not be reached. It is manifestly impossible for any group of men, no matter how well aided, even to start to investigate the "facts" of labor disputes in the coal industry within three days.

During the thirties there were created by the New Deal administration numerous so-called "experimental" programs. Some of these,

[15] See F.T.C. Ann. Rep. 19 ff. (1935); Ann. Rep. 36 ff. (1936); Ann. Rep. 220-221 (1941).

[16] Toben & Case, Operation of Ag. Conserv. Programs in Ill. (Jan. 1940) USDA, Farm Manag. Rep.—No. 4; The National Turkey Improvement Plan (Rev. Issue June, 1948) USDA Misc. Pub. No. 555; The National Poultry Improvement Plan (Rev. Issue July, 1946) USDA Misc. Pub. No. 300.

such as the studies of traffic, as seen in an earlier chapter, developed into real scientific activities, but many more, such as the tree shelter-belt to run across the Midwest, experimental housing plans and others, were simply attempts to implement pet political theories without any preliminary investigation or careful scientific check of the results of the program if and when instituted. Others started to be scientific but were killed by unsympathetic Congressional appropriation committees or by the intervention of the war before any real check could be made and proof submitted of the success or failure of the particular plan. Typical of this pseudo-experimental activity was the work of hundreds of county planning activities developed in the Department of Agriculture.[17] These took many forms, but one of the most active was the cooperative crop planning which started in 1937 with ten sample counties[18] and then spread like wildfire all over the United States.[19] Before there was any opportunity to check the success or failure of the plan by careful comparison with counties where it was not adopted, the whole activity came to an ignominious end, probably a war casualty, with little or no follow-up, and some of the studies which were attempted seemed to be devoted more to expounding the authors' theories of democracy than to discovering the real social effects of the "experiment."[20]

Many of the promising legal devices created either by Congressional act or administrative rule met a similar fate. It is hoped that at some future time they may be revised under better auspices with more careful attention to particular problems and underlying scientific verification. Some of these experiments are still going on and are producing very useful results. The remaining are too numerous to follow in detail, but some of them will be discussed to indicate the extent to which experimental methods are being attempted by the federal government.

[17] U.S. Bur. of Agricultural Economics, County Planning Series; Allin, County Planning Project—A Cooperative Approach to Agricultural Planning, 22 Jour. of Farm. Econ. 292 (Feb. 1940).
[18] 8 Ext. Serv. Rev. 90 (June 1937); Planning for a Permanent Agriculture, USDA Misc. Pub. No. 351, 21 (1939).
[19] 9 Ext. Serv. Rev. 71, 106, 130, 138 (1938); 10 Ext. Serv. Rev. 2, 36, 42, 61, 68, 75, 83, 153, 156, 178 (1939); 11 Ext. Serv. Rev. 12 (1940); 13 Ext. Serv. Rev. 6, 7, 34 (1942).
[20] Gross, A Post Mortem on County Planning, 25 Jour. of Farm Econ. 644, 652 ff. (Feb. 1943).

SCIENTIFIC PREPARATION FOR LAWMAKING

Much scientific information is being brought to bear by government agencies on social and economic problems as a basis for passing laws. Sometimes the government bureaus act on their own motion to initiate studies, and at other times they are particularly requested to make careful investigations by direction of one or both of the Houses of Congress. Of course it is clear that none of this work can be attempted without a proper Congressional appropriation. But instances in which agencies have moved to obtain such appropriations and have uncovered valuable information which appears in reports and suggestions for lawmaking are very numerous. Among the best are the forest service reports on the condition of various forest areas, such as the study of *Louisiana Forest Resources and Industries*,[21] *The Anthracite Forest Region—A Problem Area*,[22] and *Forest Resources of the Ponderosa Pine Region*.[23] These are carefully conducted scientific and statistical studies of the forest resources, including the kind of trees in the area, the amount of cut-over land as related to virgin timber and second growth, an examination of the lumbering practices and recommendations for the enactment of long-term statutes regulating activities.

On a similar plane are the surveys of the Department of Agriculture of wages and working conditions in various areas in the western states.[24] Here one may find detailed statistics on the wages and hours of workers in crops like oranges, lemons, beets and cotton. The length of the seasons, living conditions, effect of migratory labor, and attempts, both legal and voluntary, to stabilize wages are all analyzed.

A good example of instances where a number of agencies have cooperated to produce material on area problems is found in the report on *Economic and Social Problems and Conditions of the Southern Appalachians*,[25] which contains an intricately detailed descriptive an-

[21] Winters, Ward & Eldredge, La. Forest Resources and Industries, USDA Misc. Pub. No. 519 (1943).

[22] Ineson & Ferree, The Anthracite Forest Region, A Problem Area, USDA Misc. Pub. No. 648 (1948).

[23] Forest Resources of the Ponderosa Pine Region, USDA Misc. Pub. No. 490.

[24] Metzler, Wages and Wage Rates of Farm Workers in the Citrus Harvest, Los Angeles Area, Calif., April-June, 1945, USDA Bur. of Ag. Econ., Survey Rep. No. 5 (1945); Wages and Wage Rates of Farm Workers in the Potato, Sugar Beet, and Cotton Harvests, Calif., 1945, USDA Bur. of Ag. Econ., Survey Rep. No. 14 (1946); Ducoff, Wages of Agricultural Labor in the U.S., USDA Tech. Bull. No. 895 (July 1945).

[25] Economic and Social Problems and Conditions of the Southern Appalachians, USDA Misc. Pub. No. 205 (Jan. 1935).

alysis of the population resources and community activities of the area studied. Here, as is often the case, agencies of the Department of Agriculture and Interior pooled their resources to make a detailed report on resources, temperature, farming practices, social habits, educational facilities, family income, housing and a thousand other factors in the patterns of individual and mass actions in the societies involved. Although this report contains a few suggestions for changes in the laws, like thousand of others, it is oriented more toward description than toward lawmaking.

Instances are legion where bureaus, at the request of Congress, have gathered material to be used for future lawmaking. Timber depletion and the problem of lumber prices and exports were studied meticulously in response to a Senate resolution,[26] and the report carries with it recommendations for both federal and state legislation.[27] Scientific publications of experiment stations dealing with erosion and control of land[28] are, of course, well known and offer an excellent scientific basis for legislation. The history of flood control also contains numerous examples of careful scientific study being implemented by later statutes.[29] The Army Engineers, the Geological Survey and the Bureau of Reclamation are constantly conducting detailed studies which precede the adoption by Congress of appropriations for rivers and harbors, construction of flood-control devices and power and reclamation projects. Here scientific research comes to the aid of lawmaking in a truly experimental manner, and the results can be expected to have wide effect upon the social habits and activities of the people of the areas involved.

[26] Timber Depletion, Lumber Prices, Lumber Exports, and Concentration of Timber Ownership, USDA Rep. on Sen. Res. 311 (June 1920).

[27] Timber Depletion, Lumber Prices, Lumber Exports, and Concentration of Timber Ownershop USDA Rep. on Sen. Res. 311, pp. 69-70 (June 1920). For other studies made by the U.S. Tariff Commission upon Congressional request see Alcoholic Beverages Misc. Series (1934); Hides and Skins and Leather Rep. No. 13 (1946); Petroleum Rep. No. 17 (1946).

[28] Hill, Peevy, McCall & Bell, Investigations in Erosion Control and Reclamation of Eroded Land at the Blackland Conserv. Exp. Sta., Temple, Tex., 1931-41, USDA Tech. Bull. No. 859 (Jan. 1944); Browning, Norton, McCall & Bell, Investigation in Erosion Control and the Reclamation of Eroded Land at the Mo. Valley Loess Conserv. Exp. Sta., Clarinda, Iowa, 1931-42, USDA Tech. Bull. 959 (Oct. 1948); Borst, McCall & Bell, Investigations in Erosion Control and the Reclamation of Eroded Land at the Northwest Appalachian Conserv. Exp. Sta., Zanesville, Ohio, 1934-42 USDA Tech. Bull. No. 888 (May 1945).

[29] The Land in Flood Control, USDA Misc. Pub. No. 331, pp. 13, 36 ff. (1939).

There should be distinguished the hundreds of scientific research projects which may later become the basis of legislation but which are not initiated with immediate legislation in mind. Typical of such projects is the $30,000,000 appropriation authorized by Congress to the Bureau of Mines of the Department of the Interior to set up synthetic oil shale plants and processes which might later become the basis of establishing a new industry.[30] Although the results of such research in the future might be used as a basis of creating a system of laws, at the present time they are little more than the authorization of pilot experiments such as might be carried on by a university or an industry.

CONGRESSIONAL INVESTIGATING COMMITTEES

The scientific research conducted above also should be distinguished carefully from the efforts of Congressional committees and other legislative hearings which purport to be research for the possible creation of laws. These activities may vary all the way from pure propaganda and rabble-rousing, which has been habitually charged to the House Un-American Activities Committee, to bona fide attempts to find the social facts underlying necessary legislation; but these hearings are of little value to the jural scientists because they are operating on a non-scientific basis. They are largely sounding boards for pressure groups, and since the committee seldom indulges in research of its own but simply listens to the material which is brought to it, any scientific product is largely accidental, depending upon the evidence that particular witnesses care to offer. Seldom, if ever, does the committee have the personnel or the desire to check on its own motion the voluminous "information" and testimony which are often heaped upon it by partisan factions contending for favorable legislation. These defects apply equally to the hearing process, whether it be in regular session or special committees sitting in interim between sessions.[31] At the time the committee hearing system was devised, it was probably the best available means of collecting information, but social science research technique has now developed to the point where such methods can be regarded as little better than historical anachronisms.

There are, however, notable exceptions to the general run of the publications of legislative committees. Among the most prominent of these are the monograph reports of the Temporary National Economic

[30] 58 U.S. Stat. at Large 190-191 (April 1944).
[31] Cohen, Towards Realism in Legislation, 59 Yale L. J. 886 (1950).

148

Committee,[32] a joint body of the House, Senate and six government agencies created in the third session of the Seventy-fifth Congress,[33] with authority to investigate and report upon the concentration of economic power and financial control over production and distribution of goods and services. An initial expenditure of $500,000 was authorized for the employment of experts and for other expenses which eventually cost the committee twice that amount.[34] Although the forty-four published monographs attempted mostly to paint in broad general colors the economic conditions of the community, they are supported by a mass of carefully compiled and detailed statistics. The recommendations for legal action, with but few exceptions, are disappointments.[35] The reasons for this failure of the committee to achieve concrete results are probably two. First, like so many similar fact-finding expeditions, the base of operation is too broad. Aimed at what is wrong with the whole system, it is too vague to effect concrete changes in the law. Much better results might be expected from the study of the operation and social effects of a single statute. This is probably the reason the monographs on the patent system[36] and the enforcement of the Sherman Act[37] are the two containing the most outstanding recommendations. The second difficulty is that the directing head of the committee was made up of politicians rather than scientists. Under our present system, politically appointed or elected officials may have to determine ultimate policy, but when they are placed in a position of being required to find facts and make recommendations thereon, their scientific judgment is undoubtedly tainted by their political points of view. A careful examination of the final reports and recommendations of the committee will show the extent to which political discretion has interfered with or destroyed factual analysis and recommendation.[38] Until such committees are given full independence to discover facts and make recommendations on the basis of their discoveries, investigations of this type are likely to yield little besides an uncorrelated mass of informative data.

---

[32] TNEC Monographs 1-44, published as Senate Documents 76th & 77th Congress (1940-41); see Business Week 27 (March 22, 1941).

[33] 52 Stat. 705 (1938).

[34] Twilight of TNEC, 37 Time 85-87 (April 14, 1941).

[35] Stone, The TNEC Recommends—What? 152 The Nation 463 (April 19, 1941); TNEC—Magnificent Failure, Business Week, 22-31 (Mar. 22, 1941).

[36] Patents and Free Enterprise, TNEC Mono. No. 31 (1941).

[37] Anti-Trust in Action, TNEC Mono. 16 (1940).

[38] Final Report and Recommendations of the TNEC, 77th Congress Sen. Doc. No. 35 (Mar. 31, 1941).

In spite of such committees' failure to produce concrete results in the form of better laws, the vast amount of valuable information buried in the text of the studies conducted by experts on a lower level in this and similar reports is gradually changing the legislative habits of the Congress. Enlightened lawmakers are coming to realize that laws affecting the economic and social welfare of the country cannot be enacted without a careful study of the phenomena to be regulated. The same kind of careful scientific investigation before the enactment of laws which has become an obvious necessity in the fields of flood control, conservation and military planning is rapidly appearing as a prerequisite to laws regulating economic and social conditions. If the federal government is going further on the way toward social planning, then more and more it must adopt the technique of Experimental Jurisprudence which requires reliance on the research and recommendation of impartial experts before lawmaking. We are now in an era where it is recognized that the fact-finding methods of Congress must be changed and that the enactment of law cannot safely be based solely upon popular sentiment or the demands of unchecked pressure groups.

MOVEMENT TOWARD SCIENTIFIC FACT-FINDING

In many fields Congress has already moved to create more scientific fact-finding as a basis for law- and rule-making. The growth of activity of this sort is usually found in coincidence with delegations of power to expert commissions and bureaus of government, the theory being that the complicated nature of the regulations involved is such that they can only be properly administered by a group of experts devoting a large amount of attention to the scientific and the factual aspects of the situation controlled by law or regulation. The manner in which such delegation has made possible the growth of real jural science under the direction of the Bureau of Roads and in traffic control in the District of Columbia has already been discussed.[39] There are many other branches of the federal government where the possibility of similar scientific development may be found lurking beneath the delegation of power to government agencies. Among these are the Tariff Commission, with its power to change the rates by fifty per cent, independent government agencies with strong rule-making power, such as the Interstate Commerce Commission, Federal

---

[39] See Ch. VI, fns. 81, 87, 43 Stat. 1119 § 6 (a) (1925); D.C. Code (1940 § 40-603. Laforest v. Board of Comm'rs, 92 F. 2d 547 (App. D.C., 1937), cert. denied 302 U.S. 760 (1937).

150

Trade Commission, the Civil Aeronautics Board and numerous other like organizations. The manner in which the Treasury Department is able to control currency, the powers of the Board of Governors of the Federal Reserve System, the directors of the Reconstruction Finance Corporation, the managers of the Federal Deposit Insurance Corporation and those in control of many other government banking and financial institutions offer opportunity for scientific development of economic controls, any one of which could be made the subject matter of a treatise.

Many of the departments of the cabinet, like the Department of the Interior, which is charged with great reclamation projects similar to the TVA, also contain within their authority illustrations of Experimental Jurisprudence. Critical studies and comparisons of methods of research of many of these departmental activities would prove a fruitful source of material for an experimental jurist. It is impossible to review here even a few of the products of these organizations, but a comparative study of their work, either by governmental agencies or independent research organizations, should prove a fertile source of jural science.

USING LAWS AS ADMINISTRATIVE DEVICES FOR DISSEMINATING SCIENTIFIC INFORMATION

EDUCATIONAL ACTIVITIES

In examining the purpose of particular laws, it will be discovered that there are many federal statutes whose chief function is to issue to the public information developed by the sciences. The Department of Agriculture administers a vast system of experiment stations and appropriations for the encouragement of agricultural research in hybrid corn, animal breeding and new farming methods, among others. In these instances the purpose of the law is simply to educate the farmer in the use of any discoveries which will eventually change his habits, increase his productivity and his happiness and improve living conditions. While these activities are very numerous and valuable, little effort has yet been expended to check upon their effectiveness as legal devices. But they do represent one important aspect of scientific jurisprudence, viz., the use of laws to disseminate information developed by the sciences to remold the legal and social habits of the body politic.

The Departments of Commerce, Interior and many other government agencies administer laws with a similar purpose. Not the least of these is the Public Health Service in the Department of Health, Education and Welfare which not only disseminates the scientific results of research but also has much lawmaking power delegated to its head, the Surgeon General.

In the matter of collecting and disseminating scientific information, the work of the Public Health Service in the field of milk production and sanitation is an excellent example of the complete workings of Experimental Jurisprudence in a field where science comes forcibly to bear upon lawmaking.

Since shortly after the beginning of the twentieth century, the Public Health Service has been studying the effect upon health of the production and distribution of milk. The early efforts began with the problem of the incidence of milk-borne diseases and the effect of pasteurization.[40] In 1923 the Division of Scientific Research set up an Office of Milk Investigation to cooperate with state and local governmental units. Due to the divisions of power in our system of federal government, it was believed impossible at this time for the federal Public Health Service to recommend federal statutes to control the production and distribution of milk in local areas. Due to this legal and governmental difficulty, the Milk Investigation office studied the various types of milk ordinances and their effect upon the industry in different localities.[41]

As a culmination of this effort, there was developed a standard Milk Ordinance and Code based upon the information obtained from the continuing research. In due time the experimental ordinance[42] had reached sufficient perfection to be adopted. It was recommended to the various cities and towns throughout the country.

By the year 1950, as a result of the efforts of the Federal Security Agency, the recommended milk ordinance was in effect in over fourteen hundred municipalities and three hundred counties and districts scattered over an area of thirty-eight states and one territory. It had also been adopted as state law or regulation in thirty-two states and two territories, in thirteen of which it had statewide enforcement. Included within the jurisdiction of these laws are fifty-five cities of over one hundred thousand and thirty-eight between fifty thousand and one

---

[40] Moss, Milk Investigations of the U.S. Public Health Service, 3 Jour. of Milk Technology 145 (1940).

[41] Moss, supra 147 ff.

[42] Milk Ordinance and Code, Pub. Health Bull. 220, F.S.A. (1939).

hundred thousand. In total it affected an area with a population of over fifty-eight million.[43]

After these statutes and regulations were adopted, the Public Health Service then devised a means of checking up on the effectiveness of enforcement under the new regulations. This process corresponds to Step Three in the procedure of Experimental Jurisprudence explained in Chapter II. Inspectors of the federal agency and also of the state and local agencies were provided with large score sheets[44] covering the major points of the statutory provisions. These were filled out in full and returned to the supervising agency. When reports came in, they were summarized by agents of the bureau, which then set up milk sanitation rating[45] for the various areas. There were also careful before-and-after studies[46] based upon health conditions and the status of milk sanitation in various local areas before and after adoption of the code. Reports were also compiled on the effects on general health,[47] trade barriers[48] in the industry and like subjects and their relation to the regulations.

As a result of these continuing studies, amendments[49] are constantly being suggested to the standard milk code; the amendments are put into force, and the studies begin over again,[50] showing both the actual effect and contemplated effect[51] of changes in methods. Here one can easily recognize Steps Six, Seven and Eight of Experimental Jurisprudence.

This entire process, at the suggestion of the Public Health Service, is now being studied in cooperation with the Department of Agricul-

[43] List of American Communities in which the Milk Ordinance recommended by the Public Health Service is in effect, Div. of Sanitation, F.S.A. (Nov. 1950).

[44] For example see F.S.A. Form P.H.S. 842 (SE) Rev. 3-50, Pub. Health Serv.

[45] Communities Awarded Milk Sanitation Ratings of 90 Percent or More, 66 Pub. Health Rep. 1087 (Aug. 1951).

[46] For example see Fuchs and Koeze, Results of the Operation of the Standard Milk Ordinance in Mississippi, 45 Pub. Health Reports 1412 (June 1930); Clark and Johnson, Results of the Operation of the Standard Milk Ordinance in Missouri, 46 id. 1413 (June 1931).

[47] Andrews and Fuchs, Pasteurization and its Relation to Health, 138 Jour. of Am. Med. Assn. 128 (1948).

[48] Fuchs, Trade Barriers in the Milk Industry, 10 Jour. of Milk and Food Technology No. 4, 195 (July 1947).

[49] For example see Fuchs, Recent Amendments of the U.S. Public Health Service Milk Code, 11 Jour. of Milk and Food Technology, No. 3, 149 (May 1948).

[50] See Thomas, Levine and Black, Studies Showing the Effect of Changes in the New (9th) Edition of Standard Methods in Regulation of the Bacteriological Analysis of Milk, 38 Am. Jour. of Pub. Health. No. 2, 233 (Feb. 1948).

[51] Black, Effects of Contemplated Changes in Standard Methods, 11 Jour. of Milk and Food Technology No. 4 (July-Aug. 1948).

ture and the National Research Council. A preliminary bulletin on the state of sanitary milk and cream regulation was published in 1950 and a final report of the whole study appeared in the early spring of 1953.[52] These reports illustrate one of the many fields in which government agencies have cooperated with private scientific organizations to produce purely scientific results. While the report itself was done by scientists and not by jurists, nevertheless it contains many suggestions both for jural research and for corrections in the laws studied.

In the final process one will recognize all of the steps in Experimental Jurisprudence set out in Chapter II.

In this case it should be noted that the agency created by federal law is acting only as a scientific research body, while the enactment of the rules themselves, which are left to states, cities and counties, form the laboratories and the controls. The Public Health Service is likewise operating along these lines in many other fields where the legal jurisdiction is wholly in the hands of local government. Among these are restaurant sanitation,[53] control of drinking water, water pollution, air pollution, pest control, refuse control, school and rural environment, protection for travelers and industrial health.[54]

Similar activities are carried on in the field of interstate commerce where the federal government has complete legal jurisdiction. Here the lawmaking power delegated to the Surgeon General has been extensively used. The Interstate Quarantine Regulations governing communicable diseases, land and air conveyances and inspections of all types have been codified in the Code of Federal Regulations.[55] These controls and accompanying instructions cover such additional areas as railroad servicing,[56] dining-car operations,[57] passenger-car construction,[58] and sanitation in the operation of vessels[59] where the Public

[52] Preliminary Report, Dahlberg and Adams, Sanitary Milk and Ice Cream Legislation Bull. No. 121 Nat. Research Council (July 1950); final Dahlberg, Adams and Held, Sanitary Milk Control, Pub. No. 250 (1953).

[53] Fuchs, Restaurant Sanitation Program of the United States Public Health Service, 62 Pub. Health Rep. No. 8, 261 (Feb. 1947); Ordinance and Code Regulating Eating and Drinking Establishments, P.H.S. Pub. No. 37 (1943); Form P.H.S. 72 SE. (5-47) F.S.A. Pub. Health Service, Sanitation Rating of Eating and Drinking Establishments.

[54] See Fed. Security Agency P.H.S. pamphlet, Environment and Health (1951).

[55] Tit. 42, Parts 71-73 (1949-50).

[56] See Railroad Servicing Areas, F.S.A., P.H.S. Pub. No. 66 (1951).

[57] See Handbook, Dining Cars in Operation, F.S.A., P.H.S. Pub. No. 83 (1951).

[58] See Handbook, Railroad Passenger Car Construction, F.S.A., P.H.S. Pub. No. 95 (1951).

[59] Handbook, Vessels in Operation, F.S.A., P.H.S. Pub. No. 68 (1951).

Health Service, as a result of its scientific investigations both of health problems and of the operation of regulations controlling them, is daily improving conditions of living and travel.

In spite of the handicaps of divided sovereignty and the wails of certain interests against interference in local affairs by the federal government, Experimental Jurisprudence is an established procedure in many of the fields of operation of the Public Health Service.[60]

A meticulous study of similar activities in other governmental agencies should reveal much more progress toward the ends indicated by the theories of experimental social science.

ANNUAL REPORTS OF OFFICERS AND HEADS OF BUREAUS

A common source of information used by Congress in determining future governmental policy is the reports of heads of government agencies on the progress of their activities.[61] Many of these reports are based upon the careful examination and assembly of information by competent social scientists and experts, and although they contain much valuable data, they are likely to fall short of scientific standards for a number of reasons known to those with experience in government administration.

1. The reports of most heads of government agencies are too closely tied to political parties and party policies to be stated in an unbiased fashion.

2. It is always necessary for the administrator to make a showing to Congress of his success in directing his responsibilities.

3. Every ambitious executive is under the temptation to develop a powerful bureaucracy through which he can hand out largess to the faithful and increase the scope of his leadership.

4. The resulting absence of objectivity in agency reports makes it almost impossible, short of a declaration of unconstitutionality or a complete political upset, to terminate a government bureau once it gets started. Even though a Supreme Court holding of unconstitutionality eventually aided in stopping the NRA,[62] it had no effect

[60] Divided sovereignty, a bad handicap in getting laws adopted originally, may be an aid to objectivity when a U.S. agency is studying the efficiency of enforcement of the laws adopted by the states. Objectivity has been further encouraged in this field by the cooperation of National Research Council, Note 47, supra.

[61] For example, see FCC Ann. Rep., 11-19 (1948); id. 89 (1939); id. 23, 24 (1940). CAB Ann. Rep. 20, 21 (1946); id. 29, 30 (1947); id. 33, 34, 36, 37 (1948); Ann. Rep. of the Sec. of Commerce 3, 4 (1948); FPC Ann. Rep. 119-121 (1947); id. 108 (1948). FTC Ann. Rep. 19, 20 (1941); id. 12 (1946); FHA Ann. Rep. 1-19 (1948); SEC Ann. Rep. 8 (1944); id. 17-20 (1948).

[62] Schechter Corp. v. U.S., 295 U.S. 495 (1935).

whatsoever upon the AAA, which went forward to accomplish its purpose in spite of a similar Supreme Court decision[63] and a ruling of the Comptroller General[64] that he would not pay its bills, simply by the device of a Congressional appropriation.[65] The Reconstruction Finance Corporation, Social Security, the military clique and other huge bureaucratic organizations containing within themselves their own research and propaganda departments span political upsets and continue to flourish whether the country is at war or peace.

SCIENTIFIC POLICY DETERMINATION

THE TARIFF COMMISSION AS A SCIENTIFIC BODY

One of the most controversial aspects of government regulation of business throughout the history of our country has been the protective tariff. In 1916[66] it was thought that the tariff could be removed from politics by creating an administrative agency to study the economic effect of particular tariff regulations and by delegating to the President power to raise or lower the tariff as indicated by the studies and recommendations of the Committee.[67] The flexible Tariff Act set up a research commission with authority to raise or lower the tariff to meet the necessity of putting American industry on a fair footing in competition with foreign producers. Undoubtedly this law contained germs of what might have developed into an excellent experiment in scientific government, but, although the commission in theory was equipped to do impartial work, in the early stages it was never possible to remove the pressure of political interference, especially in light of the fact that final decisions on the result of the studies had to be made by the President, who was the leader of the party in power.[68] In more recent times it shows promise of developing into a fact-finding organization of considerable reliability,[69] but still it remains in the shadow of cash-and-carry lobbying.[70] So, although the

[63] U.S. v. Butler, 279 U.S. 1 (1936).

[64] Ag. Adjust. Act—Unconstitutionality—Availability of Appropriations, Comp. Gen. Op. (A-69, 783) (Jan. 14, 1936).

[65] 49 Stat. 1116 (1936).

[66] 39 Stat. 795-798 (1916).

[67] 19 USCA § 1336 (1930).

[68] Schattschneider, Politics, Pressures and the Tariff 59 ff. (1935); Villard, Free Trade—Free World c. 21 (1947); Herring, The Political Context of the Tariff Commission, 49 Poli. Sci. Quar. 421 (1934); Taussig, The U.S. Tariff Commission and the Tariff, 16 Am. Econ. Rev. 171 (1926).

[69] Villard, Free Trade—Free World 225-227 (1947).

[70] Id. 40, 41; Schattschneider, Politics, Pressures and the Tariff c. 3 (1935).

Tariff Commission has the possibility of developing into a workng example of Experimental Jurisprudence, until it is entirely removed from the reach of the political pressure boys, it is doubtful whether it will be more than an example of conditions under which Experimental Jurisprudence cannot work in our present form of government.

RESEARCH TO DETERMINE POLICY WITHIN AGENCIES

Many government agencies have become so large and cover such a vast field of activity that the administrators themselves cannot determine policy intelligently without first indulging in complicated social research to find out what is going on within their own jurisdiction. Good examples of this sort of effort to determine what sound policy ought to be can be found in the studies of the Bureau of Reclamation to establish the directional course of the Columbia Basin Reclamation projects[71] in the state of Washington. Here studies of at least twenty-eight topics involved in the basic decisions were undertaken. The titles of some of these reports are indicative of the research involved. For example, there are: *Problem No. 2, Types of Farming; Problems 4 and 5, Irrigation, Water Requirements; Problem 9, Standards of Living; Problem 19, Highway Development*. Similar work has been carried on in the Central Valley where studies were made of twenty-four[72] basic divisions of information bearing upon later administrative decisions; and in both instances the end of fruitful policy-determining research is not yet in sight.

Although investigations of this type are highly useful in determining bureau policy, they are often slanted by basic legal requirements which are an historic accident. For example, many of the studies are devoted to proving that the highly controversial one-hundred-and-sixty-acre requirement for farms on reclamation projects is the proper limitation for the best social development in the area,[73] when as a matter of fact this figure is simply an anachronism going clear back to the old homestead statutes[74] and is yet to be subjected to a scientific analysis based upon the facts and requirements of modern farming, which undoubtedly will vary from area to area. These policy-determining studies are subject also, of course, to the difficulty that the administrator sometimes finds himself under the necessity of supporting party

---

[71] Columbia Basin Joint Investigations, USDI Bur. of Reclamation (1945-46).

[72] Central Valley Project Studies, USDI Bur. of Reclamation (1946-49).

[73] Farm Size and Adjustment to Topography, Columbia Basin Investigations, Probs. 6 and 8, USDI Bureau of Reclamation 5 (1946).

[74] 12 Stat. 392 (1862).

157

policy, which was determined in advance solely by intuitive or other non-scientific methods. But in spite of this handicap, the information turned up in such research is gradually having effect upon the basic postulates of governmental policy.

THE NECESSITY OF SEPARATING RESEARCH FROM ADMINISTRATION

Scientific jurisprudence, of course, requires impartial studies of the social results of the enactment of statutes, and this is impossible where the persons directing the studies have a stake in the result to be accomplished through the administration of the statutes in question. The best products of social research by the federal government seem to have evolved in fields where the researcher was not interested in the outcome of his investigations. There are many sharply devised studies directed toward the operation of a particular law or laws, not under the direction and control of the agency making the study. The report of the Bureau of Labor Statistics on prices as affected by the price control acts and administrative regulations[75] is a classic example of the third step of Experimental Jurisprudence in action on a wide scale. The Bureau of Labor Statistics' report on the effect of the statutes and administrative orders releasing rent controls,[76] showing the extent to which rates of rent immediately rose in typical American cities on removal of restrictions, illustrates well the manner in which social science research can illuminate the immediate results of the change in the law.

The Tennessee Valley Authority's Department of Regional Studies, Government Research Division's analysis of the administration of county governments in the region under its jurisdiction[77] is a fine instance of how scientific research and analysis can be applied to the administration of the particular activities of counties. In this one report can be found illustrations of all the first six steps of the process of scientific jurisprudence. Since the TVA itself was not involved in county administration, it was able to evaluate impartially the major aspects of this legal device in use in seven states and to assemble and study in detail significant developments in administration, together

[75] The General Maximum Price Regulation, Bull. No. 879, USDL, Bur. of Labor Statistics (1946).

[76] Report on Rent Increases in Seven Decontrolled Areas, USDL Bureau of Labor Statistics (Jan. 18, 1950).

[77] County Government and Administration in the Tennessee Valley States, TVA Dep't. of Regional Studies (July 1940); Cf. Columbia Basin Joint Investig., Local Gov't. Units, Prob. 28, USDI Bur. of Reclamation (1945).

with projected jural laws[78] evolved from carefully compiled reports. The result was a series of suggestions for improvement in the laws.[79] It is unfortunate that the recommendations made in the report have not yet been attempted by any of the counties involved.

In like fashion, the Bureau of Agricultural Economics of the Department of Agriculture has made an excellent analysis of the effect of the land acquisition policies for military and war production purposes during World War II,[80] showing in detail the expenditures, the amount of land involved and the effect upon the owners. There is an exposition of the social impact of this very important activity.

The Bureau of Labor Statistics' bulletins contain many excellent studies of the effect of the workings of statutes on particular problems; for example, workmen's compensation as a protection for seamen,[81] maximum price regulation,[82] and many others. Even though these bulletins are primarily directed at description, they often contain expositions of the operation of particular laws on particular facts which can be the basis of scientific study of law.

The Research Department of the Federal Reserve Banks also has produced a number of excellent surveys of the operation of state statutes. Two of these which should be especially noted are the *Alabama State Docks,* [83] which is a study of the operation of a statute in the state of Alabama authorizing state docking facilities in the port of Mobile. This one report shows *in extenso* the effect of that statute and the growth of the commerce of that port due to its influence. In like manner another study of the *Mississippi BAWI* plan[84] gives detailed information on the manner in which a statute of the state of Mississippi, attempting to encourage the importation of industry, actually succeeded in its purpose. It may be indicated here that studies of this sort would be vastly improved if the researchers not only had described what went on in the localities where the statute was applied but also had gone on and made a comparison of similar localities where

[78] County Gov't. and Administration in the Tennessee Valley States 27, 45, 67, 69, 77, 83, 90, 91, 93, 105, 127 ff. (July 1940).

[79] County Gov't. and Administration in the Tennessee Valley States 25, 50, 67, 78, 83, 94, 105-107 (July 1940).

[80] Acquisition and Use of Land for Military and War Production Purposes, War Records Mono. 5, USDA Bur. of Ag. Econ. (Aug. 1947).

[81] Workmen's Compensation and the Protection of Seamen, USDL Bull. No. 869 (1946).

[82] The General Maximum Price Regulations, USDL Bull. No. 879 (1946).

[83] Alabama State Docks, Fed. Res. Bank of Atlanta (1945).

[84] Hopkins, Mississippi's BAWI Plan, An Experiment in Industrial Subsidization, Fed. Res. Bank of Atlanta (Jan. 1944).

the statute was not in operation. If this had been done, the success or failure of the statute itself to accomplish its purpose would have been brought into much bolder relief, and the influence of other factors such as general prosperity caused by the war could have been largely eliminated. When the social scientists engaged in either governmental or private research are willing to devote more attention to the factor of the effect of the law itself and less to the description of uncorrelated general social phenomena, reports of this type will be vastly improved.

The success of the enumerated studies demonstrates the principle that research as to the effectiveness of the law must be separated from the direction of the executives responsible for its administration. Such research is possible within the government in a permanent organization created for that purpose which might be a branch of the Bureau of the Budget, or it could be conducted wholly outside the government by foundations such as the Brookings Institute, whose work in the field of county organization and administration, to name only one, has been outstanding.

SCIENTIFIC POLICY DETERMINATION

Scientific policy determination might also be possible by the further development of an experiment such as the Board of Economic Advisors which is part of the Executive Office of the President.[85] Since this experiment is just in its infancy, it is hard to measure its success. At the present time, unfortunately, the advisors must rely upon experts from other government bureaus of more or less doubtful independence for their basic materials. But if this organization is able to develop an expert research staff of its own and to maintain its independence of party policy, it may prove a valuable step in the direction of government based upon scientific need rather than popular clamor. At any rate, it deserves continued scrutiny by jural scientists.

THE TWO "HOOVER" COMMISSIONS

The Commissions on the Organization of the Executive Branch of the Government, usually called the Hoover Commissions, deserve more than passing mention because they illustrate in their two stages much that is good and bad in the so-called government research for policy determination. The first Hoover Commission was created in 1947 with a mandate of Congress to study the executive branch of the government and to make recommendations for changes.[86] The commission of

---

[85] 15 USCA §§ 1023, 1024 (Supp. 1949).
[86] 61 Stat. 246 (1947).

twelve members was appointed, four by the President, four by the President of the Senate and four by the Speaker of the House.[87] The enabling statute required that it be strictly nonpartisan, made up of an equal number of Republicans and Democrats.[88] It was limited in its authority to making recommendations for administrative change and was not charged with so-called policy determinations.[89] With adequate appropriations[90] and under the chairmanship of former President Herbert Hoover and Vice-Chairman Dean Acheson,[91] its work was divided among twenty-four task forces of experts who reported to the commission, which in turn made its own recommendations to Congress.[92] After two years the commission reported the desirability of multitudinous changes in the organization of the executive branch of the federal government.[93] Since these changes were based upon careful study and facts determined and weighed by experts, they were received with peons of praise alike by political scientists and the Congress.[94] One authority has called this report "the most monumental product of government research in American history."[95] Within the next four years, seventy per cent of the suggestions were enacted into laws which have done much to improve government administra-

---

[87] Id. § 3.

[88] Id. § 3 (b).

[89] Id. §§ 1 and 10.

[90] Id. § 8.

[91] Concluding Report, Com. on Org. of Ex. Br. of Govt. (May 1949).

[92] Heady, The Operation of the Mixed Commission, 43 Am. Pol. Sci. Rev. 940, 944 (1949). The task forces, in the order of their creation, were: (1) Presidency and Departmental Management; (2) Post Office; (3) Federal Supply; (4) Transportation; (5) Veterans Affairs; (6) Public Welfare; (7) Fiscal, Budgeting, and Accounting; (8) Federal-State Relationships; (9) Public Works; (10) Federal Field Offices; (11) Revolving Funds and Business Enterprises; (12) Lending Agencies; (13) Federal Personnel Management; (14) Foreign Affairs; (15) Natural Resources; (16) Regulatory Agencies; (17) Agricultural Activities; (18) Public Relations Activities; (19) Medical Services; (20) Indian Affairs; (21) Government Statistical Services; (22) Records Management; (23) National Security Organization; (24) Territories and Dependencies.

[93] There are thirty-seven of these reports consisting of the commission reports to Congress and the task reports to the commission which are printed and many more in typescript.

[94] See for example, Aikin, Koenig, Heady, Gaus, Millett, Cheever, Haviland, Pritchett, Sims, The Hoover Commission a Symposium, 43 Am. Pol. Sci. Rev. 933-1000 (1949); Finer, The Hoover Commission Reports, 64 Pol. Sci. Quar. 405, 579 (1949); Flemming, The Challenge of Government Inefficiency, 266 Annals (Nov. 1949) 25; and see President Truman's letter to Ex-President Hoover Nov. 12, 1948, 43 Am. Pol. Sci. Rev. 939 (1949).

[95] Aikin and Koenig, The Hoover Commission, 43 Am. Pol. Sci. Rev. 933 (1949).

tion and encourage economy, and many more suggested changes have been adopted by administrative action.

The experience of the second commission by the same name, which was authorized by an almost identical statute,[96] is exactly the opposite. Like its predecessor, it had Herbert Hoover for chairman, and five of the members, three Republicans and two Democrats, were members of the previous commission,[97] but there the similarity ends. It was not nonpartisan. Although it was appointed in the same manner as its predecessor, but by a Republican administration,[98] it turned out to have a Republican chairman, and seven out of its twelve members were Republicans.[99] It never elected a vice-chairman, although it was required by law to do so,[100] and like any other political body it contained a predominant majority of the dominant political party. It was also packed with conservatives and friends of big business. Another striking difference between it and its predecessor was that Congress gave it somewhat broader powers to recommend constitutional and statutory changes.[101] With this as an excuse and relying upon some committee reports to that effect, the commission took onto itself "policy-making functions."[102]

With this policy-making power, Mr. Hoover immediately took over. Probably relying on the prestige resulting from the success of the previous commission, he supervised the appointment of the task forces, and the commission went to work. With the subpoena power and authority for public hearings, which it used only in one instance,[103] and an appropriation of over two and one-half million dollars to spend,[104] it again delved into the executive branch and its related agencies. The work, like that of the previous commission, was divided among nineteen task forces, which,[105] as was the case in the previous

---

[96] 67 Stat. 142 (1953).

[97] Final Report to the Congress, Com. on Org. of Ex. Br. of Gov. (1955) v.

[98] 67 Stat. 142 § 3 (1953).

[99] See list in Report cited note 97 supra.

[100] 67 Stat. 142 § 4 (1953).

[101] Cf. 67 Stat. 142 § 9 (b) (1953) with 61 Stat. 246 § 9 (b) (1947).

[102] See Final Report supra note 97, p. 5 ff. and Congressional reports there cited.

[103] See Commissioner Holifield's Dissent, II Water Resources and Power, Com. on Org. of Govt. Rep. to Congress (1955) 10, 27.

[104] It spent a total of $2,848,534, see Final Rep. supra note 97, p. 4.

[105] Id. p. 7. The subjects were: (1) Budget and Accounting; (2) Federal Activities Competitive with Private Enterprise; (3) Committee on Business Organization of the Department of Defense; (4) Depot Utilization; (5) Intelligence Activities; (6) Legal Services and Procedure; (7) Lending, Guaranteeing, and Insurance Activities; (8) Medical Services; (9) Military Procurement; (10) Overseas Economic Operations;

commission, made numerous recommendations for changes. The commission in turn made its own recommendations, which often differed with those of its task force, and which involved many basic deviations in governmental policies over the subject matter involved. They were immediately met with storms of partisan protest that Mr. Hoover was using the prestige of the commission to express his own prejudices and not conclusions based upon sound facts discovered after impartial research.[106]

It is impossible here to analyze in detail the difference between the two reports which run into a whole book shelf of printed volumes, but this is strikingly illustrated by the parts on water resources and power. The first commission made no recommendations for change in government policies in this field but confined itself simply to recommendations for economy.[107] The second recommended complete change, such as turning the water resources over to the states and forcing federal power projects not to compete with private enterprise in their rates.[108] The final report of the second commission contains compilations of figures purporting to show that the federal projects are losing millions of dollars and are a burden on the taxpayers.[109] This part of the report looks like a power lobby presentation to Congress.[110] Nothing need be said here about this, except to point out that it is not an objective study of the facts or a fair comparison of the benefits of private versus public power. Representative Holifield, a member of the commission, in his dissent blasts it for what it really is, simply a hurried rationalization of certain views held by the so-called free-enterprise group of politicians.[111]

(11) Paperwork Management; (12) Personnel and Civil Service; (13) Personnel Problems in the Department of Defense; (14) Real Property Management; (15) Research and Development; (16) Subsistence Services; (17) Transportation; (18) Use and Disposal of Federal Surplus Property; (19) Water Resources and Power.

[106] See, for example, the strong dissent of Commissioner Holifield, supra note 103; see also summary, The Second Hoover Commission, Back to '32, Democratic Digest 25 (Sept. 1955); and see Mr. Hoover's rather lame reply, id. 25 (Nov. 1955).

[107] See Federal Business Enterprises, Com. on Org. of Govt. (March 1949) Part Four.

[108] See, I Water Resources and Power, Com. on Org. of Govt. 36 ff. (June 1955), and see the three-volume task report submitted at the same time together with Rep. Holifield's remarks infra note 111.

[109] Id. p. 101 to 107.

[110] See, II id. Dissent of Commissioner Holifield, 64 ff.

[111] See, II id., 10 ff. Even Commissioner Farley, a well known conservative Democrat, could not stomach the extreme private power slant of the majority, see, II id. 7 ff. In like fashion the report on Federal Medical Services, id. (Feb. 1955) and its task report take the American Medical Association line, which is to get government

Without discussing the reports or their merits further, it is significant that these two commissions, created under almost identical laws with the same chairman and with five out of twelve of the same commissioners, showed results in the first case which were almost unanimously hailed as excellent, and in the second, denounced alike by its own members and by a large segment of the public. These two reports and the procedures underlying them illustrate the difference between the scientific approach and a politically motivated attempt to solve problems of government. The first commission was nonpartisan by law, its membership carefully distributed to represent all factions. It confined itself to recommendations based upon carefully collected facts and did not attempt to enact private prejudices under the guise of policy. The second was packed with a majority of the dominant political party and a huge majority of conservatives representing one point of view. It did not confine its recommendations to the evidence but freely chose its "facts" to fit political conclusions and boldly recommended its prejudices as policy.

No matter how "good" their values or how sincere their beliefs, the recommendations of Mr. Hoover and his colleagues on the second commission based on their political conclusions probably will go a long way toward setting back the program of scientific governmental investigations.

The first report was a triumph for the methods of Experimental Jurisprudence, the second a tragedy of substituting personal "values" for scientifically determined facts.

CONCLUSION

Viewed as a whole, this brief summary would tend to indicate that although the United States government spends fantastic sums for research, it will be the rare exception rather than the rule to find an instance where its lawmaking follows the lines of the theories of Experimental Jurisprudence; but the exceptions and the impact of such research indicate that scientific lawmaking in the federal government is on the increase.

---

out of all medical services, again with no supporting facts as to comparative services of government and private medicine. See again Commissioner Holifield's dissent id. 73 ff.

CHAPTER VIII

The Development of Scientific Jural Methods and Research Institutions

The cure for the lag between science and law and the backwardness of our legal system, as discussed in Chapters V and VII, seems to lie in two fields of activities. There is an immediate necessity for more widespread and extensive cooperative research in which lawyers and scientists team together to collect and apply scientific discoveries to the improvement of the legal system. Second, there is an immediate need for increased education to spread the results of current and completed studies and to pass on the newly developed material to places where it could do the most good to improve the structure of our legal system.

These two steps must be undertaken before there can be any hope that comprehensive government machinery will be set up to transpose scientific technique into the legal procedures. Although these two activities are simultaneous and interacting and should be undertaken together, for the purpose of convenient discussion, some of the problems of developing research will be discussed in this chapter. The necessary changes which must be taken to make it possible to apply the results to the enlightenment of the educational system are postponed to a later time.

As previously indicated, experimental methods and effective research agencies are now operating in the fields of public health, traffic control, crime detection and police methods and educational administrative methods, among others; but little is being done in the last to affect the legal system. Research to carry science into war effort both on its physical and psychological sides has also received tremendous impetus since the last war in the fields covered by atomic energy, operations research,[1] military government and attitude of army personnel.[2] Although the development of these experiments has had only slight effect on education, the success of experimental methods in changing the administration of the law in fields where they have been attempted shows that the time is ripe to move boldly into others which more intimately affect the ordinary processes of government and law.

SIMPLE PROBLEMS THE KEY

If we are to learn anything from the advancement of scientific methods, it seems clear that research to establish an experimental science of law must begin with the isolation of simple problems arising in the field of law enforcement and administration. The scientific method requires attention to the most elementary detail. For example, Galileo started with the motion of the pendulum and the dropping of shot to determine his laws of motion and acceleration, and Newton progressed from the apple to the heavenly bodies. In like fashion, traffic engineers started with observance of movements at particular corners, the effect of specific stop lights and the reaction of drivers and pedestrians on individual streets. From these details there has been a steady progress to the statewide freeway and area planning. Police science moved from individual smudges to the present great fingerprinting system of the FBI, or from scratches on bullets to our present knowledge of ballistics. Similarly, jural science will probably prove most fruitful if research is begun with simple problems, such as auto theft as set out in Hall's *Theft, Law and Society*.[3] Other fruitful studies might be made of the veracity and usefulness of witnesses and juries in particular cases, such as prosecution of alcohol violation and the like, the usefulness of rules of evidence in solving problems of paternity of children, the efficiency of cigarette licensing statutes to prevent sale to minors and the effectiveness of a single legal device such as juvenile court.[4] The manner in which the solutions of problems of this sort are now attempted and the efficiency of the legal means, if used as a basis of study, should start one on the road to discovery of jural laws which will be useful in creating new methods for the practice of law.

---

[1] Salow, Operations Research, 43 Fortune 105 (April 1951); Morse and Kimball, Methods of Operations Research (1950).

[2] Stouffer, Lamsdaine and others, The American Soldier, in four volumes (1949-50).

[3] Chapter VI (1935).

[4] Glueck, One Thousand Juvenile Delinquents (1939), while not directed at the court, throws much light on methods such a study might use. Cf. also Tappan, Delinquent Girls in Court (1947).

ADAPTING SCIENTIFIC DISCOVERIES TO JURAL PROBLEMS

This indicates that as legal or other education for social control begins to teach experimental methods, there will have to be set up more research units to design experiments and to learn how they can be applied to problems of law enforcement. Policy determination in its broader aspects, which is intriguing, is now too far off even to be considered.

As suggested in Chapter V, one of the first problems to be encountered in such a program will be the discovery of the ways in which modern scientific knowledge can be helpful in the practical solution of the problems to be examined. It so happens that current scientific information available from studies and researches of present workers in the field of physical and social science is not now oriented to the solution of legal problems.

Pertinent data must be found, and when it is discovered new techniques will have to be devised, received and oriented to use the data to solve legal problems. This will require great originality and imagination on the part of the researchers. At a glance one can see that the fields of science which may be applied to any particular problem are so great, so complicated by scientific techniques and so scattered throughout the areas in which they may be available that the individual worker in any one area alone cannot hope to be successful in exposing them. For example, a recent federal budget[5] shows that the Federal Bureau of Investigation uses over fifty high-grade technical specialists and as many assistant technicians in its criminal and scientific laboratory, covering professions including physicist, chemist, metalurgist, petrographer, spectrologist, dermatologist, agronomist and many others, all directing their cooperative efforts to the identification of criminals. Similar teamwork will be necessary in other fields. People with present legal training may be able to help compile the questions which need to be answered,[6] but they will have to have cooperation from many other specialists to determine the direction which the research should take to solve a problem and further to produce the pertinent materials now available to be applied to such a solution.

[5] The Budget of the United States 705 (1951-52); Id. Appendix, 281. Personnel and Services of the FBI Laboratory, FBI Law Enforcement Bulletin (Oct. 1947).

[6] See Lovinger, Jurimetrics, 33 Minn. L. Rev. 455, 484 (1949) for some interesting suggestions; and for methods of finding answers, see Morse and Kimball, Operations Research (1951).

167

COOPERATIVE RESEARCH

The task of getting cooperation from physical and social scientists will not be easy because the demands of scientific search for jural laws will cut across the present classification of the sciences themselves, will upset the bureaucracy of educational and research institutions as now organized and will demand a re-orientation of thinking of the individual workers. Many of our current social scientists and physical scientists, for these reasons, will prove more of a detriment than a help to the development of Experimental Jurisprudence methods. The initial objections of the leaders of the profession and the practitioners of medicine to new and scientific methods in that field are illustrative of the attitude that may be expected from lawyers and social scientists toward anyone rash enough to attempt the organization of institutions of Experimental Jurisprudence. The task, however, is not hopeless. The complete triumph of scientific methods in the fields of medical practice and medical teaching are indicative of the possibilities for success of similar methods in the more complicated field of jural experimentation.

The diverse nature of the scientific data to be collected and the wide areas of complicated legal procedures to which it is to be applied will require different combinations of talent, depending upon the nature of the problems being studied. The solution of problems involving the facts of parentage may require a preponderance of the use of medical data to be integrated with legal procedure. The reform of jury methods will have to lean heavily on experimental psychology. The studies of the Gluecks, Tappan and others demand the cooperation of doctors, social workers, anthropologists, criminologists, statisticians and lawyers. At the outset, then, any research organization will need to be flexible and will require cooperation of various combinations of experts in relationships to be controlled by the nature of the data relevant to the problems studied.

PERSUADING THE LAWYERS

The development of experimental methods and experimental education in the use of scientific methods and materials, as indicated in Chapter V, will be further handicapped by the necessity of proving to the legal expert what seems obvious to the scientist. This is illustrated by such situations as the Chaplin case,[7] in which judges upheld the jury in rejecting scientific proof of paternity in spite of

[7] Berry v. Chaplin, (Cal. App. 1946) 169 Pac. (2d) 442.

the fact that, although the present scientific method of determining paternity has never proved to be wrong,[8] no experimental proof whatsoever exists as to the correctness of jury votes. The judges relied solely on the social inertia and previous cases. In like fashion, although lie detectors have been scientifically proved to be correct in over seventy-five per cent of all controlled experiments,[9] courts stubbornly refuse to admit their use to replace similar jury findings of facts,[10] for the accuracy of which there is no scientific proof.

This state of mind is also shown by the fact that the courts and the legal profession are constantly attacking arbitration and administrative procedures of all kinds because they are not like courts. Although the court has nothing of scientific nature to support it other than sheer survival and professional prejudice, the feeling that judicial methods are the best means of resolving disputes still exists even where many administrative practices have been adopted to solve problems in areas where court procedures have failed utterly,[11] and where many of the current administrative procedures are based upon scientific fact-finding.[12]

One of the earliest problems of an experimental approach to jural science will be the necessity of studying and demonstrating the relative value of these new methods of fact-finding as compared with older "tried and true" judicial schemes. When a comparative test is made of the two methods, the usefulness of scientific organizations for the solution of specific problems will appear to all but the most stubborn legal minds which rely simply on blind precedent. The data and experience collected from such experimental studies of the efficiency of problem-solving legal devices will gradually emerge in the form of jural laws which can be collected and transposed into teachable form in texts, laboratory problems, research devices and the like which will make lawyers and law students conscious of the problems involved and

---

[8] Dudley, Weight to be Given Blood Test Evidence in Paternity Proceedings, 4 Wash. and Lee L. Rev. 199, 201 (1947), and numerous authorities there cited.

[9] Inbau, The Lie Detector, 26 B. U. L. Rev. 265, 268 (1946).

[10] Id. 270.

[11] For example, labor dispute, see Frankfurter and Green, The Labor Injunction (1930); valuation of utilities, Beutel, Due Process in the Valuation of Utilities, 13 Minn. L. Rev. 409, 434 (1929), and see Mr. Justice Black's dissent, in McCarl v. Indianapolis Water Co., 302 U.S. 419, 423 (1938); and the Fellow Servant Rule.

[12] The administration of the Pure Food and Drug Act is a good example in point. Although almost all of its "facts" are of highly scientific and chemical nature, it is given no special consideration in the Administration Procedure Act, 60 Stat. 237 (1946), wherein the American Bar Association succeeded in getting Congress to pass a bill imposing judicial standards on administrative agencies.

of new methods of solution. Then this new scientific material can be used to build legal methods abreast of current scientific advancement. If this stage of research and teaching can be brought to the law schools, the next generation of the bar will not be as prejudiced against innovations of all kinds as are its present leaders but will be willing to cooperate in research and innovation.

Any hope that scientific research may eventually change the direction and emphasis of legal education lies very far in the future. Such considerations in themselves pose new problems which will need examination far beyond the scope of a preliminary discussion such as this; but it can be noted here that fundamental changes in instructional methods may be predicted.

GROUPS OF PROBLEMS TO WHICH PRESENT DATA MAY BE APPLIED

When the individual problems for study have been isolated and attempts have been made to study them, they will probably fall into classifications which make possible the simultaneous grouping and solution of problems under research institutions composed of experts in the particular category into which the problems can be conveniently gathered. Just what the classifications should be and what should be the nature of the subject matter to which teams of scientists and lawyers working in such institutions should devote their attention will themselves be matters to be determined by experiment. However, a number of tentative groupings might be attempted at this time. Such combinations might prove useful as follows:

Problems of proof involving research to improve, enlarge and completely revise our present fact-finding machinery both in courts and administrative bodies certainly could form one central classification around which teams of expert workers could be collected.

Criminal administration, including criminal courts, penal institutions, systems of parole[13] and crime prevention certainly offer another category where teams of scientists working together could produce worthwhile results. Here the psychologists, psychiatrists and doctors, working in cooperation with prison executives, law enforcement officers, courts and parole supervisors, could greatly advance the science of criminology. The work of the Gluecks and many others in this field and the suggestions contained in their writings show the possibility for organizing such research units.

---

[13] See Ohlin, Selection for Parole (1951) and authorities there cited p. 131 ff.; Wechsler, The Challenge of a Model Penal Code 65 Har. L. Rev. 1097 (1952).

170

Legislative methods, including a study of the present antiquated machinery by which the legislatures grind out laws, an examination of the records, the research, the hearing process and the effect of pressure groups and other organizations upon the end product of the legislature, its laws, offer another fruitful field. Such groups might devote their attention to the efficiency of laws creating various types of legislative machinery, the pertinence of popular methods of election, initiative, referendum and recall and the affect of these particular devices upon problems of social control. Here a great amount of cooperative effort on the part of political scientists, public opinion experts and lawyers might develop information that would make it possible for us to correct some of the defects that are so obviously present in the Congress and the state legislatures.

City planning beyond traffic control, which is already an experimental science, area development and zoning offer a growing field for cooperative research by city officials, social workers, engineers, architects and professional city planners.[14] State[15] and national planning receive much attention, but the scientific techniques are not sufficiently developed to assure a proper engineering approach to the problems.

Reorganization of building codes and laws pertaining to the structure, materials and operations of buildings offers a broad field for cooperation of scientists. Here the architect, engineer, lawyer, physicist and chemist, together with the sociologist and social worker, could combine their talents to study and reorganize a host of laws closely touching human activity.

Weights, measures and standards prescribed by law offer a virgin area for research as illustrated by the preliminary investigation set out in Chapter IX. Most of these laws were passed before modern developments and before national organizations of manufacturers began to set standards for their members. It would be possible for lawyers, scientists and engineers to cooperate with committees of trade societies and government to overhaul completely the laws in this field for the benefit of consumers, producers and law-enforcement officials.

Labor relations laboratories, where the success of numerous devices now used in solving the problems of friction in the field of relationships between employee and employer, a field in which the current

---

[14] For an example of what can be done in these fields, see A Proposed Housing Ordinance Regulating Supplied Facilities, Maintenance and Occupation of Dwelling Units, by the Committee on Hygiene of Housing of the American Pub. Health Assn. See also Bauer, Clients for Housing, Progressive Architecture p. 61 ff. (May 1952).

[15] For an attempt along these lines, see Schulz, Conservation Law and Administration (1953).

legal devices have been constantly stretched to the breaking point, offer another opportunity for endless study and experiment. Lawyers, administrators, economists and many types of engineers would have to cooperate in such an effort.

Social relief problems very easily fall into a classification where lawyers, social workers, psychologists, doctors, biostatisticians and other scientists could cooperate to solve problems in the application of laws and other devices to legal aid, care of the sick, aged, mentally deficient and incompetent. Here the operation of laws for institutionalization, sterilization and many other legally approved devices offer a field of operation, study and research which could be most fruitful not only to legal science but to social advancement and control as well. Public health administration, which already has grown into separate institutes, would be glad to cooperate.

It would be impossible to begin now to outline in detail the techniques, organizations and devices necessary to create such institutions. The organization of such institutes will have to wait further study and cooperation of people attempting to solve particular problems; however, the time is now ripe to begin consideration of the creation of such research organizations. An indication of the type of problems which they will be expected to solve will go a long way toward pointing out the direction which their organization, study and attention should take. These will be discussed in later chapters.

CREATION OF TECHNIQUES AND EXPERIMENTAL METHODS

After research groups have collected information from other fields and have begun to apply it to jural problems, the second great task will be the creation of the techniques and methods of an experimental jural science itself. In Chapter II a tentative general theory of the directions such inquiry should take, as indicated by the analogy of the scientific method in other fields, has been outlined. Particular methods and techniques will have to be developed to fit the problems to be studied. The necessary experimental design must be accommodated to the nature of the subject matter studied.

A few principles seem to be emerging already. First, success appears to be indicated if simple problems are the basis of starting experiments. Foreign policy, world peace, general constitutional revision, labor relations in general, capitalism versus socialism, democracy versus dictatorship and all similar generalities and grandiose plans which so intrigue the theoretical policymaker will have to be omitted for the present because they involve a maze of theories and speculations which have no tangible foundation in the present status of social science.

When the attention of the researchers is devoted to very simple rules of law and their effect on society, it will be discovered that answers to pertinent questions and the experimental designs[16] necessary to reach such answers will command the combined attention of experts from many fields. Some of the indicated organizations and the direction which research should take are set out in detail in a later chapter.

One illustration here will suffice.

One of the most intriguing problems for sociologists, law enforcement agencies and the public in general has been juvenile delinquency; but this subject is far too general to yield to scientific treatment. If one cares to examine it, he is immediately met with the question, "Delinquent as to what? Filial obedience? School rules? Social conduct? Law-breaking? Or general hoodlumism?" Even if one chooses one of these subjects, he is led into all kinds of speculation about home environment, slum districts versus the other side of the tracks, psychological equality, physical and mental hazards, religion and social mores. Much pious talk and even conferences result, but at the end of general inquiries nothing more is known or done than at the outset.

When one begins to examine the characteristics of particular delinquents so defined because of apprehension for violation of specific statutes, one may be able to expose some useful information and perhaps to predict that young persons possessing particular characteristics of personality, physique and environment are likely to become delinquent in the defined sense.[17] But still there is little progress toward correcting the conditions which cause and fail to prevent that particular type of delinquency.

On the other hand, if a detailed study is made of legal devices used to correct or prevent delinquency, such as the juvenile court[18] or laws prohibiting sale of cigarettes, liquor or narcotics to minors, concrete information about the effectiveness of a particular device to prevent specific evils emerges in a form which makes possible the advocacy of a sensible change of the law as the result of an experimental study.

The beginnings of such work by Tappan and the Gluecks have already been mentioned, and an outline of an experimental study of the sale of cigarettes to minors will be set out in Chapter IX.

[16] Cf. Chapin, Experimental Design in Sociological Research (1947); Young, Scientific Social Surveys and Research (1949).
[17] Glueck, Unraveling Juvenile Delinquency 257 ff. (1950).
[18] Tappan, Delinquent Girls in Court (1947).

These studies of what appear to be simple legal devices, when examined in detail, will prove to be extremely complicated projects involving the use of experts and materials from many fields of science but promising tangible results within the grasp of experimental methods.

DETAILED ATTENTION TO ACTUAL SOCIAL FACTS

When a problem has been chosen, there must be careful collection of the basic factual data. Mere speculation or casual observation will not suffice. The simplest problem becomes extremely complicated when one attempts to get the basic information. Any one of a thousand simple statutes might be taken as an illustration, but as a matter of convenience let us choose for example the rather elemental problem from the field of city planning, the planting of shade trees along city streets. This seems to be a civic habit all over the country, and at first blush one would not expect it to be regulated by law.

Any person who has traveled in the great plains area of the United States is struck by the absence of natural trees and also by the abundance of shade trees lining the streets of towns and cities. The problem of obtaining trees along the streets was considered of such importance that every state in the area has a statute covering the subject.[19] No two are identical, and various public authorities are delegated the supervision of the problem with different powers, among which are payment of bounties for planting trees,[20] power to plant,[21] power to regulate or supervise,[22] to tax[23] and to rebate taxes,[24] authori-

---

[19] Ill. Ann. Stat. c. 24, § 23-9, c. 34, § 24 (6th), c. 127, § 40-11 (Smith-Hurd, 1942); Ind. Stat. Ann. § 11915 (11) (Baldwin, 1934); Iowa Code §§ 416.134, 420.57 (1946); Kans. Gen. Stat. §§ 12-1611 (a), (c), 13-429, 14-404, 15-428 (1935); Minn. Stat. § 448.55 (1947); Mo. Rev. Stat. §§ 6952, 7172 (1943); Neb. Rev. Stat. §§ 18-801 to 807 (1943); N.Dak. Rev. Code §§ 40-2408, 40-3201 (1943); Okla. Stat. Tit. 11, §§ 7,644, 660, 1004 (1936); S. Dak. Code § 45.0201 (99) (1939); Tex. Civ. Stat. Art. 1015 (32) (Vernon, 1942).

[20] N. Dak. Rev. Code § 4-2102 (1943).

[21] Ill. Ann. Stat. § 23-9 (Smith-Hurd, 1942); Ind. Stat. Ann. § 11917 (Baldwin, 1934); Iowa Code § 420-57 (1946); Kansas Gen. Stat. § 12-1611 a (1935); Minn. Stat. §§ 448.56 (3), (4) (1947); Neb. Rev. Stat. § 18-801 (1943; N. Dak. Rev. Code § 40-3201 (1943); Okla. Stat. Tit. 11, § 644 (1936).

[22] Kans. Gen. Stat. §§ 13-429, 15-428 (1935); Minn. Stat. § 448.51 (2) (1947); Mo. Rev. Stat. §§ 6952, 7172 (1943); Okla. Stat. Tit. 11, § 7 (1936); S. Dak. Code § 45.0201 (99) (1939); Tex. Civ. Stat. Art. 1015 (Vernon, 1942).

[23] Iowa Code § 416-138 (1946); Kan. Gen. Stat. §§ 12-1611c, 14-404 (1935); Minn. Stat. §§ 448.36 (4), (5) (1947); Neb. Rev. Stat. § 18-802 (1943); N. Dak. Rev. Code § 40-2408 (1943).

[24] Neb. Rev. Stat. § 18-805 (1943); N. Dak. Rev. Code §§ 4-2101 ff. (1943).

ty to enforce criminal penalities for destroying trees[25] and various combinations thereof.

Here is a line of comparative law which, when studied, should yield much information upon the usefulness and efficiency of the legal devices involved in the solution of this simple problem.

A complete study would require an examination of the operation of the statutes in each state and a comparison of results, but it will at once appear that the magnitude of the task is beyond the reach of any but the most heavily endowed research. A preliminary examination in the form of a pilot study of the statute of a single state therefore seemed advisable.

As a matter of convenience the Nebraska statute, which was passed in 1871 and reads as follows, was chosen:[26]

> *18-801. Trees; planting; duty of city.* The corporate authorities of cities and villages of the state of Nebraska shall cause shade trees to be planted along the streets thereof.
> *18-802. Trees; planting; tax.* For such purpose a tax of not less than one dollar, nor more than five dollars, in addition to all other taxes, shall be levied upon each lot adjacent to which trees are to be planted as aforesaid and collected as other taxes.
> *18-803. Trees; planting; number.* Trees shall be annually planted when practicable on each side of one-fourth of the streets in each city and village in the state of Nebraska, until all shall have shade trees along them not more than twenty feet apart.
> *18-804. Trees; planting; regulations.* The corporate authorities aforesaid shall provide, by ordinance, the distance from the side of the street that trees shall be planted, and the size thereof.
> *18-805. Trees; planting by landowner; exemption from tax.* The owner of any lot or lots may plant trees adjacent thereto where ordered in the manner provided in sections 18-803 and 18-804, and, on making proof thereof by affidavit to the collector, he shall be exempt from the payment of the tax authorized by section 18-802.
> *18-807. Trees; planting; business lots excepted.* Sections 18-801 to 18-806 shall not apply to any person that is an occupant of any business lot, without his consent.

A proper determination of the effectiveness of this statute would require, among others, the discovery of the following facts:

---

[25] Ind. Stat. Ann. § 2503 (Baldwin, 1934); Neb. Rev. Stat. § 18-806 (1943).
[26] Neb. Rev. Stat. (1943).

(1) The extent to which corporate authorities in the cities and towns of the state have taken action in accordance with the statutes.
  (a) Ordinances, if any covering intervals between trees and distances from street.
  (b) Executive action under the statute covering the same area.
  (c) Extent to which taxes have been levied for the purpose.
  (d) Exemption from taxes, if any, because of tree planting by the owner.
(2) The extent to which trees have been planted, and whether at the intervals prescribed by the statute.

A full check of the factors of (1) above would require an examination of the ordinances of all cities and towns in the state, a check of all the tax rolls and interviews with the officials involved to find out how they are enforcing the statutes. It would also be necessary to examine old records to find out how officials have acted toward this statute in the past.

The answers to the second problem, (2), would require a census of shade trees along streets of the cities and villages to see what effect, if any, the statute had on the actual number and location of trees. This latter, of course, would require sampling techniques, since the counting of all trees would involve a tremendous expense. The botanical information as to the nature of a "shade tree" would have to be assembled, the scientific advisability of the twenty-foot interval would have to be studied; and if it were studied, the optimum interval would probably be found to differ depending upon the species of tree chosen for planting.

Thus a research team for this simple problem should include persons with knowledge of or some expertness in sampling, statistics, law and tree culture.

It may also appear that the operation of the statute is infringed by city zoning ordinances or federal regulations or publications, all of which will have to be investigated.

When this myriad of facts and regulations is assembled, then one will be in a position to draw conclusions as to the effectiveness of this simple law in Nebraska, and from there to make comparisons of some aspects of enforcement in other states from which jural laws on the working of such regulatory statutes might tentatively be set up.

With this information at hand, recommendations for change could be made; and if complete research of all the state statutes disclosed the laws like the one recommended had been adopted elsewhere, such laws could be studied to test further the validity of the tentative jural laws and the suggested remedial statutes.

Thus the experimental study of even the simplest law develops into a large but not impossible task.

A very inadequate preliminary investigation of the operation of this Nebraska statute has been attempted, so it might be worth while to digress for a moment to see what results might be expected from a complete study.

On inquiry, the authorities responsible for the records in six cities scattered over the state disclosed no knowledge of the statute and no attempt to comply therewith. No ordinances complying with Section 18-804 specifying distance from the street were disclosed.

In the city of Lincoln, which has a particularly beautiful stand of shade trees, there was a city ordinance collateral to and contradicting the state statute, prohibiting planting except on written permit by the Superintendent of Parks.[27] Although the ordinance prescribes that the city council may make further rules, the Superintendent of Parks has established a set of rules for intervals in feet for planting the following trees: American elm, forty-five to fifty feet; English moline elm, thirty to thirty-five feet; honey locust and pin oak, forty to forty-five feet; linden, thirty to thirty-five feet; Norway maple and hackberry, thirty-five to forty feet; Chinese elm and cottonwood are prohibited. It should be noted that none of these intervals correspond with those required by the state statute.

That there is little scientific basis for either set of intervals is shown by the fact that the federal Department of Agriculture bulle-

---

[27] City of Lincoln Ordinance 3850 (1941).

30-601, *Planting, Removal and Destruction of Trees and Shrubbery.* It shall be unlawful for any person either for himself or for another to plant, remove, or destroy, or cause to be planted, removed or destroyed, any tree or shrubbery in or on any street, parkway, or publicway within the city without first having obtained a wriitten permit to do so from the Superintendent of Parks.

That every applicant for permit shall at the time of making application agree in writing to in all ways save the City harmless and to protect the City and the public at all times in connection with said planting, removal or destruction of trees or shrubbery.

That the provisions of this section shall be applicable to any and all persons, in any manner engaged in such operations.

That the City Council may, by resolution, establish requirements, rules, and regulations other than and in addition to those set forth herein and governing operations herein permitted.

This ordinance was probably passed under authority of Neb. Rev. Stat. § 15-201 (1943).

tin[28] on the subject makes the following recommendations. "A common practice is to set trees 35 feet apart. If it were practicable to remove one half of the trees at the proper time, this would be a good distance, but for most trees 50 feet is close enough; for the larger growing trees 60 to 70 feet would be better."

A preliminary examination of books on forestry and tree planting yields no scientific information on the subject either of interval or distance from the street or sidewalk. And it is doubtful if one can be determined even for the same type of tree in the varying conditions of pavement, etc., to be found even in a single city or town.

An examination of the actual condition of the location and interval of the trees would be even more revealing. Such a study was made in Lincoln. Here again it was impossible to check each tree on each of the thousands of blocks in a city of one hundred thousand inhabitants, but since the streets in that city parallel section lines, a block at the corner of each section was examined. This rough sampling disclosed that there was no complete uniformity, even within many blocks, of the interval or distance from the street, while in many residential blocks in the "poorer" part of the city, no trees at all were planted. In the older areas, especially close to the site of the old capitol, there were indications that the trees planted before 1900 complied with the statute as to the interval of twenty feet, positions tending to smaller intervals, but many other blocks in the vicinity seemed to indicate that trees had been planted two or three to each fifty-foot lot. In the newer parts of the city, the intervals of planting indicated some compliance with the park commissioner's rules and therefore violation of the state statute. The distance from the curb was often uniform within blocks, but a careful check by experts on the variety of trees involved would have to be made to determine whether or not even the park commissioner's regulations are being followed.

The tax rolls disclosed no variations in taxes for tree planting as allowed by the statute.

A preliminary survey, then, indicates that a complete study supported by proper statistical material might reveal the following:

(1) Insofar as the statute prescribes exact intervals, it was almost completely useless, suggesting the possible jural law, to be verified in other fields, that exact details in regulatory statutes cannot be enforced but should be left to administrative discretion. So far as tree planting is concerned, this could be verified by

---

[28] U.S. Dept. of Ag. Farmers Bull. No. 1209, Planting and Care of Street Trees 9, 10 (1937 rev.).

a study of the amendment[29] and later repeal[30] of a Washington statute[31] also prescribing exact measurement and the effect of similar current North[32] and South Dakota[33] statutes.

(2) The facts found here seem to indicate that statutes regulating common phenomena are likely to be covered by unnecessary, overlapping and contradictory state, city and federal laws and administrative actions.

(3) This statute may be entirely without present effect and perhaps never need to have been passed. This could be checked by comparing the condition of tree planting in states, if any, where there are no tree-planting statutes. If there are no such states, then like cities and towns where the authorities either never heard of or ignored the statutes could be compared with those where there was some effort at compliance. So also the condition of trees in like geographical areas where different types of statutes exist could be compared. If no difference appeared in the condition of the shade trees under different laws in similar types of areas, then one might easily conclude that this was a field where personal pride made the interference by the legal authorities unnecessary.

(4) On the other hand, if differences did appear, the utility or disability of city planning in this area could be demonstrated. So also there could be a comparative evaluation of the effectiveness of various types of enforcement devices.

(5) With this data available, the experts would be ready to recommend amendment or complete repeal of the state statutes.

This brief summary indicates that complicated factual situations are bound to appear even in the simplest problems, and the complication will probably be found to increase in proportion as the law studied covers broader fields.

STATISTICAL DATA THE BASIS OF FACTUAL CONCLUSIONS

It is also clear even from this simple illustration that, as in other sciences, mathematics, here largely in the form of social statistics, will play an important part. Since large numbers of individuals subject to legal action are the objective facts at which almost all laws are directed, the statistical compilation and arrangement of individual data will

[29] Wash. Laws c. 242, p. 370 (1927).
[30] Wash. Laws c. 53, p. 192 (1937).
[31] Wash. Laws c. 118, §§ 1, 2, pp. 221-2 (1930).
[32] N. Dak. Rev. Code § 4-2102 (1943).
[33] S. Dak. Code § 4.1302 (1939).

constitute the "facts" upon which the conclusions are ultimately based. The work of the Johns Hopkins Institute and the results of myriads of traffic studies show conclusively that under mass statistical treatment the effect of individual variations is completely submerged. The individualization of the law to fit particular people is a problem of administration and not of scientific generalization. However, the success of such administrative devices as may be created for these purposes is not necessarily beyond the ken of Experimental Jurisprudence. As indicated above, though many other disciplines may play a part determined by the nature of the subject matter studied, statistics certainly will have a place in the solution of almost every problem. Although new statistical methods will undoubtedly appear with the development of Experimental Jurisprudence, it is certain that enough progress has been made in the social application of this science to offer an adequate working tool for the beginning efforts of the experimental jurist.

MEASURING DEVICES

One of the greatest objections to experimental social science has been that accurate measuring devices are not available. While it is to a large extent true that measuring devices need to be developed in almost every field of social science, these tools are much further advanced than is usually believed, and although they appear to be of a different nature, they serve a purpose similar to that which they have in physical sciences.

Although it is elemental to the experts in their own fields, many people do not seem to realize that the primary purpose of measurement is one of comparison. With this in mind, the following material is offered simply to open up the possibilities of the subject of measurement necessary in Experimental Jurisprudence. It is not intended either as a learned discussion or as an exhaustive catalog of the devices for measurement now available.

Measurement, as indicated above, is simply a device for comparing one thing or phenomenon with another. The yard, for example, is said to have evolved from the length of the king's arm to a stick of thirty-six inches. The process of measurement of distance was simply a comparison of the unit, the arm or stick, with the object to be measured. As science advanced, it became easily recognized that the arm or stick varied under different conditions, such as temperature. In like manner, measuring weight is simply comparing or balancing one heavy object against another. The fact that the standard may change due to atmospheric density, pressure and other conditions may or may not be important, depending upon the nature of the object measured.

180

The most important requirement is that the unit of measurement be relevant to the purpose for which the measurement is devised.

Similarly, in social science one culture itself may be used to measure another. The operation of a law in one city or other governmental unit may be the standard against which success or failure of a corresponding law elsewhere may be measured.

The fact that the unit used for the basic comparison may itself be constantly changing is not fatal to its usefulness as a measuring device. For example, in the fields of social activity where law applies, the problem is one of measuring mass reactions rather than of applying a ruler with pinpoint accuracy to individual situations. Many of the measuring problems will be of a nature of comparison of one group activity against another. For example, where the civil rights acts require that negroes be given equal service with whites in restaurants,[34] the effectiveness of the law can be measured by comparing the reactions of the restaurant service personnel to chosen groups of negroes and whites demanding equal service.

A similar method has been found to be very fruitful in the matching techniques used in studies of juvenile delinquency by the Gluecks and others.[35] Here groups of young people are carefully examined by all available devices of education, medicine, psychology and other sciences. Then individuals and groups are matched one against the other, and one group is given a particular treatment while the other is not. In this way the effectiveness of the treatment is measured by comparing the record of performance of the control with that of the tested group. Powers and White have described this and other measuring devices used in a recent study of juvenile delinquency.[36] All of these methods are available, where pertinent, to the experimental jurist.

Again in the field of the study of traffic law, as explained in Chapter VI, where measuring devices have been highly developed, they are in the nature of graphs showing traffic flow, accident frequency charts, average speeds and other devices to take into account such items as direction, speed and volume of mass movements. Similar ingenious schemes have been or can be developed in other fields. The measurement of public opinion, intelligence tests, consumer demands, intensity and frequency of listening to the radio and other advertising schemes and comparative intensity of feelings of groups as developed in

---

[34] Neb. Rev. Stat. §§ 20-101, 102 (1943).

[35] See Glueck, Unraveling Juvenile Delinquency c. 4-7 (1950), and authorities there cited.

[36] Powers & White, An Experiment in the Prevention of Delinquency (1951).

sociometry[37] are all illustrations of the nature of measuring devices which can be used. It should also be kept in mind that practically all of the divisions of statistics in their present and future development will find immediate application in this field.

Any attempt at determining the effectiveness of rules of law will, of course, require a measurement of individual and mass reactions to the law. For a long time it has been believed that the factors involved in the impact of a rule of law upon its subjects are so numerous as to make measurement impossible. Any such doubts should be permanently put to rest by the recent *Studies in Social Psychology in World War II.*[38] Here are collected some of the results of the operations of the Research Branch, Information and Educational Division of the United States Army. These volumes show that the comparatively small team of psychologists, other research scientists and laymen, working sometimes under the most adverse conditions and limitations, were able to measure not only intelligence, emotional and educational conditions but also the volume and intensity of the soldiers' reactions to army life, regulations, their officers and noncoms, battle conditions and a myriad of other results of the application of military "laws." Among others, they were able through research to create the point system for discharge at the end of the war,[39] to lay the basis for the G. I. Bill of Rights[40] with its vast system of subsidized education for veterans and to guide and predict the success of these and other regulations governing the conduct of soldiers during and after the war.

Out of these great experiments there has emerged a vast amount of information in the field of social psychology upon the techniques of measurement and prediction[41] which is spoiling to be used on problems of civilian law enforcement.

The desire for minute accuracy in measurement, sometimes said to stand in the way of social science, is largely a fetish which has been developed from certain aspects of physics, chemistry and machine operation. But even in these fields the chronometer that measures

---

[37] For example, see Moren and Jennings, Sociometric Measurements of Social Configurations (1945); see also the Journal of Sociometry, now in its ninth volume; Chapin, Experimental Design in Sociological Research c. 6 ff. (1947).

[38] Stouffer and others, in four volumes (1949-50).

[39] Stouffer, 2 Studies, supra c. 11 (1949).

[40] Cottrell and Stouffer, 2 Studies, supra c. 13 (1949); Clausen, 4 Studies, supra c. 15 & 16 (1950).

[41] Stouffer, Guttman, Schuman, Lazarsfeld, Star and Clausman, 4 Studies supra (1950); see also Feitzer, Katz and others, Research Methods in the Behavorial Sciences (1953).

to a millionth of an inch is in fact a crude device if one is attempting to deal with atoms and electrons. So even in physics itself where measurement is most minute, when we consider the nature of physical matter, this so-called accuracy becomes only a gross estimate. The same principle will apply with even greater force to measuring social activity under laws.

Even in cases where the individual reactions to social conditions are involved, gross measuring devices have proved experimentally effective. An example of the value of crude measurement in this field is shown by the tables used in studying the possibility of predicting parole violations in the state of Illinois.[42] Although it is clear that parole violations can vary in all degrees from a mere routine failure to report to the commission to a most heinous crime, "the most widely used measure of success or failure on parole has been the issuance or non-issuance of a parole violation warrant."[43] In like manner, although the family connections of criminals are subject to all sorts of variations, the extremely rough classification of family relationships as "very active" and "none"[44] were the only ones used or useful in setting up family factors in a prediction table. So also it was discovered that where simple gross classifications were used as a basis of measurement they were more useful in prediction of parole behavior than complicated measuring systems.[45] It was likewise discovered that prediction tables based upon such gross measuring devices, if they had been used, "could yield up to thirty-six percent greater accuracy in making parole selections than if this information were ignored."[46]

The problem of measuring devices for Experimental Jurisprudence, then, is not so much one of creating techniques as of building upon the material already available. When the problems are chosen and the experts from the fields of specialization involved are called in, the measuring devices may appear to be at hand or will be capable of construction from known data.

STATE OF THE RECORDS

A matter very closely associated with social measurement, if not really a part thereof, is the condition of the public records. Any ex-

[42] Ohlin, Selection for Parole (1951).

[43] Id. p. 43. In like manner, the Gluecks successfully used the presence or absence of further criminal acts; see authorities cited at p. 42.

[44] Op. cit. supra note 42.

[45] Id. p. 56.

[46] Id. p. 88.

perimental jurist must necessarily take into account the records of federal and state legislatures, counties and the myriads of administrative bodies. It is a well known fact to all researchers in the field of social activity that records are seldom adequate and often are entirely nonexistent. If one desires to look into the reason and purpose behind legislation, the *Congressional Record* and the reports of hearings before federal committees are in pretty good shape, but when one turns to state legislatures or city and county legislative bodies, the journals and other material of this nature become steadily worse until, on the lower level, one can say they are almost nonexistent.

A similar condition exists in the records of judicial activity. The researchers at Johns Hopkins Institute found that they practically had to create a set of records to get the facts which they needed, and the same experience has been the lot of almost all investigators into the activity of the judiciary.

Administrative records will also be found to be in a very haphazard state. Many federal agencies like the Public Health Service, the Department of Agriculture, the Bureau of Labor Statistics and the Census Bureau, to name only a few, keep very complicated sets of statistical records for the purpose of exposing the prevalence of disease, predicting crops and estimating agricultural price controls, measuring the cost of living, recording basic facts on commerce and industry and for myriad other purposes. All of these offer mines of ready-made information for the preliminary work of experimental social scientists. Beyond these, although every federal agency has a set of files that are staggering in their proportions, and though there is a National Archives Establishment which attempts to preserve the more important records of the activity of various federal organizations, past and present, anyone taking the trouble to delve into this material will be shocked at its inadequacy to disclose the data desired. One must look through mountains of seemingly irrelevant papers and files to expose the simplest of facts. Again, when one descends from the federal to the state, city and county levels, the inadequacy of the records becomes progressively greater.

This absence of records of the pertinent activity of current institutions for social control has always been discouraging to the social scientists, but as a matter of fact it should not be a cause for any great worry. Much pertinent data may be collected from existing records, but no set of records, however intricate, can yield all the information for the solution of all problems of social research. Experimental researchers will find it necessary in almost every instance to create the records and to collect the data which they consider pertinent to the

184

particular problem that they are studying, and no amount of improvement in public records will ever eliminate this step completely. Likewise, there is little use in reforming records until, by theory, research design and experiment, one has determined what data are needed. The collection of material pertinent to the problem studied requires long and tedious experimental research. The work of the Gluecks in getting the basic facts for their books on juvenile delinquents and criminal careers illustrates how this problem will face almost every researcher into social activity.

Though the design set up for particular studies may point the way to improvement in public records, the research will always have to precede the change in record-keeping if it is to result in any purposeful improvement.

NECESSITY FOR PRELIMINARY AND PILOT INVESTIGATION

Almost any scientific research problem will have to be preceded by preliminary or pilot studies. After the problem to be studied has been analyzed and the group has come to an agreement on the particular phenomena to be examined and the information necessary to yield the facts desired, there will always have to be a preliminary investigation to see whether or not it is possible to obtain the pertinent information. It may be discovered that the deciding factors of a particular problem lie in the field of electrical engineering, mathematics, chemistry, psychoanalysis, medicine, sociology, psychiatry or any one of the numerous specialities into which research on problems touching society have been divided. Quite often a preliminary investigation and analysis will show that a problem of the social effect of the law and its usefulness cannot be solved because this information is beyond the reach of the combined sciences touching the field. For example, a study of the effect of divorce laws, when properly analyzed, will immediately carry one into questions of human conduct, psychology, psychiatry and medical information bearing on the personality of married couples which is probably too complicated to be within the reach of anything but the most expensive and protracted research. On the other hand, as indicated in Chapter IX, the question of the effect and efficiency of laws requiring sterilization of barbers' instruments is entirely within the reach of information which can be gleaned from sociological interviewing techniques, medical and chemical sciences. Thus, before the solution of any problem is undertaken, there must be a preliminary pilot study to see if a projected experimental design to reach the results desired is within the joint possibilities of the group involved. These preliminary studies are an absolute necessity if experimental method is to succeed at all in the field of jurisprudence.

After the preliminary studies, there will emerge the task of building up the organization or team of experts to undertake the particular problems to be solved. Once the team is at work, the ramification of finding the answers to apparently simple questions, the collection of related data and the testing of developing hypotheses and jural laws may lead to the creation of permanent research institutions. Beyond the research institution lies the question of reorganization of the educational system to take into account the data which research may assemble; but discussion of the foreseeable problems in this area may be left to a later time.

It may be interesting now to turn to a practical study to show the nature of a possible implementation of the theories so far considered.

PART II

Illustrations of Experimental Methods as Applied
to New Legal Problems

Illustrations of Experimental Methods
as Applied to New Legal Problems

INTRODUCTION TO PART II

As indicated in Part I, Experimental Jurisprudence may be said to extend to two main fields of activities: (1) bringing the discoveries of other sciences, both physical and social, into such a focus that they can be used as tools to aid in lawmaking and enforcement; (2) conducting legal research into the effectiveness of statutes as actually enforced to accomplish the purpose for which they were enacted, and, as indicated in Chapter II, to develop by research and experiment the jural laws controlling such social phenomena.

Transposing the products of science to be used by the legal system as shown in Chapter V is proceeding slowly, but there seem to be no insurmountable obstacles in this area. It is doubtful if anybody will deny that, with the proper funds and organization, studies and whole institutions devoted to adapting the products of all sciences to increasing the efficiency of the legal machinery are theoretically and practically possible.

In the field of the second division of Experimental Jurisprudence lies the area of the most controversy. It seems that it has been shown that where there is a large amount of scientific data developed in areas outside of jurisprudence, experimentation with the enactment of laws and testing of their enforcement is entirely possible. The progress of milk control statutes, provisions for fluoridation of water, the success of vaccination laws for the prevention of smallpox, the structure of reclamation statutes founded on engineering data, discussed in Chapters V and VII, all testify to the success of scientific method when applied to lawmaking and enforcement. The critics may object that in these areas the highly developed scientific techniques of the natural sciences underlying the social problem are fundamental, and lawmaking is only the obvious and rather simple result of the independently created data, so Experimental Jurisprudence does not itself have a separate technique but relies wholly on the highly developed science

189

which gives the lawmaker obvious and complete data. Be that as it may, it is clear that in these fields the overwhelming results of experiments in the sciences underlying the social and legal problems tend to obscure the relevant techniques of jural science.

On the other hand, where the social problem lies in a field in which the underlying scientific facts are not fully developed, the jural techniques stand out in bold relief. No place is this clearer than in the area of traffic control. As indicated in Chapter VI, a complete experimental science of lawmaking was developed there, and the creation of scientific gadgets and methods used in the field developed along with the jural techniques. But the critic may argue again that traffic control is a unique and particular field where the methods of Experimental Jurisprudence, as outlined in Chapter II, seem to apply, but that this is a mere exception which cannot be extended into other areas of lawmaking and enforcement.

With this in mind, it seemed wise to attempt to find a statute lying in a field of social control not dominated by any existing scientific discipline which could be expected to yield ready answers to current questions of the efficiency of present regulatory legal devices. If such a statute could be discovered, and if the techniques of Experimental Jurisprudence could be applied to it, it was felt that there would be demonstration of the feasibility of a more widespread application of that science in determining the usefulness of current laws.

POSSIBLE FIELDS FOR STUDY

The social problems to which attempted solutions in the form of laws have been applied are as various as the activities of civilized man himself. As indicated in Chapter VIII, the testing of the effectiveness of some of the laws governing human conduct like marriage, divorce, inheritance, economic systems of private ownership versus socialism and many others are obviously beyond presently developed techniques. There are, however, many attempts to solve by law other problems of the body politic which are within easy reach of methods of the experimental jurist even with the crude tools now available to him. At first glance it seemed that these might be laws governing various fields of activity such as public health, some aspects of morals, fairness in the market and city-planning, including building codes.

Most of the individual laws regulating activities of this sort were passed late in the nineteenth or early in the twentieth century when the state of scientific knowledge was not as advanced on the regulated subjects as it is today. Many of the statutes have been revised and re-enacted, so a study of their efficiency to solve the problems for which

190

they were passed might yield much fruit in the form of illustration of the extent to which they are enforced or enforceable, suggestions for improvement and even light upon the advisability of attempting to solve such problems by legal devices.

In order to illustrate the methods of Experimental Jurisprudence as applied to a particular law, a search was made to find a law which was of current importance to our present civilization, but which at the same time was sufficiently simple in its administration to have social effects capable of being observed without the use of complicated and expensive scientific devices. It also seemed advisable that a field of law be chosen where tangible results might be expected without the necessity of organizing a large and expensive staff of experts and where the data to be collected would be such that the conclusions from it could not easily be attributed to a scientific discipline other than Experimental Jurisprudence.

With this in mind, a number of pilot studies were made of laws in the field of public health like acts requiring sterilization of barbers' instruments and building codes, for example, the regulation of the installation of plumbing. In both of these, after preliminary study, it seemed that tangible results would be governed largely by the sciences of medicine and engineering. Moral questions, like laws prohibiting smoking or drinking by minors, were also examined; but here the state of medical knowledge, the social prejudice and the obviously wide disregard of the laws by all concerned caused the subjects to be rejected. On the economic side, statutes providing for standard weights, measures and the like seemed to offer a fruitful field; but on closer scrutiny it developed that regulation in these areas was so enmeshed with the activities of trade associations and scientific bodies as to cause considerable complication of the matter studied and to raise doubts whether such regulation still needed legal sanctions. A brief summary of the methods and findings of four of these pilot studies is set out in the following chapter.

After preliminary examination of the foregoing and many other laws, it was finally decided that the Nebraska statutes regulating the issue of bad checks, which, as indicated below, are similar to those in other states, offered a field of fruitful inquiry.

Upon completion of a number of pilot studies by the writer and volunteers, the University of Nebraska appropriated a modest sum to meet the cost of the research. With the aid of one regular full-time research and teaching staff member of the Law School, this study was undertaken. The material which follows is the result of three years' work in the field by the writer in his spare time, aided by three successive full-time assistants, the first a lawyer and sociologist, the second an economist and statistician and the last a political scientist.

For convenience and ease of reading, the description of the study is divided into two parts: (1) analysis and methods and (2) a running account of the results gathered from the research based thereon. The former is supplied for scientists and technicians who may desire to criticize the methods used. The latter is for the use of jurists, lawmakers, administrators and businessmen who may want to apply the findings to improving the administration of justice.

There is no pretext that this is a perfected bit of research. Less than $15,000 was spent on the compilation of the whole study, divided approximately as follows: about 30 per cent for technical help in interviewing persons and gathering data, nearly 15 per cent for travel expenses connected with interviews, 25 per cent for statistical aid and compilation of data, about 20 per cent for printing and publication of forms and completion of the manuscript published herewith, and the balance for postage, secretarial help and miscellaneous expense. The methods of social research adopted are therefore subject to much refinement. With more resources, the techniques could be improved to meet the most rigorous requirements of modern social science and statistics. The results are in a sense only a larger pilot study of the problem of the effectiveness of bad-check laws and an indication of the direction further experimentation should take.

The whole is set out here as a modest illustration of the possibilities of the application of Experimental Jurisprudence to the practical problems of law enforcement.

CHAPTER IX

A Brief Description of the Experimental Pilot Studies

In an effort to find the law which would be a fit subject for experimental research within the modest resources available, the writer and his students in a class in jurisprudence have conducted preliminary studies of the workings of various statutes picked almost at random. Many of these investigations have led into blind alleys. Others have indicated that the subjects chosen were too complicated for any but the most heavily endowed and continuous research. But in at least the four fields mentioned above, the preliminary studies seem to indicate that it is possible, without too much effort and expense, fruitfully to apply experimental methods to testing the operation and effectiveness of current statutes. In each of these fields it appeared from the preliminary studies that the real solution lay in an area which would be dominated by an existing science, and if developed to its indicated end, the research would demand expensive equipment and results determined by the techniques of the controlling science. To illustrate the nature and methods of Experimental Jurisprudence, one problem upon which there has been some preliminary research has been chosen from each field. Because of lack of funds and scientific organization, no completed studies are available, but preliminary or pilot studies which have been made are described here to illustrate the possibility of the application of Experimental Jurisprudence to each type of problem.

It should be constantly borne in mind that the material which follows is only a description of preliminary investigations. It is not offered as illustrations of complete statistical studies of the various problems involved; neither are the conclusions anything other than suggestive indications of what might be expected from more complete studies or experiments dealing with the laws here examined.

Exposition of the nature of such investigations might be either a short summary of the methods and results or a detailed reproduction of each step in the process. The former is informative but perhaps too brief; the latter might be overly tedious to all but technicians interested in methods. The material which follows is a compromise between the two but tends to lean toward a short summary because it is possible to illustrate briefly both the strength and weakness of the methods which might be used and available and also to point graphically toward the results to be expected from further research.

PUBLIC HEALTH PROBLEMS

As indicated in Chapter VIII, all states have laws or administrative devices created by law regulating the conduct of various businesses which directly affect the public health, such as restaurants, grocery stores, meat markets, beauty parlors, barber shops, cigar stores, pool rooms and many others. Studies of the effectiveness of all these laws are easily within the grasp of students using known techniques.

As an illustration of the possibilities of such studies, the laws of a single state regulating sanitation in barber shops have been chosen for preliminary examination. This should tend to show what can be expected from standard and properly directed experiments in the field of health regulation, many of the like of which are now being conducted by established authorities.

STERILIZATION OF BARBER INSTRUMENTS

The Problem[1]

There are a number of common diseases of the skin which can be spread by barber tools; among these are barbers itch, boils, ringworm, impetigo and possibly venereal diseases.[2]

The competent dermatologist who would have to be part of a team of experts conducting the completed study could add much more information to illustrate the nature of the infections which sanitary laws on the subject attempt to control and prevent.

The Law

Laws enacted to solve this problem take many forms, which, in a complete study, could yield to comparative techniques; but for the purpose of a preliminary investigation the Nebraska law was examined.

---

[1] The writer is greatly indebted to Glen A. Fiebig and Joseph V. McAneny, members of the Nebraska Bar, for the preliminary research on this problem, which was conducted in the class on jurisprudence in their senior year in law school.

[2] This material is summarized from the following sources: Sutton and Sutton, Synopsis of Diseases of the Skin (1942), Gardiner's Handbook of Skin Diseases, Kenner's edition (1943); Andrews, Diseases of the Skin (2nd ed. 1943).

A pilot study using Lincoln as a base disclosed that there were parallel laws on the sanitation of barbers at the city and state level. The Lincoln City Ordinance, set out in the margin,[3] was adopted in December of 1915. While the apparent purpose of the ordinance is the prevention of the spread of diseases through barber shops, it appears that the City Council passed it only as routine health legislation. A check of the health records kept by the City Health Department shows that there was no outbreak, at least of epidemic proportions, of barbers itch or other diseases which might be spread by barber tools during 1915 or the years immediately preceding. It is quite possible that the council adopted the ordinance verbatum from some other city's health regulations.

The state of Nebraska has adopted a regulation which is identical with the Lincoln ordinance. This current regulation was set up in March of 1947 by the Board of Examiners under authority granted them by law.[4]

The city regulation does not provide specifically for punishment if it is not obeyed. The enforcement agency is the Board of Health, which could conceivably take action against the barbers under its power to "investigate the existence of infectious diseases and adopt measures, with the approval of the Department of Health of the State, to arrest the progress of the same."[5] What action it could take in this case is nowhere set out, and there has never been occasion for it to attempt a specific punishment because it apparently has never attempted enforcement of the ordinance. The state regulations do set out penalties which provide that a violator, upon conviction, shall be fined not less than $15 nor more than $100 for each offense. Furthermore, under Section 71-217(8) of the statutes,[6] the State Department of Health may revoke a certificate of registration if a barber violates "any valid regulation promulgated by the Board of Barber Examiners

---

[3] Chapter 11, Art. 4, Sec. 11-403. "The owner or manager of every barber shop . . . shall cause all tools and instruments, such as razors, tweezers, contact cups or pads or massage machines, hair brushes and combs, clippers and shears or any other tool or instrument used in a barber shop . . . to be sterilized by immersing in a recognized disinfectant solution such a liquor cresolis compositur 4% Formalin or (formaldehyde) 25% or phenol (carbolic acid) 5% and kept in a sanitary condition at all times. When instruments are not in use they shall be kept in an enclosed cabinet."

[4] Neb. Rev. Stat. § 71-223 (1943).

[5] City Ordinance, Lincoln, Nebraska, No. 4007, April 24, 1945.

[6] Revised Statutes of Nebraska 1943.

pertaining to service charges and the elimination of unfair and insanitary practices."

As stated above, the City Health Department has never attempted enforcement of the ordinance, nor has it set up any system of inspection to determine whether the barber shops were obeying the law. The reason for this lack of enforcement does not seem to be any feeling of lack of power on the part of the Administration, nor does the Administration feel that the ordinance is one which should not be enforced; rather the absence of enforcement comes from a shortage of manpower to do the job. An interview with the head of the City Health Department disclosed that in his view the ordinance was a good thing and should be enforced. However, since the skin diseases spread by barber tools were not believed to be of serious proportions in Lincoln and since matters thought to be of more importance to the general health of the city took up all of his time and that of his limited staff, he has not and does not intend to set up an enforcement or inspection procedure.

The state has set up an inspection procedure. Inspections are made by three examiners who are appointed by the governor under his powers set out in the statutes.[7] This statute provides that each member must be a practicing barber who has followed the occupation of barber in this state for at least five years prior to his appointment, that he shall serve for a three-year term and that his compensation shall be six dollars per diem plus traveling expenses, but not to exceed $1,200 per annum. An interview with the Director of the Board of Examiners of the Nebraska Department of Health and the inspector for the Lincoln area showed that time permits the inspectors to make visits to every shop in the state about one and one-half times per year. Furthermore, the office of inspector is appointive and most governors rely mainly upon the recommendations of prominent barbers and barber unions when making their selections. Therefore, according to the opinion of many of the barbers interviewed in the survey, most of the inspectors have held themselves out as being "easy to get along with" before their appointment in order to obtain the support of their fellow barbers and thus take office with obligation to overlook the less obvious faults of any barber shop. These inspectors look into all aspects of sanitation in the barber shop; they are not inspecting for violations of the rules concerning the sterilization of tools alone.

[7] Neb. Rev. Stat. § 71-221 (1943); but see id. § 71-222.

The Effect of the Law on the Barber Shops of the City of Lincoln, Nebraska

The brief examination of skin diseases above shows beyond a doubt that many skin diseases could be spread by infected barber's tools and instruments and that many of these diseases are quite common. Therefore, the next step in the pilot study was to see if the statutory methods were being used in the barber shops of Lincoln to prevent the spread of these contagious skin diseases. The state law and the municipal ordinance each set out the same method for the sterilization of the barber's tools and instruments.

In order to discover if the law was being followed, it was decided to conduct a survey of a sample of all the barber shops in the city. There was, at first glance, no list of all of the shops in Lincoln. At the State Examiner's office, however, it was discovered that if such a list existed the state inspector would have it. The inspector indicated that he had never made a list of all the shops,[8] but he did tell enough to enable the choice of a valid sample. There are 75 barber shops in the city, and of this number 60 shops are located in the "downtown area." When reduced to percentages, it appeared that 80 per cent of the barber shops in Lincoln are in the downtown area, and 20 per cent are in the suburbs. Therefore, an attempt was made to set up the same ratio in the selection of shops to be interviewed. As the sample turned out in its final form, interviews were had with 24 per cent of all the shops in the city, and of these, 74 per cent were in the downtown area and 26 per cent were in the suburbs.

It was also desirable to see if there was any noticeable difference in the standard of sanitation in the large shops over the "one-chair" type of shop or the normal two- or three-chair shop. Therefore it was decided to conduct a stratified type of sample. On this point, the survey ranged all the way from the appointment shops in the large office buildings and the hotels to the one-chair basement shops on Ninth Street.

After deciding that the interview was the best method to follow, it seemed desirable to set up certain questions that each barber should answer. The following were picked because it was felt that they would show if the law was being followed, and if not, to what degree it was being violated.

The questions were:

[8] An apparent failure to carry out the mandate of Sec. 71-224, **Revised Statutes of Nebraska 1943**, requiring such a record held open to the public.

1. How often do you sterilize your instruments?
2. Do you use a sterilizing liquid? If yes, what liquid?
3. If you use a liquid, is it in any way hard on your instruments?
4. If you do not use liquids, what do you use?

A point was made of observing if the tools were kept in an enclosed cabinet when not in use, and if not, where they were kept.

The final task on the list was to try to keep a note of any comment the barbers had on the law as it now exists.

The results of the survey were rather shocking when one is aware of the possible diseases that can be passed in a barber shop. The fact was pointed up continually that most barbers do not feel that their instruments can spread diseases and that, if they do at all, it is in a rare case. They apparently feel no obligation to stop those rare cases.

The results reduced to percentages are as follows:

PER CENT

1. Violated the law in whole or in part.................................100
2. Liquids used to sterilize instruments
   a. Soap and water..50
   b. Statutory liquids 33⅓
   c. Other commercial liquids.....................................16⅔
3. How often the liquids are used
   a. Once a day 44½
   b. After each customer who looks diseased........................50
   c. When the barber thinks they need it..........................5½
4. Per cent of barbers who felt that razors need special care ...39
5. Per cent of barbers who kept their tools in an enclosed cabinet 12

These results show beyond the slightest doubt that the law is being violated and in some cases is being completely ignored. The survey was difficult to tabulate completely because many of the barbers did sterilize the razors but completely ignored their clippers and scissors. They would clean their scissors once every two or three days.

While the law requires that the instruments be sterilized after each customer, the very best shop found only changed instruments after every four or five customers. The barbers all seem to feel that they run a clean shop and that no skin disease is ever spread through their tools, but the medical testimony indicates that unless sterile procedure is followed they could not help spreading disease in some cases.

It should also be noted that a large percentage of barbers use only soap and water as their sterilizing agent. While these are of some help, it is doubtful if they do a complete job. Complaints on the statutory liquids ranged from statements that they cost too much to the fact that the liquids dulled their tools. Some of these grievances might be justified, so the next step in the study of the law would be an examination of the efficiency and usefulness of the statutory disinfectants.

The Efficiency of the Legally Required Disinfectants

The fact that preliminary interviews indicate that the city ordinance and rules of the Board of Barber's Examiners, which are identical, are being violated at almost every point causes one to question the thoroughness of the enforcement machinery and the efficiency of the legal antiseptics. The former is clearly weak, understaffed and underpaid.[9] One of the causes of the widespread violations is clearly the resulting incompetency of the inspection system; but the best inspector's organization could not hope to get good results unless the required sterilization agents were efficient, practical and easy to use.

A complete study of the law would require a scientific examination by chemists and pharmacologists of the usefulness and efficiency of the statutory liquids and also of all other available disinfectants for use on barber instruments. This would not be either difficult or too costly; but for the purpose of the pilot study interviews were had with members of the faculty of the Colleges of Medicine and Pharmacy and staff members of the Department of Bacteriology of the University of Nebraska. These, with the aid of reference to a few standard texts on the subject,[10] yielded interesting preliminary results.

The following chemicals are set forth in the statute, and they or others like them are to be used by the barbers to sterilize their instruments. They are liquor cresolis compositus, four per cent, Formalin (or formaldehyde), 25 per cent, and phenol (carbolic acid), five per cent.

The interviews and texts may be briefly summarized as follows: Some of the liquids prescribed would be harmful to the barber's equipment. Both phenol and cresol would attack the newly developed plastic combs and brush bristles. The first effect they have on a comb is to force the teeth to cross; then the teeth become brittle and snap out. On a more expensive hard-rubber comb the effect is not so noticeable,

---

[9] The members of the board apparently do the inspection, and Section 71-222 of the statutes limits their compensation to six dollars a day and travel not to exceed $1,200 a year.

[10] Pharmacopeia of the United States of America (13th ed. 1947); Modern Drug Encyclopedia and Therapeutic Index (4th Ed. 1949); Soloman, A Manual of Pharmacology (7th Ed. 1948).

but in time these two compounds will soften the rubber and make it useless.

The barber's clippers are built to be immersed in these liquids. On many models one can snap off the cutting parts and put them in the liquids. On others the entire head is simply put in the liquid, and it is so built that the antiseptics are drawn in and around the cutting edges and forced out through the sides when the motor is turned on. The statutory liquids are in no way harmful to these clippers, but the survey shows that the clippers are very rarely sterilized.

The sterilizing cabinets in the barber shop which may be contemplated by the rules work on the fumigation principle. A small tray of formaldehyde is placed in the cabinet, and the door is closed. The fumes penetrate to all parts of the cabinet and should kill all the germs present. The idea is that the fumes combine with the moisture on the tools and equipment, giving the same effect as dipping the tools. Naturally, this method is slower, and the fumes are lost each time the door to the cabinet is opened. The odor is strong and is released into the shop and is not pleasant for the customers. It was also found that in about half of the barber shops these cabinets were not used, the cabinets contained no formaldehyde or barbers would store towels, cigarettes and gum in them, but no disinfectant.

It was the opinion of the experts interviewed that of the three disinfectants set out in the statute, the cresols would probably be best, in spite of their very bad odor.

A complete study by a competent staff of chemists and pharmacologists would probably disclose among the thousands of methods and chemicals now available one or more practical and efficient antiseptics which the Board of Barber Examiners might prescribe.

The Necessity for Any Kind of Sterilization

Although the pilot investigation disclosed numerous cases of skin disease having appeared in barber shops and at least one case of infection traced directly to barber instruments, a complete study of the effectiveness and necessity of the legal requirement of sterilization of barber instruments would require a census of the diseases listed above and others which are spread by barber shops. This, of course, would be the province of the medical members of the research team. Techniques for conducting this part of the experiment are surely within the knowledge of present medical science.

The extent to which diseases spread by barbers were found in the community would have an important bearing upon the necessity for recommending the tightening of enforcement procedures and the advisability of further studies of the problem.

Organizations for This Research

The preliminary study shows that measuring the statewide effectiveness of the law requiring sterilization of barber's instruments is entirely possible with a team of workers including a lawyer, a dermatologist, a pharmacologist, a number of interviewers, a social statistician to determine the proper sampling for a statewide study and sufficient medical personnel to conduct a census of the diseases involved. Sufficient laboratory factilities would be available at any first-class university or medical school.

Results to Be Expected from a Complete Study

A complete study conducted by a team of experts organized approximately as indicated above should yield the following results:

1. The extent to which the law was being violated could be accurately determined for the whole state.
2. The reasons for violations would appear in proper focus.
3. The efficiency of legally required sterilization agents would be determined.
4. The necessity for tighter enforcement would become apparent.
5. Recommendations for improvement in the law based upon scientific data would be forthcoming.
6. Jural laws as to effectiveness of detailed regulations in accord with or contrary to scientific knowledge and the efficiency of paid inspectors might begin to emerge.
7. A comparative study of similar sanitary measures in other states might yield further jural laws as to the proper type of administration of such health devices.
8. If recommendations were enacted into laws or changes in regulations, their efficiency could be further studied with fruitful results.

Studies of Other Types of Health Regulations

An organization once set up to study the rules requiring the sterilization of barber's instruments or similar regulations could turn its attention with very little reorganization to the myriad of problems which grow out of the enforcement of all sorts of public health laws. If the solutions of such related problems were attempted, it would be possible to build a permanent research unit to operate simultaneously on the thousands of problems of law enforcement in the vital field of public health and to cooperate with existing public health officials and research units.

It should also be noted that such a team of experts would be expensive, and to operate efficiently it would have to study simultaneously a number of problems. For these reasons, a complete experiment in this field had to be rejected.

A MORALS PROBLEM

The attempts are legion to use law to enforce the moral codes desired by the dominant classes in society. They range from the more drastic criminal penalities against adultery, fornication and prostitution, which the Kinsey reports have shown to be in a bad state of failure of enforcement, through all sorts of criminal penalties, licensing and inspection of the production, sale and consumption of liquor, narcotics and tobacco, to the Sunday blue laws and many other minor interferences with human conduct. Among these acts and the myriad of agencies attempting to enforce these various legal controls are countless subjects for study by the experimental jurist which it seemed should yield immediate scientific fruit at comparatively little cost.

LAWS ON USE OF TOBACCO BY MINORS

The problem of controlling the early use of tobacco by minors, which appears to be a symptom if not a cause of juvenile delinquency,[11] is one of the many which has resulted in laws in almost every state in the Union, at either state or city levels, or both. These take numerous forms, such as licensing the sale of cigarette and other tobacco products, criminal penalties for sale or gift to minors at various ages and many other types of restraints. A complete catalog of the various devices used for control of this one activity would prove an interesting and enlightening part of a complete study of the problem. Here again comparison of the operations of the various laws should yield much fruitful scientific data. Cursory investigation indicates that a study of these legal devices seems to be entirely within the range of present techniques.

As material for a preliminary examination, the laws of Nebraska on the subject of sale of cigarettes to minors were used.[12] These

[11] Glueck, Unraveling Juvenile Delinquency (1950) p. 161, shows that 90 per cent of juvenile delinquents began smoking at an early age, while only 21 per cent of matched non-delinquents smoked at such ages.

[12] The writer is greatly indebted to Fred A. Hodek and Donald E. Morrow, members of the Nebraska Bar, whose preliminary report on their subject is in part quoted below.

statutes have gone through a series of revisions not important at the present time.[13] The current laws provide for the following controls.

The Nebraska Law as It Exists Today

1. The state[14] statutes:

"Tobacco; use by minors; penalty. Whoever being a minor under the age of eighteen years, shall smoke cigarettes or cigars, or use tobacco in any form whatever, in this state, shall be fined in any sum not exceeding ten dollars; *Provided,* any minor so charged with the violation of this section may be free from prosecution when he shall have furnished evidence for the conviction of the persons or person selling or giving him cigarettes, cigars or tobacco."

Similar to this statute is the penalty under the licensing statute,[15] which provides as follows: "Any person under the age of eighteen years who shall obtain cigars, tobacco, cigarettes or cigarette material from a licensee hereunder by representing that he is of the age of eighteen years or over, shall be guilty of a misdemeanor, and upon conviction thereof shall be punished by a fine of not less than five nor more than twenty-five dollars."

The above statutes deal only with the effect of the laws on the minor as a direct result of the minor's own activity. A statute which pertains to the selling and giving of tobacco[16] provides: "Tobacco; sale to minors; penalty. Whoever shall sell, give or furnish, in any way, any tobacco in any form whatever, or any cigarettes, or cigarette paper, to any minor under eighteen years of age, shall be fined, for each offense, not less than twenty nor more than fifty dollars, or be imprisoned for not less than ten nor more than thirty days."

The last statute was enacted prior to the law pertaining to licensing, yet it still remains in effect even though it in part duplicates a similar law in the licensing section,[17] which provides: "License for sale of tobacco; rights of licensee. The license provided for in sections 28-1023 and 28-1024, when issued, shall authorize the sale of cigars, tobacco, cigarettes and cigarette material by the licensee and employees, to persons over the age of twenty-one years, at the place of business

---

[13] The statute seems to have had its origin in an act of 1885 prohibiting the sale of tobacco to minors under 15 years of age. It has had numerous amendments, Laws of Nebraska 1885, c. 105 p. 394; 1895, c. 80, p. 326; ed. (1897) c. 101, p. 389; id. 1903, c. 138, p. 643; and the current acts cited infra.

[14] Neb. Rev. Stat. § 28-1020 (1943).

[15] Id., 28-1029.

[16] Id., 28-1021.

[17] Id., 28-1026.

described in such license, for a period of one year from the date of such license, unless the same be forfeited in section 28-1027."

Here the licensee is enjoined from selling to those not "over the age of twenty-one years," which in a sense varies Section 28-1021, *supra,* which prohibits the sale of tobacco to those under 18. Of course the penalty is different, viz, for sale to a person under 21, the licensee is subject to $100 fine or ten to 60 days imprisonment and may forfeit his license; for sale to those under 18, the vendor or supplier, be he licensed or otherwise, is subject to fine of $50 or imprisonment from ten to 30 days.

It is interesting to note the no man's land between 18 and 21 where one may purchase with impunity, but a vendor may not sell under penalty of law. This was apparently meant to put the vendor on his guard so that he would not sell to anyone under 18, which may lead to the conclusion that 18 and not 21 was the age limit which the legislature probably had in mind in enacting these statutes.

2. The Lincoln city ordinances:

The Lincoln city fathers were apparently of the same mind as the state legislators concerning the problem of minors and tobacco. In most aspects they closely duplicate the state statutes. The city prohibitions are set out in the margin.[18]

The Effect of the Law on Its Administration

A preliminary investigation of the administration of the law has yielded some revealing aspects of the problem.

During the entire history of the statute and city ordinance above cited, not one single complaint, arrest or conviction seems to have been had under either in Lancaster County.

---

[18] Lincoln, Municipal Code (1936).

20-101. *Minors under eighteen not to use tobacco.* It is hereby declared unlawful for any minor under eighteen years of age to smoke or use cigarettes, whether made of tobacco or other material, cigars, or tobacco in any form whatever within the limits of the city of Lincoln.

20-102. *Tobacco not to be furnished to minors under eighteen.* It shall be unlawful for any person to sell, give, or furnish in any way any tobacco in any form whatever, or cigars or cigarettes, or cigarette paper, to any minor under eighteen years of age within the corporate limits of the city.

20-103. *Policemen to arrest for violations.* It is hereby made the duty of each police officer while on duty, to arrest, without warrant, any person found violating any of the provisions of this article, and detain such person a sufficient length of time within which a complaint can be made, warrant issued, and arrest made thereunder.

The city ordinances above cited do not seem to contain any penalty provisions.

The statute prohibiting sale to minors has been in effect since 1885, the current licensing statute since 1919 and the ordinance since 1902, yet according to available records no official violation of either has been noted in Lancaster County.[19]

This is indeed an "administrative change" in the law. As subsequent findings easily support, it amounts to a complete disregard of the law by some of the authorities who are bound to enforce it.

Another administrative change on the licensing level is of significance, as it demonstrates the state of mind of those charged with the printing and issuing of tobacco licenses. Section 28-1026 of the state law, *supra,* states clearly that the licensee may not sell tobacco to anyone under 21 years of age, yet the licenses issued to tobacco vendors in Lancaster County in 1951 stated that the licensee is "authorized to sell cigars, tobacco, cigarettes and cigarette material . . . to persons over the age of eighteen years."

When this obvious error was called to the attention of the licensing officials by one of the investigators, they announced their certainty that 18 and not 21 was the age limit for purchasing tobacco and even went so far as to state that either the previous year's licenses which contained 21 as the age limit were in error or else the law had been changed. The matter was then referred to the city attorney's office, which settled it by reading the statute, affirming that 21, not 18, was the age limit.

The section of the statute pertaining to licensing and the payment of fees for licensing is apparently strictly adhered to. That is, everyone in the county examined who sells tobacco is careful to obtain a license. It is not certain why this part of the law is complied with much better than that portion concerning the sale of tobacco to minors, as there seem to have been no prosecutions in the county for selling tobacco without a license.

Support for the inference that enforcement is equally lax in the rest of the state is shown by the fact that, although cases under earlier statutes and the licensing provisions have reached the Supreme Court, none involving the present provisions as to sale to minors seem to have been appealed to that body. A complete experiment covering the state would, of course, require careful examination of properly sampled communities along lines indicated by the pilot study hereinafter discussed.

---

[19] That there were convictions under the earlier laws in other counties is shown by the fact that the Supreme Court in Apperson v. Whalen, 74 Neb. 680 (1905) sustained the constitutionality of the 1903 version of the act.

The Effect of the Law on Consumption of Tobacco by Minors

In order to determine the effectiveness of the law, it would be necessary to find out the extent to which tobacco was used by persons within the prohibited age groups. To get an insight into the problem involved, two senior law students attempted a pilot study in the city of Lincoln.

Explanation of the Results

The questionnaire used is set out in the margin.[20] It contained 11 questions, and the results were obtained from 155 students ranging in age from 16 to 20 years. The compilation here was made in percentages of smokers, with the exception of the answers to Questions 10 and 11, where the total number of those questioned was used as the denominator. Some of the results are stated below. The numbers refer to the questions set out in the margin.

3. 55 per cent of those questioned smoke, while 38 per cent of those smoking are females.

5. 10 per cent of the smokers indicated they smoke over 10 cigarettes a day.

   16 per cent smoke between 6 and 10.

   21 per cent smoke less than 6.

   53 per cent of the smokers did not answer this question.

---

[20] The questionnaire was as follows:

Dear Student:

    We greatly apreciate your help on our project. We are Law College Seniors seeking information on the need, if any, and the "workability" of the laws which prohibit a certain age group from purchasing and using tobacco. Feel free to give us full information, as you will *not* sign this questionnaire.

1. Age:................. 2. Sex: Male................, Female.................
3. Have you ever used tobacco in any form? Yes................, No.................
4. If answer is "Yes," at what age did you first use tobacco in any form?............
5. Do you now smoke an average of 3,4,5,6,7,8,9,10, over 10, cigarettes per day? (Circle number used.)
6. If you smoke a pipe, how many pipe loads do you average per day? 2,3,4,5,6, over 6. (Circle number used.)
7. Do you make your own purchases of tobacco? Yes................, No.................
8. If answer is "Yes," have you ever been refused tobacco when seeking to purchase it? Yes................, No.................
9. At what sort of place do you obtain most of your tobacco? A. Cafe................, B. Drug Store................, C. Grocery Store............, D. Vending machine ...., E. Parents................, F. Other Sources................ .
10. How do your parents regard your use of tobacco? A. Opposed................ . B. Indifferent................ .
11. What is the age at which you may legally purchase tobacco?................ .

7. 55½ per cent of those smoking indicated that they make their own purchases, while 22 per cent indicated they did not and 32½ per cent did not answer.

8. 23 per cent of the smokers have been refused at least once, and that is all the question will determine. 36 per cent had never been refused, and 41 per cent did not answer.

9. 15½ per cent of the smokers purchased their tobacco at a cafe.
   39 per cent at a drugstore.
   18 per cent at a grocery store.
   10 per cent at a vending machine.
   (This answer casts doubt upon the results of this question, since the only vending machines in Lincoln were in private clubs.)
   9 per cent obtained the tobacco from their parents.
   8½ per cent indicated other sources.

10. 50 per cent of the entire group indicated that their parents were opposed to their smoking, and the other 50 per cent checked the "indifferent" answer.

11. 57½ per cent of the entire group thought 18 was the legal age to purchase tobacco, while 18 per cent thought it to be 21. The remaining 24½ per cent indicated ages all the way from 14 to "any age," or did not answer.

The Reasons for Widespread Failure of Enforcement

The above data, meager as it is, points to the eventual discovery of widespread violation of the statute[21] and serious breakdown of enforcement. Further data when collected might reveal many of the reasons for violations, but a number of burning scientific questions will remain.

(1) Is smoking injurious to adults?

(2) Is it more injurious to young people?

(3) Is it progressively more injurious as the smoker's years decline?

(4) At what age, if any, is smoking by minors so injurious that it should be prohibited because it endangers health or bodily or mental functions?

---

[21] Casual observation at the tobacco counter at the Student Union at the University of Nebraska indicates that over 50 per cent of the sales are made to persons under the legal age of 21.

It should be noted that the statute has attempted to answer Question (4) by placing the age at 18 and has answered Questions (2) and (3) by attempting to restrain smoking between the ages of 18 and 21.

One of the main causes of the lack of enforcement and the violations of the statute probably is the fact that there is no widely known proof of the validity of the assumptions underlying the law.

The scientific, quasi-scientific and moral literature on the subject of smoking tobacco in general and cigarettes in particular is legion; but whether or not Questions (1) to (4) can be answered in presently known reports is a question for experts, including doctors and psychologists. If the answers are available, great light will be thrown upon the causes of the present apparent breakdown of the law and the type of amendments which should be suggested. If no answers are available, then properly devised experiments should be set up to get them. If they can't be attained, then it is clear that the law is based entirely upon old wives' tales and prejudices, in which case there would be no more reason for prohibiting smoking by minors than by adults.

If it turns out that the latter is the case, then repeal would be indicated unless a public opinion poll showed that the peace of the body politic would be disrupted by such action. If this latter were the case, which is highly unlikely, an "educational" campaign would be indicated which, no doubt, the tobacco companies would be glad to finance.

At any rate, it is clear that the answer to all the pertinent scientific questions on the usefulness and effectiveness of this law and the purposes for which it was created are available to a team of experts made up of lawyers, doctors, psychologists, polling experts, statisticians and interviewers. When the results were in, the information on the advisability of using laws to enforce moral concepts of this kind and the predictability of the success of such attempts would be better understood. Thereafter jural laws could be further developed by studying other attempts to enforce moral concepts by law. Similar techniques and like organizations could be developed to work out experiments in all fields where law attempts to enforce moral concepts. But it should be noted that the type of "team" necessary to conduct such a study would be complicated and the research equipment various and expensive.

PROTECTION OF THE MARKET

All states and the federal government have numerous legal devices for protecting the fairness of the dealings on the market. Probably the most numerous and uniform in appearance of these laws are the ones classed under the general heading of weights and measures. Here one will find acts regulating the size of a pound, a ton and a bushel and the standard measurements of such staple products as bread, milk, potatoes and grain of various kinds. But though the subject of weights and measures appears uniformly in the indices of the compiled statutes of the states, the variation in details from state to state is surprising.[22]

Here is a treasure of material for the experimental jurist. The standard regulations of each unit of measure, their effect upon the business world, and their usefulness, if any, as a regulation are fit studies for the juridical scientist.

STATUTES REGULATING STANDARD SIZE FOR BRICKS

To check the usefulness of these statutes and to illustrate methods available, a pilot study has been made of the comparatively simple Nebraska statutes prescribing the standard size for bricks. The law reads as follows:[23]

> *89-137 Brick; standard size.* The standard size of brick sold in the State of Nebraska shall be eight and one-fourth inches long, four inches wide, and two and one-half inches thick.
> *89-138 Brick; selling other than standard size; notice to purchaser.* No person shall sell any brick of any size other than that specified in section 89-137 without, at the time of the sale, notifying the purchaser, in writing, of the size of such brick.
> *89-141 Violations; penalty.* Any person, firm or corporation violating any of the provisions of sections 89-101 to 89-141, shall

---

[22] For example, almost all the states have a statute specifying the standard weight per bushel of various commodities, yet the variations of standards from state to state even in contiguous areas is shocking. Taking seven states at random in the Mississippi Valley, they specify the weight per bushel of the following number of commodities: Nebraska, 68; Ohio, 41; Indiana, 53; Illinois, 83; Kentucky, 35; Iowa, 72; and Tennessee, 100. In none are the specifications uniform, even in the most widely produced commodities. For example, the following are the weights in pounds per bushel of the named commodity specified by the states: Corn: Nebraska 70, Ohio 68, Indiana 68-70, Illinois 70, Kentucky 68-70, Iowa 70, Tennessee 70; Popcorn in Ear: Nebraska 70, Ohio 42, Indiana 56, Illinois 70, Kentucky none, Iowa 70, Tennessee 70; Turnips: Nebraska 55, Ohio 60, Indiana 55, Illinois 55, Kentucky 60, Iowa 55, Tennessee 50. See Neb. Rev. Stat. §§ 89-112 (1943); Ohio Code § 6418 (Page 1945); Ind. Stat. §§ 69-305 (Burns 1936); Ill. Ann. Stat. §§ 147-84 (Smith-Hurd 1936), See id. § 147-34; Ky. Rev. Stat., § 363-040 (Baldwin 1943); Iowa Code Ann. § 210.10 (1949); Tenn. Code § 6649 (Williams 1943).

Just what is the effect upon all this and like state legal standards of 15 USC c. 6 on Weights and Measures is also a nice question of Experimental Jurisprudence as well as constitutional law.

[23] Neb. Rev. Stat. (1943).

be punished by a fine of not less than ten dollars nor more than one hundred dollars, or by imprisonment in the county jail for not more than thirty days; *Provided, however,* that upon the second conviction for the violation of any of the provisions of said sections, such offender shall be punished by a fine of not less than fifty dollars nor more than one hundred dollars, or by imprisonment in the county jail not less than thirty days nor more than ninety days.

These sections can be traced back to the session laws in 1901, which, so far as can be discovered, was the first time they appeared as law in the state of Nebraska.[24] The original law when passed carried a penalty for violation of a maximum $500 fine and had an emergency clause. This would seem to be evidence that at the time the law was passed 50 years ago it was considered by the legislature to be a very important regulation. The reasons why this may have been considered more important then than now cannot be determined with exactness but can only be a subject of speculation. However, this pilot study was not concerned primarily with the problem of whether the law was needed at the time it was passed, but it is concerned with the value of the law at the present time.

The Effect of the Law

To determine the effect of the law upon present business practices and its usefulness, if any, it seemed necessary to find out (1) to what extent, if any, it is being enforced; (2) whether or not, regardless of enforcement, the prescribed dimensions are useful in the brick trade; (3) whether there are any scientific or trade reasons for these or similar dimensions; (4) whether standardization at any size is useful or desirable; and (5) whether or not it should be attempted by law.

Enforcement of the Law. The enforcement of the Weights and Measures statutes, of which this is a part, is entrusted to the state Department of Agriculture and Inspection. Upon inquiry there, it appeared that the Department was ignoring the statute.

Inquiries among the retailers of bricks in the city of Lincoln disclosed that they had never heard of the statute and consequently paid no heed to it. The principal brick manufacturer in the state, located near Lincoln, also expressed complete ignorance of the law, as did samples taken among architects, contractors, persons buying bricks for homes and brick masons. This leads to the conclusion that the statute is an absolute dead letter.

[24] Laws of Nebraska, 1901, p. 471.

Usefulness to Trade of Such Regulations. As is well known, bricks are a ceramic product made by cooking a moist clay which has been mixed carefully in various combinations to produce the desired size and color. The size is produced by the dimension of the die into which the clay is pressed for molding and cutting, and the color comes from the chemicals in the mixture and the degree of exposure to heat in the burning process.

The size of brick can be changed easily by changing the die through which the clay is forced in the manufacturing process. There are limits, however, to the size that brick can be made. Huge bricks would be extremely difficult, if not impossible, to make, due to problems of burning them evenly.

There is another practical problem involved in determining the size of brick. The clay from which the brick is cut shrinks during the drying process, and it shrinks even more during the burning process. This shrinkage cannot be definitely determined in advance. There are many factors involved, such as the temperature at which the bricks were burned, the length of time they were burned and the type of clay from which the bricks were made, since some clays are more subject to shrinkage than others. Due to these considerations, individual bricks made from the same batch and burned in the same kiln will not necessarily be the same size at the end of the manufacturing process. This is true because the bricks in the top part of the kiln are hotter and therefore tend to shrink more, while the various chemical substances in the clay are not mixed evenly throughout, and this causes some bricks in the same layer in the kiln to be a trifle different in size. Brick manufacturers state that this difference in size sometimes ranges as much as one-half inch in length from the smallest to the largest.

From the above discussion, it can be seen that it is not possible, let alone practical, to decree by statute that a standard brick shall have certain "definite" dimensions. The statutes allows no tolerances for variation in the brick, and the Department of Inspection in Agriculture is not given the power to establish tolerances regarding the measurements of bricks.[25] For this reason alone, it would be impractical and impossible to enforce the statute.

If it were useful, it would, of course, be possible to amend the statute to allow for tolerance to take care of the fact of variation of the size of bricks in the process of manufacture. In fact the provision for a written statement of variation in a sense already allows for this

---

[25] Neb. Rev. Stat. § 89-101 (1950).

difference if necessary. This raises the question of whether or not such a statement offers any protection to the purchaser, and this in turn involves the question of sizes of bricks on the market.

The prescribed size of bricks as set out in the statute is 8¼ inches long, 4 inches wide and 2½ inches thick. For purposes of definiteness in this problem, this size brick will be referred to as the "statutory" brick.

Other sizes of brick are being manufactured and sold in Nebraska. The size which most nearly corresponds to the statutory size is what is referred to by persons in the trade as a "standard" brick, which is 8 inches long, 3¾ inches wide and 2¼ inches thick. In this study, when reference is made to the standard brick, it will refer to this size, which is ¼ inch less than the statutory brick on all three dimensions.

Some architects and engineers have come out in favor of yet another size of brick with dimensions of 7⅝ inches long, 3½ inches wide and 2¼ inches thick, which is known as a "modular" brick. This brick is not at the present time made in Nebraska, but it is becoming popular in the East. Presently available information indicates that there is no demand for it as yet in this state.

In addition to these common bricks, there are also manufactured and used in the state the so-called Rancho and Roman bricks, and these bricks were not exactly the same size at the two large plants in the state; however, the difference in size was only 11/16 inch in thickness, ⅛ inch in width, and length was the same. (The sizes were 11⅝ x 3½ x 2¼ inches and 11⅝ x 3⅝ x 1 9/16 inches.)

With the exception of Roman bricks and other fancy non-standard tiles used for facing of buildings, there is one ratio in the size of ordinary bricks which seems to remain constant. Though the size of bricks will vary an inch in all dimensions from place to place and occasionally from brickyard to brickyard in the same city, they are always in a ratio so that the length of the brick will double the width plus the thickness of one mortar joint. Therefore, regardless of the size of the bricks, various standard styles of bond may be used in laying them.

Mortar joints vary from ⅛ to ⅞ inches in thickness. The narrower joint is used with a smooth, uniform pressed brick and the extremely wide joint with a rough textured brick. The standard width of mortar joint for all ordinary brickwork is about ½ inch. The width may be slightly under this dimension when smooth effects must be emphasized and slightly wider—⅝ inch for rough textured bricks. Bricks of standard size, approximately 8 x 3¾ x 2¼ inches, work out well in combination with mortar joints for all of the pattern bonds when an average width of mortar joint (½ inch) is used. When mortar joints of greater or less width than the average are used in the face of the wall, the backing-up masonary requires considerable cutting in order that the headers may be placed in the proper condition.[26]

Even this ratio seems to spring from a customary way of laying bricks to meet certain standard designs or bonds and seems to be supported by no basic scientific requirements.

Scientific Requirements

Standard texts show that there seem also to be no scientific requirements as to the size of bricks.[27]

The federal government has formulated standard specifications covering structural clay products.[28] These specifications are slightly different from those of other testing organizations such as the American Society for Testing Materials[29] or the Standard Clay Products Institute. However, there are no mandatory specifications as to size. Common, paving, sewer and modular, however, are listed. This would seem to indicate that size is not a significant factor as far as the trade is concerned. Naturally they would not want a brick 4 x 2 x 1 inches when ordering common brick, but they know that will not happen. There may very well be a brick that size, but it is not known as "common" brick. They know that when they order common brick from a brickyard that it is going to measure 8 x $3\frac{3}{4}$ x $2\frac{1}{4}$ inches with not more than $\frac{1}{4}$ inch variation on any one dimension, depending on the brickyard and the location.

The federal specifications have been approved by the Federal Specification Board for use by all federal departments. They are very often incorporated into the specifications on private projects and are the result of conferences held with leading architects, engineers and manufacturers, as well as architects and engineers employed in the various construction divisions of the federal government.

Usefulness of Standard Sizes

From the previous discussion it seems clear that a standard size for bricks is not useful within the market as it appears to operate today. A number of standard trade names for various bricks within variable limits might prove useful for purposes of trading specifications, but

---

[26] George A. McCarvey, Brick Laying, U. S. Government Printing Office (1940) p. 120; cf. Standard Clay Products Institute, Brick Engineering.

[27] Serle, The Clayworkers Handbook (3rd ed. 1911).

[28] Palmer, Structural Clay Products, Govt. Printing Office, Trade Info. Bull. 842 (1939) p. 1g.

[29] American Society for Testing Materials Bull. (Mar. 1941) p. 17.

even this does not appear necessary on a state level, because this has already been taken care of on a national level by a voluntary organization of manufacturers and the trade, such as the American Society for Testing Materials and the Standard Clay Products Institute; and it should be noted that their attention is centered on physical properties rather than measurements.[30] In addition, for those who want a more impartial testing, the specifications of the federal government are much better able to bring about standardization than could any single state law.

There would therefore appear to be no need whatsoever for this particular law, and repeal seems to be the proper scientific recommendation.[31]

APPLICABILITY TO OTHER WEIGHTS AND MEASURES STATUTES

In this single case, it appears that all the research necessary to determine the usefulness of the law could be conducted in a simple pilot inquiry of a few intelligent people at little cost. The necessary scientific work was all completed, just awaiting its application to the jural problem at hand.

If similar attempts were made to study other problems of market control, many other areas might develop where law reform could be suggested easily after a careful examination of the social facts surrounding the particular regulation.

Thus it seems that the studies of the experimental jurist may be short or long, simple or complex, depending upon the material of the law and social problems studied. The next and last problem illustrates a field in which such studies will prove both long and complex.

BUILDING CODE PROBLEM

One of the oldest and most active areas of legal interference in the form of direct regulation is in the field of city planning. Although the fairly new zoning ordinances, as an outgrowth of traffic study and airport building, are beginning to feel the impact of Experimental Jurisprudence, building codes, which are much older, continue to retard city expansion by imposing nineteenth-century methods upon

---

[30] See notes 26 to 29 supra.

[31] It should also be noted here that, due to the changes in building practices caused by the introduction of structural steel and other new materials, bricks as bearing walls are rapidly disappearing and are now used principally for facing and curtain walls. In these capacities they meet stiff competition from newer substances. Since this is the case, there is little need for standardization by law to protect the trade or the public.

many aspects of twentieth-century construction. While their main purpose is protection of the public, some of these laws which usually appear in city ordinances serve to perpetuate trade and labor practices of a bygone era. But since they are part of the structure of the craft system, they may have the solid support of some branches of organized labor and of many of the older entrenched contracting firms. For these reasons, if the law is to keep abreast of the emerging industrial revolution in the building industry, these ordinances must be revised to make room for new materials and methods, such as prefabricated houses, trailer houses and various types of other factory-assembled installations.

The extent to which the building codes are retarding progress can only be determined by a careful scientific comparison of the lawfully prescribed methods with those available as the product of modern materials and methods. Whether or not they are being enforced and whether such enforcement is necessary are questions subject to checks similar to those used on other laws.

THE PLUMBING CODE

The building code as a whole in all states and cities covers many details too numerous for complete study in a preliminary examination, but it seems to include items which are within the reach of present techniques and methods.

In order to test the possibility of experimental study, that small portion of the code specifying the type of pipes to be used by plumbers was chosen for a pilot investigation. To further limit the areas of preliminary investigations, only the law on pipes for Lincoln, Nebraska, was used as a test.

The State and City Laws

The laws of Nebraska,[32] like other states, provide for rigid control and inspection of the installation of plumbing in metropolitan and primary cities, of which Lincoln is one. Control of plumbing is in the jurisdiction of a board of plumbing examiners made up of the city health officer, the plumbing inspector, a master plumber and a journeyman plumber. The board is appointed by the mayor and recommends to the city council rules and regulations to be passed as ordinances governing plumbing installations. It also examines and licenses plumbers. The plumbing inspector is secretary of the board on a salary and must be a licensed plumber. It is his duty to see that the plumbing code is enforced. Plumbing by others than those licensed

---

[32] Neb. Rev. Stat. §§ 19-301 to 314 (1943).

is prohibited, and the inspector, through board action, has power to stop or remove work which does not conform to the rules. The statute also provides penalties by fine and forfeiture of license for violations.

Those portions of the City Plumbing Code adopted in accordance with this law governing the use of pipes are set out in the margin.[33]

[33] *Plumbing Code, as Amended, 1947.*
Article VIII—Materials
§33-801—*Materials, Quality of.* All materials used in any drainage or plumbing system, or part thereof, shall be free from defects.
§33-802—*Cast Iron Pipe.* All cast iron pipe and fittings shall be what is commercially known as Extra Heavy, and shall be coated with asphaltum or coal tar pitch; provided that the Plumbing Inspector may approve the use of Standard Cast Iron Pipe and fittings when he determines that such Extra Heavy Pipe and fittings are not available.
§33-803—*Wrought Iron Pipe.* All wrought iron and steel pipe shall not be lighter than standard weight and shall be galvanized.
§33-804—*Brass and Copper Pipe.* Brass and copper pipe shall conform, respectively to standard specifications.
§33-805—*Lead Pipe, Diameter, Weights.* All lead pipe shall be of best quality of drawn pipe, of not less weight per linear foot than shown below. All lead Traps, Bends and Ferrules shall be what is known as Extra Heavy. [table following is omitted]
§33-906—*Material in Soil, Waste, and Vent.* All main or branch soil, waste, and vent pipes within the building shall be of cast iron, galvanized steel, wrought iron, lead, brass, or copper except that no galvanized steel or wrought iron pipe shall be used for underground soil or waste pipes. All culinary sink waste or stack shall be of soil or lead pipe and no fixture other than sinks or lavatories shall be connected to the same, provided however that in old work or where it is necessary that such culinary sink waste and vent stack be exposed, the soil waste may terminate at the floor line on which such fixtures are installed, and such waste and vent stack may be continued from said floor line to the roof or main vent stack with galvanized iron, and said waste to be fully two (2) inches in diameter to the waste opening at the fixture, and if said fixture is located on the first floor said vent may be reduced in size to one and one-half (1½) inches, but where the fixture is located above the first floor the waste stack shall continue full size through the roof, or connect with the main soil or waste vent.
§33-101—*Penalty.* Any person upon whom a duty is placed by the provisions of this code, who shall fail, neglect, or refuse to perform such duty or who shall violate any of the provisions of this Code, for which a penalty is not otherwise specifically provided, shall be deemed guilty of a misdemeanor and upon conviction thereof shall be fined in any sum not to exceed one hundred ($100.00) dollars and shall stand committed to the city jail until such fine and costs of prosecution are paid. Each day that a violation of this Code continues shall constitute a separate and distinct offense and shall be punishable as such.
The penalty provided in this chapter shall be cumulative with and

To determine the state of enforcement of this statute, a preliminary pilot study was made.[34]

Present State of the Records and the Application of the Plumbing Code

From the very beginning, the study faced a very limited source of information on the Code itself and from records kept. Actually, there is at present only one true and up-to-date copy of the Code available to the city of Lincoln which exists partly in the mind of the building inspector and partly in a booklet of printed pages, typewritten pages and appended newspaper clippings. Records of permits granted and work inspected are only partially indexed and partially retained. Consequently, much of the information obtainable could at best be had by interviews with the plumbing inspector, other city officials and members of the plumbing trade.

Thus the provisions of the Code set out in the margin are only an approximation of what the "Code" requires. Administrative variations are numerous and frequently made by the building inspector. The building inspector seems in practical effect to have assumed an omnipotent position with respect to administering the Code and frankly admits that he allows variations from the Code whenever he becomes convinced that they should be made. What form of evidence is required to convince him could not be ascertained. No record of the variations is kept, and the inspector does not take the trouble to note in the Code permanent changes which he makes. Therefore, the study was limited to that portion of the Code which does appear of record, recognizing that the possibility of error in the analysis is incalculable.

No record of any legal action involving the Code could be found. While the plumbing inspector thought that some court orders had been obtained in the past, he could not recall whether any portion of the Code had received judicial construction. Furthermore, he could not point to where this information might be found, and as a matter of fact he was quite sure it could not be found, as the legal action taken was probably through justice of the peace court with no records.

---

in addition to the revocation, cancellation, or forfeiture of any license or permit elsewhere in this Code provided for violation thereof.

(The usual provisions requiring licenses, permits and inspections are not set out here as they are the general form found in all codes.)

Municipal Code, 1936, As Amended by Ordinance 4562

§44-601—All supply pipes shall be double extra strong lead pipe, copper pipe, or cast iron pipe, not lighter than 150 pounds working pressure . . . .

[34] The writer is indebted to Richard L. Berkheimer and Jess C. Nielsen, members of the Nebraska Bar, for the research connected with this pilot study.

Other Nebraska court dockets were spot-checked with no result.

The expected procedure for the installation of new plumbing or remodeling of old plumbing is that the owner of the building or unimproved property shall file a request for a permit. The building inspector usually grants this permit as a matter of course, and the work is begun. If the owner offers to pay the expense, the building inspector will make periodic inspections as the work progresses; otherwise the inspector makes only a final inspection upon completion of the work. No special or determined procedure is used to insure that all plumbing work is inspected. The usual procedure is to be on the general lookout for new building construction and to rely on informers. The building inspector believes that neighbors are usually inquisitive enough to discover and report suspected failures to secure permits. If, however, the owner secures a permit, the inspection is certain to be made. Occasionally plumbing craftsmen report suspected violations.

In order to determine the quality of the inspective enforcement of the law, a survey of existing structures would be necessary; but the physical and legal difficulties of such a study are apparent.

However, a pilot study was attempted by questionnaire which would seem to indicate an enlightened estimate of what one might expect to find if the full and complete experiment were conducted.

Proceeding on the theory that most of the plumbing installed in Lincoln is done by Lincoln plumbers (licensed) and the materials are

SOIL, WASTE AND VENT PIPES (ABOVE GROUND)

How often do you use the following types of pipe for soil, waste, or vent pipes which are installed above ground? Check which applicable.

	Often	Occasionally	Never
Cast Iron			
Extra heavy	(6)	(4)	( )
Victory	(9)	(10)	( )
Standard	(6)	(4)	( )
Galvanized Steel	(9)	(1)	( )
Wrought Iron	(3)	(5)	(2)
Lead	(3)	(6)	(1)
Brass	(3)	(5)	(2)
Copper	(10)	( )	( )
Other	( )	( )	( )

Specify _____ none

Does the plumbing inspector refuse to allow any of these pipes? _____

Which? (Galvanized pipe for sink wastes: 3; Wrought iron sink waste: 1, "no": 5; "no victory or standard cast iron in 'normal times' ": 2)

Are there any other types of pipe which you would like to use for above ground soil, waste, or vent pipes which the plumbing inspector will not approve, but which you believe to be satisfactory? If so, what are they? (4" aluminum pipe: 1)

SOIL, WASTE AND VENT PIPES (UNDERGROUND)

How often do you use the following types of pipe for soil, waste or vent pipes which are installed underground? Check which is applicable.

	Often	Occasionally	Never
Cast Iron			
Extra heavy	(6)	(5)	( )
Victory	(10)	(1)	( )
Standard	(5)	(6)	( )
Galvanized Steel	(4)	(2)	(5)
Wrought Iron	(2)	(4)	(5)
Lead	(5)	(4)	(2)
Brass	(4)	(4)	(3)
Copper	(10)	(1)	( )
Tile	(9)	( )	(1)
Tar-Fibre	(1)	(1)	(7)
Other	( )	( )	( )

Specify _____ none

Does the plumbing inspector refuse to allow any of these above pipes? _____

Which? (7 indicated tar-fibre; 1 indicated galvanized iron)

Are there any types of pipe which you would like to use for underground soil, waste, or vent pipes which the plumbing inspector will not approve, but which you believe to be satisfactory? If so, what are they? (Tar-fibre: 1; "Would like to experiment with tar-fibre": 1)

purchased either through them or from Lincoln jobbers or retailers, questionnaires were mailed to all of the licensed plumbers listed in Lincoln, Nebraska. The copy of such questionnaire above with the total results of answers indicated is self-explanatory.

It should be noted that the questionnaire uses only two broad classifications in determining what kind of pipe was used; i.e., above-ground and below-ground.

The purpose of the questionnaire was to obtain information on three primary issues: administrative variations, violation even in terms of administrative variations being considered good law, and suggestions of plumbers as to other materials that they would like to use but felt constrained not to do so. As for administrative variations, it should first be noted from the Code that the plumbing inspector is authorized to make such variations only when the material specified by the Code is not available. By interviews with plumbing supply houses in Lincoln, it was first determined that all of the materials specified in the Code were available to prospective purchasers in the Lincoln area. Thus all of the variations made by the plumbing inspector are technically a violation of the Code as such—in fact, so far as could be determined, the plumbing inspector has made no consistent attempt to ascertain whether there is any problem of supply, although it might

219

be that such a consideration entered into his decisions occasionally.

As for installations which were even a violation of the Code as interpreted by the plumbing inspector, it cannot be determined whether the respondent plumbers answered truthfully or not. However, according to the provisions of the Code, this second type of violation is only more flagrant than the type discussed in the next preceding paragraph and therefore would only serve to show that the Code is violated to a greater degree.

The composite results obtained from the questionnaire are noted on the appended questionnaire, and the following observations can be made therefrom:

Questionnaires were mailed to 24 plumbers (those which appear in the Lincoln telephone directory) and from those, 12 answers were returned. There are three general weights of cast iron pipe manufactured: Extra Heavy, Victory (lighter than the former) and Standard (lightest of all), while Extra Heavy cast iron pipe is the only type allowed by the Code. Approximately 90 per cent of the plumbers indicate that they are using Victory weight "often." The remainder were using it "occasionally." Furthermore, the results indicate that between 50 per cent and 60 per cent of the plumbers were even using Standard weight "often" while the remainder were using it "occasionally." These estimates indicate that the Code is being grossly violated as to the requirements for cast iron pipe, which is further substantiated by the fact that from the questionnaire, only an estimated 60 per cent made any effort to use the Extra Heavy weight required by the Code.

Although the results indicate that 90 per cent of the plumbers answering do use galvanized steel, the results also indicate that 30 per cent of the plumbers believe that, or have found that, the plumbing inspector will not allow the use of such pipe for sink wastes. Yet such use is permitted by the Code.

The results indicate that lead and brass pipes are used either only "occasionally" or "never" by approximately 70 per cent of the plumbers. The reason for this non-use should be checked, since the Code permits their use.

The above results were taken from answers for above-ground pipes. A further discrepency was noted with respect to below-ground pipe. The Code specifically excludes the use of wrought iron and galvanized steel below ground. The results indicate that 50 per cent of the plumbers were using wrought iron and galvanized steel underground, and 40 per cent were using galvanized steel often.

From the discrepencies and open violations of the Code indicated by this questionnaire, it seems reasonable to conclude that sufficient evidence has been presented to justify a complete full-scale inspection of plumbing conditions in Lincoln. It also seems reasonable to conclude that at present the Code has little application to what is actually happening and therefore is either grossly archaic or grossly wrong. However, it is interesting to note that the questionnaire disclosed that the majority of the plumbers (only three of those reporting suggested new types of pipe) are satisfied with the Code as interpreted by the plumbing inspector, as indicated by their failure to disclose a desire to use other types of pipe. This result is quite significant and probably can best be explained as emblematical of the conservatism of the craft.

This brief report of part of the pilot study is both revealing and suggestive.

Due to the fact that plumbing installations are usually hidden within the walls, a check of violations as suggested in this preliminary report would be difficult and costly but probably not impossible.

Since the state law gives the plumbing board the right to recommend changes in the Code, it seems rather shocking that even such an incomplete pilot questionnaire as that reported should show so many apparent violations condoned by the plumbing inspector. The failure to regularize these deviations is probably due to lack of finances or qualified personnel, which in turn may be caused partly by the fact that the state law sets such a low compensation for the plumbing inspector.[35]

Scientific Data on Optimum Materials

In contrast to the state of scientific knowledge about bricks revealed in the last study, it seems that there is little conclusive data about the best materials and methods for plumbing. One author has put it as follows:[36]

> Plumbing, an ancient and useful craft, has had difficulty finding its proper place in a modern world of engineering technique. Treated as a stepchild, it has not been properly acknowledged by any particular group, whether architects or mechanical, sanitary, and civil engineers. . . . The old methods are often unscientific, and the new theories unfortunately are very often impractical.

---

[35] Section 19-305 provides that board members, of whom the plumbing inspector is one, shall receive five dollars a day not "to exceed the sum of two hundred" and "assistant inspectors shall receive a salary of at the rate of twelve hundred dollars per annum each." Just how the city can get competent plumbers to administer the Code honestly at these rates is itself a nice question in Experimental Jurisprudence.

[36] Plum, Plumbing Practice and Design, V (1943).

There seems to be much miscellaneous data on the effect of corrosion of the various metals used in pipes,[37] and the American Society for Testing Materials has collected considerable information on this point.[38] The United States Bureau of Standards has also conducted tests in the field of underground pipes covering a period of ten years;[39] but conclusive facts will probably be found still to be in the field of experimental engineering. There is no doubt, however, that the optimum evaluation of various materials and methods used in plumbing is entirely within the reach of a team of sanitary engineers using the available testing methods. The question of whether or not the plumbing Code prescribes optimum present materials within the knowledge of modern science can be answered.

New materials, such as Tar Fibre sewer pipes, could be subjected to a central testing bureau before being offered for Code approval.[40]

NECESSARY RESEARCH UNITS

Thus a small permanent staff of lawyers and investigators working with properly qualified metallurgists, plumbers and sanitary engineers in cooperation with the American Society for Testing Materials, The Bureau of Standards and the industry could make full studies of the law over a long period of time which would result in complete modernization of the plumbing codes. New materials and methods, after a proper test, could immediately find a legal place in the industry.

What could be done for pipes could in a similar manner be applied to the whole of plumbing technique and from there be extended to the entire building industry.

In light of modern experimental methods, there is no excuse for the continued obsolescence of building codes. Here is a field ripe for the application of Experimental Jurisprudence, and there is little doubt that the industry and city fathers could be persuaded to cooperate.

Of course the cost of attempting such a study and the permanent nature of the research involved would put it beyond the reach of any but a permanent and well endowed foundation.

AREAS FEASIBLE FOR IMMEDIATE STUDY

It can readily be seen that although the areas in which lie the four pilot studies so far recounted offer a fertile field for further research,

---

[37] McKay and Worthington, Corrosion Resistance of Metals and Alloys (1936).

[38] American Society for Testing Materials 865 (1949).

[39] National Bureau of Standards, Soil Corrosion Studies, see 19 Jour. of Research 695 (1937) and authorities there cited.

[40] Sec. 2 American Society for Testing Materials 467 ff. (1949).

222

three of them are too expensive to be attempted by other than a highly endowed organization. The fourth, the brick study, was too simple to need further research. Whether or not an inexpensive and practical field for study in similar areas of standards is feasible would require further pilot studies.

While these preliminary explorations were under way, a pilot study of the bad-check laws was also in progress. It developed that these laws offered a fertile field for modest research which promised substantial results. This area was consequently adopted for a more complete illustrative study. Its details, both in the pilot and more enlarged stage, will appear in the following chapters.

CHAPTER X

Analysis and Methods of the Bad-Check Study

After many pilot studies in other fields as indicated in Chapter IX, it was determined that Nebraska Statutes of 1943, Sections 28-1212 to 28-1215, providing punishment for the issue of no-fund and insufficient-fund checks might offer a starting problem for a typical investigation of the effect and efficiency of criminal statutes. A summary of the results of this study are set out in Chapter XIII.

I. THE EXPERIMENTAL DESIGN

Since there were no precedents for such an investigation other than a few pilot studies in similar fields, and since the project required the collection of much social and economic data not currently available in census and other reports, it was necessary to grope in the dark and to improvise the design of the procedure. The data secured depended upon the analysis of the problem, and the analysis in turn would be governed largely by the data found. Since the problem involved large areas of social activity, it seemed that general impressions and rough relationships of the factors were more important than a statistically accurate description of the component parts.

In designing the study, then, an attempt was made to follow roughly the steps outlined in Chapter II. Briefly recapitulated in terms of the bad-check law, these were as follows:

1. The nature of the social problem toward which the bad-check law is directed should be isolated and examined.

2. The laws should be accurately stated.

3. The effect on society of the bad-check law should be observed and measured.

4. Hypotheses should then be constructed to explain the social reactions to enforcement of the law.

5. Jural laws growing out of the broader application of these hypotheses should be formulated.

6. If analysis shows the laws to be inefficient, then new laws to govern the bad-check phenomena should be formulated.

7. The proposed new law might be tested by enactment and further study.

8. Step Eight, the ultimate evaluation of the usefulness of this kind of bad-check law, is, of course, beyond the reach of a single study of this nature.

In designing an experiment to achieve these results, it immediately became apparent that the steps outlined here, as a practical matter, could not be taken separately without prohibitive expense. The facts underlying Step One delimiting the nature of the social problem and those surrounding Step Three, the effect of the law on society, involved interwoven factual situations which would have to be determined from data taken in the same interviews.

Finding and accurately stating the law, Step Two, involves the usual law library research. Step Four, the stating of hypotheses, of course could be undertaken only after the gathering, classification and reduction of the social data to workable form.

The jural laws likewise would be expected to appear only after the data was collected and tested. Some such suggested jural laws are set out in Chapter XII.

As stated in Chapter II, Step Six may take two forms: (1) drafting statutes and getting them adopted in the jurisdiction studied; and (2) the projection of such an adoption by studying the results of statutes like the one suggested which already might be enforced in other jurisdictions. Both of the devices suggested are used in this experiment. The second tends to obviate the necessity of an immediate adoption of an amendment suggested by hypotheses based upon the data collected. As indicated below, the use of such devices as studying different statutes in similar states was projected and tried, but not as widely as planned because of the unfortunate interference of a New England hurricane. The difference in law enforcement in similar counties under the same statutes, it seemed, would also offer excellent experimental material from which the effect of different projected legal regulations or administrative practices which various hypotheses might suggest, could be tested. It seemed wise to utilize devices of this sort to the fullest extent possible under the limitation of time and finances here available. The points at which these techniques appear throughout the following material will be self-evident.

The collection of the social data upon which the project rests, the factual business needs and the results achieved by the statutes, was, of course, basic and had to be arranged so it was possible simultaneously to gather the data needed for Steps One, Three, Four and Five.

225

The arrangement of the results of the social data has been set out in Chapter XI which follows in the order of the first five steps of the suggested techniques of Experimental Jurisprudence mentioned above.

THE SOCIAL PROBLEM

The social problem involved seemed a simple one: to discover the extent to which bad checks interfered with the functioning of the business community and the effectiveness of the criminal law in dealing with the dislocation created by bad-check writers.

Preliminary analysis indicated that there were a number of factors involved: (1) the proportion of the bad checks to the total volume of business; (2) the means which the businessmen could and did use to protect themselves from bad-check writers; (3) habits of the buisiness public, both customers and merchants, in regard to checks; (4) the sanctions which the law placed upon the writers of bad checks; (5) the extent to which the law was enforced; (6) the kind of people who wrote bad checks; (7) the way in which the law acted as a deterrent to the issue of such checks; (8) the effect of the law on the penal system; (9) the entire social cost of the bad-check phenomenon; and (10) the cost to the government of its attempts at control through the criminal law; these were some of the factors. If this data were assembled, it seemed that an evaluation of the needs, demands and desires of the business world and the public at large could be made. In that instance, it should also be possible to determine the effectiveness of the law in controlling the problem of writing bad checks, and also it might be possible thereafter to suggest useful changes in the procedure and substance of the law.

After preliminary informal consultation with teachers of criminal law, law enforcement officials and other interested parties, it seemed that there was no need to study the enforcement of statutes on confidence games, forgeries and the like. Violators of these statutes seemed to be treated differently by the law from insufficient- and no-fund check writers and to be regarded as a separate type of criminal.

SOURCES OF INFORMATION

In order to obtain information on the volume of bad checks and the business losses caused thereby, it was clear that it was necessary to get business figures from banks and various types of merchants. Although the banks kept books on deposits, clearings and the like, there seemed to be no complete totals available on the volume of checks drawn or on the number of checks dishonored. Preliminary studies disclosed further that there were divergent bookkeeping practices by the city and county banks and even that the records themselves were by no means uniform.

In like fashion, it appeared that business houses kept no count of the number of checks they received from customers or the number returned to them dishonored by the banks. Pilot studies also showed

QUESTIONNAIRE 1, BANKS

The University of Nebraska College of Law is making a study of the operation of the bad check law for the State of Nebraska. We would appreciate it if you could give us the following information from your Bank. All details are confidential; only statistical totals for the State and County will be published.

1. Name of Bank

2. Location

Could you give us the following information on dishonored checks? We would prefer totals for the calendar years. But in absence of such figures, monthly or weekly totals taken from a typical banking month or week in the year period indicated would be satisfactory.

Year 1953

Period covered full year ☐ ....
Representative month ☐ ....
　　　　　　　　　　　　　　　　　　Month

3. Total in dollars of checks charged back to your customers. $

4. Total number of checks (items) charged back to your customers.

5. Total in dollars of checks drawn on your bank for the period. $

6. Total number of items (checks) for period.

7. Percentage of total period check business to yearly check business for year indicated.　　　　Per cent

8. Percentage of total items dishonored, question 4 above.

    (a) Not sufficient fund checks.　　　Per cent

    (b) No account checks.　　　Per cent

    (c) Forgeries.　　　Per cent

9. Are the answers to question 8

    (a) An actual figure.

    (b) Your best estimate.

10. Average total deposits during period covered.

    (a) Your bank. $

    (b) Your city. $

    (c) Your county. $

QUESTIONNAIRE 2, BAD-CHECK BUSINESS PRACTICES

1. Name of business: _____

   Address: _____

   Nature of business: _____

2. Does the business accept checks? _____ (if the answer is "No," disregard remainder of the questionnaire except question 15.)

3. What were the total number and amount of checks received by the business?

   1953: Number _____ Amount _____

4. Does the business in keeping records distinguish between *forgeries, no-account* and *insufficient-fund* checks? Yes _____ No _____

5. What were the number and amount of *insufficient-fund* checks the business received?

   1953: Total Number _____ Total Amount _____

6. What were the number and amount of *forgeries* and *no-account* checks the business received?

   1953: Total Number _____ Total Amount _____

7. What is the volume of the business? (1953)

   a. Amount of check business $ _____

   b. Amount of business done on account $ _____

8. What precautions are taken in accepting checks? Does the business require: (mark those applicable)

   a. Personal acquaintance _____

   b. Identification _____

      1) Draft card or driver's license _____

      2) Photograph _____

      3) Others—explain _____

   c. Personal reference _____

   d. Maximum limit on amount _____

   e. Approval of person in supervisory capacity _____

   f. Only on local bank _____

   g. Require additional indorser _____

      1) Known to you _____

   h. Consult a bank _____

   i. Consult a credit agency _____

   j. Others—explain _____

9. a. Is the business insured against loss by bad check? _____ If so, what is the total coverage? _____

   b. Does the business have detective service or other protection against bad checks? _____ Specify _____

10. Of the bad checks which you have received, what are the numbers and amounts in which they have been collected by: (1953)

	Insuf. Fund		No Account	
	No.	Amt.	No.	Amt.
a. Sending back through the bank				
b. Contacting person giving check				
c. Collection agency				
d. County attorney				
e. Attorney				
f. Insurance company				
g. Police				
h. Other—specify				

11. Of the bad checks which you have received, what are the numbers and amounts of those which have remained uncollected?

   NOTE: If the business records do not distinguish between *forgeries, no account* and *insufficient fund* and if it is impossible to reconstruct the records to reflect such differences, use the column labeled total.

Uncollectible Checks

Insufficient Fund		No Account		Forgeries		Total
Number	Amount	Number	Amount	Number	Amount	
1953						

12. Have you brought any civil actions for any bad checks you received since 1941? _____ Explain _____

13. Do you know of any criminal charges having been filed for bad checks given to you? _____ Number filed since 1941 _____ How many? _____

14. Has the business ever paid the county attorney a fee for collecting checks? _____
   If so, give details _____

   a. Any other person connected with his office? _____

   b. Any other person designated by the county attorney? _____

15. What literature or information has been received alerting to the bad check problem?

   a. Where does it come from?

16. *Remarks*

229

that there was also the widest divergence of opinion among the members of the business community as to the seriousness of losses and the necessity for precautions in handling checks.

It immediately became apparent that if the study were to develop the volume of bad checks and the seriousness of their menace to business, the facts would have to be obtained by questionnaires or interviews. After a number of spot checks and interviews, questionnaires were developed and amended later to suit their purpose of securing the pertinent facts. The final ones used for bankers and businessmen are set out as Questionnaires 1 and 2. It also became apparent early in the game that reliable information could be had only by personal interviews. There were two main reasons for this. The first was that since businessmen and bankers had no uniform bookkeeping system and lacked a scientific terminology to describe their operations, it was impossible to devise a questionnaire which would be uniformly understood by all. An example of this was found in the use of the bankers' questionnaire. Although this is a simple one-page document and the facts required would seem to be obvious, it usually took from five to twenty minutes to explain to a banking executive the nature and extent of the information wanted, and if he in turn were left to tell the bookkeepers, the figures produced almost always varied from the type of information desired. The second difficulty was that even if a clear questionnaire could be devised, the businessmen, though they showed cordiality toward the project, could not be counted upon to do the necessary research in their records and to answer their mail. Even in instances where interviewers personally explained what was wanted and left questionnaires to be completed later with self-addressed envelopes, less than half were returned. Pilot studies demonstrated that personal interviews were necessary in all cases and by skilled interviewers who could gain the confidence of the businessmen. Even when all precautions were taken, a small minority either refused to answer or gave false information.

Similar difficulties were encountered in obtaining facts from law enforcement officials and judges. Court and penal records, of course, are public, and the information there, to the extent to which it was recorded, was entirely available; but here again the records were too voluminous and the law enforcement units too numerous to allow an exhaustive study. It also developed that, though the researchers were met with the utmost good will in almost all cases, personal contact and perseverance were essential to gain any reliable information.

SAMPLING

It at once became apparent that if personal interviews with businessmen, bankers and law enforcement officials were necessary to obtain valuable information, it would be impossible to see more than a very small fraction of them. Some kind of minute sampling, therefore, was indicated.

The writer and his assistants were aware, of course, that there are available powerful mathematical and statistical scientific devices for creating sampling techniques which are capable of producing results of approximate minute accuracy. It also developed on consultation with experts that these methods were very costly in time and manpower and quite beyond the budget limitations of this project. It also became apparent that this was the study of the operation of a law of Nebraska alone, and as such, minute statistical data on the exact numbers and amounts of bad checks circulated in the nation, in the state or in any given county were not needed. What was required was a rough estimate of the general effect of bad checks on business. Since preliminary surveys had already shown that the ratio of the volume of bad checks to total business would run to less than three decimal places, an error of 100 per cent in the total figures on bad checks would be of little significance in their relation to business as a whole. Comparatively inexpensive methods which would give an approximate over-all picture of the economic impact of the law seemed to be all that was needed. In the area of court action, official policies of enforcement and penal activities, fairly accurate records are available, and the sampling in this area, as indicated below, was on a much broader base; but it still had to be tailored to meet the demands of convenience and economy.

Spots developed later in the study, as for example where a county-to-county comparison of various enforcement methods became pertinent, where more accurate figures would have been preferable to the tentative ones developed by the method chosen; but such results, although they would have improved the nicety of certain conclusions, soon appeared to be outside the financial scope of the project. If some of the tentative results herein developed for these areas are subject to statistical doubt, there is nothing in the theory of Experimental Jurisprudence or in the methods which it was necessary to adopt here to reach any conclusion at all which prevents the construction of as minute checks as would delight the most fastidious social scientist or statistician. If finances are available for such a check, the writer would welcome it as a further step along the path toward scientific lawmaking.

The methods used in the sampling, which are briefly outlined below, represent a compromise between the scientific accuracy currently available in advanced methods of social science and statistics and the financial necessity of the situation at hand. The theoretical requirements of minute scientific accuracy would have defeated the project at the outset. The choice was between tentative approximation and nothing. It is believed that the material produced by the methods used here is sufficient for illustrative purposes. Improvements in techniques are not only welcome, they are solicited.

With these preliminary considerations disposed of, the following are the methods used.

THE BANKING SAMPLE

In order to get the total volume of bad checks issued in the state of Nebraska, it was thought advisable to visit a number of banks and inquire as to the manner in which they returned bad checks. The sample was made up as follows.

First, using the *Nebraska-Iowa Bank Directory of 1953* as a list, one bank in twenty was chosen at random. After these banks were located on the map, it was noted that 13 of them were near and similar in size to banks located in county-seat towns covered in the county-attorney sample. Thirteen of these banks were, therefore, exchanged for banks of similar size in the county-seat towns, as indicated in the list. This then gave a final list for the bank sample containing 22 banks to be visited, 17 of which were in county-seat towns.

Because the random sample contained no large banks, one bank in Lancaster County with deposits of over $30,000,000 and two in Douglas County with deposits of over $75,000,000 were added, thus making a total of 25 banks, five of which were not in county-seat towns. Their deposits ranged all the way from small western country banks with $300,000 deposits to metropolitan banks having nearly $100,000,-000 deposits.

In addition, it became necessary, in checking the extent of law enforcement in the various counties, to get figures on the number of bad checks in each of the 31 county seats in that sample in Nebraska and at least in six cities in Colorado, Vermont and New Hampshire. This made a total of 36 banks in all in Nebraska, five in Colorado and one each in New Hampshire and Vermont which were visited, and produced statistics from 11 non-sample banks in Nebraska which proved useful later in checking the accuracy of the figures from the 25 sample banks in Nebraska.

The problem of reaching a representative sample of business and professional men taking checks was more complicated.

On analysis it developed that any attempt to interview businessmen chosen on a strictly random sample throughout the state would be impossible within the financial resources available, so a simpler and more stratified selection seemed necessary. One scheme was devised for Lincoln and Omaha, the two metropolitan areas, and another for the smaller towns throughout the region.

As a basis of the Lincoln sample, the classified telephone directory for the city was used, and one business out of 20 listed was chosen. This list was then checked against the United States Census of 1948 for Wholesale, Retail, Service and Manufacturing to see if the number of businesses chosen equaled one in 20 of the numbers listed in each

TABLE 1

Types of Business and Professional People in the Lincoln Sample

Accountants	Grain and Feed Stores
Antiques	Grocers
Apartment Houses	Hardware Stores
Attorneys	Hotels
Auto Accessories	Insurance
Auto Agencies	Jewelers
Auto Repair Shops	Laundry
Bakers	Labor Organizations
Baggage Transfer	Liquor, Retail
Beauty Shops	Lumber Companies
Beer Taverns	Manufacturers
Billiard Parlors	Men's Furnishings
Book Stores	Motels
Bowling Alleys	Music Houses
Building and Loan Associations	Night Clubs
Cafes	Optical
Candy Manufacturers	Paint and Glass Houses
Caterers	Pawnbrokers
Cigar Stores	Photography Shops
Clothing Stores	Physicians and Surgeons
Dairies	Plumbers
Dentists	Printers
Department Stores	Radio Shops (Retail and Repair)
Drugstores	Railroads
Electrical Appliances	Second-Hand Stores
Farm Machinery	Service Stations
Farm Organizations	Shoe Stores
Financing	Sporting Goods
Florists	Storage
Furniture Stores	Tailors
Gas Companies	Wholesale

category. The wholesale and manufacturing category was found to be slightly under one-twentieth of the census list, so a few more chosen at random were added to bring this category up to one-twentieth of the census number. It should be noted that professional men are also included in this list, among them accountants, attorneys and the like. Here the sample relied on was one in 20 only from the classified directory. The list of business units fell into 62 categories which are set out in Table 1, covering 136 business units in all.

A similar sample was devised for Omaha, using one in 40 from the classified telephone directory.

A substantial effort was made to reach all of the Lincoln sample. This often involved returning to a similar establishment as often as four or five times, which resulted in a pattern of 79 usable questionnaires from Lincoln. The Omaha list proved much larger, containing in all over 450 firms and individual professional people; but lack of time and money made it impossible to visit all of these, and finally only 59 usable questionnaires were returned from Omaha.

In the balance of the state, the sampling technique adopted was to visit every business on one side of the street of the county-seat town where interviewers approached the legal officials and bankers. Where the county-seat cities were too large to adopt this technique, one side of half of one of the representative streets was chosen. In all, this yielded 285 complete and usable questionnaires from the balance of the state outside of Lincoln and Omaha.

THE LAW ENFORCEMENT SAMPLE

In making the law enforcement sample, it was thought wise to approach the problem in reverse order to the usual legal procedure.

There are 93 counties in the state of Nebraska, each with separate and almost independent elected law enforcement officials. There are two or more counties where the same person holds the position of county attorney in each. The number of county judges, justices of the peace, sheriffs and deputies, city police, city prosecutors, city courts and district judges varies in almost all of the counties. Though each county has its own district and county court records which are somewhat alike, the records kept by other officials vary in accordance with the personality of the official from meticulously kept books and files to nothing at all. It was clear at the outset that extracting information from all records and reconstructing those which were nonexistent would be neither fruitful nor possible. There were also no immediate criteria from which an experimental design could be constructed.

QUESTIONNAIRE 3, INDIVIDUAL PENAL RECORD

Institution _____ Year _____

1. Name: _____ 2. Number _____

3. Committed for:
   a. Insufficient _____ b. No-fund _____ c. False pretenses _____ d. Habitual _____

4. Plea: G _____ NG _____ 5. Sentence: (Yrs.) _____ (County) _____

6. Date passed: _____ 7. Date convicted: _____

8. Am't of check: _____ 9. Where cashed: (Town) _____

                                        (Type of business) _____

                                        Drinking _____

10. Age: _____ 11. Race: _____ 12. a. Married _____ b. Single _____

13. Address: _____

14. Occupation: _____ 15. Place: _____

16. Education:
    a. 8th Grade: _____ b. Hi-School: _____ c. College: _____ d. Trade School _____

    e. Other: _____

    f. Dependents: (Number) _____

17. Criminal Record: Convictions for Bad Check _____ Forgery _____

    a. Other Prior Convictions:

Offense	Sentence	Time Served	Time off for Good Behavior
_____	_____	_____	_____
_____	_____	_____	_____
_____	_____	_____	_____
_____	_____	_____	_____
_____	_____	_____	_____
_____	_____	_____	_____

    b. General Record:

Charge	Disposition
_____	_____
_____	_____
_____	_____
_____	_____
_____	_____
_____	_____

    c. Penitentiary Record:

18. Psychologist's Report:

19. I.Q.: _____

20. Miscellaneous:

235

In these circumstances, it was decided to examine first the records of the penal institutions which house part of the human end-product of the various law enforcement machines. The biennial reports of the state Board of Control contained many valuable statistics on the criminal population of the state, and, in addition, the records of the penal and corrective institutions, the State Penitentiary, the State Reformatory, the State Reformatory for Women, the Girls' Training School and the State Industrial School for boys, will yield individual case histories of the inmates. Most of these records are public, and the executives of the institutions were very cooperative in making them available. Since the number of persons in these institutions is relatively small, it was decided that the Penitentiary and Reformatory records for the life of the present law, 1942 to 1953, inclusive, should

TABLE 2

Number of Men Committed to the Penitentiary from Various Counties, Whole Twelve-Year Period 1942-1953

Douglas	110	Perkins	4
Scotts Bluff	94	Holt	4
Lancaster	70	Cass	3
Lincoln	40	Dundy	3
Hall	37	Saline	3
Cheyenne	17	Boone	2
Custer	16	Brown	2
Dawson	14	Burt	2
Gage	12	Cedar	2
Keith	11	Furnas	2
Morrill	10	Johnson	2
Saunders	10	Nuckolls	2
Richardson	10	Knox	2
Box Butte	9	Platte	2
Cherry	9	Sarpy	2
Phelps	8	Seward	2
Buffalo	8	Sheridan	2
Dodge	7	Thayer	2
Red Willow	7	Valley	2
Adams	6	Washington	2
Chase	6	Butler	1
Hamilton	6	Clay	1
Harlan	6	Cuming	1
Kearney	5	Hitchcock	1
Kimball	5	Merrick	1
Otoe	5	Polk	1
Dawes	4	Sherman	1
Jefferson	4	Thurston	1
Madison	4	Wayne	1
Nemaha	4	York	1

The remaining counties had no sentences to the penitentiary during the entire twelve-year period.

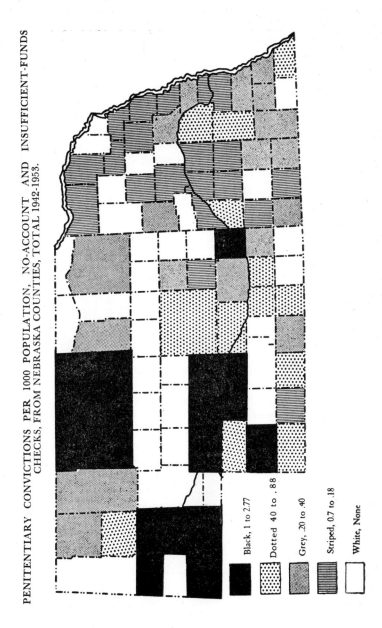

FIGURE 1

PENITENTIARY CONVICTIONS PER 1000 POPULATION, NO-ACCOUNT AND INSUFFICIENT-FUNDS CHECKS, FROM NEBRASKA COUNTIES, TOTAL 1942-1953.

Black, 1 to 2.77

Dotted 40 to .88

Grey, .20 to .40

Striped, 0.7 to .18

White, None

be examined. After preliminary pilot studies of two years of the Penitentiary records, Questionnaire 3, printed herewith, was devised to record information on individual criminals. The records of inmates of the Penitentiary and Reformatory for the entire period of those who were sentenced for violation of the no-fund and insufficient-fund statute were then taken. The other institutions were also contacted; but, as will appear later in Chapter XI on results, the number of inmates there for bad checks was not sufficiently large to use as a basis for constructing a law enforcement sample. When the answers from the Penitentiary and Reformatory to the question, "From which county was the inmate sentenced?" were tabulated, it became apparent that there was a tremendous variation in law enforcement. Table 2 shows the number of persons sentenced to the Penitentiary from the various counties; but this gives a distorted picture of the enforcement of the law because the most populous counties naturally have the most convictions. A better rating is the number of convictions per capita. This is shown in Figure 1, which is a map of the state setting out the ratio of the total number of persons sentenced to the Penitentiary to the total population of the various counties during the entire twelve years.

In making this map, the total number of inmates in the Penitentiary charged with no-account and insufficient-fund checks from 1942 to 1953, inclusive,[1] were distributed among the counties from which they came. Of the 93 counties in Nebraska, 33 had no convictions. Of the remaining 60, the number per thousand from the population of the counties from which they came was calculated. The black counties had the highest rate of convictions, 1.05 to 2.77 per thousand for the entire period; the dotted were next with .42 to .88 per thousand; followed by the grey, .20 to .41; striped, .07 to .18; and white, with no convictions at all. The counties were distributed on the map in accordance with the following table:

TABLE 3

Penitentiary Convictions per Thousand	County	Number of Counties
Over 1	Black	9
.4 to 1	Dotted	13
.2 to .4	Grey	18
.07 to .2	Striped	20
None	White	33

[1] A later check on the counties from which forgery inmates were sentenced showed a very close correlation between the number of forgery sentences from the various counties and the number sentenced for no-account and insufficient-fund checks. These figures are set out in the chapter on results p. 320 ff.

The counties on this map were then sampled to get an even geographical distribution. County law enforcement agencies to be visited were chosen from the counties as follows:

TABLE 4
County Law Enforcement Agencies Visited in Each Group

Black (9 counties)	4
Dotted (13 counties)	4
Grey (18 counties)	7
Striped (20 counties)	6
White (33 counties)	10

Of the whites, there were four counties which over the period of 12 years had sent one or two persons to the Reformatory but which had sent none to the Penitentiary. Of these four counties, one was included which had convicted two Reformatory inmates.

In making the geographical distribution, an attempt was also made to pick county seats in areas depending upon the basic industry such as oil, irrigation, dry farming, cattle ranching and industrial areas.

When the samples of county seats were checked against the retail sales volume by counties, as shown in the 1948 census, the following distribution appeared:

TABLE 5
Distribution of Sample in Relation to Retail Sales

Total Number of Counties	Retail Sales in Millions of Dollars	Number in Sample
1 (Douglas)	Over 318	1
1 (Lancaster)	Over 100	1
32	10 to 41	16
31	5 to 10	7
28	Less than 5	6

In a similar way the county seats chosen, when distributed over the population per square mile, 1950 census, in the various counties, showed the following distribution:

TABLE 6
Distribution of Sample in Relation to Population Density

Total Number of Counties	Population per Square Mile	Number in Sample
1 (Douglas)	843	1
1 (Lancaster)	141	1
29	19 to 60	12
31	8 to 18	8
31	1 to 7	9

A study was made of the operations of the law enforcement machinery, including the county attorney, sheriff, county court, district court, and justices of the peace, city police and city courts, where they were affecting the problem of bad checks in each of the sample county seats. Also, questionnaires and interviews were taken to business units and bankers in these areas, as indicated in the discussion of the business and bankers samples.

It should be noted that this sample of one county in three numerically is slightly heavy in the heavily populated and large-volume-of-conviction areas. Also, it is a bit heavy in the upper brackets of the volume-of-retail-business areas. But it seemed impractical to get a more random distribution because of the necessity of getting data from both Douglas and Lancaster counties, which are unique; and also because it so happened that an extra black county was needed to make a proper comparison with similar counties in Colorado. This will be discussed later.

In each of the sample counties, all of the courts, from justice of the peace, when they handled check cases, to the district court, were visited, and their records for the years 1952 and 1953, when available, were examined. The data required in Questionnaire 4, reproduced herewith, was taken and tabulated. There were also personal interviews with the judges to determine their attitudes and policies toward bad-check writers.

County attorneys and sheriffs in the sample counties were also visited, but owing to the divergence of operations and the lack of records kept by many, a formal questionnaire was found not to be useful. Those officials were interviewed informally, separately, privately and with the assurance of anonymity. They were asked questions to elicit their understanding of the law, their policy toward enforcement of the bad-check laws, whether or not they collected checks for the merchants, the number of collection letters and personal collections in which they participated, their habits in extraditing offenders, records, if any, which they kept, the attitude of the business community toward prosecution, the nature of criminals and the complaints against them, and generally anything on the subject of bad checks which the officials desired to discuss. These interviews lasted from 20 minutes to one or two days, depending upon the cooperation of the official and the records available. Wherever possible, which was in a large percentage of the cases, verbal statements were checked against each other and against the records which appeared in the officials' offices. Needless to say, there were many discrepancies found, and a large number of these were eliminated by further probing.

QUESTIONNAIRE 4, INDIVIDUAL COURT RECORDS

Court _____ of _____ County.
(J.P., City, County, District)

PRELIMINARY INFORMATION

A. Name of the accused _____

B. Residence
   City _____ State _____

   Street Address _____

C. Age _____

D. Sex _____

E. Amount of the check $ _____

F. Date the check was given _____ 195___

   Date of the check _____ 195___

G. Place the check was passed
   1. Town _____

   2. Business which took the check _____

   3. General nature of the business _____

FORMAL PROCEDURES

A. If the accused was not prosecuted, we would like to know why he was not prosecuted. Which of these factors influenced you not to prosecute?

   a. The accused made this check good in total ____

   b. The accused made a substantial part of the check good ____

   c. The accused's past criminal record ____

B. If the accused was prosecuted
   a. When was the criminal information filed _____

   b. Who verified the information _____

      If the information was not verified by the accuser, why was it not verified by him _____

   c. What offense was alleged in the information _____

   d. Warrant returned _____

   e. Was the accused defended by an attorney _____

   f. What plea did he enter
      1—Guilty ____
      2—Not guilty ____

   g. Was the case dismissed in court _____

      If "yes," on whose motion _____

      Why _____

   h. Was accused acquitted _____

   i. Was accused found guilty _____

   j. What sentence was given _____

   k. Was sentence suspended _____

City and state police, where their duties or activities seemed to involve bad checks, were also interviewed in much the same manner. In some of the larger cities, even city attorneys were occasionally found who played a part in the enforcement of the bad-check statutes. A typical summary of the pertinent points of these interviews was collected in memoranda for each county. These were analyzed and are now filed in the office of the writer. Lack of space prevents setting them out in detail here, but Appendix II contains a reproduction of these notes for three counties to illustrate in further detail the type of information obtained in these visits.

THE NECESSITY OF INCLUDING FORGERIES

Before the study had progressed beyond two or three counties, it became clear that forgeries as well as insufficient-fund and no-account checks would have to be included in the survey. The reasons for this were numerous. First, law enforcement officials regarded all bad checks as more or less alike. Sheriffs, police and some county attorneys usually made no distinction between the three types of bad checks either in their records or in all of their enforcement activities before they came to court. In like fashion, the business community considered all three types of bad checks as if they were the same thing and often could not distinguish between them even after a technical and legal explanation. Owing to the separate nature of the statutes, the court records usually made the distinction, and the bankers also knew the difference. Although the incidents of forgery cases were almost as numerous in the district courts as no-account check cases and far more numerous than insufficient-funds, the results were, of course, the reverse in the lower courts and in the banks. In fact, forgery occurred so seldom that a separate study had to be made to determine the number of forgeries occurring in the state, and even the figures available may be unsatisfactory because the incidents of forged checks were so scarce that neither the bankers' records nor recollection could produce an entirely accurate account; but for the purpose of this study, it is sufficient to note that this type of bad check is far more scarce than the other two, though the criminals sentenced to the Penitentiary for writing this type of check turned out to be more numerous.

It should be noted that an examination of the criminal records shows that writers of bad checks apparently do not make the distinction between the three types; and, as the final results of the penal records show, the same individual may have on his record sentences for forgery, no-account and insufficient-fund checks. Socially, therefore, it develops that forgeries, no-account and insufficient-fund checks are all part of the same phenomenon, and hereafter in this study the term "bad check" will be used to cover all three.

THE USE OF DATA FROM OTHER STATES

When the data began to come in from the Nebraska counties, the results indicated that they might support a hypothesis that the felony provisions of the statutes were not effective in checking the production of bad checks. As indicated in Chapter XI, Subpart IV, it seemed possible to check this hypothesis by turning to states which had no felony penalties but which had social conditions like Nebraska. The summary of the laws of the several states set out in Subpart II of Chapter XI showed that a number of states had no felony penalties. Of these, Colorado was adjacent to the most western Nebraska counties, which were some of those most active in enforcing the felony provisions. Four Colorado counties were therefore chosen which had physical and economic conditions and population which could be matched with four similar Nebraska counties. The institutions, set-up of public officials and all other legal devices were also similar, except that there was no general felony provision in the law governing bad checks, other than forgeries, such as existed in Nebraska. The fact that the forgery penalties were almost identical also offered a further useful control. Examining the conditions surrounding law enforcement in similar Colorado counties ought, it seemed, to yield results which might be expected if the felony laws had been repealed in the corresponding Nebraska counties. So by using these Colorado counties as a control, an experimental device could be created.

In like manner, Vermont had no criminal penalties except for forgery but had a legalized collection system, while New Hampshire had both on paper. It seemed, therefore, that like comparative results could be obtained by making studies in these two states similar to those carried out in Nebraska. These results, it was believed, would offer a simulated test of the effectiveness of legalizing the present extra-legal Nebraska collection practices.

The Colorado investigations were completed on the same basis as those in Nebraska, and the compiled results are set out together with references therefrom in Chapter XI.

Unfortunately, the fall hurricanes in 1954 prevented the completion of the planned investigations in New Hampshire and Vermont, but they progressed to a degree which throws considerable light on hypotheses concerning legalized collection, and they also yield much information on the state of enforcement in those two states as compared with that in Nebraska.

These states were not chosen with any eye to determining national bad-check practices but are used solely as an experimental test of the hypothesis on law enforcement and collection raised by the Nebraska law and its study. The results and the hypothetical deductions are explained at length in Chapters XI and XII.

IS THIS A COMPLETE EXPERIMENT?

While this study of the operation of the bad-check law contains some of the elements of experimental methods, it is, of course, only part of a complete experiment which to be concluded would require the creation of further theories and hypotheses as to the effect of the law, the drafting and enactment of a new bad-check law, then a study, after an appropriate time, of how the new law operated in Nebraska. These steps, with some of the problems raised, are discussed in detail in Chapter XII, and a model experimental statute for Nebraska is set out in the Appendix.

If the legislature of the state of Nebraska or one like it sees fit to adopt this statute, the results of the enforcement of the new law can be studied, and the experiment in bad-check laws can proceed further.

II. METHODS OF CALCULATING RESULTS

When the returns came in from the questionnaires and letters, the task of figuring state totals in the various fields was largely one of simple mathematical manipulation of the various facts and factors.

THE NUMBER AND AMOUNT OF BAD CHECKS IN RELATION TO THE TOTAL VOLUME OF BANKING BUSINESS

In calculating the number of bad checks issued yearly in the state, it was necessary to use as a basis the total bank deposits in the state. This, of course, gives a very rough estimate, but there seem to be no sound clearing figures, and because of the way the books are kept, total debits include much beside checks. The figures obtained in the banking questionnaire,[1] in answer to Questions 3 and 4, gave the total in both dollars and numbers of checks dishonored at a given bank. Questions 5 and 6 gave the total, actual count, of checks in dollars and numbers drawn on the bank for the base period, a week to a month or two, depending upon the size of the bank. Question 7 was an estimate of the ratio of these periods to the total yearly business.

Assuming that the bad-check rate was uniform, it was a simple matter to divide period figures by the fraction of the year which they rep-

[1] See p. 227, supra.

resented. By multiplying the total of bad checks thus obtained by the per cent of the whole represented by insufficient-funds, no-account and forgeries given in the answer to Question 8 (usually an actual figure for the base period), it was possible to calculate a yearly total for each kind of bad check.

State and county totals were then obtained by the following process: For a geographic unit, county, group of counties or state: $d =$ the bank deposits in the sample bank(s); $D =$ the total bank deposits in the county(ies); $n =$ the number of checks charged back by the sample bank(s); and $a =$ the dollar amount of the checks charged back by the sample banks. The number and dollar amount of total checks and bad checks for a given county, or group of counties as a whole, can then be estimated as follows:

(1) The *ratio* of the deposits in the sample bank(s) to total bank deposits in the county(ies) is determined. $R = d/D$

(2) N—The estimated number of bad checks in the county(ies) is equal to the number of bad checks reported by the sample bank(s) divided by the (above) ratio (of its deposits to total deposits). $N = n/R$

(3) A—Total dollar amount of bad checks in the county(ies) is obtained by the same method. $A = a/R$

(4) The same procedure is used to arrive at the number and dollar amount of *all* checks transacted in a given county or group of counties.

In estimating the state figures, the totals for Douglas County and for the counties outside of Douglas were calculated separately and then added together to get state totals. This was necessary because the average turnover of deposits in Omaha was much more rapid than in the rest of the state,[2] and because banking in the large metropolitan center is different from that in the remainder of the state.

The forgery figures were obtained in a similar manner, except that due to the scarcity of the forgeries, it was necessary to re-question many of the sample and non-sample banks by mail, asking for forgery figures over a six-month or yearly period. Thirty-one banks returned usable answers, so these were the basis of calculating the forgery figures for the state which appear in Table 11.[3]

It is clear that more accurate totals on the number, amount and type of bad checks could be obtained, but since what is wanted here is the proportion of convictions to total bad checks, and since the latter is so many times the former, rough estimates seem to be satisfactory.

---

[2] See p. 262, infra.
[3] See Ch. XI, Results. 258.

The rest of the figures on the per cent of bad checks to total checks per capita, and the turnover of bank deposits which appear in the chapter on results were reached by simple mathematical calculations based upon these estimated totals and upon census figures. These, in turn, in some cases, were checked against figures issued in the Federal Reserve Bulletin, where available.

The average size of bad checks, shown in Tables 14 and 15,[4] was calculated from actual tapes of checks used by 15 banks in figuring their totals to answer Questionnaire 1.[5] The mathematics of these estimates seems to be self-evident.

BUSINESS LOSSES DUE TO BAD CHECKS

The problem of calculating business losses from bad checks was much more complicated. Due to the fact that there are hundreds of different types of businesses, that many of them do not take checks, or in taking them do not receive bad checks, and that in addition there are many persons who receive checks, like itinerant truckers, farmers, workers and many others with no business addresses, the returns from the business sample explained above are necessarily incomplete. But the answers to the questionnaires submitted to the businessmen and filled in by interviewers had to be the basic starting point for obtaining a workable picture of the bad-check phenomenon.

Usable questionnaires were received from 423 businesses throughout the state. Not all of these were complete in every respect because some of the businessmen refused to answer one or more of the questions. Many of the proprietors declined to give the volume of their business. The most difficulty in this respect was encountered in obtaining volume figures from chain stores because the managers felt that the figures were the property of the home office.

The results calculated from these questionnaires may also be checked against the records of one county attorney from one of the most representative counties which yielded the names of 408 complainants on 1,535 bad checks brought to the county attorney in 1952 and 1953, and, in addition, there were figures on about one-half of the total claims shown on his records over the seven-year period during which he was in office.

The volume of bad checks and the size of individual bad checks can also be checked from the returns of the law enforcement and court record questionnaires. No special mathematical or other scientific

[4] See Ch. XI, Results p. 261.
[5] See p. 227, supra.

problems were encountered here. The tabulated results of these questionnaires are set out in Chapter XI, "Results of the Study of the Bad-Check Problem."

STATE LOSSES FROM BAD CHECKS

When one attempts to leave the detailed tabulated findings and approaches a calculation of state losses on checks, the mathematical problems and the possibility of error in the estimated totals are greatly increased. Three methods were used to reach the total of bad-check losses for the state, as indicated here and in Chapter XI on results. These were estimates based on the location of the business, the losses by types of business and losses by the size of the business. All yielded slightly different totals; but when taken together, it seems possible to reach a very workable estimate of the gross figure for bad-check losses in Nebraska. No figures are offered on national losses because the base of calculation from Nebraska figures alone is too narrow to be statistically sound.

LOSSES FIGURES BY LOCATION

In order to arrive at estimates of losses for the state in the categories of businesses, Retail, Wholesale and Service, listed in the United States Census of 1948, three area units were used—Douglas County, Lancaster County, and the state excluding Douglas and Lancaster counties. This was necessary, as each area had a different proportion of the state's trade, retail, wholesale and service, as well as differing percentage losses to business volume resulting from uncollected checks. There are different proportions of wholesale, retail and service trade in each area. Therefore, estimates were made independently for Douglas County, Lancaster County and the remainder of the state. These estimates were summed to arrive at correct state totals.

I. Basic Method: For any unit, either county or business group, the following is known: (1) the dollar volume of trade of the *sample* (businesses interviewed) (t) ; (2) the total dollar volume of trade—wholesale, retail and service (U. S. Census of Business, 1948) (T); and (3) the dollar loss from uncollected checks for the sample (u).

The estimate of the dollar loss from uncollected checks (U) for the unit (county or business group) was made as follows (using Lancaster County as an example):

(1) The *ratio* of the dollar trade in the sample to total dollar trade is estimated:

$$R = t/T$$
$$= \$15,325,637/\$236,054,000 \quad \text{(questionnaire and U. S. Census figures)}$$
$$= .0649243$$

(2) The estimated county loss from uncollected checks is equal to the loss by the sample businesses divided by the *ratio*.

$$U = u/R$$
$$= \$1,152/.649243$$
$$= \$17,744$$

II. The sample for the "State excluding Douglas and Lancaster counties" did not include wholesale establishments, although 46.7 per cent of the trade in this area is wholesale. It was assumed wholesale establishments had a negligible dollar amount in uncollected checks (this was the case in all wholesale establishments interviewed in Douglas and Lancaster counties), so the area's retail and service trade alone were used to estimate the area's uncollected-check loss. Note that the percentage of volume lost from uncollected checks changes from .02081 per cent in the *sample* (without wholesale) to .01110 per cent for the entire area (with wholesale). (Compare Tables 18 and 21 pages 266 and 268.

Now it should be noted that these figures do not include all the losses from checks in the state, but only from those businesses in the U. S. Census Retail,[6] Wholesale and Service categories. It is also clear that such gross estimates are subject to a rather large error; so to check these results, an attempt was made to reach the total in this group of businesses by calculating the losses in a series of classifications of businesses.

LOSSES CALCULATED BY THE TYPE OF BUSINESS

The businesses surveyed were arranged into 23 categories according to business type. As these types correspond to categories used in the United States 1948 Census of Business, the census definitions have been used. *Miscellaneous* includes all the kinds of business which did not fall into the 22 other categories. (The sample miscellaneous group also includes all businesses with no classification provided by the interviewer.) It is equivalent to all the census categories *not* specifically listed.

The 1948 Census (Retail, Wholesale and Service) provided information on the number of business establishments and dollar sales volume for each business category.

---

[6] It should be noted that there has been no correction of these estimates, based on 1948 information, to bring them up to date with 1953. A 1953 census of business, which will be published at some future date, could be used to correct these totals.

Following the basic method outlined above, the dollar loss from uncollected checks was computed for each business category.

The Nebraska totals are the sum of the individual business category totals. As shown in Table 7, the total losses for the census group figured by individual categories and added together for the state of Nebraska were $316,419, as compared with $256,703 when the totals for all businesses are figured from volumes by location. Thus it will be seen that the estimates made by volume and location show that the state losses are smaller by about 19 per cent than those figured by categories. Of course this was due to the fact that the percentage of losses from bad checks on the average in the various business categories varied by the type and size of business. These variations, which required no complicated calculations to reach, are set out in detail in the chapter on results.

The calculation of the total figures for the state estimated so far are also subject to error because the size of the businesses in the sample and by categories necessarily varied from the actual size of these units in the state. The extent of this variation and also the proportion of the sample to all businesses in the census categories are set out in Table 8.

Now it was further discovered that in general the proportion of losses from bad checks varied greatly with the volume of the business.

LOSSES BY SIZE OF BUSINESS

After analyzing the relationship first between business losses and location, and second between business losses and type of business, already explained, it was decided to find the relation existing between business losses and the size of business.

In this part of the study, two categories, gasoline stations and drinking places and liquor stores, were excluded, because, as shown in the chapter on results, their losses were so very high and their volume so small as to distort the picture based on size alone. This left 278 Nebraska businesses in the sample. The smallest business had an annual dollar sales volume of $700—the largest had $32,000,000. The 278 businesses were arranged into a frequency table according to size. For each size classification, the total volume of sales and the average per-business volume of sales were determined. Total losses and losses as a per cent of dollar volume were calculated.

When the values associated with average size of business and corresponding per cent of volume lost by business of that size were plotted on a graph (Figure 2), an inverse relationship between business size

TABLE 7

Nebraska Business Groups in Retail, Wholesale and Service Trades—
Losses from Uncollected Checks, State and National. (Source:
U. S. Census of Business, 1948, and Nebraska Business Survey)

Kind of Business	Number of Establishments	State Volume of Sales ($1000's)	Loss from Uncollected Checks*	Per Cent of Volume Lost*	Average per Business	
					Volume	Loss*
1. Gasoline Service Stations	2,298	100,045	$ 95,879	.09584	$ 43,536	$41.72
2. Drinking Places; Liquor Stores	1,804	62,149	41,967	.06753	34,451	23.26
3. Eating Places	1,850	48,282	22,983	.04760	26,098	12.42
4. Apparel Stores	487	54,230	22,614	.04170	111,355	46.44
5. Jewelry Stores	242	9,844	2,412	.02450	40,678	9.97
6. General Merchandise (Department and Variety Stores)	494	132,913	32,281	.02429	269,055	65.35
7. Shoe Stores and Repair (R&S)	536	11,631	2,641	.02270	21,700	4.93
8. Hotels and Tourist Courts (S)	564	20,391	4,294	.02106	36,154	7.61
9. Drug and Proprietory Stores	661	38,624	6,630	.01716	58,433	10.03
10. Sporting Goods Stores	42	2,748	375	.01366	65,429	8.93
11. Groceries and Meat Markets	2,625	222,499	27,548	.01237	84,762	10.49
12. Farm Equipment	765	97,725	11,209	.01147	127,745	14.65
13. Household Appliances; Radio Stores and Repair (R&S)	683	28,281	2,833	.01002	41,407	4.15
14. Hardware; Paint, Glass, Wallpaper	790	47,786	4,100	.00858	60,489	5.19
15. Automobiles, Parts; Repair, and Garages (R&S)	2,297	243,542	11,528	.00473	106,026	5.02
16. Furniture Stores	275	34,051	688	.00202	123,822	2.50
17. Cleaning, Dyeing; Laundries (S)	332	13,319	161	.00121	40,117	.48
18. Lumber Yards	500	69,557	639	.00092	139,114	1.28
19. Barber, Beauty Shops (S)	1,692	6,820	0	0	4,031	0
20. Dairy Products; Milk Dealers (R&W)	168	35,690	0	0	212,440	0
21. Hay, Grain, Feed	242	28,299	0	0	116,938	0
22. Florists	74	2,334	0	0	31,541	0
23. Miscellaneous—All other census groups (R,W,S)	7,150	2,460,475	25,637	.00104	344,122	3.59
NEBRASKA	26,571	3,771,235	316,419	.00839	141,930	11.91
UNITED STATES	2,681,498	334,296,780				

* Estimated from results of questionnaires; see Chapter X on methods.
R. = retail; S = service; W = wholesale.

TABLE 8

Comparison by Kind of Business of Nebraska Businesses, 1953, with the Census of Nebraska Business, Retail, Wholesale and Service, 1948.

Kind of Business	Number of Businesses			Volume of Sales			Average Per-Business Sales Volume	
	Total (Census)	Sample	Sample as per cent of Total	Total (Census) ($1000's)	Sample ($1000's)	Sample as per cent of Total	Census (dollars)	Sample (dollars)
Column Number	(1)	(2)	(3)	(4)	(5)	(6)	(7)	(8)
NEBRASKA	26,571	326	1.23	3,771,235	111,006	2.94	141,930	340,509
1. Gasoline Service Stations	2,298	16	.70	100,045	972	.97	43,536	60,781
2. Drinking Places; Liquor Stores	1,804	32	1.77	62,149	1,651	2.66	34,451	51,601
3. Eating Places	1,850	8	.43	48,282	305	.63	26,098	38,075
4. Apparel Stores	487	23	4.72	54,230	2,556	4.71	111,355	111,146
5. Jewelry Stores	242	13	5.37	9,844	828	8.42	40,678	63,731
6. General Merchandise Group (Dept. & Variety Stores)	494	14	2.83	132,913	1,902	1.43	269,055	135,879
7. Shoe Stores & Repair (R&S)	536	9	1.70	11,631	207	1.78	21,700	23,001
8. Hotels & Tourist Courts (S)	564	8	1.42	20,391	2,303	11.29	36,154	287,863
9. Drug & Proprietory Stores	661	25	3.78	38,624	2,529	6.55	58,433	101,147
10. Sporting Goods Stores	42	6	14.29	2,748	1,493	54.33	65,429	248,833
11. Groceries & Meat Markets	2,625	26	.99	222,499	3,764	1.69	84,762	144,762
12. Farm Equipment	765	6	.78	97,725	1,151	1.18	127,745	191,797
13. Household Appliances	683	11	1.61	28,281	629	2.22	41,407	57,182
14. Hardware; Paint, Glass, Wallpaper	790	22	2.78	47,786	2,518	5.27	60,489	114,434
15. Automobiles, Parts; Repair, and Garages (R&S)	2,297	28	1.22	243,542	26,725	10.97	106,026	954,453
16. Furniture Stores	275	7	2.55	34,051	495	1.45	123,822	70,714
17. Cleaning, Dyeing; Laundries	332	6	1.81	13,319	414	3.11	40,117	69,017
18. Lumber Yards	500	3	.60	69,557	1,850	1.84	139,114	616,667
19. Barber, Beauty Shops	1,692	2	.12	6,820	37	.54	4,031	18,550
20. Dairy Products; Milk Dealers (R&W)	168	2	1.19	35,690	10,352	29.01	212,440	5,176,000
21. Hay, Grain, Feed	242	3	1.24	28,299	490	1.73	116,938	163,333
22. Florists	74	5	6.76	2,334	231	9.90	31,541	46,149
23. Miscellaneous (All other Census Groups, R.W.S.)	7,150	51	.71	2,460,475	47,604	1.93	344,122	933,410

R—Retail; W—Wholesale; S—Service.

251

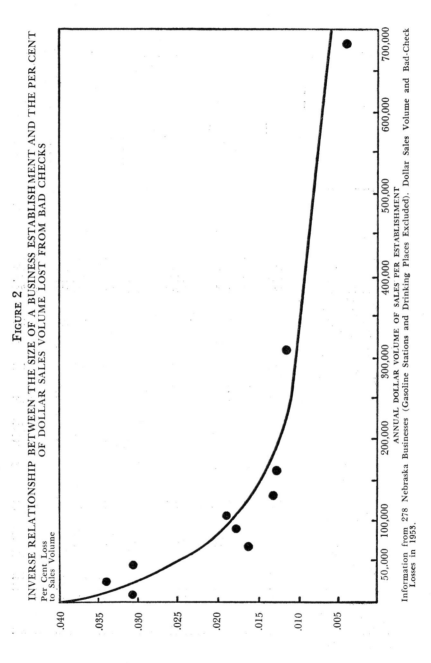

FIGURE 2

INVERSE RELATIONSHIP BETWEEN THE SIZE OF A BUSINESS ESTABLISHMENT AND THE PER CENT
OF DOLLAR SALES VOLUME LOST FROM BAD CHECKS

Per Cent Loss
to Sales Volume

ANNUAL DOLLAR VOLUME OF SALES PER ESTABLISHMENT

Information from 278 Nebraska Businesses (Gasoline Stations and Drinking Places Excluded). Dollar Sales Volume and Bad-Check Losses in 1953.

and the per cent of volume lost appeared. Table 9 shows the statistics from which this graph was plotted.

A free-hand curve fitted to the data describes the general character of the relationship. Using the regression line, it can be predicted that businesses of a given size will lose, *on the average,* a given per cent of sales volume from uncollected checks, as shown in Table 10.

TABLE 9

Bad-Check Losses by Size of Business Volume, 1954*

Size of Business	Number in Class	Total Volume in Class	Total Loss in Class	Per Cent Volume Lost	Average per Establishment	
					Volume	Loss
Under $19,999	42	$ 416,009	$ 128	.03077	$ 9,905	$ 3.05
$ 20,000-$ 39,999	37	991,945	339	.03418	26,809	9.16
40,000- 59,999	31	1,492,577	456	.03055	48,148	14.71
60,000- 79,999	30	2,011,256	331	.01646	67,042	11.03
80,000- 99,999	22	1,891,500	335	.01771	85,977	15.23
100,000- 119,999	23	2,329,244	430	.01846	101,271	18.70
120,000- 149,999	18	2,371,337	289	.01219	131,735	16.06
150,000- 199,999	18	2,903,000	340	.01171	161,278	18.89
200,000- 499,999	27	8,304,274	976	.01175	307,366	36.15
500,000- 999,999	14	9,544,334	386	.00406	681,738	28.54
1,000,000 and over	16	76,066,500	1,733	.00228	4,750,406	108.31

* Results of 278 questionnaires.

Furthermore, this relationship raises the question of whether or not the sample of Nebraska business was biased by containing too large a

TABLE 10

*Per Cent of Volume Lost through Bad Checks
in Relation to Size of Business*

Size of Business (Sales Volume)	Per Cent of Volume Lost through Uncollected Checks
$ 10,000	.036
20,000	.032
40,000	.027
80,000	.020
160,000	.0130
320,000	.0100
640,000	.0065

proportion of very large or very small firms. If so, the state estimates would be accordingly distorted.

Table 8 was set forth to test the representativeness of the sample when classified by kind of business. The average sales volume of business of a given type (e.g., gasoline stations) in the sample is compared with the average sales volume of the same type of business as obtained from the 1948 Census of Nebraska Business. For almost all types of business, the average size was larger in the sample than in the census. Apparently the sample contained too many larger-than-average business establishments. Percentagewise, these larger establishments typically have smaller losses in proportion to volume. (See Figure 2.) This means that the original estimate of total dollar loss to Nebraska business is understated.

However, the graph in Figure 2 describing the relationship between business size and per cent of volume loss also provides a method of adjustment.

The procedure and results were as follows:

(1) The 1948 Nebraska Business Census was used to determine the average sales volume per establishment for each kind of business. See Table 8, Column (7).

(2) An estimated per-cent loss for each kind of business was obtained by using the graph in Figure 2.

(3) Total dollar losses for each type of business were then obtained. (Per cent of volume lost times total sales volume, by kind of business.)

Conclusion:

(4) These losses by kind of business were then added, and equalled $378,456. This is a corrected estimated total loss from bad checks to all business in Nebraska covered by the census.

It should be noted that the two groups, (1) drinking places and liquor dispensaries, and (2) gasoline stations, were not included in determining the graph. Therefore the original estimates for these businesses were used in reaching the corrected total. Of course the results obtained by the above method were not accurate for any specific kind of business, as they were based only upon size differences. However, the results seem valid for Nebraska business as a whole. This is verified by the following test: Using the average size of business by type given by the sample (see Table 8, Column (8)), and calculating state totals by the above method, business losses in Nebraska were estimated to be $310,027, which corresponds quite closely to the $316,419 obtained by the original business-by-type analysis. (See Table 7.)

Thus the highest calculated loss from bad checks for the census categories of businesses, based upon the sample results and the census average size, is about $379,000. Now it should be noted that the census average, being an arithmetic average of size, is likely to be distorted in favor of the larger businesses, which are fewer in number but which cause an arithmetic average to be larger than the median.

It may well be, and probably is, true that the median business in Nebraska in all categories is much smaller than the census arithmetic average; but on the other hand Table 9 shows that over 95 per cent of the volume of business is found in the larger businesses above the median size. Since this same ratio undoubtedly obtains in the entire state, the actual total loss figures might not be higher than $379,000.

Therefore it is safe to say that, at the outside, Nebraska losses from bad checks in the census category of businesses (Retail, Wholesale and Service) will range around $400,000 a year.

Since the data from the representative county attorney's office shows that 75 to 80 per cent of all complaints on bad checks came from this census category of businesses, the total loss in the state from all bad checks would be somewhere around $500,000. Totals for the United States as a whole calculated from such a base are too speculative to be sound. No fast conclusions on national losses are suggested here.

SOCIAL RESULTS OF ENFORCING THE BAD-CHECK LAWS AND THEIR EFFECT ON SOCIETY

No special techniques or methods other than those revealed in Chapter XI on results were necessary to assemble the material on the results of enforcing the bad-check laws. The interviews with many businessmen and officials, of course, involved considerable skill, but only that which comes after long practice and contact with persons having confidential information. Compiling the data also involved certain exercise of judgment in choosing materials which seemed relevant to the purposes of the study. The methods used in assembling the numerous tables involved are self-evident or sufficiently apparent from the data itself. The raw materials from which these tables were drawn are found in the public records of the penal institutions, the courts and the officials. That which came from their experience was assembled in county memoranda for each county visited.

It should be repeated again that the author and his co-workers make no claim to perfection of the methods or finality of the data presented in this study. It is offered not as a model of detailed technical procedure but rather as an indication of the general direction in which more technically perfect methods can lead. If there are defects in the conclusions reached, it is hoped that the development of more accurate techniques by persons better equipped with the tools of social science may be applied to achieve a more useful Experimental Jurisprudence.

CHAPTER XI

Results of a Study of the Bad-Check Problem

THE NATURE OF BAD CHECKS

A check, as almost everyone knows, is an order on a bank to pay a sum of money to a designated person. The bank is under contract obligations to the drawer of the check to pay it when presented if the drawer has an account containing sufficient funds to cover the check. If such is not the case, the bank is under no obligation to honor it and usually refuses to do so. When a check is dishonored for any reason whatsoever, it is usually termed a "bad check" and is returned by the bank to the holder. In that case, the law provides two remedies. The holder has a civil action against the drawer for the full amount of the check and damages. In addition, under the laws of most states, there are usually criminal sanctions. This study is concerned chiefly with the latter, their enforcement and effect on society and the possibilities of improving the laws better to meet the needs of business, the public at large, the drawers and the law enforcement officials.

There are many grounds upon which banks may reject checks, among which are: incompleteness of the fundamental requirements on the face of the check, stopped payment, improper endorsements, patent alterations, improper signatures, forgeries, insufficient funds and no account in the name of drawer. The last three, constituting well over 90 per cent of all the reasons given for dishonoring checks, are the ones where the state statutes place criminal sanctions upon the drawer. This study is confined to the effect upon business in the state of Nebraska of these three types of defective checks and to the impact of the criminal law in this area upon business and society. Hereafter whenever the term "bad check" is used, it refers collectively only to forged, insufficient-fund and no-account checks. These three component types of bad checks will be designated by the individual terms: (1) forgery, when the signature of the drawer of the check is falsified or placed thereon without his authority; (2) insufficient-fund, when the drawer has an account, but the bank has rejected the check because the balance therein is not large enough to pay the check; and

(3) no-account, when the drawer has no account at all in the drawee bank at the time when the check is presented for payment. The latter type of check is sometimes given the name of "no-fund check" by both businessmen and lawyers, and quite often they use the generic term "bad check" indiscriminately to cover all, some or any of the three types.

1. THE NATURE OF THE PROBLEM OF BAD CHECKS

Popular literature is full of stories about writers of bad checks who are pictured as "Fancy Dan" forgers, annually extracting millions from gullible businessmen. One recent article[1] which has gained wide circulation and credence has placed these losses to businessmen in the United States from bad checks between $500,000,000 and $600,000,000 annually. There is little scientific discussion of the problem by writers other than experts on forgery. The average businessman, when questioned about it, inclined to regard the problem very seriously. If he has been duped into cashing a bad check, and few have not, he feels that he has been "had." His blood pressure rises, and he usually joins with the majority of law enforcement officials in demanding more stringent penalties aimed at preventing the repetition of the outrage.

What are the real facts?

In order to find the true impact of bad checks upon the community, hundreds of businessmen, bankers, lawyers, judges and law enforcement officials from Nebraska, Colorado, Vermont and New Hampshire, carefully chosen by random and stratified sampling as explained elsewhere,[2] were interviewed. The state of Nebraska, for convenience, was chosen as the principal area for the study of their activities. Over a period of approximately six months their books were examined, their records sampled and their personal experiences obtained through the medium of letters, questionnaires and interviews. Each bit of information was voluntarily given and was cross-checked against the records and testimony of others. The results were collected, statistically correlated and reduced to this report, which offers some educated guesses indicating the real state of affairs in the enforcement of the criminal law of Nebraska relating to bad checks.

---

[1] Nolan, Big Business in Bad Checks, N.Y. Times, Mag., Aug. 29, 1954, p. 15. The source of these figures may be a "survey" made by a company selling check protectors, see Newsweek 75 (June 7, 1954). See also Yoder, You'd Never Think They Were Crooks, Saturday Evening Post 17 (April 4, 1953), which is typical of the literature on the subject. But see note 6, infra.

[2] See Ch. X, Analysis and Methods.

THE NUMBER AND AMOUNTS OF BAD CHECKS IN RELATION TO
THE TOTAL VOLUME OF BANKING BUSINESS

There are no complete records kept in the state by either business-men or bankers which will give the exact volume and kind of bad checks. To set up such a system of records would require an astronomi-cal amount of accounting, so this material is necessarily based upon the records of banks chosen as indicated in the chapter on analysis and methods.[3]

CHECKS DISHONORED BY THE BANKS

In order to determine the volume of bad checks in the state of Nebraska, a sample number of carefully chosen city and country banks were interviewed, and from their records the actual numbers of checks dishonored by them during a given period, a week to a month, depend-ing upon the size of the bank, were obtained. The estimates for the year's total for 1954 then were calculated. As a check on the list of sample banks, there were also further interviews with banks which were outside of the sample but conveniently located in the county-

TABLE 11

*Estimated Number and Amount in Dollars of Bad Checks Compared
with Number and Amount of Total Checks, and Total Bank
Deposits, State of Nebraska and Douglas County, 1954*

	State,† (Sample)§	State,‡ (Non-Sample)**	Douglas County††
Number of Banks*	412	412	14
Deposits (Amount in Millions)	$1525.7	$1525.7	$523.9
Total Amount of Checks	$18,768,544,000	$19,648,732,000	$10,698,584,000
Amount of Checks Charged Back	$ 25,338,247	$ 31,311,587	$ 8,528,294
Total Number of Checks	83,182,626	92,482,403	19,014,825
Number of Checks Charged Back	410,730	451,244	97,630
Insufficient-Fund Checks	371,074	395,917	83,503
No-Account Checks	36,026	51,697	13,540
Forged Checks (31 Reporting Banks, Sample—Non-sample)	3,630	3,630	587

* Figures on number of banks and deposits from *Nebraska Iowa Bank Directory (1953)*.
† Sample estimates plus Douglas County estimates.
‡ Non-sample plus Douglas County.
§ Sample: Twenty-two banks, selected at random, and one Lancaster County bank. (See chap-ter on methods.)
** Non-Sample: Eleven banks that were also visited.
†† Douglas County: Three banks.
Since the deposits in Douglas County are ⅓ of the deposits in the state, independent estimates were made for Douglas County and were added with the appropriate sample and non-sample estimates to arrive at the estimates for the state.

[3] Nebraska-Iowa Bank Directory (1953 ed.) was the basic material used.

seat towns where interviewers visited district attorneys and public officials falling within that part of the study. Estimates were then calculated from this group and compared with the results obtained from the sample banks. This, of course, is not a completely accurate statement of the number and amount of bad checks in the state, but it gives a working estimate which will show the distribution of bad checks between the rural areas of the state and Douglas County, situs of Omaha, the state's one large metropolitan area.

As set out in Table 11, there are 412 banks in the state with total deposits of about $1,526,000,000. It is estimated that during the year they handle around $20,000,000,000 worth of checks and charge back a total of $25,000,000 to $30,000,000 worth of bad checks. The total number of checks drawn in the state is around 90,000,000, and 450,000 of these are bad. These figures indicate that one check in 200 drawn on the banks of the state is a bad check. Of these rejected checks, about 90 per cent are dishonored for insufficient funds. A bit over nine per cent are no-account checks and less than one per cent are forgeries. The per cent of the three types of bad checks to the total checks in the state is shown in Table 12.

TABLE 12

Per Cent of Bad Checks to the Total Number of Checks Cashed

	All Bad Checks	Insufficient-Fund Checks	No-Account Checks	Forgeries
1. State (sample)	.49	.45	.04	.004
2. State (non-sample)	.46	.41	.05	.004
3. Douglas County	.51	.44	.07	.003
4. State exclusive of Douglas County (sample)	.49	.45	.03	.005
5. State exclusive of Douglas County (non-sample)	.45	.40	.05	.004

The incidence of bad checks as compared with the total number of checks cashed appears slightly greater in Douglas County (51 out of every 10,000) as compared with the rest of the state (49 out of 10,000).

The proportion of no-account checks is about twice as great in Douglas County (seven out of every 10,000 checks cashed) as compared with the rest of the state (three out of 10,000 checks cashed). (Estimates are from sample.)

However, there are about the same proportion of insufficient-fund checks cashed in Douglas County (44 in every 10,000) as in the rest of Nebraska (45 out of 10,000).

The number of forged checks as compared with total checks is smaller in Douglas County (three out of 100,000 checks) as compared with the rest of the state (five out of 100,000 checks, as estimated from sample banks).

In terms of the number of people in the state, the number of rejected checks averages one-third check per capita per year. Table 13 shows the annual proportion of the three classes of bad checks to the population.

TABLE 13

Number of Incidents of Bad Checks per Capita,
Nebraska and Douglas County, per Annum

	Bad Checks	Insufficient-Fund Checks	No-Account Checks	Forgeries
State (sample banks)	.31	.28	.03	.003
Douglas County	.35	.30	.05	.002
Nebraska excluding Douglas County (sample banks)	.30	.28	.02	.003

Figures calculated from Table 11, using U. S. Census, 1950.

Annually, there are 31 instances of bad checks for every 100 people in Nebraska; 28 of these checks are insufficient-fund, three are no-account. There appear to be three forgeries a year for every 1,000 people in the state.

On a per-capita basis, Douglas County has a few more instances of bad checks (35/100 of a check per person) than the remainder of the state (30/100 of a check per person); but Douglas County has over twice as many no-account checks per capita as the rest of the state. Thus, for every 100 people in Douglas County, there are 30 insufficient-funds checks and five no-account checks per year, whereas in the rest of Nebraska for every 100 people there are 28 insufficient-funds checks and two no-account checks a year.

Annually there are about the same number of checks drawn per capita in Douglas County (67.6) as compared with the remainder of the state (61.4), but the size of the checks as shown below is much larger in the city of Omaha.

FINANCIAL SIGNIFICANCE OF BAD CHECKS

When one turns to the financial significance of bad checks, it immediately becomes apparent that, measured against the total banking business, they are insignificant.

SIZE OF BAD CHECKS, STATE OF NEBRASKA AND DOUGLAS COUNTY

The average size of bad checks, as shown in Table 14, is about one-third the size of the average good check.

TABLE 14

*Average (Arithmetic) Size of Bad Checks Compared with Good Checks
Derived from Total Estimates Given in Table 11.*

	Bad Checks	Good Checks
Nebraska..(sample)	$62	$226
(non-sample)	69	202
Douglas County....................................	87	563
Nebraska, excluding Douglas		
County.. (sample)	54	125
(non-sample)	64	114

Note that in Douglas County the average bad check was about $30 larger than the average bad check in the rest of the state.

The average (arithmetic) size of forged checks for the state was $34.60.

Table 15, taken from a different sample, shows that three-fourths of all bad checks returned throughout the state outside of Lincoln and Omaha were less than $30.00 each, and the most numerous amounts are from $5.00 to $10.00.

TABLE 15

Size of Bad Checks

Arithmetic Average Amount.......................................	$52.23
Median Amount..	10.00
First Quartile..	5.00
Third Quartile..	28.00
Mode (181 Checks)..	5.00

Thus, 50 per cent of the bad checks received were $10.00 or less, while 25 per cent were $5.00 or less and 75 per cent were $28.00 or less. Notice that ¾ of the checks were considerably below the arithmetic average of $52.23.

Source: Fifteen banks provided tapes which recorded the number and size of the bad checks received in given time periods. There is a record for 1,113 checks totaling $58,288. The banks were in the following counties: Colfax, Custer, Red Willow, Brown, Hall, Holt, Scotts Bluff, Garfield, Dakota, Cass, Thomas, Dodge, Webster (two banks) and Douglas (1954).

RATIO OF DOLLAR VALUE OF BAD CHECKS TO THE TOTAL CIRCULATION
OF CHECKS

The ratio of the dollar value of bad checks to the total volume of check business is very small. Table 16 shows these proportions.

TABLE 16

Ratio of Dollar Value of Bad Checks to Total Circulation of Checks

	Sample	Non-Sample	Both Sample and Non-Sample
Nebraska	.00135	.00159	
Douglas County			.00080
Nebraska, excluding Douglas County	.00208	.00255	

Calculated from the total volume of checks set out in Table 11.

In the state as a whole, 1.3 mills out of each dollar of checks drawn are bad, and in Douglas County .8 of a mill per dollar are bad, while in the state outside of Douglas County, 2 mills per dollar are bad. Thus, the proportion of the dollar value of bad checks to the total checks in the rural areas is one and one-half times larger than in the metropolitan area.

TURNOVER OF BANK DEPOSITS AND PER-CAPITA DOLLAR VALUE
OF CHECKS

Though Douglas County shows a greater number of bad checks per capita, and though the bad checks average larger than the rest of the state, in proportion to the banking business, the losses are much smaller.

Douglas County has only 21 per cent of the population of the state, but it has 34 per cent of the bank deposits, and 57 per cent of total volume in dollars of checks.

The bank deposits in Douglas County turn over at a rate of 20 times in a year, while in the rest of the state the annual turnover is only nine times, and for the state including Douglas County only 13.

Likewise, the annual per-capita total of checks drawn in Douglas County is $38,100, while in the rest of the state it is only $8,600; for the state as a whole it is $14,800.

So, proportionately to the banking business done, there are many more incidents of bad checks in the smaller towns and rural areas. Thus the potential crime rate related to the amount of checks in circulation is much higher in the non-metropolitan areas.

It is clear, of course, that not all of the bad checks returned by the banks are criminal or represent financial losses to the businesses receiving them. A large proportion, well over 98 per cent by number and dollar volume, are collected either by the business itself or through attorneys and collection agents.

BUSINESS LOSSES DUE TO BAD CHECKS

In order to determine the ultimate losses to businessmen from bad checks, a questionnaire was devised,[4] after a number of pilot surveys, and the businessmen in each sample county-seat town[5] where district courts and law enforcement officials were located were interviewed to determine the volume of their business, the number of checks which they received and the number and amount of their losses on bad checks. It was, of course, manifestly impossible to interview even a small fraction of the businesses interested, so a sample was devised. The method is explained in detail elsewhere.[5] In all, businessmen in 31 counties were contacted, but the Lincoln (Lancaster County) results, being the most complete, are the most reliable.

As was to be expected, no businessmen kept books showing the number of checks received during a year. So where these figures appear, they are estimates by the proprietor or represent a figure calculated from the actual number of checks received over a short period. As to the numbers and amounts of checks uncollected, however, the figures are more accurate. Each business had a record for income tax and other purposes of their unpaid checks. More often than not, they still held the actual bad checks themselves. Some of the proprietors were loath to give the figures on the volume of business for the year, but 344 out of 423 interviewed offered such totals, and they were usually straight from the books of the establishment. While the sample may be too limited to estimate accurately the losses for the entire state, it seems large and diversified enough to give an adequate picture of the losses in relation to the volume of various types of businesses.

The results were also checked by a very intensive study of the records of a county attorney in one representative Nebraska county. These contain the names of all the check writers and the amounts of the checks upon which the businessmen complained during the years 1952 and 1953. Also, there were taken from these records the names of approximately half of the complaining firms and the amounts of the checks which they brought to the county attorney over a period of seven years.

The court and law enforcement records of 31 counties in the sample for the years 1952 and 1953 and the figures for the penal institutions referred to later also offer an excellent check on the nature and amount of losses suffered by various types of businesses. Taken all together,

---

[4] See forms set out in Ch. X, p. 228 ff.

[5] See Ch. X, Analysis and Methods as to the manner in which these samples were chosen.

these give a very satisfactory picture of the nature of the bad-check problem. The estimated losses for the state, which follow immediately, are perhaps less accurate in dollars and cents, but have been calculated only to offer the problem in its proper perspective.

STATEWIDE LOSSES TO BUSINESSES ON BAD CHECKS

According to the United States business census of 1948 (last figures available at present writing), the statewide list of businesses in Nebraska in the categories compiled by the census (retail, wholesale and service trades), which roughly correspond to the businesses interviewed, had a total volume of business of $3,771,235,000. This is approximately one-fourth of the estimated dollar volume of checks passing through the banks in 1954. This, of course, is accounted for by the fact that the census figures omit manufacturing, contracting, banking, finance, many of the facets of agriculture and all of the public payrolls. Data from the representative records of the county attorney's office, mentioned above, show, however, that about 75 per cent to 80 per cent of the dollar volume of complaints on bad checks came from those businesses listed in these census categories. In other words, about one-fourth of the businesses by volume of check turnover seem to suffer four-fifths of the total losses on bad checks.

Although it is not necessary to this study, it might be interesting to estimate the total loss to business in Nebraska from bad checks. Table 22, below, shows that, figured by the classes of business interviewed and broken down to include selections from the 1948 census sub-classifications, there was an estimated total loss of $316,419 in unpaid bad checks for the state in 1953. Now as shown in Figure 2, page 252, the proportional losses in bad checks increased rapidly as the volume of individual businesses decreased. So, adjusting these figures to take account of those situations where the average volume of the businesses interviewed varied from the 1948 census averages, the total loss from bad checks is increased to around $378,456. Since this is approximately four-fifths of the total of all unpaid bad checks, the total loss for the state of Nebraska in this field would appear to equal about $473,000.[6]

---

[6] See infra. p. 271. It is, of course, clear that this study covers only Nebraska; but if one is interested in attempting on as narrow a basis as this to calculate the total check loss in the United States, a pure conjecture not based on sound statistics, this would raise the estimated loss for the United States calculated from figures in Table 22 from $28,048,619 to about $44,000,000. That this is an outside figure is shown by the fact that the larger businesses have a lower ratio of loss than do the smaller ones. Since Nebraska is primarily a small business state, national figures based on the Nebraska averages should be decreased proportionately. Also the losses

This figure is a little small because of the fact that the collection of a great majority of the bad checks which were returned to the merchants must have entailed some expense. The interviews, however, showed that in many instances this collection involved no cost other than simply calling or notifying the drawer, but where the checks had to be placed in the hands of civil collection agencies, the fees amounted to from one-third to one-half the amount collected. As shown later, the number and amount of checks collected privately was almost negligible; so it would be an outside estimate to say that the annual loss from bad checks in the state of Nebraska was less than one-half million dollars, or about 38 cents per capita per year.

AMOUNT AND PERCENTAGE OF LOSSES

Leaving speculation and returning to Nebraska business figures, a number of interesting features immediately emerge from the questionnaires. In the first place, Table 17 shows that less than two-fifths of the businesses interviewed suffered any losses at all from unpaid bad checks.

Fewer of the businesses interviewed in Douglas County (one-third) had uncollected checks in 1953 as compared with Lancaster County

TABLE 17

Number of Businesses Affected by the
Problem of Uncollected Checks, 1953

	Number of Businesses that Took Checks	Number of Businesses with Uncollected Checks	Per Cent of Businesses with Uncollected Checks
State (excluding Douglas and Lancaster counties)	282	115	40.8
Douglas County	58	17	32.8
Lancaster County	75	30	40.0
Total	415	162	39.0

The results for the state (excluding Douglas and Lancaster counties) are obtained from 29 counties; 285 businesses were interviewed. In Douglas County, 59 businesses were interviewed; in Lancaster County, 79 were interviewed.

in New England, which is partially covered in the study, see infra. p. 356, run much below those in Nebraska, which would also lead to the conclusion that the United States estimate based on Nebraska ratios is likely to be too large. Even if an amount be added to take care of additional costs of collecting checks civilly, the figure of $44,000,000 for bad-check losses in the United States may still be a little small, but it is nowhere near the $500,000,000 to $600,000,000 figure being widely bandied about. This sum would seem to be about five to ten times larger than any possible figure which could be based on any calculation from the information found in this survey.

and the remainder of the state, where two-fifths of the respective businesses were affected.

Not all the businesses revealed their total volume, but of those that did, Table 18 shows that the ratio of losses from uncollected bad checks to the total volume of business runs to four or five decimal places.

TABLE 18

Dollar Volume of Business Compared with Losses Resulting from Uncollected Checks to Nebraska Businesses Reporting for 1953

	Number of Businesses Reporting	Sales Volume	Loss from Uncollected Checks	Ratio of Total Volume to Uncollected Checks	Average per Business		Average Size of Uncollected Checks
					Volume	Loss Uncollected Checks	
State (excluding Douglas and Lancaster)	241	$22,780,002	$4,740	.0002081	$ 94,523	$20	$16
Douglas	37	73,924,244	1,913	.0000259	1,997,953	52	56
Lancaster	66	15,325,637	1,152	.0000752	232,207	17	12

Losses to businesses interviewed reporting uncollected checks compared to total sales volume were very small, with a loss of .02 per cent of sales volume in the state (not including Douglas and Lancaster counties), a loss of .003 per cent of sales volume in Omaha, and a loss of .008 per cent in Lincoln. The estimated ratio of these losses to volume from uncollected checks was one-eighth as great in Omaha, and three-eighths as great in Lincoln, as in the rest of Nebraska.

Note that the average annual volume of sales per business is much greater in Omaha ($1,997,953) and Lincoln ($232,207) than in the rest of Nebraska ($94,523). (The Lincoln and Omaha establishments interviewed include wholesale businesses, but see Table 20.) The average yearly loss per business is also large in Omaha ($50) as compared with Lincoln ($17) and the rest of the state ($20).

The ratio of uncollected checks to the total number received by the businesses reporting such checks is also small. The figures set out in Table 19 show the ratio of bad checks to the total checks received by the less than 40 per cent of businesses which reported such losses.

In the state, excluding Douglas and Lancaster counties, .03 per cent of the checks taken by these businesses remained uncollected in 1953. Similarly, in Lincoln .03 per cent of the checks were uncollected, whereas in Omaha only .01 per cent of the checks taken were not collected.

TABLE 19

Total Number of Checks Accepted by Businesses Compared with the Number of Uncollected Checks, 1953

	Number of Businesses Reporting	Total Number of Checks Accepted	Number of Uncollected Checks	Ratio of Uncollected Checks to Total Number of Checks	Average per Business	
					Total Number of Checks	Number of Uncollected Checks
State (excluding Douglas and Lancaster)	199	852,628	254	.0002979	4,285	1.28
Douglas	42	379,611	39	.0001027	9,028	.93
Lancaster	45	213,831	66	.0003087	4,752	1.47
Totals	286	1,446,070	359			

Note that the average number of checks taken per business was greater in Omaha (9,038 checks) than in the rest of the state (4,285 checks). However, the number of uncollected checks per business was small in Omaha (.93 of a check) as compared with the rest of the state (1.28 of a check).

When the figures are adjusted to correspond to the state estimated totals, covering all businesses, whether or not they hold uncollected business checks, including wholesale, retail and service trade on a statewide distribution as indicated in the last census (1948), Tables 20 and 21 show that the total effect of bad checks on these businesses as a whole is further reduced by about one-half.

TABLE 20

Number of Businesses Affected by the Problem of Uncollected Checks, 1953 (Estimated State, Douglas and Lancaster Counties; Retail, Wholesale and Service)

	Number of Businesses*	Per Cent with Uncollected Checks†	Estimated Number with Uncollected Checks
STATE	26,571	34.9	9,270
State (excluding Douglas and Lancaster counties)	20,081	36.0	7,236
Retail and Service	17,912	40.4	7,236
Wholesale	2,169	negligible	negligible
Douglas County	4,701	28.8	1,354
Lancaster County	1,790	38.0	680

Source: * U.S. Census of Business, 1948 (Retail, Wholesale and Service).
      † Sample—Business Survey Interviews for 423 Establishments.

This estimate, based on census figures and the results of the interviews, shows that approximately 35 per cent of Nebraska businesses in the census categories had uncollected checks in 1953—9,270 of the 26,571 establishments. In Douglas County, where there is a concentration of wholesale business, fewer businesses were affected (29 per cent). In Lancaster County, 38 per cent of the businesses had uncollected checks; in the remainder of the state, 36 per cent had uncollected checks (assuming that outstate wholesale establishments which were not reached by the interviewers had practically no uncollected checks, which assumption seems valid, based upon Douglas and Lancaster

TABLE 21

Dollar Volume of Retail, Wholesale and Service Trade Compared with Losses Resulting from Uncollected Checks, Nebraska Businesses, 1953 (Total Estimates)

	Number of Businesses	Volume in Sales	State Loss from Uncollected Checks	Per Cent of Business Volume Lost from Uncollected Checks	Average per Business	
					Volume in Sales	Loss Uncollected Checks
State (excluding Douglas and Lancaster counties)	20,081	$1,732,937,000 (46.0%)	$192,321 (74.9%)	.01110	$ 86,297	$9.58
Douglas County	4,701	1,802,244,000 (47.8%)	46,638 (18.2%)	.00259	383,375	9.92
Lancaster County	1,790	236,054,000 (6.2%)	17,744 (6.9%)	.00752	131,874	9.91
STATE TOTALS	26,571	3,771,235,000 (100.0%)	256,703 (100.0%)	.00681	141,930	9.66

Source: 1) U.S. Census of Business, 1948.
2) Business Survey.

wholesale results). Losses to Nebraska businesses in the census classification from uncollected checks were quite small—with a loss of .007 per cent of sales volume, or $256,703, in the state. In Douglas County, there was a .003 per cent loss ($46,638); in Lancaster County, a .008 per cent loss ($17,744), and the remainder of the state, a .011 per cent loss ($192,321). Percentage loss to volume appeared to be less than one-half as large in Douglas County as in the state of Nebraska; Lancaster County percentage of loss about equalled that in the state; the percentage loss was about 1.6 times greater in the remaining area compared to the state including Douglas and Lancaster counties.

Douglas County, with 48 per cent of the dollar volume of trade in the state, had only 18 per cent of the state dollar losses from uncollected checks. Lancaster County had 6 per cent of the trade and 7 per cent of the losses. The remainder of the state, with about half the volume of trade (46 per cent), had 75 per cent of the state's dollar loss to business resulting from bad checks.

Thus it appears that both individually and collectively bad-check losses to business are of no commercial consequence. In fact, they are probably the smallest expense the business suffers, so small that not a single business interviewed outside of banks was found to insure itself against such losses.

DISTRIBUTION OF LOSSES AMONG VARIOUS TYPES OF BUSINESSES

When losses are distributed over the various types of businesses, it will be seen that there are a few businesses which are particularly susceptible to bad-check writers.

Table 22 shows the results of the questionnaires as distributed among the various types of businesses listed by the United States census. These were then arranged in the order which their per cent of loss bears to the total volume of business. Then the state losses were calculated to give the overall picture.

Table 23 shows the per cent of the total state loss suffered by each business, and Figure 3 shows these estimated losses projected against the total yearly volume of each kind of business. It is significant to note that the losses had to be blown up by 200 times their proportional size even to be seen on the chart.

As shown by Table 24, six business categories accounted for over three-fourths of the state's wholesale, retail and service business losses for uncollected checks.

These all are retail businesses, compose one-third of the business establishments of the state by number and have about one-sixth of the trade volume in the state. In fact, gas stations and liquor dispensaries together suffer over 43 per cent of the state's total losses, although they have only 15 per cent of the businesses by number and about four per cent of the trade by dollar volume.

Although the department stores as a group suffered a loss almost as large as the liquor dealers (ten per cent of the total losses in the state), their volume of business was so large that their individual losses were proportionately microscopic. One of the pilot studies showed that a department store in Lincoln, although it was one of the biggest in the state and had such a liberal policy on checks that it took

FIGURE 3

CHECK LOSSES IN RELATION TO BUSINESS VOLUME

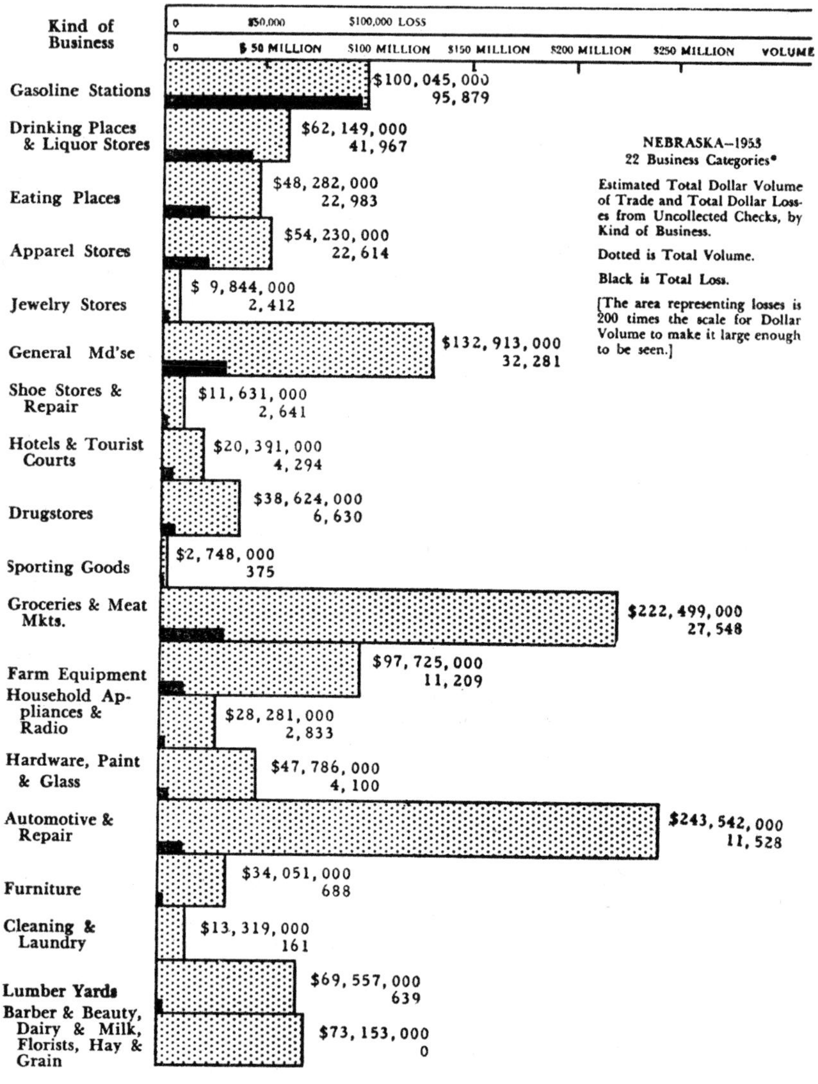

Kind of Business						
	0	$50,000	$100,000 LOSS			
	0	$50 MILLION	$100 MILLION	$150 MILLION	$200 MILLION	$250 MILLION VOLUME

Gasoline Stations — $100,045,000 / 95,879

Drinking Places & Liquor Stores — $62,149,000 / 41,967

Eating Places — $48,282,000 / 22,983

Apparel Stores — $54,230,000 / 22,614

Jewelry Stores — $9,844,000 / 2,412

General Md'se — $132,913,000 / 32,281

Shoe Stores & Repair — $11,631,000 / 2,641

Hotels & Tourist Courts — $20,391,000 / 4,294

Drugstores — $38,624,000 / 6,630

Sporting Goods — $2,748,000 / 375

Groceries & Meat Mkts. — $222,499,000 / 27,548

Farm Equipment — $97,725,000 / 11,209

Household Appliances & Radio — $28,281,000 / 2,833

Hardware, Paint & Glass — $47,786,000 / 4,100

Automotive & Repair — $243,542,000 / 11,528

Furniture — $34,051,000 / 688

Cleaning & Laundry — $13,319,000 / 161

Lumber Yards — $69,557,000 / 639

Barber & Beauty, Dairy & Milk, Florists, Hay & Grain — $73,153,000 / 0

NEBRASKA—1953
22 Business Categories*

Estimated Total Dollar Volume of Trade and Total Dollar Losses from Uncollected Checks, by Kind of Business.

Dotted is Total Volume.

Black is Total Loss.

[The area representing losses is 200 times the scale for Dollar Volume to make it large enough to be seen.]

Sources: U. S. Census of Business, 1948; Sample survey of Nebraska business, 1953.

* The remaining miscellaneous businesses had $2,460,475 in volume and $25,637 in losses from uncollected checks.

TABLE 22
(Duplicates Table 7)
Nebraska Business Groups in Retail, Wholesale and Service Trades—
Losses from Uncollected Checks, State and National. (Source:
U. S. Census of Business, 1948, and Nebraska Business Survey)

Kind of Business	Number of Establishments	State Volume of Sales ($1000's)	Loss from Uncollected Checks*	Per Cent of Volume Lost*	Average per Business	
					Volume	Loss*
1. Gasoline Service Stations	2,298	100,045	$ 95,879	.09584	$ 43,536	$41.72
2. Drinking Places; Liquor Stores	1,804	62,149	41,967	.06753	34,451	23.26
3. Eating Places	1,850	48,282	22,983	.04760	26,098	12.42
4. Apparel Stores	487	54,230	22,614	.04170	111,355	46.44
5. Jewelry Stores	242	9,844	2,412	.02450	40,678	9.97
6. General Merchandise (Department and Variety Stores)	494	132,913	32,281	.02429	269,055	65.35
7. Shoe Stores and Repair (R&S)	536	11,631	2,641	.02270	21,700	4.93
8. Hotels and Tourist Courts (S)	564	20,391	4,294	.02106	36,154	7.61
9. Drug and Proprietory Stores	661	38,624	6,630	.01716	58,433	10.03
10. Sporting Goods Stores	42	2,748	375	.01366	65,429	8.93
11. Groceries and Meat Markets	2,625	222,499	27,548	.01237	84,762	10.49
12. Farm Equipment	765	97,725	11,209	.01147	127,745	14.65
13. Household Appliances; Radio Stores and Repair (R&S)	683	28,281	2,833	.01002	41,407	4.15
14. Hardware; Paint, Glass, Wallpaper	790	47,786	4,100	.00858	60,489	5.19
15. Automobiles, Parts; Repair, and Garages (R&S)	2,297	243,542	11,528	.00473	106,026	5.02
16. Furniture Stores	275	34,051	688	.00202	123,822	2.50
17. Cleaning, Dyeing; Laundries (S)	332	13,319	161	.00121	40,117	.48
18. Lumber Yards	500	69,557	639	.00092	139,114	1.28
19. Barber, Beauty Shops (S)	1,692	6,820	0	0	4,031	0
20. Dairy Products; Milk Dealers (R&W)	168	35,690	0	0	212,440	0
21. Hay, Grain, Feed	242	28,299	0	0	116,938	0
22. Florists	74	2,334	0	0	31,541	0
23. Miscellaneous—All other census groups (R,W,S)	7,150	2,460,475	25,637	.00104	344,122	3.59
NEBRASKA	26,571	3,771,235	316,419	.00839	141,930	11.91
UNITED STATES	2,681,498	334,296,780				

* Estimated from results of questionnaires; see Chapter X on methods.
R = retail; S = service; W = wholesale.

TABLE 23

Nebraska Business Groups in Retail, Wholesale and Service Trades.
Business by Category and the Per Cent of Nebraska's Total Dollar
Loss from Uncollected Checks. (Source: U.S. Census, 1948,
and Business Survey)

Kind of Business	Per Cent of Nebraska's Total		
	Number of Establishments	Dollar Volume of Sales	Dollar Loss from Uncollected Checks
NEBRASKA	100.0	100.0	100.0
1. Gasoline Service Stations	8.65	2.65	30.30
2. Drinking Places; Liquor Stores	6.79	1.65	13.26
3. Eating Places	6.96	1.28	7.26
4. Apparel Stores	1.83	1.43	7.15
5. Jewelry Stores	.91	.26	.76
6. General Merchandise Group (Dept. and Variety Stores)	1.86	3.52	10.20
7. Shoe Stores and Repair (R&S)	2.02	.38	.83
8. Hotels and Tourist Courts (S)	2.12	.54	1.36
9. Drug and Proprietory Stores	2.49	1.02	2.10
10. Sporting Goods Stores	.19	.09	.12
11. Groceries and Meat Markets	9.88	5.90	8.71
12. Farm Equipment	2.88	2.59	3.54
13. Household Appliances; Radio Stores and Repair (R&S)	2.57	.75	.90
14. Hardware; Paint, Glass, Wallpaper	2.97	1.27	1.30
15. Automobiles, Parts; Repair, and Garages (R&S)	8.64	6.46	3.64
16. Furniture Stores	1.03	.90	.22
17. Cleaning, Dyeing; Laundries (S)	1.25	.35	.05
18. Lumber Yards	1.88	1.84	.20
19. Barber, Beauty Shops (S)	6.37	.18	0
20. Dairy Products; Milk Dealers (R&W)	.63	.95	0
21. Hay, Grain, Feed	.91	.75	0
22. Florists	.28	.06	0
23. Miscellaneous—All other census groups (R,W,S)	26.91	65.24	8.10

R = retail; W = wholesale; S = service.

TABLE 24

Per Cent of Uncollected-Check Losses by Six Businesses

	Business Establishments (Per Cent)	Dollar Volume of Trade (Per Cent)	Loss from Uncollected Checks (Per Cent)
Gas Stations	8.65	2.65	30.30
Drinking Places and Liquor Stores	6.79	1.65	13.26
Eating Places	6.96	1.28	7.26
Apparel Stores	1.83	1.43	7.15
General Merchandise	1.86	3.52	10.20
Groceries and Meat Markets	9.88	5.90	8.71
Total	35.97	16.43	76.88

more checks than its total volume of business, had losses of only $415 for a year, or .008 per cent of its total volume of business. These check losses were so small that it would not pay the store to keep a book account of the uncollected checks.

No instance was found where fees were charged by businesses other than banks for cashing checks.

DISTRIBUTION OF LOSSES OF BUSINESS FIRMS COMPLAINING TO A REPRE-
SENTATIVE COUNTY ATTORNEY

Another study which shows the losses by types of business was taken from the notebooks of a county attorney in a representative Nebraska county who performed the unusual feat of keeping complete records of check complaints.

Over the seven years which the county attorney kept records, there were many complaints from businessmen on bad checks. The name of each firm and the number and amount of checks which were brought

TABLE 25

Complaints from Types of Businesses, County Attorney's Notes for Seven Years, 1948 to 1954, Inclusive

Type of Business	No. of Business Units	No. of Checks	Checks per Unit	Average Size of Checks	Total Complaints	Total Per Unit 7 Years	Amt. per Unit 1 Year
Gas Station	46	207	4.5	$ 20	$4,116	$ 89	$13
Misc. Businesses	42	78	1.8	41	3,165	75	11
Groc. & Super Mkt.	36	181	5	15	2,819	78	11
Merchandise	33	125	3.8	25	3,105	94	13
Liquor & Tavern	30	225	7.5	15	3,476	116	19
				(64) 29 ⎱		(22) 68 ⎱	(22) 3 ⎱
Auto Repair & Parts	23	65	3	54 ⎰	3,506	152 ⎰	22 ⎰
Cafes	11	41	4	13	520	47	7
Hardware	10	22	2	26	567	57	8
Farm Equipment	9	16	2	100	1,612	179	26
Hotels	8	61	8	16	957	146	21
Dept. Stores	7	227	32	21	4,800	686	98
Drugs	7	64	9	12	752	107	15
Farm Products	5	10	2	147	1,477	293	42
Banks	4	12	3	38	452	113	16
Jewelry	3	6	2	24	147	49	7
Florists	3	11	4	12	131	43	6
Individuals*	131	184	1.4	33	6,175	46	7
Totals	408	1,535			$37,777		
Averages			3.8	$ 25		$93	$13

* This figure undoubtedly includes a number of small businessmen and farmers who were listed by name rather than by type of business. Wherever possible, these individuals were classified under the type of business in which they were engaged, but the 131 here are a residue which could not be classified on the basis of the information available.

to the county attorney were put down in a notebook in alphabetical groupings. In order to get a good sample of this activity, the alphabetical groups B, C, F, G, L, M, P, S and T, were Photostated in full and classified. This constituted a little over 50 per cent of all of the complaints coming to the county attorney's office on checks during the seven-year period. In all, the notes showed that there were a total of 408 business units who brought in 1,535 checks for prosecution or collection. This averaged 3.8 checks per business unit complaining, and the mathematical average size of the checks was $25, making the average claim of the businessman $93 for the seven years, or an average of $13 per single year. The spread of these classes of claims was $131 by three florists on 11 checks to $4,800 by seven department stores on 227 checks, making the spread of average claims per year $6 by the florists to $98 by the department stores. Table 25 shows that in total amounts of claims for the sample, the department stores were the highest, followed by gas stations, auto repairs, and liquor dealers, including taverns. Among the largest claimants who had an average of three or more checks a year were four department stores, two supermarkets, a tavern, a gas station and a hotel. The number of checks, total amount of claim, and the dollar total of claims submitted per year are set out in **Table 26 below.**

TABLE 26

Representative-County Establishments Having Largest Bad-Check Complaints in a Seven-Year Period

	Seven-Year Number of Checks	Seven-Year Total Amount	Yearly Average Claim
Department Store			
A	57	$1,157	$165
B	59	990	141
C	38	895	128
Supermarkets			
A	52	906	129
B	43	613	88
Tavern	75	965	138
Gas Station	26	698	100
Hotel	28	425	61

It should be noted again that, as shown in Table 25, department stores, supermarkets, liquor dealers and gas stations had the largest number of complaints on bad checks.

Since this county attorney collected over half the amount of all bad checks brought to him and did it without charge (see law enforcement reports below), the yearly losses to the local businesses were negligible.

LOSSES BY SIZE OF BUSINESS

There is one other fact in the business picture which is worthy of note. The total returns showed that the proportional losses from bad checks among the 344 businesses which had measurable losses varied in inverse ratio to the size of the business. The curve in Figure 4 shows that this ratio of losses rises very rapidly as the volume of business grows smaller. This is another reason why the larger incidents of losses are found outside the metropolitan areas where the big businesses are concentrated.

CHECK WRITING AND HANDLING HABITS OF THE COMMUNITY

Sophisticated bankers and businessmen are aware of the inconsequential losses from bad checks and govern themselves accordingly.

The bankers in many small towns honor almost all overdrafts, so the percentage of insufficient-fund checks in these areas is very small. In the larger cities, many banks advertise freely that if customers will adopt their "pay-as-you-check" system, the banks in turn will honor overdrafts up to $50 by any customer using this type of checking account.

Businessmen, both in the cities and towns, are very liberal in cashing checks for customers. Because many customers object to producing identification or to being questioned about their checks, merchants regard it as a valuable good-will item to cash checks without question, regarding such a reputation as one of the cheapest forms of advertising. For this reason, many firms have a total of checks cashed considerably in excess of their full volume of business. One tavern in a small town admitted to cashing over $10,000 worth of paychecks a week, but such practice is not limited to drinking places. Department stores, chain groceries and many apparel stores will cash checks almost without question.

On the questionnaire for businessmen, set out in the chapter on analysis and methods, there were questions involving fourteen different means which might be used of identifying drawers of checks, limiting the amounts which would be cashed and attempting to discover what precautions, if any, the organization interviewed used. The interviewers soon discovered that this portion of the question-

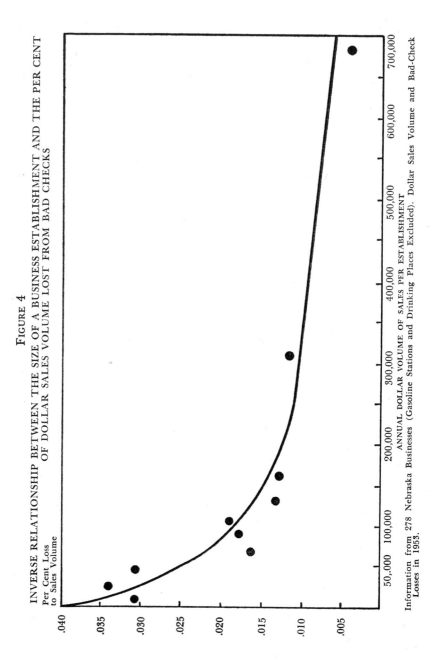

FIGURE 4

INVERSE RELATIONSHIP BETWEEN THE SIZE OF A BUSINESS ESTABLISHMENT AND THE PER CENT
OF DOLLAR SALES VOLUME LOST FROM BAD CHECKS

Information from 278 Nebraska Businesses (Gasoline Stations and Drinking Places Excluded). Dollar Sales Volume and Bad-Check
Losses in 1953.

naire was useless because none of the businessmen seemed to use such precautions. A few claimed they knew the drawers of checks personally, and others occasionally asked for drivers' licenses or addresses of the writers, but most were so anxious to receive checks that they took them under almost any conditions. Most of the stores in the rural areas carried pads of counter checks on all adjacent banks, and in many instances the merchants themselves filled in the check and handed it to the customer to be signed. In one instance a proprietor of a store had signed his own name to such a check, and at the end of the day was totally unable to recall any identifying characteristics of the customer who had walked out with the merchandise. In Scottsbluff one banker, attempting to explain the high ratio of no-account checks drawn on his bank, suggested that another bank in the area had counter checks of the same color and that many people in asking for checks to sign simply called for the pads by color and not by name of the bank.

Businessmen were also fantastically careless in the types of paper which they took for checks. One sheriff produced an instrument signed "U. R. Stung" which an irate merchant had asked him to collect. Another displayed a receipt for $45 with the word "RECEIPT" printed on it in red ink, in letters a quarter of an inch high, which an ice cream merchant had taken for a quart of ice cream and returned a little over $44 in cash. Another produced a magazine salesman's receipt for a small amount which looked like a check but contained no name of a drawee bank. This piece of paper was cashed in one store, endorsed to another, deposited for credit in the local bank, and reached the Omaha clearing house before the fact that there was no drawee was caught. In one western county, a crew of forgers passed a number of forged instruments purporting to be payroll checks of an Oklahoma oil company. The printing on the checks, which approximated $65 each, was so crude that anybody acquainted with commercial paper should have suspected forgery, but this group of rascals cashed between ten and twenty of these checks in one western town in one day, and some of the merchants even wanted to argue with the sheriff that the checks were good after he found them in their possession. These are only a few of many similar examples of carelessness in handling commercial paper.

The banking habits of the citizens are also extremely lax. Thousands of individuals and hundreds of businessmen sign counter checks indiscriminately, keeping no records of their check stubs but relying on the banks to notify them when their account becomes overdrawn. Many are insulted if the bank refuses to pay their overdrafts.

277

Neither businessmen nor customers seem to regard insufficient-fund or no-fund checks as a serious matter. Many take checks drawn upon known deficient accounts with an agreement to hold the paper to a later date like a note or time draft. This practice is so common throughout the western areas that the expression "hold check" is a well known business term.

II. CRIMINAL LAW GOVERNING BAD CHECKS

Unlike the laxity of the business world in dealing with bad checks, the Nebraska criminal law is very strict. The principal Nebraska statutes on the subject, which are of interest here and set out in full in the margin,[1] clearly provide that issuing or indorsing a forged check or forging an indorsement on a check of any amount with intent to defraud is a felony punishable by one to twenty years in the penitentiary and by a fine up to $500.[2] Drawing a no-account check of any amount is also a felony punishable by one to ten years in the penitentiary, or a misdemeanor with a penalty of from one to six months in jail or a fine of from $50 to $500.[3]

[1] Nebraska Citations are to Revised Statutes of Nebraska (1943) and later editions and reissues thereof. Hereafter in this chapter these will be cited simply by section numbers.

[2] 28-601. *"Forgery," defined; penalty.* (1) Whoever falsely makes, alters, forges, counterfeits, prints or photographs . . . bank bill or note, check, draft, bill of exchange, contract or promissory note, for the payment of money or other property; . . . (e) any acceptance of a bill of exchange; . . . (q) any signature to a letter, paper or writing of whatsoever kind, with the intent to defraud or bring into disrepute or disgrace any person or persons in their personal, social, civic or business relations; or (2) whoever shall utter or publish as true and genuine or cause to be uttered or published as true and genuine or shall have in his possession with intent to utter and publish as true and genuine, any of the above-named false, forged, counterfeited, falsely printed or photographed matter, above specified and described, knowing the same to be false, altered, forged, counterfeited, falsely printed or photographed, with intent to prejudice, damage or defraud any person or persons, body politic or corporate, shall be imprisoned in the penitentiary for any space of time not exceeding twenty years nor less than one year, and pay a fine not exceeding five hundred dollars.

[3] 28-1212. *No-fund checks, assignment of funds and drafts; drawing, uttering; penalty.* Any person who, with intent to defraud, shall make or draw, utter or deliver any check, draft, assignment of funds, or order for the payment of money upon any bank, cooperative credit association, or other depository knowing, at the time of such making, drawing, uttering, or delivering, that the maker or drawer has no account or deposit in such bank, cooperative credit association, or depository, upon conviction thereof, shall be imprisoned in the penitentiary for not less than one year nor more than ten years, or imprisoned in the county jail not less than thirty days nor more than six months, or be fined not less than fifty dollars nor more than five hundred dollars. (1953 Supp.)

The penalties are more complicated for issuing insufficient-fund checks with intent to defraud. If the check is not more than $35, the crime is a misdemeanor punishable by a fine of from five dollars to $100 or imprisonment not over 90 days in jail or both. If the check is over $35, then the same act becomes a felony subject to a fine of from $100 to $5,000 or imprisonment not to exceed seven years in the penitentiary.[4] The statute further provides that if the bank refuses payment on grounds of insufficient funds and the drawer does not pay within five days of securing protest or notice of dishonor, then the protest or notice shall be presumptive proof of both the lack of funds and intent to defraud.[5]

---

[4] *28-1213. Insufficient-fund checks and assignment of funds; drawing, uttering; penalties.* Any person who, with intent to defraud, shall make or draw, utter or deliver any check, draft, assignment of funds or order for the payment of money upon any bank, cooperative credit association or other depository knowing, at the time of such making, drawing, uttering or delivery, that the maker or drawer has not sufficient funds in, or credit with, such bank, cooperative credit association or other depository for the payment of such check, draft, order or assignment of funds in full upon its presentation, shall upon conviction be punished as follows: (1) If such check, draft, order or assignment of funds so issued be for a sum not exceeding thirty-five dollars, then and in that case, the person so convicted shall be fined in any sum not less than five dollars nor more than one hundred dollars or shall be imprisoned in the county jail not more than ninety days, or both such a fine and imprisonment, at the discretion of the court, and shall pay the costs of prosecution; or (2) if such check, draft, order or assignment of funds so issued be for a sum greater than thirty-five dollars, then and in that case, the person so convicted shall be fined not less than one hundred dollars nor more than five thousand dollars, or be imprisoned in the penitentiary not exceeding seven years, or both such a fine and imprisonment, at the discretion of the court.

[5] *28-1214. Insufficient-fund checks and assignment of funds; rules of evidence; presumptions; protests; notice of dishonor.* In any prosecution under section 28-1213, as against the maker or drawer thereof, the making, drawing, uttering or delivering of a check, draft, order or assignment of funds, payment of which is refused by the drawee because of lack of funds or credit, shall be presumptive evidence of intent to defraud and of knowledge of insufficient funds in, or credit with such bank, cooperative credit association or other depository; *Provided,* such maker or drawer shall not have paid the payee thereof the amount due thereon, together with all costs and protest fees, within five days after receiving notice that such check, draft, order or assignment of funds shall have been protested; and the notice of protest thereof shall be admissible as proof of such presentation for payment, nonpayment and protest; and if such notice of protest, or the drawee's notice of dishonor thereof, shall state that payment of such check, draft, order or assignment of funds was refused because of lack of funds or credit of the maker or drawer, then such notice of protest or notice of dishonor shall be presumptive evidence that there was a lack of funds in, or credit with, such bank, cooperative credit association or other depository for the payment of such check, draft, order or assignment of funds.

There are other statutes, such as that covering the obtaining of money under false pretenses[6] and the habitual-criminal statute,[7] which might also apply in some cases, but the forgery, no-fund and insufficient-fund statutes are the ones under which most of the prosecutions in this field are brought. The statutes are clear and simple in their execution and need not be discussed at length here except to point out a few provisions which become obvious in their enforcement.

Since intent to defraud must be proved except where the presumptions are effective and not rebutted, mistakes are not criminal. The prosecuting attorneys have usually ruled that no fraud is committed unless the offending check was given in return for some present value. Thus a bad check given in payment of a pre-existing account involves no crime unless it was larger than the account and something else of value passed at the time it was written. The famous "hold" check is not criminal if the drawer bona fide intends to pay it at a later date, but of course if the holding was merely part of the fraudulent scheme, passing such a bad check would be a crime. The legal technicalities involved are discussed at length in Chapter XIII.

It is important to note that, as is the case in most crimes, making restitution does not wipe out the offense nor affect the question of guilt of the accused.[8]

It is also worthy of observation that in the case of many financial crimes, such as larceny, the line between misdemeanors and felonies is set at $100;[9] but where bad checks are involved, as indicated above, a forgery or no-fund check in any amount or an insufficient-fund check of over $35 may be the basis of a felony charge. This is the more surprising when it is considered that in the ordinary financial crime the victim is usually helpless, but in the case of bad checks he actually and willingly takes part in the transaction upon which the crime is based.

Thus it is clear under the statute that the crimes are well defined, easy of proof and the penalties are severe. The duties of the prosecuting officers are not shrouded in any ambiguity or complicated technicalities.

28-1215. *Insufficient-fund checks and assignment of funds; "credit," defined.* The word "credit" as used in sections 28-1213 and 28-1214 shall be construed to mean an arrangement or understanding with the bank, depository or cooperative credit association for the payment of such check, draft, order or assignment of funds.

[6] 28-1207, 28-1211.

[7] 29-2221, 29-2222.

[8] See Haines v. State, 135 Neb. 433, 281 N.W. 860, 864 (1938); May's Criminal Law § 20 (4th ed. Sears and Weihofen 1938).

[9] See 28-506, 28-512 (1953).

The law in Nebraska on bad checks is quite similar to those of other states. Like Nebraska, the statutes of all the states provide that forgery is a felony punishable by up to 20 years in the penitentiary.[10] In the case of no-fund and insufficient-fund checks, the laws of other states are more various. As shown in Table 27, penalties range from mere tort action in Vermont to 14 years in prison in Montana. As seen below,[11] these variations in penalties offer an excellent opportunity to study and project what might be the effect of changes in the law in any of the several states.

The federal statutes authorize no prosecution of writers of bad checks unless they are transported in interstate commerce. The activity of the F.B.I., which is considerable in the field, is authorized by the National Stolen Property Act, pertinent parts of which are set out in the margin.[12] This statute has been interpreted by the courts to be

---

[10] Penalty for forgery in the various states. The figures immediately after the name of the state compilation indicate the number of years sentence prescribed by statute. Ala. Code 10-20, Tit. 14, § 207 (1940); Alaska Comp. Laws, 1-20, § 65-6-2 (1949); Ariz. Code, 1-14, § 43-2501 (1939); Ark. Stat. Ann., 2-10, § 41-1806 (1947); Calif. Penal Code, 1-14, § 473 (1949); Colo. Rev. Stat., 1-20, 40-10-1 (1953); Conn. Gen. Stat., 1-5, § 8684 (1949); Del. Code, -5, Vol. 11, § 543 (1953); D. C. Code, 1-10, § 22-1401 (1951); Fla. Stat. Ann., -10, § 831.01 (1944); Ga. Code Ann., 2-10, § 26-3910 (1936); Ida. Code, 1-14, § 18-3604 (1948); Ill. Stat. Ann., 1-20, § 38-279 (Smith-Hurd, 1953); Ind. Stat. Ann., 2-14, § 10-2102 (Burns, 1942); Iowa Code Ann., 0-10, § 718.1 (4th) (1954); Kans. Gen. Stat., 1-10, §§ 21-608, 631 (Corrick, 1949); Ky. Rev. Stat., 2-10, § 434-130 (Baldwin, 1955); La. Rev. Stat., 0-10, § 14:72 (West, 1951); Me. Rev. Stat., 0-10, (1954); Md. Ann. Code, 1-10, § 27-51 (Flack, 1952); Mass. Gen. Laws, 0-10, c. 267, § 1 (1932); Mich. Stat. Ann., 1-7, §28-448 (1936); Minn. Stat. Ann., -20, § 620.09 (1947); Miss. Code Ann., 2-15, §§ 2170, 2172, 2187 (1944); Mo. Ann. Stat., 2-10, §§ 561.030, 561.080 (1949); Mont. Rev. Code, 1-14, §§ 94-2001-2006, 2009 (1949); Nev. Comp. Laws, 1-14, § 10369 (1929); N.H. Rev. Stat., 1-7, c. 581, § 1 (1955); N.J. Stat. Ann., -7, §§ 2:132-1, 2-103-5 (1951); N.Mex. Stat., 1-5, § 40-20 (1953); N.Y. Penal Code, -20, §§ 884- (5), 886 (McKinney, 1954); N.Car. Gen. Stat., 1-10, § 14-119 (1953); N.Dak. Rev. Code, 1-10, § 12-3927 (1943); Ohio Rev. Code, 1-20, § 2913.1 (1953); Okla. Stat. Ann., -10, § 21-1577 (1937); Ore. Rev. Stat., 2-20, §§ 165.105, 165.115 (1955); Pa. Stat. Ann., -15, § 5010 (Purdon, 1954); R.I. Gen. Laws, 1-10, c. 609, § 1 (1938); S.Car. Code, 1-7, § 16-351 (1952); S.Dak. Code, -5, §§ 13-4101, 4106 (1939); Tenn. Code Ann., -5, §§ 39-1721, 4203 (1955); Tex. Penal Code, 2-7, Art. 995 (Vernon, 1948); Utah Code, 1-20, 76-26-4 (1953); Vt. Stat., -10, § 8344 (1947); Va. Code, 2-10, § 18-26 (1950); Wash. Rev. Code, -20, § 9.44.020 (1949); Wis. Stat., 1-7, § 343.56 (1951); Wyo. Comp. Stat., -14, § 9-1009 (1945).

[11] P. 353.

[12] § 2311 As used in this chapter: . . . "Securities" includes any . . . check, draft, warrant, traveler's check . . .

§ 2314 Whoever, with unlawful or fraudulent intent transports in interstate commerce . . . any falsely made, (or) forged, . . . securities knowing the same to have been so falsely made, (or) forged, . . . Shall be fined not more than $10,000

TABLE 27

Penalties for Insufficient-Fund and No-Fund Checks in the Various States*

STATE	PENALTY	TYPE OF OFFENSE	AUTHORITY
Alabama	Fine not more than $1000 paid in money only and 6 months at hard labor for the county.	Not sufficient funds or no funds, misdemeanor.	Ala. Code tit. 14, §§ 232 to 234 (2) (3) (1940).
Alaska	$50 or less, 1 yr. jail or $25-$100. $50 or more, 1-10 yrs. in pen.	Offense is entitled larceny.	Alaska Comp. Laws, 65-5-48 (1949).
Arizona	Not more than 1 yr. in county jail, or in state prison for not more than 14 yrs.	Misdemeanor and felony, 43-109.	Ariz. Code § 43-2613 (1939), cf. id. § 43-2614.
Arkansas	Not more than 1 yr. and/or $1000 or, if check is mentioned in sec. 743, Crawford and Moses Digest and between $25-$500, crime is misdemeanor. Otherwise, if over $25 it is a felony and punished by 6 mo.-2 yrs. in state pen.	Misdemeanor and felony.	Ark. Stat. Ann. §§ 67-714 to 718 (1947).
California	County jail for not more than 1 yr. or state prison for not more than 14 yrs.	Misdemeanor and felony, sec. 17.	Cal. Penal Code §§ 476, 746 (a) (1949).
Colorado	Not more than $500 and/or imprisoned in county jail not more than 6 mo.	Misdemeanor.	Colo. Rev. Stat. 40-14-10 (1953), cf. id. 40-10-1.
Connecticut	Not more than $1000 and/or 1 yr.	Misdemeanor, sec. 8873.	Conn. Gen. Stat. § 8697 (1949).
Delaware	Less than $100, not more than 1 yr. and/or $1000. More than $100, judge's discretion.	Misdemeanor.	Del. Code, vol. 11 § 555 (1953).
District of Columbia	Not more than 1 yr. and/or $1000.	Misdemeanor.	D.C. Code § 22-1410 (1951).
Florida	If check is $50 or more, state pen. not more than 1 yr. or $1000. If less than $50, county jail not more than 6 mo. or $500.	Felony or misdemeanor.	Fla. Stat. Ann. §§ 832.01, 832.02 (1944), § 832.02 (Supp. 1955).
Georgia	Not more than $1000, imprisonment not more than 6 mo., or to work on chain gang not more than 12 mo. Any one or more.	Misdemeanor.	Ga. Code Ann. § 13-9933 (1936), § 27-2506 (1953).
Idaho	If no funds or not sufficient funds, not more than 5 yrs. and/or $5000. If less than $25 and not sufficient funds, county jail not more than 6 mo. and/or $300; if more than $25 and not sufficient funds, state prison not more than 5 yrs. and/or $5000.	Misdemeanor or felony.	Ida. Code § 18-3106 (Supp. 1955), cf. id. § 18-3604 (1948).

* The writer is indebted to Messrs. Paul Douglas and William E. Morrow, Jr., of the Nebraska Bar for aid in compiling this material.

TABLE 27—(Continued)

Penalties for Insufficient-Fund and No-Fund Checks in the Various States

STATE	PENALTY	TYPE OF OFFENSE	AUTHORITY
Illinois	Not more than $1000 and/or 1 yr.	Misdemeanor.	Ill. Stat. Ann. c. 38, § 256 (Smith-Hurd, 1935), § 255 (Supp. 1954).
Indiana	1-10 yrs. pen., if $25 or more. Less than $25, 1-5 yrs. in pen. and fined not more than $500; or county jail not more than 1 yr. and $500.	Misdemeanor or felony.	Ind. Stat. Ann. § 10-2105 (Burns, 1942), cf. id. § 10-3002.
Iowa	If over $20, not more than 7 yrs. and/or $500; or in county jail not more than 1 yr. and/or $500.	Felony and misdemeanor.	Iowa Code Ann. §§ 713.3, 713.4 (1950).
Kansas	Less than $20, fine $25-$100 and/or county jail 10 days to 6 mo. Over $20, fine $100-$5000 and/or state pen. 1-5 yrs.	Felony or misdemeanor.	Ken. Gen. Stat. §§ 21-554 to 556 (Corrick, 1949).
Kentucky	Less than $20, not more than $100 and/or 90 days. Over $20, 1-2 yrs.	Misdemeanor or felony.	Ky. Rev. Stat. § 434.070 (Baldwin, 1955).
Louisiana	Not over $1000 and/or 1 yr.		La. Rev. Stat. § 15.428 (West, 1951), § 14.71 (Supp. 1955).
Maine		Misdemeanor.	Me. Rev. Stat. c. 133, §§ 14, 15 (1954).
Maryland	Not more than $1000 and/or 11 months.	Misdemeanor. No funds and insufficient funds.	Md. Ann. Code Art. 27, § 167 (Flack, 1952), § 165 (Supp. 1954).
Massachusetts	More than $100, not more than 5 yrs. in the pen., or not more than $600 and jail for not more than 2 yrs. Less than $100, jail for not more than 1 yr. or fine not more than $300.	Larceny. Making the check is attempted larceny.	Mass. Laws Ann. c. 266, §§ 30, 37 (Supp. 1955).
Michigan	If no-fund check, not more than 2 yrs. If with intent to defraud one makes 3 or more insufficient-fund checks within a period of not more than 10 days, not more than 2 yrs.	Felony.	Mich. Stat. Ann. §§ 28.326 to 28.328 (1938), § 28.326 (1) (Supp. 1955).
Minnesota	Not more than 1 yr. and/or $1000.	Misdemeanor.	Minn. Stat. Ann. § 620.41 (Supp. 1955), cf. id. §§ 622.03 to 622.05, 622.07 (1947), § 622.06 (Supp. 1955).
Mississippi	Less than $25, not more than 6 mo. and/or $500. $25 or more, not more than 3 yrs. and/or $500.	No funds and insufficient funds. Felony or misdemeanor.	Miss. Code Ann. § 2153 (Supp. 1954).
Missouri	Insufficient funds, not more than 1 yr. and/or $1000. No-funds check, not more than 7 yrs.	Misdemeanor or felony.	Mo. Ann. Stat. §§ 561.450 to 561.470 (Vernon, 1953).

TABLE 27—(Continued)

Penalties for Insufficient-Fund and No-Fund Checks in the Various States

STATE	PENALTY	TYPE OF OFFENSE	AUTHORITY
Montana	$50 or less, not more than 6 mo. and/or $500. Over $50, 1-14 yrs. in state pen.	Larceny or misdemeanor.	Mont. Rev. Code §§ 94-2702, 2706, 2707 (1949).
Nebraska	As explained in this chapter.		
Nevada	Up to 1 yr. in county jail, or 1-5 yrs. in the state pen., in the discretion of the court.	Misdemeanor or felony. Felony, but if sent to jail considered a misdemeanor for all purposes after judgment.	Nev. Comp. Laws § 10359 (1929).
New Hampshire	Imprisonment under 3 degrees of larceny. Body execution lies if failure of payment. Applies to either maker or deliverer. (Obsolete.)	Not a crime but a tort. Also larceny if not paid in 10 days.	N.H. Rev. Stat. c. 507, §7 (1955), cf. id. c. 582, §§ 3 to 5, 12, 13.
New Jersey	Not more than $1000 and/or 1 yr.	Misdemeanor. Both no-fund and insufficient-fund.	N.J. Stat. Ann. §§ 2A:111-15, 2A:111-16 (1953).
New Mexico	Under $20, $100 fine or 3 mos. in jail. Over $20, $500 fine or 5 yrs. in pen.	Misdemeanor or felony.	N. Mex. Stat. Ann. 40-21-8 (1953).
New York	More than $500, not more than 10 yrs. $100-$500, not more than 5 yrs. Less than $100, not more than 1 yr. and/or $500.	Felony or misdemeanor.	N.Y. Penal Code §§ 1292(a), 1294(3), 1295 to 1299, 1937 (McKinney, 1944).
North Carolina	No funds, fine or imprisonment at the discretion of the court. Insufficient funds, 4 mo.-10 yrs. or fine at the discretion of the court, except, in some counties, not more than $50 or 30 days.	Felony or misdemeanor.	N. Car. Gen. Stat. §§ 14-3, 106, 107 (1953).
North Dakota	Not more than $100 and/or 30 days in county jail.	Misdemeanor.	N. Dak. Rev. Code §§ 6-0816, 12-0107 (1943).
Ohio	$50-$200 and/or 1-3 yrs.	Felony.	Ohio Rev. Code §§ 1115.23, 1115.99 (1953).
Oklahoma	If $20 or less, $100 fine and/or 30 days in county jail. More than $20, $500 fine and/or 7 yrs.	Misdemeanor or felony.	Okla. Stat. Ann. § 21-1541 (Supp. 1955).
Oregon	Up to 1 year and/or $1000.	Misdemeanor.	Ore. Rev. Stat. § 165.225 (1955).
Pennsylvania	$1000 and/or 2 yrs.	Misdemeanor.	Pa. Stat. Ann. tit. 18, § 4854 (Purdon, 1945).
Rhode Island	$100 or less, not more than $500 and/or 1 yr. More than $100, not more than $1000 and/or 1 yr.	Felony or misdemeanor.	R.I. Sess. Laws c. 144, § 2 (1950).

TABLE 27— *(Continued)*

Penalties for Insufficient-Fund and No-Fund Checks in the Various States

STATE	PENALTY	TYPE OF OFFENSE	AUTHORITY
South Carolina	$100 or 30 days for less than $20 if tried in a magistrate's court. More than $20 fine and imprisonment at discretion of court.		S. Car. Code §§ 8-176, 8-177 (1952), § 8-178 (Supp. 1955).
South Dakota	Not more than $100 and/or 30 days.	Misdemeanor.	S. Dak. Code § 13-4204 (1939).
Tennessee	$60 and more, 3-10 yrs. Under $60, 1-5 yrs.	Misdemeanor and felony.	Tenn. Code Ann. §§ 39-1722, 1916, 4203, 45-2122 (1955), § 39-1904 (Supp. 1955).
Texas	First offense, $5 or less, $200 fine; $5-$50, $1000 and/or 2 yrs. Second offense, $50 or less, 30 days-2 yrs. and $2000. Third offense, $50 or less, 2-10 yrs. in pen. and $5000. Any offense over $50, 2-10 yrs. and $10,000.	Misdemeanor and felony.	Tex. Penal Code c. 567B, §§ 1 to 4 (Vernon, 1952).
Utah	Not more than 1 yr. in county jail or 14 yrs. in state pen.	Misdemeanor or felony.	Utah Code 76-20-11 (Supp. 1955).
Vermont	Imprisonment on body attachment till payment.	Tort action. No-fund checks a felony by devious interpretation of sec. 8321, if over $25.	Vt. Stat. §§ 8329, 8330 (1947), cf. id. § 8321.
Virginia	Less than $50, 10 days-12 mos. in jail and/or $5-$100. More than $50, 1-5 yrs. in pen. or not more than 12 mos. in jail and $500.	Larceny or grand larceny.	Va. Code §§ 6-129 to 131, 18-164 (1949).
Washington	$25 or more, not more than 15 yrs. Less than $25, not more than 1 yr. and/or $1000.	Larceny.	Wash. Rev. Code §§ 9.54.050, 9.54.090, 9.92.020 (1952).
West Virginia	$20 or less, 5-60 days and/or not less than $100. More than $20, 1-5 yrs. and not more than $1000.	Felony and misdemeanor.	W. Va. Code § 5980 (1949).
Wisconsin	Not more than 1 yr. and/or $1000.	Misdemeanor.	Wis. Stat. § 343.401 (1951).
Wyoming	More than $25, not more than $5000 and/or 5 yrs. First offense of $25 or less, not more than $100 and/or 6 mos. Second offense of $25 or less as if more than $25.	Felony and misdemeanor.	Wyo. Comp. Stat. § 9-910 (1945), §§ 9-908, 909 (Supp. 1955).

effective against instruments signed with false names[13] and not with the real name of the maker and dishonored because of insufficient funds[14] or no funds.[15]

Since the federal law covers only a small portion of the field, the activities of the F.B.I., the federal law enforcement officials and the federal courts are not included in this study.

III. THE SOCIAL RESULTS OF ENFORCING THE BAD-CHECK LAWS

When one tries to measure the social effects of the bad-check laws, he is immediately met with two factors: (1) the behavior of the officials and the public toward the law, and (2) the more subtle problem of the interaction caused by the rules of law between the component parts of the public, the officials, the business community and that element of the population whose behavior may be affected by the enforcement of the statute. Both of these factors will have to be measured primarily by the activity of the county attorneys, sheriffs, judges, penal institutions and the type of people who fall into the clutches of the criminal law or so adjust their actions as to avoid its consequences.

THE ROLE OF THE COUNTY ATTORNEYS AND THE SHERIFFS

The prosecuting attorney, in Nebraska the county attorney, probably more than any other official, determines the course of law enforcement. He, with the sheriff, receives complaints of violations, advises the sheriff on investigating the cases, directs the swearing out of warrants, makes decisions to prosecute or grant clemency, conducts the prosecution in court, advises the judge in the matter of sentencing and sometimes takes part in parole and pardon deliberations. The personality and policies of the county attorney, therefore, become the key to the nature of law enforcement in any given county, but it should be obvious that he is subject to every kind of political and social pressure. Elected to a term of four years with the right to conduct a private practice of law while in office, he is often a young attorney just starting his professional career; but whether young or old,

---

or imprisoned not more than ten years or both.

§ 2315 . . . whoever . . . disposes of any falsely made, (or) forged, . . . securities, moving as, or which are a part of, or which constitute interstate or foreign commerce, knowing the same to have been so falsely made, (or) forged . . . Shall be fined not more than $10,000 or imprisoned not more than ten years or both. Title 18, Ch. 113, U.S.C.A. Supp. III (1950).

[13] Sheridan v. U.S., 329 U.S. 379 (1946).

[14] Wright v. U.S., 172 F.2d 310 (1949).

[15] Martyn v. U.S., 176 F.2d 609 (1949).

he is dependent upon the business community for re-election and for the future of his practice. This makes him particularly sensitive in shaping his law enforcement policies to the demands of the business-men. In no place is this more apparent than in the handling of the bad-check problem.

As indicated below, there is a wide variation in the extent to which county attorneys prosecute cases, the forums which they use, the fees, if any, which they charge and the attitude which they take toward literally enforcing the law. The reasons why a public official follows one policy rather than another are determined by the impact of a myriad of pressures, personal and political considerations, the practica-bility of enforcing the law and the like, upon the personality, ethical standards and ambitions of the official himself. It is, of course, im-possible to get frank statements from politicians about policies based on these considerations, which in some cases may range all the way from venal corruption for individual gain to great personal sacrifice based upon strongly felt ethical considerations. The reasons for policies adopted by the official are his personal concern and private secret and are largely irrelevant in a study of this type. The following ma-terial attempts to report only objective conduct as shown by tangible evidence.

THE COLLECTION OF BAD CHECKS

The result of the interviews with law enforcement officials shows that there is great variation, county to county, in the per cent of bad checks which are brought by businessmen to the county attorney or sheriff for action. Table 28 indicates that, on the average in the 31 counties in the sample, only 2.2 per cent of the bad checks returned by the bankers came to the legal officials. The actual figures ranged from .3 per cent to 8.5 per cent. (It is significant that the counties which had the lowest per cent per capita of bad checks seem to have the highest percentage of bad checks brought to the legal officials.) Those not appearing here were probably collected (1) by the business-men themselves, (2) by their attorneys, (3) by private collection agencies or (4) simply held by the businesses, which took the loss and made no further attempt to collect. The extent of the total losses to the businessmen from this process has already been discussed.

The number of checks collected by private attorneys could not be ascertained, largely because lawyers did not keep accurate records of their activity. On the whole it can be said that they collected only large checks because they could not afford, except as a favor to their clients, to devote the time necessary to recover on the smaller ones.

287

TABLE 28

Collection Activities by County Attorneys and Sheriffs Compared to the Total Number of Bad Checks, 1953

County*	NUMBER OF BAD CHECKS					COLLECTIONS					
	Total in County	To the Officials			Per Cent Given Officials[4]	County Attorney			Sheriff		
		Total	County Attorney[4]	Sheriff		Letters Sent	No. Collected[4]	Per Cent Collected	Letters Sent	No. Collected	Per Cent Collected
1	5,500	60	47	12	1.1	47	33	70	12	....	....
2	3,684	50	....	24	1.3	....	2	....	....	....	....
3	3,440	....	3	....	....	3	3	100	(effective)		....
4	4,252	150	36	100	3.5	36	20	56	100	33	33
5	27,744	80	15	52	.3	0	0		....	26	....
6	2,586	65+	....	....	2.5+	....	....	....	65	52	80
7	2,703	100	50	50	3.7	43	33	75	50**	17	33
8	3,671	80	12	68	2.2	0	0		60**	12	20
9	5,419	226	126	100	4.2	126	105	83	100	80	80
10	3,475	100	100	....	2.8	30	20	67	....	....	....
11	2,523	40	20	....	1.6	20	3	15	....	....	....
12	3,171	25	....	20+	.8	12	4	33	11	9	80
13	16,274	200	200	0	1.2	210	140	67	0	0	
14	97,630	2,800	104	55	2.9	104	54	50	55**	....	....
15	2,705	30	0	28	1.1	0	0		28	....	....
16	1,138	44	....	20	3.9	....	3		0	20**	....
17	1,183	100	22	0	8.5	22	16	73	0	0	
18	10,447	167[2]	....	....	1.6	67[2]	38	57	97[2]	80	83
19	4,042	200	135	65	4.9	150[1]	115[1]	77	65	39	60
20	1,698	70+	60+	10	4.1+	60+	30+	50	10	0	0
21	35,772	667	630	37	1.9	305	360	57	0	87**	....
22	714	60	10	52	8.4	10	5	50	52	52	100
23	4,986	85	50	25	1.7	50	....	....	25	17	67
24	5,288	90	32	9	1.7	32	14	44	9	25**	....
25	4,657	17+	17	....	.4+	17	8	47	....	....	....
26	20,902	400	32	50+	1.9	32	11	33	16	50**	....
27	1,536	30	24	0	2.0	24	16	67	0	0	
28	5,562	25	18	0	.4	18	....	....	0	0	
29	1,427	44	19	25	3.1	19**	12	63	25**	18	72
30	917	70	60	0	7.7	60	45	75	0	0	
31	1,301	100	30	37	7.7	30	28	95	37	28**	....
Total	282,907[3]	6,175[3]			2.2						

[1] Through justice of the peace courts.
[2] Eighty-three of these were collected after criminal charges were filed.
[3] County Number 3 omitted from totals.
[4] This does not include settlements made face to face in county attorney's office, which were numerous but not recorded.
* Each county is assigned a number from 1 to 31.
** Includes contact by methods other than by letter (i.e., by telephone or personal contact).
.... This indicates no record.

The private collection agencies taking checks for collection seem to be active in only nine Nebraska counties in the sample. Their fees were from one-fourth to one-half the amount of the check. In Omaha and Lincoln they collected around 350 and 65 checks a year totaling roughly $30,000 and $6,500. In the other seven counties they collected only from 25 to 60 checks for each, totaling for the whole state not over 1,000 checks, worth about $50,000. On the average they collected less than .5 per cent of the total bad checks in these nine counties and .3 per cent of their money value. This will be recognized as about one-fifth the average number coming to the legal official, and since the private collection agencies operated in less than one-third the counties, their influence on trade outside of Omaha is negligible.

Theoretically, the duties of the county attorney and the sheriff are limited to the prosecution of crime. Specifically applied to bad checks, this means that it is not part of their official work to collect the amount due on the checks. In fact in situations where the writing of the check is felonious, which includes all forged and no-account checks, and insufficient-fund checks over $35, if the official takes payment for the check and then dismisses the charges, such action seems a clear violation of his statutory duty to prosecute all cases and comes pretty close to the crime of compounding a felony.[1] In like fashion, threatening a check writer with criminal prosecution if he does not pay the check might be considered a type of blackmail.[2]

While there are technical ways of avoiding the criminal charges and still getting the results, such actions on the part of prosecuting attorneys sometimes have been made the basis of disbarment proceedings.[3] But regardless of the technicalities involved, attempts by legal officials to collect checks in circumstances where criminal charges are involved are regarded by most prosecuting attorneys as bad legal ethics, and almost all of them would prefer not to have any part of collecting bad checks in the present state of the law. It is fair to say that most sheriffs also feel the same way.

The professional ethics and the general feeling of the law enforcement officials toward the collection of bad checks, of course, made it difficult for the interviewers to get the entire truth of the activities of law enforcement officials along these lines; but when the official was assured of anonymity and felt confidence in the interviewer, the real facts of his activity usually appeared. For example, one sheriff, upon

---

[1] As to the statutory duty which seems to deny discretion, see Neb. Rev. Stats. 1943 § 23-1201 (Re-issue 1954) and for compounding a felony, see Black, Dictionary of Law (1891) 240; Balentine, Law Dictionary 250 (2nd ed. 1948); cf. Neb. Rev. Stat. 1943, § 28-709 (Re-issue 1948).

[2] Neb. Rev. Stat. 1943 § 28-441 (Re-issue 1948); cf. State v. Seville, 123 Neb. 457, 243 N.W. 269 (1932).

[3] People ex rel Colorado Bar Assn. v. .... Attorney at Law, 90 Colo. 440, 9 P (2d) 611 (1932); Costigan, Cases on the Legal Profession 406, n. 7 (1933).

being approached, said flatly that he never collected checks, but on further discussion it developed that he did get the money on bad checks for the Veterans of Foreign Wars Club and a few of his friends. Pursuing the subject, it developed that regarding checks, all of the businessmen in town were veterans, and the sheriff didn't have an enemy in the world. He then produced a set of books giving the whole story and showing that he ran a complete collection agency in his office. Similar experiences were had with other officials. The sum total of the interviews in 31 Nebraska counties developed the following facts on the practices of the county attorneys and the sheriffs.

Out of 31 counties interviewed, 25 county attorneys, when they received complaints from businessmen, wrote collection letters to the drawer of the check. Such a letter and the receipt required by one county attorney are set out in Forms 1 and 2. Eighteen sheriffs also wrote similar collection letters; two sheriffs were not interviewed, and two either had no records or the interview was inconclusive. In two counties there appeared to be no collections by either the sheriff or the county attorneys, and in one, the collections by both were negligible.

In 15 counties both the county attorney and the sheriff actively collected checks for businessmen; in ten the county attorney alone was the collection agency; in three the sheriff alone collected, and, as indicated above, in two there were no collections by either, and in one, collections were negligible. The summary set out in Table 28 shows that in 28 of the counties there was active collection of bad checks for the businessmen either by the county attorney, by the sheriff or by both.

In regard to the county attorneys' private practice in the field of collecting checks, it was difficult to get conclusive information. In

FORM 1
County Attorney's "Collection" Letter

Dear Sir:

Complaint has been made to this office that you gave a no fund check to

under date of

in the amount of   . This check was returned by the

This letter is for the purpose of giving you the five (5) days notice as mentioned in Section 28-1214 Revised Statutes of Nebraska, 1943, as amended, to establish a presumption of guilt. If you have any reason to give why prosecution should not be started I shall expect to hear from you within the five (5) day limit.

Very truly yours,

County Attorney

FORM 2

County Attorney's Receipt

RECEIPT

I hereby acknowledge receipt of $ .... from .... ,
County Attorney, in payment of the no fund check given to me by ....
....

Dated this .... day of ...., 19 ....
....

four counties the county attorney readily admitted that he took private cases for the collection of checks for a fee; in 14, the county attorneys took no such cases; in 12, it was not clear from the interviews just what the attitude of the county attorney was in regard to such collections; in one, the county attorney collected checks where they were part of other accounts brought to him, and in one, he collected checks for a private fee "where there was no crime involved."

The cases of the sheriff receiving fees for the collection of checks is more complicated. There are a number of ways in which the sheriff might legitimately receive fees for this activity. (1) If a warrant is sworn out and the sheriff goes after the culprit, he is entitled to his regular fees and mileage, even though the check writer, upon being apprehended, pays the damages, and the county attorney dismisses the case. (2) If the culprit has committed a felony and left the state, the sheriff, on extradition proceedings, is entitled to the entire costs of the trip to bring him back, whether he is prosecuted or not. There are a number of situations where the sheriff's compensation for collecting checks may lie on the borderline between legality and petty graft or extortion. If no warrant has been sworn out for the drawer of the bad check, and the sheriff apprehends him for the businessman and makes collection, he might do a number of things: (1) charge his mileage to the businessman or defendant at the same rates as if a warrant had been issued; (2) charge a private fee just as does a collection agency; or (3) accept gifts for his trouble. Out of the 31 counties visited, the following information on sheriffs' compensation for collecting checks was discovered. In seven there was no available information; in three the sheriff admitted collecting mileage or other fees when no warrant was issued (two or three said they received no such mileage, but sheriffs in the neighboring counties did); 12 positively denied receiving any compensation whatsoever unless a proper criminal warrant was sworn out against the culprit; in five the results of the interview were inconclusive; in two or three the sheriff admitted receiving "presents" for his services to the businessmen in this respect; and two of the sheriffs were not available for interview.

On the whole it will be seen then that in the great majority of the counties either the sheriffs or the county attorneys are busily engaged in collecting bad checks for the businessmen, all of which is *ultra vires* their office. It should be said in their behalf that the preponderant majority of these officials seem to be carrying on this activity without any charge, simply as a free service to the businessmen. The amounts collected ran from a few dollars in small rural counties to over $17,000 yearly in larger cities. This practice of collecting checks by officials charged with enforcing the criminal law seems to be nationwide. The most effective collection encountered in the study was by a sheriff in a small city in Colorado where writing short checks is only a misdemeanor,[4] but who nevertheless collected over $13,000, or 83 per cent of all claims brought to him in one year.

It might be interesting to assess further the efficiency of county attorneys and sheriffs as collection agencies. The county attorneys have the following score. Twenty-three out of 25 who wrote collection letters, as shown by their records and testimony, had from 12 to 100 per cent efficiency where they attempted collection. Most of these figures are verified by carbon copies of letters in the county attorneys' files and notations thereon of collection. Their arithmetic average of efficiency was a collection of 60 per cent on all the letters written, and the median was 57 per cent. The sheriffs showed an even better score. Eleven out of the 18 who indulged in collection had a low of 33 per cent and a high of 100 per cent collection. Their mathematical average was about 70 per cent of successful collections on all attempts, with a median of 72 per cent. These figures likewise were supported by records kept in the sheriffs' offices of letters written, receipt books or check stubs where the sheriff paid the amount collected to the businessman by his personal check. The slight advantage of the sheriff's office in efficiency on collection of checks probably is due to the fact that the sheriff and his deputies get around more than the county attorney, and so he is able to contact the bad-check writers personally and accordingly make more collections.

For those who regard this free collection of checks by public officials under the obvious threat of prosecution as an evil, the answer received from the officials is approximately this: The businessman is interested chiefly in getting his money out of the checks. In many in-

---

[4] See Colo. Rev. Stat. 40-14-10 (1953), cf. id. 40-10-1.

stances, when he asks the county attorney or the sheriff to collect, he refuses to swear out an information because he does not want to lose his customers' business. Even in cases where the businessman agrees to swear out a warrant, if he receives payment it is almost impossible to get him thereafter to testify in a criminal action against the check writer, and the fact that the check has been paid serves as a mitigation which makes conviction highly doubtful.

Regardless of the professional ethics involved in this collection of checks by law enforcement officials, it should be borne in mind that in the counties where the officials actually engage in the practice, they are rendering the businessmen a free service which often saves on this item alone much more than the entire salary which the officials receive from the state or county. Many county attorneys and sheriffs would earn much more than their salaries, if paid at commercial collection agency rates on checks; and, throughout the state, this item, as they now operate, would probably equal or exceed the cost of maintaining these offices. It is small wonder, therefore, that the pressure on officials to collect is intense, that those who yield to it are popular and that those who do not, find re-election difficult and sometimes impossible.

Due to these and other factors, it will be seen that the collection process, in most cases, goes right on through the entire procedure of enforcing the criminal law, even through the district court and sometimes after sentencing. The extent of this latter practice will appear from the court statistics which are set out below.

PRE-TRIAL PROCEDURES

Procedures used by the county attorneys in processing bad-check complaints very as much as the penitentiary sentences shown in Figure 5. There are many ways of handling a businessman's complaint on a check. Some county attorneys merely take the check and try to collect it. Failing to do so, they swear out an information or complaint and warrant served by the sheriff. If the culprit is apprehended and still refuses payment or cannot pay, they prosecute on their own initiative. Others require complaining businessmen to fill in forms which run all the way from a simple notation of facts, shown in Form 3, to complicated sworn complaints, illustrated in Form 4. In the latter instance, the county attorney is likely to require the businessman to sign the formal information in court, upon which the warrant for arrest is issued and may demand that he appear as prosecuting witness, whether or not the drawer pays the offending check or checks. The last procedure, which is the one theoretically required by law, is followed in

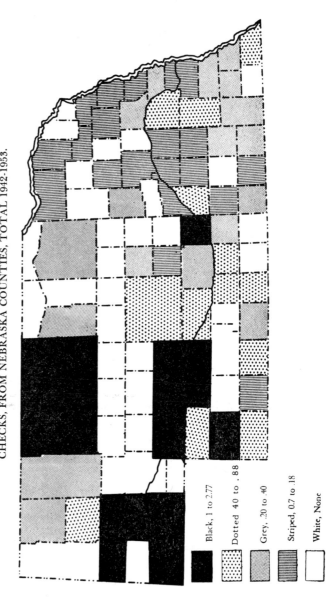

FIGURE 5
(Duplicates Figure 1)

PENITENTIARY CONVICTIONS PER 1000 POPULATION, NO-ACCOUNT AND INSUFFICIENT-FUNDS CHECKS, FROM NEBRASKA COUNTIES, TOTAL 1942-1953.

Black, 1 to 2.77

Dotted 40 to .88

Grey, .20 to .40

Striped, 0.7 to .18

White, None

FORM 3

CHECK RECORD

Name of Maker..

Address ....

Date of Check .... Date Received..

Check drawn on what bank..

Has check been presented to bank for payment..

Reason check was not paid by bank...

In what town and county was check issued...

....

What was check given to you for..

Who is check payable to..

Was check endorsed to you by some third person;

    If so, give name of endorser..

Have any payments been made on this check..

    If so, give dates and how much...

....

How many times have you written or requested maker to pay check................................

....

Dates of Notice ....

Was check post-dated ....

Did you agree to hold the check for any length of time
    before cashing it ....

Is this the first bad check you have had on this person..

    I hereby request the County Attorney of .... County, Nebraska, to immediately file a complaint against the maker of the above check.

Dated this .... day of ...., 195............

....

less than ten per cent of the counties, while the entirely informal approach first indicated is used by well over 70 per cent of the county attorneys. The others are variations of the extremes devised to fit local situations.

Sheriffs likewise may collect checks on their own initiative without the issue of warrants, paying the proceeds directly to the complaining business; or they may turn the complainants directly over to the county

Form 4

STATE OF NEBRASKA vs. ....

STATE OF NEBRASKA)
) SS.
COUNTY OF   )

The undersigned having requested a prosecution to be instituted against the above-named individual, being on oath duly sworn, deposes and says that the following are true answers;

Amount of check...................................Date of Check...

Check made payable to whom?...

Address .... Ph...........................

Check actually given to whom?..

Address ....

Check given by whom?...

Address...

Have you written to maker of the check or given him any notice of the fact that the check was returned unpaid?...

....

Description: Age............... Weight................. Eyes.................. Hair....................

         Complexion .... Build & Height...........................

Previous record or address ....

Where was check given?..
                      City   County   State

Was check given on same date it bears?..

If not, when was check given?..

Were you requested to hold this check?...

What did you give in return for check? Cash?........................... Mdse?...................

Was check given in payment for old account or loan?...

Other pertinent information?..

....

....

                         By..

Subscribed and sworn to before me this .... day of ....,
A.D., 195.............. .

                              ....
                                        Notary Public

— —

DISPOSITION: ....

....

....

            COMPLAINT FILED:..

attorney, refusing to touch the checks or proceeds or to approach the culprit without a warrant or only as directed by the county attorney. The latter again seems to conform to strict legal requirements, but it also is followed by less than ten per cent of the sheriffs. The informal procedure is the type followed by more than half of the peace officers, the rest mixing the two types to suit their purposes.

In the matter of extradition of felonious check writers, there is also a wide divergence of practice. Some county sheriffs, with the approval of the county attorneys, will go anyplace in the state or nation to bring back a culprit who seems to be guilty of a check felony; others will make such trips only within the state; and many will not leave the county to return such a felon. Some rely upon neighboring sheriffs to perform this function, in which case the courtesies are usually reciprocal. Others will not even go this far, preferring to apprehend only wrongdoers found within the borders of their own county.

TYPES OF PROSECUTION

The forums chosen by the county attorneys in which to prosecute and the nature of the charges brought there also vary greatly. Theoretically the justice of the peace courts have jurisdiction over cases in insufficient-fund checks under $35.[5] Some city courts and county courts have jurisdiction finally to sentence for misdemeanors on checks;[6] but felonies can only be disposed of by dismissal for lack of probable cause, or if such cause exists, the defendant must be bound over to the district court for trial.[7] There is, of course, right of appeal from the lower court's decision in misdemeanor cases to the district court,[8] though none such were found; and the district court has jurisdiction to sentence for both misdemeanors and felonies, which can be brought directly into this court by the county attorney, if he so desires.[9] The grand jury might also be used,[10] but no examples of this procedure were found.

It is clear that the county attorney had his choice of procedure in prosecuting. Every legally possible way, except the grand jury, was used in one or more of the counties, and in addition a number of il-

[5] Neb. Constitution Art. V § 18, Neb. Rev. Stat. §§ 27-101 to 105 (1942); cf. id. § 28-1213.

[6] Neb. Constitution Art. V § 16, Neb. Rev. Stat. §§ 826-118; 26-204 (1948); cf. id. § 28-1213.

[7] Neb. Rev. Stat. §§ 29-503, 29-506 (Re-issue 1948).

[8] Id. § 29-611.

[9] Id. § 24-302.

[10] Id. §§ 29-1408; 29-1407; id. §§ 29-1503 to 1506.

legal ones made their appearance. Twenty-six of the county attorneys in the sample of 31 brought their original cases in the county court, but two county attorneys brought no cases in the county court, using only the justice of the peace and district courts for trial of check cases. Three county attorneys used the justice of the peace courts regularly, some when the county judge was not available; one used the municipal court; and in over twenty counties the justice of the peace court did not seem to be used at all for criminal check cases. Eight county attorneys prosecuted only on misdemeanors in justice of the peace or county courts, while in 12 there were no misdemeanor convictions. Eight district courts had no cases at all on checks, and in four counties there were no convictions on any level under the bad-check laws. Ten brought no-fund or forgery charges in the county or justice courts, which occasionally found the defendants guilty and gave final sentences (in about 20 cases), clearly an illegal practice.[11] In at least one county, the county attorney made a practice of bringing charges on no-account checks as felonies in the justice of the peace court; but if the defendant would plead guilty and pay up, the charge was changed to insufficient funds, and the culprit was dismissed with a fine, a highly questionable procedure.

Thus in over a third of the counties visited, the criminal law on checks was not enforced at all or only in a spotty manner in the courts; but as shown in Table 28, in many counties where there were no court actions or only spotty prosecutions on checks, the county attorney or the sheriff or both enforced the law through the *ultra vires* sanction of running effective collection agencies. It is also significant that, as shown by Table 29, where collection was the practice, the per-capita rate of bad checks ran lower than in the counties where there was vigorous criminal prosecution but little collection activity.

The number and manner of handling such cases in the courts themselves is discussed more fully under the heading "Court Procedures" below.

TWO YEARS' ACTIVITY IN A REPRESENTATIVE COUNTY ATTORNEY'S OFFICE

A number of county attorneys kept very good records of their work in prosecuting bad-check cases; others kept none. The following is a summary of the activities of one county attorney's office located in an average-sized Nebraska city which used all of the current procedures for handling bad checks, showing the types of cases which came to him and their disposition.

[11] Neb. Constitution Art. V § 16, cf. Neb. Rev. Stat. § 28-1212 as amended (1951).

TABLE 29

Relationship between Population, Collection Activities of County Officials and Sentences of Imprisonment[1]

Population Size	County Number	Number of Bad Checks per Capita	Per Cent of Bad Checks Given Officials	Per Cent of Total Bad Checks Collected by County Attorney and Sheriff	Number of Imprisonment Sentences Misdemeanor and Felony	
					Per 1000 People	Per 1000 Bad Checks
Average for All		.37	2.2	1.1	.206	1.603
1,000-8,000	29	1.18	3.1	2.1	0	0
	17	.41	8.5	1.4	0	0
	16	.28	3.9	2.0	0	0
	3	.67	....	....	0	0
	15	.51	1.1	....	0	0
	27	.24	2.0	1.0	.156	.651
	22	.11	8.4	8.0	0	0
	31	.18	7.7	4.3	0	0
	20	.23	4.1	1.8	.268	1.178
	Average			2.5	.006	.333
8,000-14,000	30	.11	7.7	4.9	0	0
	6	.30	2.5	2.0	.115	.194
	12	.35	.8	.4	0	0
	11	.26	1.6	....	.366	1.387
	7	.27	3.7	1.9	0	0
	10	.33	2.8	.6*	.096	.288
	28	.53	.4	....	.378	.719
	5	2.30[2]	.3	.1	.456	.198
	2	.30	1.3	....	.448	1.493
	24	.41	1.7	.7	.116	.284
	8	.28	2.2	.3	.077	.272
	Average		(1.1)[2]	.5[2]	.192	.517
14,000-40,000	25	.33	.4*	....	.071	.214
	19	.27	4.9	3.8	.101	.371
	4	.26	3.5	1.3	.062	.235
	9	.28	2.2	3.4	.287	1.015
	23	.25	1.7	....	.076	.301
	13	.62	1.2	.9	.172	.276
	1	.19	1.1	.6*	.208	1.091
	18	.32	1.6	1.1	.482	1.483
	26	.62	1.9	.3	.665	1.071
	Average			1.2	.289	.970
100,000 and over	21	.30	1.9	1.2	.355	1.188
	14	.35	2.9**	.1*	.110***	.317***

[1] Population from 1950 census; convictions are an average of 1952 and 1953, number of bad checks are 1954 estimates.
[2] If County 5, which was unusual, were dropped, the average of this group would be 1.1.
* There was a record from only one official.
** Includes checks given police officials.
*** These are underestimates, as the record was not complete on misdemeanor sentences.

299

During the two-year period from January 1, 1952, to December 31, 1953, the county attorney's notebook showed complaints from businessmen on 756 checks written by 335 drawers (39, or 12 per cent, were women) totaling $21,300. Of these he collected 384 checks totaling $12,549 or 59 per cent, and there remained uncollected 372 checks totaling $8,751 or 41 per cent. The arithmetic average of checks on which he received complaints during this period was $28, on checks collected, $33, and on uncollected checks, $23.

Table 30 shows that over half of the defendants wrote only one bad check, and the most written by any one was 15. The total claims

TABLE 30

Distribution of Number of Bad Checks Written by Defendants for 1952-1953

Number of Checks to Defendant	Number of Drawers	Total Checks Written
1	196	196
2	53	106
3	28	84
4	14	56
5	10	50
6	15	90
7	6	42
8	5	40
9	2	18
10	1	10
11	1	11
12	2	24
14	1	14
15	1	15
Totals	335	756

Average Number of Checks Per Defendant	
Arithmetic Average	2.2
Median	1
Mode	1 (196)
Spread	1 to 15

Average Amount of Total Claims Charged Against Each Defendant Spread from $1 to $1,315	
Arithmetic Average	$63.58
Median	$25
Mode	$10 (29 claims)
1st Quartile	$10
3rd Quartile	$64

are small, with a median of $25, and three-fourths of them less than $65. There were only eight such claims over $350: $475, one check; $509, three checks; $548, six checks; $569, one check; $622, one check; $624, three checks; $1,075, one check; $1,315, two checks. All but three of these 18 checks seem to have been collected or settled out of court.

It should be noted, as shown in Table 31, that over half of the complaints were on single checks which constituted 40 per cent of the total dollar loss.

TABLE 31

Distribution of Defendants' Checks in Relation to Claims

	No. of Drawers	Per Cent of Drawers	No. of Checks	Per Cent of Total Checks	Dollars Total	Per Cent of Whole Amount in Dollars Reported in Each Group	Average Size Check	Average Charge per Person
Single Check	196	59	196	26	$8,490	40	$43.34	$43.34
2 Checks	53	16	106	14	$3,610	17	$34.06	$68.12
3 to 15	86	25	454	60	$9,200	43	$16.60	$106.98
Totals	335	100	756	100	$21,300	100	$28.17	$63.58

There were 454 checks cashed by 86 writers who drew three or more checks. These were the upper quartile of the writers (25 per cent), and contain most of the criminal element. These individual checks on the average range from $1 to $208. The arithmetic average of all is only $16.60. The median check in this group is $14, first quartile $10, third quartile $22. Thus three-fourths of the checks written by habitual bad-check writers were for less than $23 each.

The claims against each defendant who wrote three or more checks run from $4 to $624, both totals for three checks. The median for the claims was $70, the first quartile $40, and the third quartile $130. None of the 86 claims ran over $624, which was the highest and was for three checks. It appears that even here the average loss was only $107, and the highest claim was for less than $700.

The actual records of persons prosecuted during the two-year period show 61 prosecutions on 216 checks. The county attorney's notebook showed 46 convictions in two years of defendants who wrote 195 checks. Table 32 shows the distribution of their sentences.

It also shows that the checks were small; of the total claims against each defendant, the average was below $60 and three-fourth of the claims were below $120. On a yearly basis this was a total of 23 prosecutions, involving less than $3,500, in a county with population of over 30,000 and a higher than average bad-check-per-capita rating.

TABLE 32

Distribution of Sentences and Amounts Involved

17, or 37%, sentenced to penitentiary.
4, or 9%, sentenced to reformatory.
1, or 2%, sentenced to women's reformatory
12, or 26%, probation or parole.
12, or 26%, sentenced to jail.

These 195 checks on the average had a spread of from $1 to $1,450.

Arithmetic Average	$35+
1st Quartile	$10
Median	$15
3rd Quartile	$18

These 46 claims against individuals totaled $6,680.

Spread	$1 to $1,450
Arithmetic Average	$149
1st Quartile	$ 22
Median	**$ 60**
3rd Quartile	$115

There were also 15 cases which were dismissed, totaling claims of $1,653 for 21 checks, with a spread of from $5 to $622, both on the size of the checks and the claims. Most of these were paid or settled, but a few were dismissed because of lack of evidence or because the defendant could not be served.

A small number of these men were prosecuted and convicted more than once within the two-year period. The county attorney's notebook is very closely corroborated by the court's records.

Table 33, which gives the records of prosecutions in more detail, shows that, if $100 be taken as the lower limits of felony charges,[12] two-thirds of these defendants should be in the misdemeanor class; and it further shows that 14 of 22, also about two-thirds, receiving felony sentences with no parole were sentenced for recorded offenses, the total money value of which was less than the upper misdemeanor rate. So on the whole, the figures show that in this representative county, as throughout the state, the large preponderance of bad-check writers are petty criminals.

All the facts here set out point clearly to the conclusion that there is no uniform criminal procedure in dealing with bad checks; and further, as has already appeared in the discussion of mercantile losses above, most of the bad-check writers are in the petty misdemeanor

[12] This is now the law in larceny and similar crimes, id. § 28-506 as amended (1953).

TABLE 33
Writers of Bad Checks Who Were Prosecuted, County Attorney's Notebook, 1952 and 1953

Sentence:	Penitentiary		Reformatory		Women's Reformatory		Probation or Parole		Jail		Dismissed	
	No. Cks.	Amt. of Claims	No. Cks.	Amt. of Claims	No. Cks.	Amt. of Claims	No. Cks.	Amt. of Claims	No. Cks.	Amt. of Claims	No. Cks.	Amt. of Claims
	8	$ 85	1	$ 25	2	$25	8 pd.	$105	1	$ 31	1	$622
	15	224	7	173			1	2	3	624	4 pd.	40
	5	132	3	112			3	20	8	90	1	25
	5	310	4	59			3 pd.	115	3 pd.	28	1	5
	12	202					4	9	2	4	1	5
	7	129						1	1	10	1 pd.	500
	1 f.	5					4	7	2	22	1	5
	1 f.	60					2	1317	5	60	1	32
	4	60					1 f.	500	6	40	1	30
	7	70					9 pd.	145	3	14	1	10
	9	138					6 pd.	76	1 pd.	1450	3 pd.	245
	5	81					2 pd.	20	1	50	1	5
	1 f.	83									2 pd.	29
	2	95									1	80
	4	29									1	20
	7	55										
	5	68										
Totals / Total Defendants 61,	98	$1826	15	$269	2	$25	44	$2317	36	$2423	21	$1653
	17		4		1		12		12		15	
Average Checks per Defendant	6		4		2		4		3		1½	
Average Claims per Defendant		$105		$67		$25		$193		$202		$110

NOTE: f. means charge was forgery; pd. means checks were paid; but not all forgery charges are recorded as such, nor are all payments noted.

class. Many of them are so trivial that a few county attorneys refuse to be bothered with them. Others take the position that the bad-check laws are so strict and so far out of line with the community activities that these statutes are harder to enforce than was prohibition.

The financial significance of the county attorneys' and sheriffs' activities in handling bad-check cases lies in the extra-legal collection processes in which most of them are busily engaged.

CITY POLICE

The function of the city police in the bad-check problem is not entirely clear, but in general it can be said that they take the place of and augment the activities of the sheriff's office.

In the largest cities they cooperate with the city attorney in his collection of checks and in the apprehension of criminals. In the smaller cities they seem to take little part in this activity in the county-seat towns because the sheriff and his deputies are available immediately to the businessmen complaining on bad checks. In the larger centers which are not big cities nor county seats and not readily available to the sheriff's office, of which there are very few in Nebraska, city police may be a bit more active in collecting checks and arresting offenders. On the whole, most of the police activity is in the felony field, handling forgeries and no-account checks. They also call upon the F.B.I. for aid in identifying forgers and cooperate with sheriffs and other city police in catching fugitive check writers.

In one of the largest cities, the police kept records showing that they received complaints on about 200 bad checks a year, totaling nearly $12,500. Fifty-six per cent of the writers were arrested, and their checks amounted to 71 per cent of the total money value of all the check complaints to the police. This was about one-half the amount collected by the county attorney on letters in that county. The practice in this city was for the police to take the arrested offenders directly to the county attorney, who dealt with them face to face, either collecting or prosecuting in the city, county or district courts, as he saw fit. In this situation, the contention of the police that they did not collect money on bad checks was close to 100 per cent true and is further supported by the fact that they hardly ever dealt with writers of insufficient-fund checks, which is the largest area of collection.

The picture in the other large city was different. Here the police files indicated that they received about 300 complaints a year, involving one to 15 checks each, over twice as many as shown in the county attorney's records. Although they are extremely reticent about the facts and deny collection activity, and though their files show no record of it, there is abundant evidence that they were actively engaging in collection. Two or three officials intimately acquainted with the work of the police testified flatly that they did collect. The collection letters written by the county attorney are a mere fraction of the complaints, and the physical distance from the county attorney's office to the police station adds credence to the fact that the police finally disposed of checks in the cases where the defendants were willing to pay. It is clear also that the police themselves took the responsibility of prosecuting bad-check defendants in the city court in much the same manner as they handle speeders, vagrants and the like. Although the city court had excellent records of the felony cases bound over to the district court, they kept no records at all of misdemeanor charges on bad checks. These were all thrown together under the classification of "vagrancy," which seemed to be a catchall for dozens of minor crimes prosecuted in the city court. There was also evidence that some defendants brought into the city court on the felony charge of writing no-fund or forged checks who were willing to pay up were convicted merely of vagrancy and given a light fine when they made good the damages.

Since the police were active in the check field in so few counties in the sample and probably less so in the others because the sample contained most of the largest population centers, it is hard to reach any definite findings other than to observe that they are probably serving about the same function in the enforcement of the bad-check law as do deputy sheriffs.

THE FUNCTIONS AND RECORDS OF THE COURTS

The role of the courts in the enforcement of the bad-check laws, as already indicated, depends to a large extent upon the practices and policies of the county attorneys. As shown in the material on county attorneys and sheriffs, there is a great variation in the manner in which defendants in bad-check cases are presented to and sentenced by the individual courts of the different counties and at various levels.

It was pointed out there that no special pattern was followed by the county attorneys in the prosecution of cases. This is further confirmed by Table 34, showing the number of cases and sentences arranged by order of population of the counties. It is significant that there were seven counties which, over the two-year period, had an average of less than one sentence of any sort per year and that three-fourths of the counties, regardless of size, had less than ten convictions of any kind for a similar period. It should be noted further that there is no correlation between the size of the counties and the number of convictions

TABLE 34

Number of Court Cases and Number of Sentences Given in the Courts of Thirty Nebraska Counties per Year

County by Number (by Population Size)	Number of Cases—All Courts			Number of Sentences		
	Total One Year*	Per 1000 People	Per 1000 Bad Checks	Total One Year*	Per 1000 People	Per 1000 Bad Checks
(Average) All 30 Counties 1,000-8,000 pop.						
29	3.5	1.244	1.051	1.0	.829	.707
17	2.0	.687	1.680	.5	.172	.423
16	2.5	.608	2.192	1.5	.365	1.318
3	12.0	2.342	3.489	0	0	0
15	1.0	.190	.370	0	0	0
27	3.5	.548	2.278	3.0	.579	1.953
22	3.0	.445	4.202	0	0	0
31	2.5	.676	1.922	.5	.068	.384
20	25.5	3.424	15.018	10.5	1.410	6.184
Average		1.190	3.665		.364	1.123
8,000-14,000 pop.						
30	20.5	2.386	22.356	9.0	1.048	9.815
6	3.0	.345	1.160	1.0	.194	.387
12	3.0	.328	.946	.5	.053	.157
11	11.0	1.134	4.360	4.5	.464	1.784
7	8.5	.940	3.515	0	0	0
10	11.0	1.058	3.166	1.5	.144	.432
28	15.0	1.420	2.697	9.0	.852	1.618
5	23.5	1.945	.847	10.0	.829	.360
2	16.5	1.344	4.476	7.0	.570	1.900
24	23.0	1.772	4.349	5.0	.385	.946
8	3.0	.231	.817	2.0	1.539	.545
Average		1.175	2.250		.807	.422
14,000-40,000 pop.						
25	3.5	.249	.752	1.5	.107	.322
19	11.5	.774	2.845	3.0	.202	.742
4	18.0	2.200	4.234	8.5	.520	1.999
9	21.5	1.122	3.968	6.5	.339	1.199
23	13.0	.653	2.608	3.5	.178	.702
13	36.5	1.390	2.243	18.5	.704	1.137
1	13.0	.450	2.364	7.0	.243	1.434
18	84.5	2.626	8.089	35.0	1.087	3.350
26	126.5	3.728	6.052	71.0	2.092	3.397
Average		1.598	4.295		.751	2.020
100,000 and over pop.						
21	131.0	1.094	2.662	62.5	.522	1.747

* Average of 1952 and 1953 totals.

per capita or per the number of bad checks. The figures show that, so far as cases in court are concerned, there is no uniformity of enforcement either in the individual counties or in counties of similar size.

THE COMPOSITE COURT PICTURE

A true report of the procedures of the courts in the state as a whole is hard to reach. Since there are no judicial statistics in Nebraska, the figures taken from the 31 counties in the sample from records for

TABLE 35

Number of Check Cases Classified by Type of Crime, Thirty-one Nebraska Counties, 1952 and 1953

Courts	Number	Per Cent
TOTAL—ALL COURTS*		
Total	1,445	100.0
Forgery	306	21.2
No-Account	519	35.9
Insufficient-Fund	585	40.5
No Record of Type	35	2.4
LOWER COURTS		
Total	1,383	100.0
Forgery	280	20.3
No-Account	446	32.2
Insufficient-Fund	563	40.7
No Record of Type	94	6.8
DISTRICT COURTS		
Total	477	100.0
Forgery	197	42.3
No-Account	228	47.8
Insufficient-Fund	47	9.9

* The number of cases in the total for all courts is equal to the sum of the District Court cases and the Lower Court cases minus the cases bound over from the Lower Courts to the District Courts. A total of 415 cases were bound over to the District Courts—176 forgery, 155 no-account, 25 insufficient-fund and 59 cases with no record of type. These totals are also understated because the records in one large city court are not available.

the years 1952 and 1953 unfortunately will have to serve as a basis for projecting the judicial activity for the entire state in the field of bad-check law.

Table 35 shows that in all of the courts in the sample counties, there were, in two years, 1,445 cases involving bad checks.[13] The sample

[13] Owing to the absence of proper records, this figure does not contain the information from the city courts in one of the state's largest cities, so the number of cases in the lower courts is smaller than it should be. The absence of this figure is taken into account in calculating the state totals which follow immediately.

counties contained about 58 per cent of the population of the state and 44 per cent of the estimated number of bad checks written in the entire state. They also sent 55 per cent of the criminals to the Penitentiary and the Reformatory during this time. Using these ratios as a composite basis, it would appear that there were in the courts of the state as a whole between 2,500 and 2,800 bad-check cases. If they were divided in the same proportion as those appearing in the sample, that would make between 700 and 800 district court cases and between 1,800 and 2,000 in the lower courts in all the counties of the state.

Returning to the sample figures and taking all of the cases both in the lower and upper courts, as shown in Table 35, about 21 per cent of the prosecutions were on forgeries, 36 per cent no-account, and 41 per cent insufficient-fund checks. Of these 1,445 sample cases, 415 appeared both in the lower courts and district courts. These consisted of

TABLE 36

Disposition of Bad-Check Cases in All Courts—Justice of the Peace, Municipal, County and District—Thirty-one Nebraska Counties, 1952 and 1953

Disposition	Check Cases Classified by Type of Crime									
	Total		Forgery		No-Account		Insufficient-Fund		No Record of Type of Check	
	No.	Per Cent	No.	Cent Per	No.	Per Cent	No.	Per Cent	No.	Per Cent
Total	1,445	100.0	306	100.0	519	100.0	585	100.0	35	100.0
Without Sentence	810	56.0	146	47.7	297	57.2	342	58.5	25	71.4
No Warrant Returned	405	28.0	90	29.4	160	30.7	149	25.5	6	17.1
Dismissed	340	23.5	51	16.7	114	22.0	158	27.0	17	48.6
Paid	22	1.5	1	.3	5	1.0	16	2.7		
Acquitted	1	.1			1	.2				
Warrant Collected, No Other Record	28	1.9			14	2.7	14	2.4		
No Record	14	1.0	4	1.3	3	.6	5	.9	2	5.7
With Sentence	635	44.0	160	52.3	222	42.8	243	41.5	10	28.6
Penitentiary	167	11.6	72	23.4	89	17.1	6	1.0		
Reformatory	52	3.6	28	9.2	20	3.8	4	.7		
Probation or Parole	105	7.2	43	14.1	44	8.5	18	3.1		
Suspended Sentence	11	.7			8	1.5	3	.5		
Women's Reformatory	7	.5			7	1.4				
Mental Hospital	4	.3	1	.3	3	.6				
State School	7	.5	4	1.3	1	.2	2	.3		
Jail	82	5.7	4	1.3	33	6.4	44	7.5	1	2.9
Fine	194	13.5	2	.7	17	3.3	166	28.4	9	25.7
Other Sentence	6	.4	6	2.0						

TABLE 37

Disposition of Bad-Check Cases Filed in the Lower Courts—Justice of the Peace, Municipal and County—Thirty-one Nebraska Counties, 1952 and 1953

Disposition	Check Cases Classified by Type of Crime									
	Total		Forgery		No-Account		Insufficient-Fund		No Record of Type of Check	
	No.	Per Cent	No.	Per Cent	No.	Per Cent	No.	Per Cent	No.	Per Cent
Total	1,383	100.0	280	100.0	446	100.0	563	100.0	94	100.0
Without Sentence	729	52.7	103	36.8	270	60.5	331	58.8	35	26.6
No Warrant Returned	404	29.2	90	32.1	159	35.7	149	26.5	6	6.4
Dismissed	264	19.1	9	3.2	90	20.2	148	26.3	17	18.1
Paid	22	1.6	1	.4	5	1.1	16	2.8		
Warrant Collected, No Other Record	28	2.0			14	3.1	14	2.5		
No Record	11	.8	3	1.1	2	.4	4	.7	2	2.1
Bound Over Cases	415	30.0	176	62.8	155	34.8	25	4.4	59	62.8
With Sentence	239	17.3	1	.4	21	4.7	207	36.8	10	10.6
Jail	42	3.0			6	1.4	35	6.2	1	1.0
Fine	186	13.5	1	.4	13	2.9	163	28.9	9	9.6
State School	2	.1					2	.4		
Probation or Parole	5	.4					5	.9		
Suspended Sentence	4	.3			2	.4	2	.4		

felony cases bound over to the district courts for final disposition. It should be noted that in the lower courts the most numerous cases were on insufficient-fund checks, 41 per cent; no-account, 32 per cent; and forgeries, only 20 per cent; but in the district courts, this trend was reversed. Only ten per cent were insufficient-fund cases; 48 per cent, no-account; and 42 per cent, forgeries.

It is interesting to observe that although both forgeries and no-account checks are felonies, and although there were ten times as many no-account checks as forgeries written in the period of a year,[14] the number of prosecutions on each were about equal. Even though there were more no-account checks than forgeries, which might be innocent mistakes, this still shows a complete disparity of standards of law enforcement involving the two types of felonies.

Turning to the final decisions, one is struck with more interesting facts. Tables 36, 37 and 38 show the dispositions as a whole, in all courts, in the lower courts and in the district courts.

[14] See Table 11, p. 258, *supra*.

TABLE 38

Disposition of Bad-Check Cases Filed in the District Courts—Thirty-one Nebraska Counties, 1952 and 1953

Disposition	Check Cases Classified by Type of Crime							
	Total		Forgery		No-Account		Insufficient-Fund	
	No.	Per Cent	No.	Per Cent	No.	Per Cent	No.	Cent Per
Total	477	100.0	202	100.0	228	100.0	47	100.0
Without Sentence (total)	81	17.0	43	21.3	27	11.8	11	23.4
No Warrant Returned	1	.2			1	.4		
Dismissed	76	16.0	42	20.8	24	10.6	10	21.3
Acquitted	1	.2			1	.4		
No Record	3	.6	1	.5	1	.4	1	2.1
With Sentence (total)	396	83.0	159	78.7	201	88.2	36	76.6
Penitentiary	167	35.0	72	35.5	89	39.1	6	12.8
Reformatory	52	10.8	28	13.9	20	8.8	4	8.5
Probation or Parole	100	21.0	43	21.3	44	19.3	13	27.7
Suspended Sentence	7	1.5			6	2.6	1	2.1
Women's Reformatory	7	1.5			7	3.1		
Mental Hospital	4	.8	1	.5	3	1.3		
State School	5	1.1	4	2.0	1	.4		
Jail	40	8.4	4	2.0	27	11.8	9	19.1
Fine	8	1.6	1	.5	4	1.8	3	6.4
Other Sentence	6	1.3	6	3.0				

In spite of the fact that proof of the case against a bad-check writer is so simple that over 95 per cent of the defendants entering a plea either plead guilty or *nolo contendere*[15] and there was only one acquittal of record in all of the courts, over 56 per cent of the cases were disposed of without sentence. While the practices in the lower courts varied widely from county to county in cases without sentence, the figures as a whole are revealing. Table 37 shows that about 53 per cent of all the complaints in the lower courts and, as shown in Table 38, 17 per cent of all the complaints in the district courts never reached the sentencing stage. While a large number of these fell into the no-warrant-returned class, it should be noted that only 36 per cent of the forgery cases in the lower courts were disposed of without sentence, while 60 per cent of the no-fund and 59 per cent of the insufficient-fund cases were in this latter group. Add to this the further fact that in the case of insufficient funds, the lower courts dismissed over 28

---

[15] See Table 39, p. 312, infra.

per cent of the defendants with fines alone.[16] Almost all of these represent cases where the defendant paid the check and the court assessed a nominal fine.[17] Even though the records themselves admit openly of only three per cent collections, this high per cent of dismissals and fines in cases where proof of guilt was clear shows clearly that the lower courts were being used as part of the collection process.

In the district courts likewise, where only about 17 per cent of the cases were disposed of without decision, there is also evidence of this tendency to allow the defendants to settle and get off with no sentence at all. The dismissals here totaled about 17 per cent, running: for forgery, 21 per cent; for no-account, 11 per cent; and for insufficient-funds, 21 per cent. When these are added to the 21 per cent of cases in which the defendant was placed on probation and in which almost always he was required to make good his checks, it will be seen that even the district courts were part of the collection process, with over one-third of their cases falling into this category.

It should be further noted that in the lower courts about 30 per cent of the cases were disposed of on the notation "no warrant returned." Although many of these represent situations where the defendant paid the sheriff and the case was dropped without further action, others are instances where the defendants were floaters, professional check writers and general ne'er-do-wells. The fact that there are roughly seven per cent more of these in the forgery and no-fund classifications than in insufficient-funds where the writers had bank accounts and were, therefore, easily found shows that about ten to 15 per cent of the total found in all these classifications were cases against professionals and indigent types of criminals where the sheriffs could not locate the defendants. The other half of the "no-warrant-returned" category probably represents collections by the sheriffs using the court process as the final leverage to get payment.

Taking the courts' statistics as a whole, it can be ascertained that nearly two-thirds of all the cases involve collecting money for aggrieved businessmen. Ten to 15 per cent represent complete loss because the check writers are never apprehended, and the remaining one-fourth involve criminal prosecutions where the amounts of the bad checks are also almost a complete business loss.

---

[16] There were a number of cases where fines were also assessed with other sentences; this seemed to occur in about ten per cent of the cases, about equally divided between jail and penitentiary sentences.

[17] This information was had mostly from informal interviews with county attorneys and judges.

OTHER SIGNIFICANT PROCEDURAL OPERATIONS

. There are a number of other facts which stand out very vividly from the court records.

. The first of these is that in this field there is little use for the standard court procedural devices in criminal cases. Because the culprit, when apprehended, is faced with a direct copy of the check, usually in his own handwriting and containing a notation of the bank showing plainly whether it was an insufficient-fund, a no-account or a forgery, there is little use for the apparatus of proof. Table 39 shows that in all courts in insufficient- and no-fund cases, about 95 per cent of the defendants entering pleas pled guilty. In two years there was

TABLE 39

Record of Pleas Entered in Cases Going to Judgment on No-Account and Insufficient-Fund Checks, Thirty-one Counties, 1952 and 1953

	Number with Record of Plea	Plea of Guilty		Plea of Not Guilty		Nolo Contendere	
		No.	Per Cent	No.	Per Cent	No.	Per Cent
All Courts	411	390	94.9	19	4.6	2	.5
District Courts	215	205	95.4	8	3.7	2	.9
Lower Courts	196	185	94.4	11	5.6		

only one acquittal, and even in that case the defendant mistakenly admitted his guilt. Likewise in the entire period not a single jury case was found. Trial in the usual sense was also almost nonexistent here.

A second phenomenon is that the role of the trial lawyer loses most of its importance. Table 40 shows that in 275 recorded cases involving insufficient-fund and no-account checks in the district courts, the fact that a defense attorney did or did not take part in the proceedings appears in the record. The defendant had no lawyer in 78 per cent of these cases. The presence of an attorney in the other 22 per cent seemed to have a marked effect on the outcome of the cases only in the instances of procuring dismissals of charges on insufficient-fund checks and in the granting of probation or paroles in district court cases. In both of these situations, the lawyer proportionately seemed to be able to aid his client in mitigating the harshness of the sentence. The extent to which other sentences may have been reduced by the presence of a lawyer, of course, cannot be told from the record. Since there were only 60 recorded instances of participation by lawyers in 275 records in the

TABLE 40

Number and Disposition of Cases in District Courts with and without a Defense Lawyer, No-Account and Insufficient-Fund Checks, Thirty-one Counties, 1952 and 1953

	Per Cent of Cases with and without a Lawyer				
	All Cases	Without Lawyer		With Lawyer	
	Number	Number	Per Cent	Number	Per Cent
Total	275	215	78.2	60	21.8
No-Account	228	181	79.4	47	20.6
Insufficient-Fund	47	34	72.3	13	27.7

	Disposition of Cases with and without a Lawyer											
	All Cases (No-Account and Insufficient-Fund)				No-Account Cases				Insufficient-Fund Cases			
Disposition	No Lawyer		Lawyer		No Lawyer		Lawyer		No Lawyer		Lawyer	
	No.	Per Cent	No.	Per Cent	No.	Per Cent	No.	Per Cent	No.	Per Cent	No.	Per Cent
Total	215	100.0	60	100.0	181	100.0	47	100.0	34	100.0	13	100.0
Without Sentence	31	14.5	7	11.7	24	13.1	3	6.3	7	20.5	4	30.8
No Warrant Returned	1	.5			1	.5						
Dismissed	28	13.1	6	10.0	22	12.1	2	4.2	6	17.6	4	30.8
Acquitted			1	1.7			1	2.1				
No Record and Other	2	.9			1*	.5			1**	2.9		
With Sentence	184	85.5	53	88.3	157	86.9	44	93.7	27	79.5	9	69.2
Penitentiary	79	36.7	16	26.6	73	40.3	16	34.0	6	17.7		
Reformatory	21	9.8	3	5.0	19	10.5	1	2.3	2	5.9	2	15.4
Probation or Parole	31	14.4	26	43.3	23	12.7	21	44.7	8	23.6	5	38.4
Suspended Sentence	6	2.8	1	1.7	5	2.8	1	2.1	1	2.9		
Women's Reformatory	7	3.3			7	3.9						
Mental Hospital	2	.9	1	1.7	2	1.1	1	2.1				
State School	1	.5			1	.6						
Jail	32	14.8	4	6.7	23	12.7	4	8.5	9	26.5		
Fine	5	2.3	2	3.3	4	2.2			1	2.9	2	15.4

* *Nolle Prosequi*
** No Jurisdiction

district courts and far less in the lower courts, it is clear that the members of the bar in the role of defenders have little effect here.

FINANCIAL SIGNIFICANCE OF THE CASES

The court records do not always give a clear picture of the total amount of money involved in the prosecution of check cases. This is because it is the practice of many county attorneys to bring a criminal action on only one of a series of bad checks, with the hope that this will force the defendant to pay others which he has written or will be sufficient, since each check is a separate offense, to impose upon him the desired sentence. However, practically all of the records showed the size of the checks upon which the prosecution was based. Table 41 shows that these amounts appeared in over 1,000 cases in which the record was examined. It also confirms in its detail the figures given by businessmen and in sample counties discussed above.[18] Here, as there, the average check involved is small. Although the arithmetic average is $85, the median is only $18, and three-fourths of the amounts on which charges were based were under $40. The total recorded amount for the 1,000 cases amounted to only $86,000, which means that proportionately for all the cases in the state, the amounts reaching the

TABLE 41

Size of Insufficient-Fund and No-Account Checks for which Court Charges Were Made in Thirty-one Nebraska Counties, 1952 and 1953

Number of Cases	1,020
Median	$18
First Quartile	$10
Third Quartile	$40
Mode	$10 (195 cases)
Arithmetic Mean	$85
Total Dollar Amount	$86,235
Range	$1 to $12,040

The record is not entirely complete for all court cases involved because (a) some cases did not report the size of check, or the questionnaire was incomplete, and (b) only a tally record of the number of court cases was taken in a few courts.

court would be under $300,000.[19] Here again it is apparent that, by and large, taking into consideration all of the cases in all of the courts, most of the bad checks upon which prosecutions were based are definitely in the petty larceny class; but in spite of this, about 30 per cent of the cases in the lower courts and 70 per cent in the district courts received the felony treatment. Since about two-thirds of the cases coming to court involve collection, and since, as indicated in the discussion of the county attorney above, the checks collected are the larger ones, the total loss to the businessmen on bad checks brought to court in the state probably runs less than $100,000 a year. If the

[18] Cf. Table 15, p. 261, Table 30, p. 300, Table 32, p. 302.

[19] This can be compared with the highest calculated state loss of $475,000, supra p. 264.

total of unpaid checks for the state, as calculated from the commercial records above,[20] is considered, it appears that more than three-fourths of the losses suffered in the state came from bad checks on which the businessmen do not bother to prosecute.

Table 42 shows the types of businessmen who prosecuted cases in the courts. It is significant that the largest number of cases here came from gas stations, liquor dealers, etc., in almost the same ratio as the loss by types of businesses reported above.[21]

TABLE 42

Per Cent of Complaints Arranged by Type of Business, Insufficient-Fund and No-Account Court Cases, Thirty-one Nebraska Counties, 1952 and 1953

Business	Number of Complaints	Per Cent of Complaints
Total Number of Cases	894*	100.0
1. Gasoline Service Stations	136	15.2
2. Drinking Places and Liquor Stores	119	13.3
3. Automobiles, Parts and Repairs	114	12.8
4. General Merchandise Stores	103	11.5
5. Groceries and Meat Markets	93	10.4
6. Apparel Stores	38	4.3
7. Hotels and Tourist Courts	37	4.1
8. Drugstores	35	3.9
9. Eating Places	27	3.0
10. Hardware, Paint and Glass	12	1.3
11. Government, Local and State	12	1.3
12. Grain Companies and Elevators	11	1.2
13. Farm Equipment	9	1.0
14. Jewelry Stores	9	1.0
15. Sporting Goods Stores	8	.9
16. Furniture Stores	8	.9
17. Lumber Yards	7	.8
18. Hay, Grain and Feed	7	.8
19. Shoe Stores and Repairs	6	.7
20. Household Appliances and Radio	6	.7
21. Banks	6	.7
22. Cleaning and Laundries	4	.5
23. Florists	3	.3
24. Professionals (Doctors)	3	.3
25. Barbers and Beauty Shops	1	.1
26. Miscellaneous (All Others)*	80	9.0

* In addition, there were 54 cases with no record of the type of business and 102 cases in which the bad check was given to an individual.

[20] Supra, note 6, p. 264.
[21] See p. 269 ff.

315

SENTENCING PRACTICES

In considering the sentencing habits of the courts, it is important to note the state of the statutes under which they are operating. Forgery of a check of any size is a felony requiring a sentence to the penitentiary or a fine up to $500.[22] Writing a no-account check makes the drawer subject to either misdemeanor or felony sentences including fine, jail or penitentiary at the discretion of the court,[23] but the sentences for both forgery and no-account checks must be given only in the district court.[24] The insufficient-fund check, on the other hand, is a misdemeanor only below $35 and is a felony above.[25] So if the check is less than $35, the case can be definitely concluded at the justice of the peace or county court level by either fine or jail sentence; but if it is above $35, again it must go to the district court and for felony sentences of either fine or penitentiary.[26] It can be readily seen that the law presents the courts with a complicated maze of sentencing procedures depending upon arbitrary distinctions and makes centralized administration of similar problems impossible. It is small wonder, therefore, that, as shown in Table 34, page 306, there are no uniform practices in this regard in the various counties. Turning again to the situations in Table 36, page 308, certain trends will appear from the two-year period. The court pronounced sentence in only 44 per cent of the cases, 635 in all.

Although, as indicated in Table 41, over three-fourths of the cases involved $40 or less and were definitely in the petty larceny class, Table 36 shows that jail sentences were used only in six per cent of the total cases, in only 77 out of 465 no-account and insufficient-funds, where the law allows them, and in four forgery cases, where it was illegal. In like manner, fines were applied to less than 14 per cent of all the cases, in 194 out of 635 sentences. Taking fines and jail sentences together as the ordinary punishment for misdemeanors, it will be seen that these remedies were applied in less than 20 per cent of the total cases and in only 276 out of 635 actual sentences where these misdemeanor sentences were legally available; and 210, or over three-fourths of these, were for insufficient-fund checks where, under the law, misdemeanor was mandatory.

[22] Neb. Rev. Stat. § 28-602 (1948).
[23] Id. § 28-1212 (Supp. 1953). Until 1953 there was a mandatory penitentiary sentence up to two years, so most of the cases studied here fall under this rule.
[24] Constitution Art. V § 16 Neb. Rev. Stat. § 29-201 (1948).
[25] Id. § 28-1213.
[26] See Note 11, supra.

Felony grade sentences, on the other hand, constitute 23 per cent of all the cases, or 331 out of 1,445 cases; so felonies were well over half of all the 635 total sentences. Of these, 143 were for forgeries, 160 for no-account checks and the remaining 28 for insufficient funds. It is clear, therefore, that when the collection process failed, the courts tended to bear down heavily on the felony sentences, even though the amounts of the checks were small. Only in 20 of the felony sentences for insufficient-fund checks can it be fairly certain that the amounts involved in the criminal complaints were over $35. Of course the court records do not always show the total amount of bad checks written by each defendant; but in a representative county, set out in Table 33,[27] the records of the county attorney show that two-thirds of the felony sentences to the penitentiary, reformatory and women's reformatory were on total claims of less than $100, and the highest amount of checks written by a defendant so sentenced was $310. Thus it seems that the district courts feel that they are impelled by law, even where they have the discretion to do otherwise, to impose penalties of felony proportions in the majority of their sentences.

It should be noted also that there is little use made of the jail sentence of misdemeanor proportions. Over the period of two years, shown by the records in Table 36, there were only 82 jail sentences in the 30 counties,[28] or an average of less than two and one-half sentences per year per county, and these were usually of 90 days duration or less. So, although there are hundreds of inmates constantly in the penitentiary for writing bad checks, it is a rare occurrence to find one in a county jail, except awaiting trial on felony charges.

The absence of the use of probation is another striking feature of the records. Although Table 36 shows that this device, with suspended sentences, was used in 116 cases in the two-year period, the largest number of these occurred in one county where over half of the people on probation were bad-check writers and these, 49 in number, constituted over 42 per cent of all instances of this treatment in the sample. So in all the rest of the 31 counties, over a two-year period, there were only 67 people on probation or suspended sentence. This means, of course, that the device was not used extensively, if at all, in most of the counties.

---

[27] See p. 303.

[28] In one county the records of the city courts which handled most of the misdemeanor cases, and in large numbers, were not available, so this figure includes only the other thirty.

While a large majority of the sentences were of the standard used in all criminal cases, there were a few that deserved particular notice. The desire to collect showed itself very forcefully in the records in many cases where, in addition to sentences, the court also ordered the defendants to make restitution. It is not clear just where the court gets this authority. It is always part of the probation treatment but also appears in the records of over 100 cases where the defendants were fined, jailed or sentenced to the penitentiary.

There were also a number of cases, mostly in the lower courts, where the defendant was sentenced to jail with the mitigation that he should be released if he paid up; and in at least one county there was a practice of assessing fines which, if not paid, together with the costs and all unpaid checks, were changed to jail sentences, the length of which were measured by an amount calculated at so much per day spent in jail.

One enterprising county judge sentenced a bad-check writer to the custody of the sheriff to be locked up in jail at night but "farmed out" at labor until his checks were paid.

All in all, it can be said with rare exceptions that where there was enforcement of this law, if bad-check writers could and did pay up, their lot was an easy one; but if they did not, they were likely to find themselves sentenced for a felony.[29]

BAD-CHECK WRITERS IN THE PENAL INSTITUTIONS

As already indicated, due to the sentencing habits of the courts and to the felony provisions of the statutes, there are few bad-check writers serving sentences in various city and county jails. This is also true so far as juvenile correction institutions are concerned. While there is an occasional juvenile who writes bad checks, the average businessman will not take them; and the records of the Girls' and the Boys' Training Schools indicate that bad checks are primarily an adult problem. In the former, only 19 records out of 500 covering a period of 12 years showed any sign of bad checks, while in the latter, about five per cent of the inmates have such facts on their records. In like manner, the court records and those at the Women's Reformatory show that there are not over six or seven women a year sentenced on these charges to that institution. The only penal records then which are susceptible of statistical treatment are those at the Men's Reformatory and at the Penitentiary. These contain well over 90 per cent of all the

---

[29] This is, of course, impossible under the statutes in instances involving insufficient-fund checks under $35. See, Neb. Rev. Stat. § 28-1213 (1948).

information on the workings of the penal provisions of the bad-check laws and on the types of individuals sentenced.

THE PENITENTIARY AND REFORMATORY TOTALS

The first fact which strikes one forcefully is the high percentage of prisoners in the two state penal institutions serving sentences on bad-check charges. Table 43 shows that in the Penitentiary, out of 3,470 prisoners admitted during the last ten-year period, over 17 per cent were sentenced for forgery and about 16 per cent for insufficient-funds and no-account checks, making a total of about one-third of those convicted sentenced on check charges. It should be noted that 94 per

TABLE 43

Nebraska State Penitentiary
Number of Admissions Convicted for Forgery and Bad Checks, July 1, 1943, to June 30, 1953

Total Penitentiary Admissions	3,470
Forgery Admissions	594
Insufficient- and No-Fund Admissions	550
94% No-Account	
6% Insufficient-Funds	

Sources: (1) Board of Control, State of Nebraska, Biennial Reports Nos. 16, 17, 18 ,19 and 20.
(2) Questionnaires, Nebraska State Penitentiary.

cent of all the admissions in the group convicted under the insufficient- and no-fund laws were for no-acount checks.

In the Reformatory, which is a sort of junior penitentiary[30] for first offenders and others thought capable of reform, the over-all percentage of bad-check writers is slightly less than in the Penitentiary.

TABLE 44

Nebraska State Reformatory
Number of Admissions under Bad-Check Statutes, July 1, 1943, to June 30, 1951

Total Reformatory Admissions	1,391
Forgery Admissions	182
Insufficient- and No-Fund Admissions	141

Sources: (1) Board of Control, State of Nebraska, Biennial Reports No. 16, p. 288; No. 17, p. 357; No. 18, p. 455; No. 19, p. 242.
(2) Questionnaires, Nebraska State Reformatory.

[30] 83-455.The age limits for acceptance of inmates are 16 to 35.

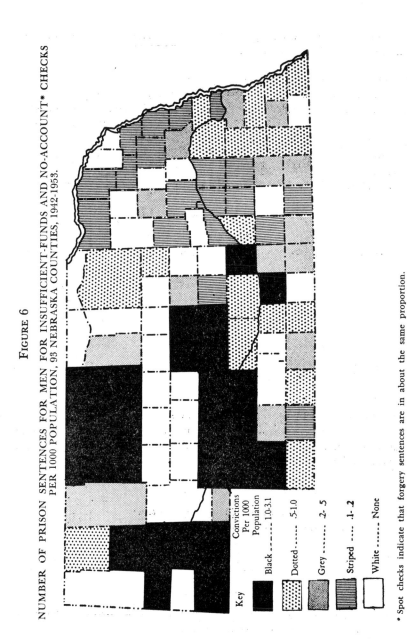

FIGURE 6

NUMBER OF PRISON SENTENCES FOR MEN FOR INSUFFICIENT-FUNDS AND NO-ACCOUNT* CHECKS PER 1000 POPULATION, 93 NEBRASKA COUNTIES, 1942-1953.

Key

Convictions
Per 1000
Population

Black ------ 1.0-3.1

Dotted------ .5-1.0

Grey ------- .2- .5

Striped ---- .1- .2

White ------ None

* Spot checks indicate that forgery sentences are in about the same proportion.

Table 44 shows that of 1,391 admissions over an eight-year period, 23 per cent were for bad checks, 13 per cent for forgeries and ten per cent for insufficient- and no-fund checks, the same proportion as in the Penitentiary records.

Since the terms of sentences of the bad-check writers are shorter than those of other criminals,[31] this means that about 28 per cent of the average daily population of the Pentientiary and over 20 per cent of those in the Reformatory are bad-check writers.

It is interesting further to note that the origin of these bad-check criminals is not the same as those of other felons. Figure 6, showing the counties from which bad-check writers were sentenced, indicates that there are as many per capita from the rural western scarcely populated areas as from the more densely populated eastern part of the state. The metropolitan areas of the state, which contain 30 per cent of the population,[32] furnished only 29 per cent of the bad-check felons.[33] In like fashion, the eight counties which have 52 per cent of the retail trade show only 59 per cent of bad-check writers in the Penitentiary and the Reformatory.[34]

Complete figures on the personal origin of all felons in Nebraska are not available, but the Reformatory records for a six-year period, as set out in Table 45, show 42 per cent of the bad-check writers came from rural areas while only 30 per cent of the other felons are from the country.

TABLE 45

Nebraska State Reformatory
Former Environment, Admissions for Six-Year Period,
July 1, 1945 to June 30, 1951

Type of Admission	Urban	Rural
Forgery	56.6%	43.4%
Insufficient- and No-Fund	59.4	40.6
Total Bad Checks	57.9	42.1
Other Non-Bad-Checks	70.0	30.0

Source: Board of Control, State of Nebraska, Biennial Reports No. 17, p. 359; No. 18, p. 457; No. 19, p. 246.

[31] See Table 49, infra p. 324.

[32] The classification and percentage used are from Rand-McNally Commercial Atlas (1953) p. 258.

[33] Percentages from questionnaires to Penitentiary and Reformatory which were used to compile Figure 6.

[34] Percentages from Rand-McNally, supra note 32, p. 260 and questionnaires, supra note 33.

It should be further noted that, according to the records of the Penitentiary, over a period of about twelve years 98 per cent of the short-check writers admitted were sentenced on guilty pleas, and only eight in over 600 pled not guilty. Of these, four seemed to have had a jury trial. In the Reformatory, over the same period, of 105 sentenced for bad checks, all were sentenced on pleas of guilty.

Also confirming the business and court statistics, the amounts of the checks on which the inmates were sentenced were small.

TABLE 46

Nebraska State Penitentiary
Dollar Amounts of Checks Involved in Convictions, 1942 to 1953*

(Records for 340 out of 614 Admissions)	
Arithmetic Average	$104
Median	20
Mode (51 convictions)	10
First Quartile	10
Third Quartile	75
Range	$2 to $7,201

(Figures rounded to the nearest dollar)
* Source: Penitentiary Questionnaires, Insufficient- and No-Fund.

TABLE 47

Nebraska State Reformatory
Dollar Amounts of Checks Involved in Convictions, 1942 to 1953*

(Record of 77 Admissions out of 187)	
Arithmetic Average	$168
Median	44
Mode	(No distinct mode)
First Quartile	13
Third Quartile	100
Range	$2 to $3,000

(Figures rounded to the nearest dollar.)
* Source: Reformatory Questionnaires, Insufficient- and No-Fund.

Tables 46 and 47 show that well over three-fourths of all those in both the Reformatory and Penitentiary were convicted on checks totaling less than $100.

LENGTH OF SENTENCES AND TIME SERVED

Although writing bad checks in most of its aspects is a felony, the sentences imposed are notably less severe than in the case of other felonies.

Table 48 shows that in the Penitentiary for a ten-year period, 70 per cent of the bad checks, 55 per cent of the forgeries and 45 per cent of the non-bad-check admissions had maximum sentences of two years or less. On the other hand, 55 per cent of the non-bad-check admissions had sentences of three years or more; 45 per cent of the forgery admissions and only 24 per cent of all the bad-check admissions had maximum sentences of this length.

TABLE 48

Nebraska State Penitentiary
Length of Sentence for Bad-Check and Non-Bad-Check Admissions, July 1, 1943, to June 30, 1953*

	Insufficient- and No-Fund Admissions (per cent)	Forgery Admissions (per cent)	All Bad-Check Admissions (per cent)	Other (Non-Bad-Check) Admissions (per cent)
Total	100.0	100.0	100.0	100.0
6-12 Months	.2	10.1	5.0	9.1
1-2 Years	94.8	44.6	71.2	35.9
3-4 Years	3.0	28.1	15.1	28.3
5-6 Years	1.0	11.6	5.3	13.8
7-8 Years	0	1.7	1.1	4.6
9-10 Years	1.0	2.9	1.9	4.0
11-14 Years	0	.2	.1	.6
15-19 Years	0	.8	.3	1.0
20-24 Years	0	0	0	.9
25-29 Years	0	0	0	.5
30 Years and Over (Including Life)	0	0	0	1.2
Death	0	0	0	.1

* Sources: (1) Board of Control, State of Nebraska, Biennial Reports No. 16, 17, 18, 19 and 20.
(2) Nebraska State Penitentiary Questionnaires.

Explanation: There is information on the sentence given to 523 out of 550 bad-check admissions, or 95 per cent, during the period July 1, 1943, to June 30, 1953.

In like fashion, Table 49 shows that at the Reformatory sentences received by bad-check admissions were also considerably less severe than those given for forgery and other crimes. Thus 80 per cent of the bad-check, 70 percent of the forgery and 48 per cent of the non-bad-check admissions had maximum sentences of two years or less. On the other hand, 52 per cent of the non-bad-check sentences were for a maximum of three years or more compared with 30 per cent for forgery and 20 per cent for all bad-check sentences. None of the no-

TABLE 49

Nebraska State Reformatory
Length of Sentence for Bad-Check and Non-Bad-Check Admissions, Eight-Year Period, July 1, 1943, to June 30, 1951*

	Insufficient-and No-Fund Admissions (per cent)	Forgery Admissions (per cent)	All Bad-Check Admissions (per cent)	Other (Non-Bad-Check) Admissions (per cent)
Total	100.0	100.0	100.0	100.0
6-12 Months	32.6	19.8	25.4	11.1
1-2 Years	60.3	50.0	54.5	36.9
3-4 Years	7.1	22.0	15.5	36.3
5-6 Years	0	5.5	3.1	11.6
7-8 Years	0	0	0	1.3
9 Years and Over	0	2.7	1.5	2.8

* Sources: (1) Records of Nebraska State Reformatory, 1942-1953.
(2) Board of Control, State of Nebraska, Biennial Reports No. 16, p. 290; No. 17, p. 362; No. 18, p. 460; No. 19, p. 254.

fund admissions had maximum sentences over four years.[35] However, eight per cent of those sentenced for forgery and 16 per cent of the non-bad-check inmates had maximum sentences of five years or more. In both these tables it is clear that the sentences for insufficient-fund and no-account checks were by far the lightest of all.

Not only were the sentences lighter for bad-check writers than for other criminals but in addition they, like the others, received time off for good behavior. Being on the whole very tractable and well behaved, their terms were further reduced for good behavior and by parole. As a matter of fact, over 70 per cent of all those sentenced to the Penitentiary and 83 per cent of those sent to the Reformatory for all types of bad checks were actually held less than a year and a half, while over half of both groups served about nine months or less. This compares to well over half the other criminals whose actual time behind bars ran in excess of over a year and a half per sentence.[36]

CRIMINAL RECORDS OF BAD-CHECK WRITERS

One of the most outstanding features of the criminal records of bad-check writers in both the Penitentiary and the Reformatory is the fact that they are habitual criminals. Although the records of the in-

[35] It should be noted that these figures are held down by the fact that before 1951, though writing any no-account check was a felony, the maximum sentence was two years. Neb. Rev. Stat. § 28-1212 (Re-issue 1948).

[36] These figures compiled from the questionnaires and from reports of the Board of Control.

mates are far from complete, those available indicate that 82 per cent of the men sentenced to the Penitentiary for insufficient- and no-account checks had previous criminal records, and 65 per cent of the total showed previous felony sentences. Even though they concern a younger group and less experienced criminals, the available records from the Reformatory for the same group of offenders show that 60 per cent of even these men had notations of prior convictions, and 28 per cent of the total already had records of previous felony convictions. A sample of those committed for forgery showed an equally high rate of previous convictions. In the Penitentiary it ran up to 90 per cent with records of prior criminal convictions, of which 79 per cent showed prior felonies with prison sentences. Thus the over-all picture shows that approximately 86 per cent of bad-check writers in the Penitentiary had records of prior convictions.

The statistics have been broken down further to show the number of prior convictions and the nature of the crimes for which the former sentences were issued. Of those in the Penitentiary for insufficient- and no-account checks, over three-fifths, as shown in Figure 7, had two or more prior criminal convictions, and 19 per cent had five or more. Figure 8 gives a like picture for a similar group from the Reformatory and shows that even among these less hardened criminals, over one-third had two or more prior convictions. Those sentenced for forgeries show a like preponderance of habitual criminals. Figure 9 shows that of those admitted to the Penitentiary on forgery sentences, two-thirds had two or more prior convictions, and 37 per cent had five or more, a record much like that of the insufficient- and no-account writers; but twice as many forgers had five or more prior convictions.

"HABITUAL CRIMINALS" UNDER THE BAD-CHECK LAWS

The Nebraska statutes set out in the margin[37] make it mandatory for a judge who has before him a defendant convicted of a felony, who has a record showing that he has been twice convicted of a similar crime, to sentence the defendant to from ten to twenty years in the

---

[37] 29-2221. *"Habitual criminal," defined; procedure for determination; hearing; penalty; effect of pardon.* (1) Whoever has been twice convicted of crime, sentenced and committed to prison, in this or any other state, or by the United States, or once in this state and once at least in any other state, or by the United States, for terms of not less than one year each, shall, upon conviction of a felony committed in this state, be deemed to be an habitual criminal, and shall be punished by imprisonment in the penitentiary for a term of not less than ten nor more than twenty years; *Provided,* that no greater punishment is otherwise provided by statute, in which case the law creating the greater punishment shall govern.

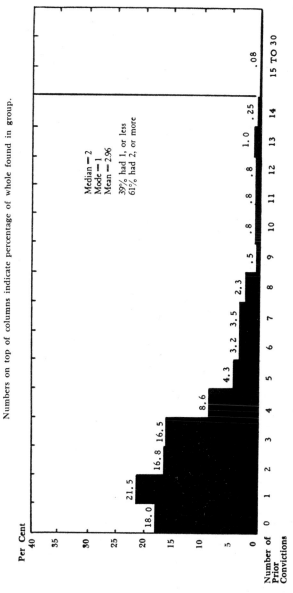

FIGURE 7

NEBRASKA STATE PENITENTIARY

PERCENTAGE OF ADMISSIONS UNDER THE BAD-CHECK LAWS (NON-FORGERS) HAVING A GIVEN NUMBER OF PRIOR CONVICTIONS

Numbers on top of columns indicate percentage of whole found in group.

Median — 2
Mode — 1
Mean — 2.96

39% had 1, or less
61% had 2, or more

Total for 12-Year Period, 1942-1953 (395 out of 614 cases, or 64.3%)

FIGURE 8

NEBRASKA STATE REFORMATORY

PERCENTAGE OF ADMISSIONS CONVICTED UNDER THE BAD-CHECK LAWS (NON-FORGERS) HAVING A GIVEN NUMBER OF PRIOR CONVICTIONS, 1942-1953

Numbers on top of columns indicate percentage of whole found in group.

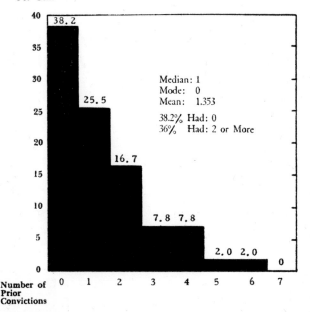

Per Cent

Median: 1
Mode: 0
Mean: 1.353

38.2% Had: 0
36% Had: 2 or More

Number of Prior Convictions

Source: Survey of Nebraska State Reformatory Records. Records were complete for 102 out of 187 admissions.

penitentiary. This habitual-criminal statute, which exists in many states, operates on the theory that it will deter felonies and remove dangerous characters from society.

The criminal records of 395 admissions to the Penitentiary under the insufficient- and no-fund check laws indicate that 134, over one third, had two or more prior felony convictions, each accompanied by a sentence of a year or more. Upon the basis of this sample, roughly 208 of the 614 admissions were thus liable for sentence as "habitual criminals." However, for the period of 1942 to 1953, only five (2½

327

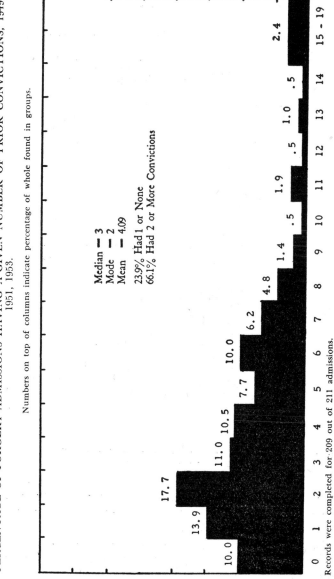

FIGURE 9

NEBRASKA STATE PENITENTIARY

PERCENTAGE OF FORGERY ADMISSIONS HAVING A GIVEN NUMBER OF PRIOR CONVICTIONS, 1949, 1951, 1953.

Numbers on top of columns indicate percentage of whole found in groups.

per cent) of the 208 admissions with records which made them habitual criminals were accordingly sentenced to ten years or more.[38]

Since forgery carries a maximum sentence of 20 years, the habitual-criminal statute needs no application there; but Table 48 shows that less than six per cent of the forgers received sentences over six years, whereas 13 per cent, or twice that many, of the ordinary criminals received sentences of six years or more. Here again the committing judges were much more lenient with bad-check writers than with persons convicted of other felonies. On the whole it would seem that for bad-check writers, even where it applies, the habitual-criminal statute is being ignored.

PERSONAL CHARACTERISTICS OF BAD-CHECK WRITERS

AGE

It is a well known characteristic of criminals that they are preponderantly people in their late teens and early twenties, but this does not apply to bad-check writers. Figure 10, taken from the Penitentiary records, shows that while the median age of admissions for offenses other than bad checks is 30 years, with the highest incidence in the 20- to 24-year category, the median age of bad-check writers is 35 years, with the highest incidence in the 30- to 34-year age group. In like fashion, the Reformatory records, illustrated in Figure 11, revealed that the median age of bad-check writers there is 23 years, three years older than that of the non-bad-check writers. It should also be noted that the highest incidence of admission is below 20 for non-bad-check writers, but between 20 and 24 years for bad checks. Turning back to the Penitentiary figures, it is further significant, as shown in Figure 12, that between forgers and other bad-check writers, the forgers are younger, with a median age of 34 years, while other bad-check writers have a median age of 37, which for a criminal is a comparatively old man (see Figure 10).

INTELLIGENCE QUOTIENT

So far as native intelligence is concerned, bad-check writers in the penal institutions seem to be about the average of the community. Table 50 shows the IQ[39] of about half the prisoners where such information was available. When the bad-check writers in the Peni-

---

[38] The sentences of more than ten years were under the habitual-criminal statute because the maximum for insufficient-funds is seven years and for no-account checks, ten years, 28-1213, 28-1212 (1953).

[39] Wechsler-Bellevue tests.

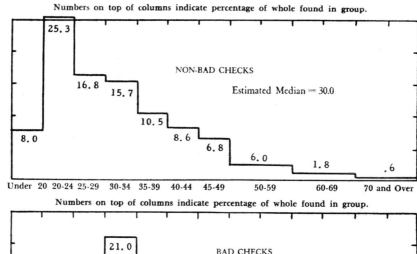

FIGURE 10

NEBRASKA STATE PENITENTIARY

PER CENT OF TOTAL ADMISSIONS IN GIVEN AGE GROUPS, BAD CHECKS
AND NON-BAD CHECKS, TEN-YEAR PERIOD, JULY 1, 1943, TO
JULY 30, 1953

Numbers on top of columns indicate percentage of whole found in group.

NON-BAD CHECKS

Estimated Median = 30.0

25.3
16.8   15.7
10.5
8.0   8.6   6.8   6.0   1.8   .6

Years   Under 20   20-24   25-29   30-34   35-39   40-44   45-49   50-59   60-69   70 and Over

Numbers on top of columns indicate percentage of whole found in group.

BAD CHECKS

Estimated Median = 35.5

21.0
15.3   16.5   15.2
10.3
7.6
1.9   8.4   3.0   1.0

Years   Under 20   20-24   25-29   30-34   35-39   40-44   45-49   50-59   60-69   70 and Over

tentiary are compared with the non-bad-check writers in the Penitentiary and with the distribution of the population as a whole, it will
be seen that the check writers are more intelligent than the other
criminals and slightly above the average intelligence of the population
as a whole.

EDUCATION

In the matter of education, the bad-check writers in prison also
rank well in comparison to the general population. Table 51 shows
the educational achievements of non-forgery bad-check prisoners in
the Nebraska Penitentiary as compared with the Reformatory and the

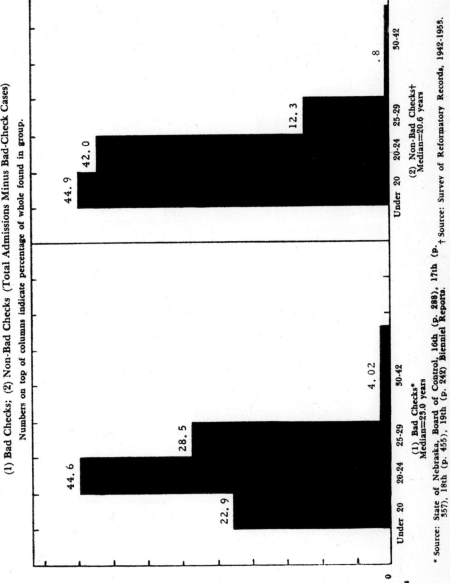

RESULTS OF A STUDY OF THE BAD-CHECK PROBLEM

NEBRASKA STATE REFORMATORY

PER CENT OF TOTAL ADMISSIONS THAT WERE IN GIVEN AGE GROUPS, CLASSIFIED BY TYPE OF OFFENSE, JULY, 1943 TO JUNE, 1951.

(1) Bad Checks; (2) Non-Bad Checks (Total Admissions Minus Bad-Check Cases)

Numbers on top of columns indicate percentage of whole found in group.

(1) Bad Checks*
Median=23.0 years

(2) Non-Bad Checks†
Median=20.6 years

	Under 20	20-24	25-29	30-42
Bad Checks	22.9	44.6	28.5	4.02
Non-Bad Checks	44.9	42.0	12.3	.8

Age Years 0

* Source: State of Nebraska, Board of Control, 16th (p. 288), 17th (p. 357), 18th (p. 455), 19th (p. 242) Biennial Reports.

† Source: Survey of Reformatory Records, 1942-1951.

331

FIGURE 12

NEBRASKA STATE PENITENTIARY

AGE DISTRIBUTION OF ADMISSIONS
TOTAL ADMITTED, TEN-YEAR PERIOD, JULY 1, 1943, TO JUNE 30, 1953,
FORGERY AND BAD-CHECK CONVICTIONS

Numbers on top of columns indicate percentage of whole found in group.

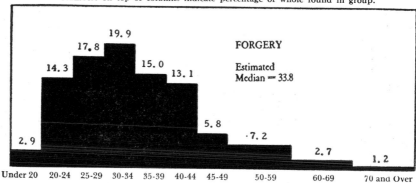

Numbers on top of columns indicate percentage of whole found in group.

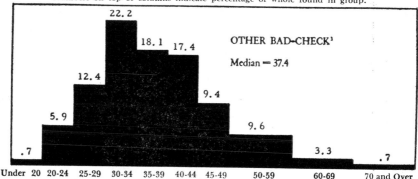

(1) Information on age for bad-check cases was available for 98.2 per cent of the total (540 out of 550).

public at large in the state. With the exception of college graduates, the table shows that bad-check-writing felons are as well as or better educated than the average members of the public, and there is no marked difference in the distribution of education throughout the two groups.

While statistics are not available for the Penitentiary, Table 52 shows the comparative educational achievements of the classes of prisoners in the Reformatory divided among the various types of bad-check writers and other felons.

TABLE 50

Comparison of Intelligence†—Penitentiary Admissions (Bad-Chck and Non-Bad-Check) with the General Population

Classification	IQ Limits	Nebraska State Penitentiary Admissions**				
		General Population*	Non-Bad-Check Offenders	Bad-Check Offenders	No-Account Insufficient-Fund Offenders	Forgers
		Per Cent	Per Cent	Per Cent	Per Cent	Per Cent
Defective	65 and below	2.2	1.5	.6	.8	.5
Borderline	66-79	6.7	10.0	6.4	7.9	4.9
Dull Normal	80-90	16.1	19.2	17.0	16.5	17.5
Average	91-110	50.0	53.1	53.4	52.0	54.7
Bright Normal	111-119	16.1	13.5	13.1	13.1	13.1
Superior	120-129	6.7	1.5	6.8	8.2	5.5
Very Superior	128 and over	2.2	1.2	2.7	1.5	3.8

† Intelligence rating is based on the Wechsler-Bellevue Intelligence Quotient system.
* "General Population"—Results obtained by D. Wechsler for the population, age 10-60. Refer to David Wechsler, *The Measurement of Adult Intelligence*, 2nd Edition, 1941, p. 40.
** Penitentiary Admissions—IQ data from: 260 non-bad-check offenders, 1953; 450 bad-check offenders, 1942-1953 (183 forgers, 267 insufficient-fund and no-account-check writers).

TABLE 51

Educational Achievements of Bad-Check Writers (Forgers Omitted) Compared with General Public

	Reformatory*	Penitentiary†	General‡ Public
Below 7th Grade	13.4%	15.2%	17.3%
Completion 8th Grade	27.4	33.2	29.9
Between 9th and 11th Grade	31.8	23.6	15.6
High School Graduate	21.2	17.7	21.4
Before Completing College	4.5	8.3	7.1
College Graduate	1.7	2.0	5.8
Median	9th Grade	9th Grade	9th Grade
1st Quartile	8th Grade	8th Grade	8th Grade
3rd Quartile	12th Grade	12th Grade	12th Grade

* 179 of 187 Admissions, 95.7 per cent.
† 589 of 614 Admissions, 95.9 per cent.
‡ U.S. Census Population Nebraska, Vol. II, Part 27, Ch. B, p. 27-36.

It should be noted that the bad-check writers include a considerably higher proportion of high school and college graduates, but that approximately one in twenty forgers is illiterate. These are probably poor misguided laborers who make crude attempts to copy or pass

TABLE 52

*Degree of Education of Nebraska State Reformatory Admissions
(Total July 1, 1945, to June 30, 1951, a Six-Year Period)
Classified with Reference to Offense*

Degree of Education	Forgery	Other Bad-Checks	All Bad-Checks	Other (Non-Bad-Checks)
	Per Cent	Per Cent	Per Cent	Per Cent
Total	100.0	100.0	100.0	100.0
Illiterate	4.6	0	2.5	3.5
Reads and Writes	18.4	10.9	15.0	14.7
Grade School	58.6	64.8	61.4	68.0
High School	17.1	23.5	20.0	13.6
College	1.3	.8	1.1	.2

Source: **Board** of Control, State of Nebraska, Biennial Reports No. 17, p. 358; No. 18, p. 456; No. 19, p. 244.

forged instruments and are, of course, immediately caught. It should also be noted that the insufficient- and no-fund group have the highest educational achievements of all.

OCCUPATIONS

Just as the educational accomplishments of other criminals show a shortage of highly educated persons, the occupations of the bad-check prisoners indicate that, as compared to total population, there is a light representation of executives, managers and proprietors. From Table 53, showing the occupations of Penitentiary and Reformatory prisoners, it is apparent that among the admissions under the bad-check law, the occupations of craftsmen, operators, service workmen, farm laborers and others typical of the labor force of Nebraska were most highly represented. It is interesting to note that the percentage of professional inmates admitted to the penal institutions is about the same as their representation in the general population. So except for those occupations that are notorious for their financial stability, the bad-check prisoners represent an even cross-check of the occupational classifications of the state.

The Board of Control reports provided a second source of occupation data. Although not strictly comparable to the census material, this source gives a comparison of the occupations of Reformatory admissions classified by offense and is therefore presented in Table 54.

The proportions of forgery admissions and the bad-check admissions in the various occupation categories were basically similar. How-

TABLE 53

Occupational Classification of Bad-Check Writers
Per Cent of Nebraska Bad-Check (No-Forgery) Admissions to Peni-
tentiary and Reformatory, 1942 to 1953 (Classified by Occupation)

	Male Experienced Civilian Labor Force, Nebraska 1950 Census[1]	Admissions to Nebraska State Penitentiary and Reformatory, Bad-Check Law, 1942 to 1953	
	(per cent)	Penitentiary[2] (per cent)	Reformatory[3] (per cent)
Total (Occupation Reported)	100.0	100.0	100.0
Professional, technical and kindred workers[4]	5.7	4.4	5.7
Farmers and farm managers	27.7	19.6	24.4 (2.2)*
Managers, officials and proprietors	10.0	.8	0
Clerical, sales and kindred	11.2	9.0	13.6
Craftsmen, foremen and kindred	14.4	19.6	16.5
Operatives and kindred	10.6	18.8	21.0
Private household	.1	.2	.6
Service workers (except private household)	4.3	6.9	6.8
Farm laborers and foremen	8.6	10.2	3.4 (25.6)*
Laborers except farm and mine	7.4	10.5	8.0

Sources: [1] U.S. Dept. of Commerce, Bureau of the Census, Population Census: 1950, Publi-cation P-B27, p. 40.
[2] Nebraska State Penitentiary Questionnaires, 1942-1953, 591 out of 614, or 96 per cent.
[3] Nebraska State Reformatory Questionnaires, 1942-1953, 176 out of 187, or 94 per cent.
[4] The "professional, technical and kindred workers" committed under the bad-check law included the following occupations: civil, structural, mechanical and diesel engineer, photographer, musician, attorney, coach, high school principal, teacher, personnel worker, T.V. actor, mortician, embalmer, radio announcer, newspaper reporter and accountant.

* The questionnaires frequently gave farm, farming, etc., as an occupation. In tabulating the data, these were listed as farmers rather than farm laborers. The figures in parentheses are more accurate and are estimates based on the ratio of farmers (2) to farm laborers (23) derived from the Board of Control reports.

ever, only seven per cent of the forgery admissions were "professional, etc.," compared with 14 per cent of the other bad-check admissions. One-third of the forgery admissions were laborers (non-farm) com-pared with one-fifth of the other bad-check admissions.

A noticeably larger proportion of all bad-check admissions was in the occupational classes of (1) professional and semi-professional, (2) clerical, sales and kindred workers, and (3) farm laborers, as com-pared with the other, non-bad-check admissions. A comparably smaller proportion of the bad-check admissions were in the "laborer" category.

On the whole it seems that the criminal records show that the bad-check writers are a separate class who do not commit violent crimes

TABLE 54

Comparison of Previous Occupations of Reformatory Admissions, Forgery, Other Bad-Check, All Bad-Check and Other Non-Bad-Check Admissions, Six-Year Period, July 1, 1945, to June 30, 1951*

Occupation	Forgery Admissions (per cent)	Other Bad-Check Admissions (per cent)	All Bad-Check Admissions (per cent)	Other, Non-Bad-Check Admissions (per cent)
Total	100.0	100.0	100.0	100.0
Professional and Semi-Professional	7.2	14.1	10.4	6.7
Farmers and Farm Managers	1.3	1.6	1.4	.8
Proprietors, Managers and Officials	0	0	0	.2
Clerical, Sales and Kindred Workers	5.9	7.8	6.8	3.7
Domestic Service Workers	5.3	7.0	6.1	6.0
Service Workers (except Domestic and Protective)	.7	2.3	1.4	2.6
Farm Laborers and Foremen	30.9	30.5	30.7	23.6
Laborers (except farm)	31.6	21.1	26.8	41.4
All Others—Truck Drivers	17.1	15.6	16.4	15.0

* Source: Board of Control, State of Nebraska, Biennial Reports No. 17, p. 361; No. 18, p. 459; No. 19, p. 251.

usually connected with the term "felon." The "Fancy Dan" forger of fiction who makes a princely income copying others' signatures and who regards himself as a professional craftsman also seems to be a scarce article in the penal institutions.

PROFESSIONAL CHECK WRITERS AND OTHERS NOT CAUGHT

It is difficult to get facts on the professional check writers, if any, who are not caught; but a county attorney's records in a representative county, which have been referred to before,[40] offer some interesting light on this subject.

As shown in Table 55 below, during the two-year period in this county, there were twenty-three check writers who wrote two or more bad checks and were not caught. These cover two classes of people, the habitual indigent check writers who were lucky enough not to get caught and the professionals who seem to make a business of cashing bad checks. The former group seemed to consist of five who wrote a total of 31 small checks (over a period of four or more days). The other 18, two of them women, appeared to be professionals. This group wrote a total of 53 checks. Both groups together wrote 84 checks totaling $1,856. The spread of checks in number was from two to 11

[40] See supra pp. 273-5, 299-303.

TABLE 55

Writers of Two or More Checks Who Got Away in Representative County, 1952 and 1953

No. Checks per Writer	Total Claims	Average Size Checks	Days Spread in Dates
2	$ 96	$16	2
2	47	23	2
3	63	21	2
2	63	31	2
3	97	32	1
2	20	10	2
3	75	25	1
2	20	10	1
3	97	32	1
5	75	15	2
4	43	10	16
2	162	81	2
7	190	27	10
3	64	31	1
4	21 f.	5	32
2	126	63	2
5	25	5	4
4	60	15	2
3	60 f.	20	1
3	22	7	1
11	141	13	19
3	169	56	1
6	120	20	2
23 writers totaled 84 checks	$1,856	$21 average	

"f." indicates cases where the record clearly shows forgery. It was probably involved in **many** more of the cases.

and in the amount from $5 to $63. The arithmetic average of the checks was $21. The average claim against individuals was $81, and the spread of the claims was from $2 to $190.

Six of the 23, as is often characteristic of the professionals, wrote all of the checks the same size, varying from $20 to $63, and two of the six were clearly guilty of forgery.

Of the 18 apparent professionals, eight wrote all of their checks on the same day, and ten, over a period of only two days. This is also characteristic of the professional's activity. He comes to town, spreads a lot of checks and leaves immediately.

The ordinary indigent bad-check writers will write checks in bunches, but they will cover periods of from four days to four years. It should also be noted that the indigents cash a very high percentage of their checks in taverns, but the 18 professionals seemed seldom to write checks in taverns or for liquor. Hotels, grocery stores, service stations and miscellaneous mercantile establishments seemed to be their chief victims.

Eight of the ten taking two days cashed the checks on weekends or holidays. Friday and Saturday, Saturday and Sunday, and holidays were the most common. Of those writing checks on a single day, Friday was the most popular—three writers—Saturday, one writer. Twelve of the 18 worked entirely on weekends and holidays. Monday and Tuesday showed a total of three operators and the middle of the week only three out of 18. About $1,200 was lost to the 18 professionals in two years. This is only six per cent of the money value bad checks coming to the county attorney during the period, and using three-fifths of the state average as the average size of the checks in this area, only one-fourth per cent of the money value of bad checks written in this area during two years was by professionals. Add to this number about $5,000 lost on those convicted[41] and $600 more on the indigents who escaped, and it will be seen that the criminal element took less than $7,000 out of the county in two years, or .0002 per cent of the dollar value of checks written, and only 0.4 per cent of the bad checks returned by the bankers, and in all, less than one-third by value and less than 12 per cent by number of the checks turned over to the county attorney.

So even professional check writers are mostly small operators who make a meager income for their efforts to keep ahead of the law. Of course these figures are from a small Midwestern town of about 20,000 population. The bad-check writers in large cities may make a bit more, but no figures are presently available on this point. They also soon get into interstate commerce where they are hunted by the city police and the F.B.I., hardly a pleasant or profitable occupation.

WOMEN BAD-CHECK WRITERS

There is a popular belief that women are notoriously bad at bookkeeping and money matters and are constantly fouling up their bank accounts and writing bad checks. Like many other popular beliefs, there seems to be little foundation for this conclusion. Even allowing for the fact that husbands occasionally bail their wives out of such difficulties, the records of the banks and prosecuting officials show that on the whole women write proportionately fewer bad checks than men. Only 11 or 12 per cent of the checks coming to county attorneys seem to be drawn by women. Table 56 shows that the number of court cases where women were charged with insufficient-funds or

[41] See supra p. 303.

no-account checks[42] was only six per cent of the total. Thus it is clear that women are haled to court on bad checks about half as often as men. This may be due partly to the fact that it was easier to collect from them and partly to the chivalry of the officials. This latter tendency is somewhat substantiated by the fact that only 36 per cent of the women defendants were sentenced as compared with 41 per cent for all cases.[43] This tendency is further illustrated by the fact that nine per cent of the women so charged were paroled or placed on suspended sentence, while only six per cent of all the cases were so treated.[43] This is not because women were less guilty than men, for in all 26 cases where women were sentenced, there were no pleas of not guilty.

It should also be noted that there were a smaller percentage of indigents and drunkards among the women. Table 57, showing the source of complaints against women, when compared with Table 42 above,[44] giving the source of all bad checks brought to court, shows that while drinking places and gas stations constitute over 28 per cent of the complaints in all cases, they amount to only seven per cent of

TABLE 56

Disposition of No-Account and Insufficient-Fund Check Cases Involving Women Defendants in All Courts, Thirty-one Nebraska Counties, 1952 and 1953

Disposition	Total		No-Account		Insufficient-Fund	
	Number	Per Cent	Number	Per Cent	Number	Per Cent
Total	71	100.0	28	100.0	43	100.0
Without Sentence	45	63.4	16	57.1	29	67.5
No Warrant Returned	16	22.6	5	17.8	11	25.6
Dismissed	24	33.8	8	28.6	16	37.3
Paid	0	0	0	0	0	0
Acquitted	0	0	0	0	0	0
No Record	5	7.0	3	10.7	2	4.6
With Sentence	26	36.6	12	42.9	14	32.5
Probation or Parole	6	8.4	5	17.9	1	2.3
Suspended	1	1.4	0	0	1	2.3
Women's Reformatory	7	9.9	6	21.4	1	2.3
Jail	1	1.4	1	3.6	0	0
Fine	11	15.5	0	0	11	25.6

[42] The forgery cases were too few to be significant.
[43] Cf. Table 36, supra p. 308.
[44] Supra p. 315.

TABLE 57

Places where Women Cashed Checks on which Charges Were Made, 1952-1953*

Type of Business	Number of Complaints	Per Cent of Total Charges
Total Number of Cases	71	100.0
1. General Merchandise Stores	22	31.0
2. Grocery Stores	11	15.5
3. Clothing Stores	8	11.3
4. Individuals	5	7.0
5. Drugstores	4	5.6
6. Gas Stations	3	4.2
7. Furniture	2	2.8
8. Liquor Stores and Taverns	2	2.8
9. Auto Repairs	1	1.4
10. Cleaners and Laundry	1	1.4
11. Shoe Stores	1	1.4
12. Lumber	1	1.4
13. Miscellaneous	4	5.6
14. No Record	6	8.6

* Court questionnaires.

the complaints against women. Department stores, grocery stores and apparel shops, on the other hand, together have proportionately twice as many complaints against women (58 per cent) as against men (26 per cent). Thus it must be admitted that while women proportionately cash far fewer bad checks for liquor and gasoline than do the males, they still cannot resist the shopping urge. Perhaps for this reason their checks seem to average a bit larger than the men's, but there were no very big ones. On the whole, however, there were not enough[45] cases to be of any firm statistical significance or to play an appreciable part in the social effects of the bad-check laws.

NATIONALITY

Another striking characteristic of bad-check writers is that, unlike other criminals, among whom there is believed to be a large number of foreign-born which is far out of proportion to their representative part of the population, the names of the defendants in the records of bad-check cases seem to show no foreign origin. This is especially noticeable in the western counties of the state, where there is a large Mexican population. Although these counties contain a larger proportion of bad-check cases than other parts of the state and have a

[45] The court questionnaires showed only 30.

higher rate of convictions, one is struck by the absence of Mexican names in the records. Apparently none of the defendants in the cases involving insufficient- and no-fund checks and only a scattered few among the forgers have Mexican names; and even in the latter instances, the number is far below the proportionate share of the population. A similar absence of other foreign representation is also striking. Most of the defendants seem to have common Anglo-Saxon and well known American names. This may be accounted for to a large extent by the fact that many foreigners, especially those in the Mexican population, do not use checks.

GENERAL CHARACTERISTICS OF BAD-CHECK WRITERS

In general, bad-check writers have about the average intelligence of the population having about the usual education, but they come from a strata of society without large financial resources or stability. They represent a group of people older than other criminals, as intelligent and well educated as the average of society, but who show a marked irresponsibility in financial matters and a considerable record of drunkenness and other minor moral maladjustments which make it difficult for them to conform to the requirements of a financially oriented society. Thus once they have acquired a criminal record, they seem to fall victim rapidly to the temptation of getting easy money by writing bad checks. Their offenses appear as all types of bad-check writing, but primarily as no-account checks or forgeries, which offenses they commit almost indiscriminately. They seem to break down into two classes: (1) those who become habitual passers of bad checks and eventually end up with one or more penal sentences, and (2) those who are simply financially irresponsible and find the temptation of easy money through writing bad checks too strong to resist.

In the first class, the kind of crimes contained in the records of bad-check writers shows that they are a unique group of criminals. Although at the Penitentiary 86 per cent of the bad-check writers have records of prior convictions, Figures 13 and 14 show that when these convictions are broken down into the types of crime,[46] 60 per cent

---

[46] Types of crime are as follows:
   (A) Prior convictions: include felonies and misdemeanors with a record that a sentence was imposed.
   (B) Convictions are classified according to the type of crime. There are five broad types:
      1. *Financial*
        A. Bad-check cases—Insufficient-fund, no-account and forgery cases.

FIGURE 13

NEBRASKA STATE PENITENTIARY

PER CENT OF ADMISSIONS CONVICTED UNDER BAD-CHECK LAWS
(NON-FORGERS) WITH PRIOR CRIMINAL CONVICTIONS,
CLASSIFIED BY THE TYPE OF CRIME, 1942-1953

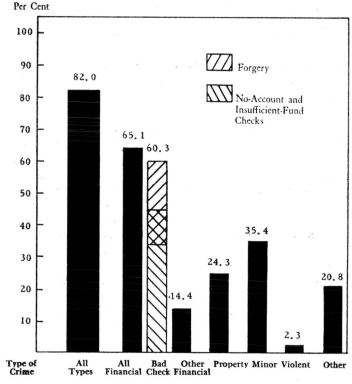

In the 12-year period, records were complete for 395 cases out of 614, or 64.3%

B. Other financial—Embezzlement, confidence game, and obtaining
money under false pretenses.
2. *Property*: These are regarded as directly related to financial crimes. Included are grand and petty larceny, burglary, car-stealing, other types
of stealing, breaking and entry, robbery, etc.
3. *Minor Crimes*: Appear to be closely correlated with financial crimes.
Include vagrancy, drunkenness (these were most numerous), non-
support, abandonment of wife and/or children, disorderly conduct,
obstructing an officer, desertion, illegal train-riding, not paying res-

FIGURE 14

NEBRASKA STATE PENITENTIARY

PER CENT OF FORGERY ADMISSIONS WITH PRIOR CRIMINAL CONVICTIONS CLASSIFIED BY THE TYPE OF CRIME, 1949, 1951 AND 1953

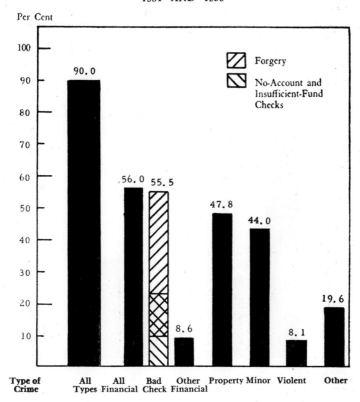

In the three years, records were complete for 209 out of 211 admissions

taurant check, delinquency, etc.

4. *Violent Crimes*: These include assault and battery, murder, manslaughter, rape, fighting, hit and run.

5. *Other Crimes*: These include sex crimes (i.e., bigamy, fornication, adultery, bastardy), parole revoked, sale and possession of liquor (illegal), AWOL, violation of Selective Service Act, fugitive from justice, escape from prison, jail break, violation of Dyer Act, opening railroad switch, escaping custody, no license for a vehicle, white slavery, insanity, federal charge re. liquor, and impersonation of officer.

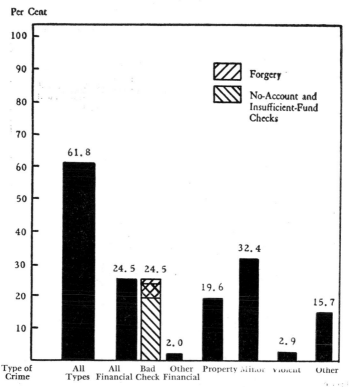

FIGURE 15

NEBRASKA STATE REFORMATORY

PER CENT OF ADMISSIONS CONVICTED UNDER THE BAD-CHECK
LAWS (INSUFFICIENT- AND NO-FUND) WITH PRIOR CRIM-
INAL CONVICTIONS, CLASSIFIED BY THE TYPE
OF CRIME, 1942-1953

In the 12-year period, records were complete for 102 cases out of 187, or 54.5 per cent.
Source: Survey of Nebraska State Reformatory records.

of the forgers and 55 per cent of insufficient- and no-account admissions
had convictions on previous bad-check charges, divided almost equally
between forgery and other bad-check charges. Sixty per cent of both
groups had previous convictions on financial charges including checks.
The next most numerous were minor crimes of which drunkenness was
the chief ingredient. The most significant fact of all is that less than
six per cent of the bad-check writers were ever convicted of violent
crimes. They are, then, a special group of prisoners whose chief offense

344

is failure to live up to the financial rules of society. They are delinquent mostly in monetary responsibility, with offenses chiefly against
property. Figures 14 and 15 show this same tendency in those in the
Penitentiary charged with forgery and among the insufficient- and no-
fund writers in the Reformatory. As a whole, they seem to be chiefly
non-violent, irresponsible ne'er-do-wells and drunkards. Of all bad-
check writers, as shown by case histories and criminal records,[47] 51 per
cent were chronic drinkers. In addition, from the remaining 49 per
cent, 18 per cent of the whole were drinking at the time the crime
was committed, making well over two-thirds under the influence of
liquor. Seventy-one per cent of all bad-check writers, 66 per cent of the
forgers and 77 per cent of the other bad-check writers had alcohol on
their criminal records.[48] Thus many of the "felons" among the bad-
check writers are simply "stumble-bums" sent to the penitentiary by
local law enforcement officials who want simply to be rid of them.

This brings us to the second class of bad-check writers who are
convicted of only minor offenses or who, under the pressure of punishment, pay their checks and escape incarceration. The preponderant
majority of these, of course, are quasi-responsible persons who are
careless with their bookkeeping, slow to pay up and generally "bad
risks." The records of county attorneys and sheriffs' offices show that
all most of these people need is a bit of pressure, and they will make
their checks good. Failure to apply such pressure in the form of prompt
collection often breeds more bad checks and leads eventually to felony
sentences. Easy money to be had at the taverns, liquor stores, gas stations and large stores seems to encourage the tendency to write bad
checks which, if not immediately deterred, may lead the writers to a
serious penal sentence, after which it is hard to get a good job but
is still as easy as ever to cash bad checks. Hence the careless check
writer in due course becomes a felon, from which status the return to
normal life is most difficult.

THE COST OF LAW ENFORCEMENT AND THE PENAL SYSTEM
IN RELATION TO BUSINESS LOSSES ON BAD CHECKS

In attempting to compare the cost of enforcing the bad-check laws
with the losses suffered by businessmen in this field, one is immediately
met with a number of estimates and imponderables. Any results, there-

---

[47] Five hundred twenty-six questionnaires.

[48] This is probably an understatement of the actual facts, since these records and
case histories are not complete.

fore, in absence of a tremendously expensive cost-accounting survey, must be in round numbers and generalities.

BUSINESS LOSSES

As indicated above,[49] business losses on bad checks are of no relative importance. Table 17[50] indicates that less than half of the businesses have any losses at all on bad checks, and, as already indicated, a rough estimate of the total business losses in Nebraska shows that they are well under $500,000[51] a year and that the ultimate losses on checks which are brought to court do not run over $100,000.[52] Thus it is clear that bad checks are so inconsequential that businessmen do not bother to bring over three-fourths of their bad checks to court. It is not surprising, therefore, that when the rate of loss is compared to the volume of business, as shown in Tables 21 and 22,[53] the ratio of check losses to volume runs between .00006 and .00008, or, as shown in these same tables, an average of less than $10 per business per year.

COST TO THE STATE OF THE PENAL SYSTEM

On the other hand, the cost to the state in enforcing its present bad-check statutes is a considerable figure, which bulks large in the total expense of law enforcement. For convenience, and to clarify this phenomenon, it seems well to divide these costs into two groups: (1) the cost of the felony aspect of the law enforcement as shown in the penal institutions, and (2) the cost of enforcing the bad-check laws in the balance of the legal organization.

(1) The yearly cost of keeping criminals in the three major institutions under the bad-check law in relation to the total costs of operating these establishments is shown in Table 58.

This shows that the total yearly cost of operating the three penal institutions is $1,463,000. Of this amount, $384,450 is the proportionate share of detaining the bad-check writers. Thus well over one-fourth of the regular inmates of the state's three institutions are bad-check writers; and if the no-fund-check writers were convicted in the same proportion as forgers, as required by the statute, the population of the penal institutions would be doubled;[54] and if the legally required de-

---

[49] P. 269, supra.
[50] P. 265, supra.
[51] P. 264 ff, supra.
[52] P. 314, supra.
[53] Pp. 268 and 271, supra.
[54] Table 11, p. 258, shows that there are ten times as many no-account checks as forgeries; but Tables 43 and 44, p. 319, show that there are less felony convictions for no-account checks than for forgeries.

TABLE 58

Yearly Cost of Maintaining Bad-Check Writers in Penal Institutions

Institution	Total Yearly Cost	Per Cent of Penal Population Bad-Check Writers†	Cost of Bad-Check Inmates
Penitentiary*	$968,473	28.2‡	$273,210
Reformatory*	449,880	20.5	92,000
Women's Reformatory*	44,727	43.0	19,240
Total	$1,463,080		$384,450

* One-half of the total from the *Biennial Report of the Board of Control, 1953*, pp. 198, 244 and 219.
† Based on the total number of prisoners and length of sentences of bad-check writers as compared to other criminals.
‡ Based on a sample of daily population and a comparison of sentences.

gree of enforcement were applied to insufficient-fund-check writers, the population of the penal institutions would equal a sizeable city.[55]

Table 58 shows that the proportionate costs of caring for bad-check writers now runs well over $350,000 annually. There must be added to this the expense suffered by the counties in enforcing the penal sections of the law by extraditing felonious check writers who have fled to other states. Figures are not available in all of the counties, but in one of those very active in enforcing the felonious aspects of the statutes, the cost of extraditing criminals for the 1952-1953 period studied was $3,500, or $1,750 per year. This county convicts about one-ninth of the felons under the bad-check law, which would make a rough estimate of the state's yearly total for extraditing them around $17,000. Add to this the mileage costs at ten cents a mile[56] for sheriffs and other law enforcement officials to bring their prisoners to the penal institutions at an average rate of 150 bad-check writers per year,[57] and it will appear that the yearly costs of administering the felony aspects of the law are almost equal to the gross business losses from all bad checks written in the state.

[55] Here again Table 11, p. 258, shows that there are over 100 times as many insufficient-fund checks as forgeries; and under the presumptions of Neb. Rev. Stat. §§ 28-1213 and 28-1214 (1948), every one of those over $35 which is not paid in five days from protest is a presumed felony, and those under, presumptive misdemeanors. So if writing insufficient-fund chesks were punished at the same rate as forgeries, there would be well over 5,000 criminal convictions a year under this statute; and if literally enforced, the rate would be much higher.
[56] Neb. Rev. Stat. § 33-117 (Re-issue 1952).
[57] See Tables 43 and 44, p. 319.

347

(2) In addition to the costs of enforcing the felony aspects of the statutes, there are also the proportionate shares of the expenses of maintaining the courts, county attorneys, police forces and other aspects of the law enforcement machinery. Here the actual costs are very elusive. It is impossible, without a complete time study, to get a fair estimate of the proportion of costs of the law enforcement offices which should properly fall to handling bad-check writers. This would be further complicated by the fact that most of these salaries are set by county officials; and in many instances, on the district court level, one judge presides over a number of counties. So here, in the present state of the records, one is in a field of complete conjecture. An effort was made, however, to find in the sample counties the relation of the number of bad-check cases to the rest of the court's docket. As already indicated, there is no uniformity at all in the policy of the courts in dealing with the bad-check laws. In the district courts, the number of prosecutions in this field ran from none at all to as high as one-third of the court's total cases, civil and criminal. If any generalization can be made at all, it might be said that the bad-check cases were well under ten per cent of the total cases docketed. In the county courts, the ratio ran again in total cases from zero to 30 per cent with an over-all average of less than seven per cent of the recorded cases. In no justice of the peace courts were criminal bad-check cases over ten per cent of the total, and in most of them there were none at all. It should be further noted that these figures are not particularly meaningful because the time spent on a bad-check case is likely to be far less than on others. This is due to the fact that the defendants almost always plead guilty. The proofs are very simple. There are practically no jury trials, in fact, seldom any trial at all in the sense in which this term is used in dealing with all civil and many other criminal cases. Taking the court system as a whole, it is clear, then, that the enforcement of the bad-check law is not a particular burden upon the judges; and, except in the two big cities, a substantial increase or decrease in this work would not materially affect the case-load.

Turning to the other law enforcement officials, the information is equally speculative. The district attorneys and sheriffs were asked to estimate the amount of their time which they spent on bad checks. These estimates almost always appeared to be too large. They were supported by no time-study or cost system, and, except in the case of the number of warrants served by the sheriffs, there was no record whatsoever to substantiate them. They are given here simply to show that, on the officials' own estimates, the bad-check work is not very large. Most of the sheriffs and district attorneys complain that collecting bad checks is one of their greatest headaches; but when asked to estimate the time which they spent on the problem, by their own estimates the county attorneys devoted from no time at all up to a maximum of 30 per cent of their efforts for the state to this law. The sheriffs' estimates ran from nothing up to 30 per cent of their time. In one or two counties most active in collecting checks, the sheriffs' records showed that half of their criminal warrants were in this field. On the average, if the averages mean anything, the district attorneys spent less than ten per cent of the time which they devoted to the state on the bad-check law, and the sheriffs, about twice this figure. When it is understood that these are, of course, overstatements, it is clear that there could be a considerable increase in the amount of work done by sheriffs and district attorneys in this field without adding much, if anything, to the costs of operating their offices.

On the whole, it seems that the cost to the public of enforcing the bad-check laws, considering all of its aspects, now runs considerably ahead of the total losses to business in this area; and that, even though there is tremendous laxity in enforcing the felony aspects of the law, bad-check cases are a substantial part of the cost of the penal system, running well over 25 per cent of the whole. In absence of proof of the deterrent effect of the law, one might well question whether this outlay is justified.

IV. HOW THE BAD-CHECK LAWS AFFECT SOCIETY AND WHAT INTERESTS ARE THEREBY REVEALED

In attempting to explain the facts revealed by a study of this kind, one is immediately faced with the problem of the extent to which the present state of the law is responsible in shaping the observable phenomena. Ultimately the law is just one of many social factors which react upon each individual's behavior. A given act by one person may be and often is the result of a complex of interests such as needs, desires and demands for action tempered by such forces as law, morals, religion, habits, competition and many other social pressures. In this state of facts, it is difficult to say which of the many factors is dominant in influencing the action of any one individual; and when the actions of many are considered, it is true that what affected one may not move another. In fact, there is no simple cause-and-effect link by which one may reason back from observable mass statistics to the manner in which any force, such as law, religion, etc., exerts a decisive influence upon observable situations. About all one may hope to do is to offer speculative hypotheses as to the reasons why certain mass activity appears and to suggest what part the state of law may have in shaping the mass reactions revealed by the statistics.

In some instances the connection between the facts and the law may be obvious; for example, there would not be any persons sentenced to the penitentiary for writing bad checks if the law did not designate that act as a felony. The fact that there are such persons there can be definitely attributed to the felony provisions of the law and their enforcement. On the other hand, the fact that a certain number of bad checks are written in one community and more in another may be influenced entirely by factors other than the state of the law; but statistical correlation of checks written in many places may reveal the simultaneous appearance of certain factors. For example, Table 59 shows a very interesting correlation between the high incidence of collection activity by officials and the low per cent of bad checks per capita. This might lead one to believe that there is a connection between the two. On the other hand, the same table shows that there is no correlation between the rate of felony convictions and the number of bad checks written in the community, perhaps pointing to the inference that neither of these two results has any relation to the other. Of course there is always the possibility that correlations, or lack of them, are the result of other dominant forces or just pure chance. Keeping in mind all of these and many other limitations of the statistical method and the observations upon which it is based, it still might be useful to attempt to find some meaningful connection between the state of the law and the facts surrounding bad checks in Nebraska and elsewhere.

Further, when such connections are found, it may be possible to offer reasons why the law does or does not influence the social facts. This in turn leads to the possibility of experimentally testing whether or not the law has the postulated effects. Such tests can readily be made in at least two ways: (1) The law could be changed and the facts reexamined to see if, with the enactment of the new law, there are any changes in social conditions. (2) It may be possible to find another state or legal unit where other social conditions are about the same but where the law is different. By subjecting this new jurisdiction to the same studies, it may be possible to determine whether the law in the state first studied has the postulated effects.

The first process of testing hypothetical explanations is slow and difficult, to say the least, because it involves getting the legislative bodies to make the desired changes and then waiting until the officials learn of the change, act under it and, in turn, till the effect of

TABLE 59

Relationship between the Number of Bad Checks per Capita, Collection Activities of Officials and Sentences of Imprisonment†

Group		Counties by Number	Number of Bad Checks Per Capita	Per Cent of Bad Checks Collected	Number of Imprisonments Misdemeanor and Felony Sentences per 1000 Bad Checks
Total Average		1-31	.30**	1.1	1.063
I		22	.11	8.0	0
		30	.11	4.9	0
		31	.18	4.3	0
		1	.19	.6*	1.091
	I	Average	.16**	5.4	.710
II		20	.23	1.8	1.178
		27	.24	1.0	.651
		23	.25	....	.301
		4	.26	1.3	.235
		11	.26	....	1.387
		7	.27	1.9	0
		19	.27	3.8	.371
		8	.28	.3	.272
		9	.28	3.4	1.015
		16	.28	2.0	0
	II	Average	.26**	2.1	.352
III		2	.30	....	1.493
		6	.30	2.0	.194
		21	.30	1.2	1.118
		18	.32	1.1	1.483
		10	.33	.6*	.288
		25	.33	....	.214
	III	Average	.31**	1.3	1.105
IV		14	.35	.1*	.317***
		12	.35	.4	0
		17	.41	1.4	0
		24	.41	.7	.284
		15	.51	....	0
		28	.53	....	1.438
	IV	Average	.41**	.7	.316
V		13	.62	.9	.267
		26	.62	.3	1.076
		3	.67	....	0
		29	1.18	2.1	0
		5	2.30	.1	.198
	V	Average	1.75**	.4	.464

† Population 1950 census; convictions are an average of 1952 and 1953; number of bad checks are 1954 estimates.
* Record for only one official. These counties are not used to obtain group averages.
** Medians.
*** Underestimates; no complete record of misdemeanor sentences was available.

these acts reaches the consciousness of the public, a long process which is sometimes never complete.

The second test, that of examining another jurisdiction where the law is, and for some time has been, different, offers an immediate method by which the effectiveness of the bad-check laws of Nebraska may be tested under what seem to be laboratory conditions. With this possibility in mind, the administration of the laws of other states was used to test possible theories as to effectiveness of provisions of the Nebraska statutes. This technique is subject to minute and far-reaching comparisons; but for a study of the limited scope of this one, it was possible to examine only some of the most outstanding features of the law.

HOW THE FELONY PROVISIONS OF THE LAW AFFECT BUSINESS PRACTICES

One of the most outstanding characteristics of the Nebraska bad-check law is its stringent felony provisions. Writing a forged check or a no-account check of any size or an insufficient-fund check above $35 is a felony.[1] As already shown, these provisions have resulted in one-third of the felons in the state being sentenced on bad-check charges and have caused one-fourth of the prison population to be bad-check writers.[2] Although the enforcement of the penal provisions of the law have been sporadic and at many times and in numerous counties nonexistent,[3] the cost of the state has been greater than the total loss to business from bad checks.[4] The resulting increase in the criminal population has been such that the prosecutors and judges are refusing to enforce against bad-check writers the plain provisions of the habitual-criminal statutes,[5] and many refuse to bring felony charges at all.[6] In this state of the law, there must be valid reasons for such strict punishment, or the provisions ought to be repealed.

Theories as to why the law ought to be so strict are not hard to find. A number of plausible explanations have been offered. (1) Many businessmen and law enforcement officials demand strong penalties because they believe the existence of felony provisions deters crime and

---

[1] Neb. Rev. Stat. §§ 28-601, 28-1212 (1953 Cum. Sup.), id. 28-1213.
[2] Supra p. 319.
[3] See Figures 1 and 6, supra pp. 237, 320.
[4] Supra p. 347 ff.
[5] Supra p. 329.
[6] Supra p. 298.

cuts down the number of bad-check writers.[7] (2) The fact that felony provisions are available makes it possible more easily to collect a bad check because the writer, being faced with prison, will make every effort to pay up. On the other hand, it is argued (3) that strict penalties in the penal law offer the businessman such protection that he gets more careless in taking checks and thus increases his losses and the burden upon the officials. It might be well to examine these hypotheses in relation to data which point to discoverable facts.

HEAVY FELONY PUNISHMENT AND THE INCIDENCE OF BAD CHECKS

The figures gathered in Nebraska counties where the enforcement of felony provisions of the law varies from almost nothing at all to high incidence of criminal sentences lend no support to the theory that felony provisions deter the writing of bad checks. The second and last columns of Table 59 show that there is no correlation between felony sentences and the number of bad checks written per capita in the various counties, and Table 60 shows further that in the case of no-account checks, which is an all-felony classification in Nebraska and only a misdemeanor in Colorado, there was likewise no correlation between the number of checks per capita and the strictness of the penalties imposed. Although there are no true figures on recidivism in the penal institutions, those available in Figures 7, 8 and 9 [8] show that the incidence of habitual-criminal tendencies among the check writers in the Penitentiary is so high that the courts do not even attempt to enforce the habitual-criminal statutes against them. So in Nebraska itself there is no evidence that felony provisions deter bad-check writing.

Better evidence of the deterrent force of felony statutes is available elsewhere. As shown in Table 27 above,[9] there are 13 states in which the writing of bad checks other than forgeries is merely a misdemeanor. If there is any restraining force in the felony provisions, it should be apparent, other things being equal, that there would be more bad checks per capita or per volume of business in such states than in those like Nebraska which have strict felony penalties for bad checks. In order to test this deterrence theory, four counties were selected in Colorado where short (insufficient-fund and no-account) checks are

---

[7] These arguments are stated as facts in almost every legislative hearing on bills attempting to cut the penalties. Statements of this nature were made by the representative of the Bankers Association at a hearing opposing L.B. 417, 67th Session, passed by the Nebraska Legislature making no-account checks below $35 a misdemeanor only, and were repeated by the governor in vetoing the bill.

[8] Supra pp. 326-28.

[9] Supra pp. 282-85.

TABLE 60

Number of Short* Checks, Actual and "Normal" Estimates, Nebraska and Colorado, Four Counties and Four Cities, 1953†

Area	Deposits (Millions of Dollars)	Number of Short Checks			No. Short Checks Per Capita	
		Actual	Estimate	Actual as Per Cent of "Normal"‡	Actual	"Normal" Estimate‡
Short Checks						
State of Nebraska (Minus Douglas County)	1001.8	310,056	(310,056)	100.0	.3	(.3)
Nebraska (4 Counties)	107.5	64,593	33,269	194.2	.6	.3
Colorado (4 Counties)	122.7	40,126	37,950	105.7	.3	.3
Nebraska (4 Cities)	83.7	47,690	25,890	184.2	.8	.4
Colorado (4 Cities)	83.2	23,046	25,766	89.4	.5	.5
No-Account Checks						
State of Nebraska (Minus Douglas County)	1001.8	22,486	(22,486)	100.0	.02	.02
Nebraska (4 Cities)	83.7	3,259	1,878	173.5	.054	.031
Colorado (4 Cities)	83.2	2,581	1,868	138.5	.053	.039

* "Short check" is a Colorado statutory term covering insufficient- and no-fund checks.
† Estimates for state of Nebraska made from sample of 23 banks.
‡ "Normal" refers to the number of short checks which would have occurred if the figures had conformed to the Nebraska averages.

a misdemeanor. (The forgery statutes of the two states are almost identical.) These counties were subjected to the same study as were the 31 Nebraska counties. The statistics were then compared with four counties in Nebraska having similar population, geographical, race, transportation, economic and business conditions. In fact, every attempt was made to get like counties so that the only substantial difference would be the state of the laws. The combined results of the four Colorado counties were also compared with the total statistics for Nebraska.

Table 60 shows the results of the banking questionnaire in the four Colorado counties as compared with four Nebraska counties, also in four cities from each of the two states chosen because they had like social characteristics. In most instances the cities and the counties chosen were less than one hundred miles apart and in like territory. It should be noted that in each estimated case the Nebraska cities and counties had more short checks than their Colorado counterparts. It should be noted likewise that in the calculations of all short checks, the Nebraska cities and counties were all above the Nebraska "normal," while the Colorado counties and cities were at or below the Nebraska "normal." In the case of no-account checks, the indicated difference is more marked. Here the Nebraska penalty for all no-account checks is a felony, but in Colorado it is only a misdemeanor; yet no-account checks show a slightly higher percentage in Nebraska than in Colorado.

In like manner, Table 61 shows the comparative bad-check losses for retail and service businesses taken from the results of the business questionnaire. Here the results, when averaged, are almost identical. These results also contain further significance when it is realized that Nebraska Counties 5, 18 and 26 were among those having the highest felony convictions for short checks. Colorado, of course, has no such felony convictions. It should also be noted that the highest percentage of estimated loss occurred in Nebraska County 5, which has recently struck oil, and where the county attorney enforces the felony penalty strictly and refuses to collect checks. The Colorado oil Counties 2 and 4 also had high incidence of losses, but they were at less than half the rate of Nebraska County 5.

All available figures tend to show that the differences in the felony provisions of the check laws do not affect the number of bad checks in the two states. If anything, there are fewer short-check losses in Colorado where the penalties are more lenient.

TABLE 61

Four Nebraska and Four Colorado Counties:
Dollar Volume of Retail, Wholesale and Service Trade Compared with Estimated Losses from Uncollected Checks, 1953

	Population*	Number of Businesses†	Volume in Sales†	Loss from Uncollected Checks‡	Per Cent of Volume Lost from Uncollected Checks (Retail and Service)
NEBRASKA					
Four Counties	106,981	2,322	$290,231,000	$25,329	.01676
1	28,856	533	56,782,000	2,114	.00606
5	12,081	291	34,764,000	8,854	.06055
18	32,200	699	108,462,000	7,198	.01797
26	33,900	799	90,223,000	7,163	.01595
COLORADO					
Four Counties	146,254	2,917	$237,837,000	$22,267	.01503
1	43,554	1,013	56,647,000	5,647	.01261
2	18,000	379	33,958,000	6,955	.02615
3	67,500	1,170	104,443,000	4,319	.00691
4	17,200	355	42,789,000	5,346	.02571

* U. S. Census, 1950.
† U. S. Census of Business, 1948.
‡ Survey of Business, 1953.

Studies were also made in Vermont and New Hampshire. By the state laws of the former,[10] the writing of a short check is only a tort, which gives the injured party only the right to attach the body of the offender until he pays. The statutes of New Hampshire have like provisions,[11] but by a peculiar interpretation of the larceny laws and refusal of the bar to use body attachments of debtors,[12] the actual enforcement of the laws by the courts and officials is almost identical to Nebraska. Table 62 shows the comparative number of estimated bad checks in four Nebraska and Colorado cities and in one each of similar size in Vermont and New Hampshire, and also the number of bad checks per capita in these cities. At a glance it should be noted in the first column that Vermont, where short checks are not a crime, has less than half as many bad checks per hundred checks as Nebraska and slightly over half of the Colorado rate, where such checks are respectively felonies and misdemeanors. This might lead one to jump to the conclusion that the higher the penalties, the more bad checks; but when one looks at New Hampshire, which enforces its laws like Nebraska but has a bad-check ratio like Vermont, one is led to the conclusion that the severity of the penalties has nothing to do with the number of bad checks. This ratio seems to be determined by factors wholly outside the law or its methods of its enforcement.[13]

THE EFFECT OF FELONY PROVISIONS ON THE EFFICIENCY OF COLLECTION

Turning to the argument that felony provisions are necessary to make it easier to collect checks, the figures again will lend no support to this belief. As already pointed out, in spite of the legal ethics which frown upon public officials collecting bad checks under threat of criminal prosecutions, this is a nationwide practice because of the pres-

[10] Table 27, supra p. 285.

[11] Supra p. 284.

[12] There seem to be two reasons why the body attachment is not widely used in New Hampshire. In the first place, prominent members of the bar frown upon it as imprisonment for debt; but, most important, by local practice the complaining creditor is required to give bond to cover the state's cost of arrest and imprisonment in case the debtor cannot pay.

[13] One of the obvious factors here would be the habits of the merchants in taking checks. The study as originally planned called for as complete a check on this factor in certain counties in New Hampshire and Vermont as was made in Nebraska, but the completion of this work was stopped by one of the hurricanes, and it could not be resumed. As far as it went, which was not conclusive, there was no evidence of greater care on the part of the New England merchants than that exhibited in Nebraska and Colorado. See the discussion of this point later in this section.

TABLE 62

Comparison: Ten Cities in Colorado, Nebraska, New Hampshire and Vermont

Per Cent of Total Checks that Were Charged Back and Number of Bad Checks per Capita

	Per Cent of Total Checks Charged Back (Sample Banks)	Number of Bad Checks Per Capita (Cities)
NEBRASKA		
1	.30	.27
5	.89	3.51
18	.64	.41
26	.68	1.21
Four-City Total	.65	.79
COLORADO		
1	.37	.45
2	.69	1.26
3	.43	.44
4	.26	.69
Four-City Total	.42	.66
NEW HAMPSHIRE		
One City	.279	.17
VERMONT		
One City	.232	.19

sure from businessmen for this service.[14] Now if the threat of felony penalties causes the drawer to make good more quickly, then the officials in the states where such penalties are in the statutes should find collection easier. Table 63 shows just the opposite. In the four counties in Nebraska which are compared with four similar counties in Colorado, the number of checks collected by officials in Nebraska is only .38 per cent of the calculated short checks; while in the four counties in Colorado, it is 1.5 per cent. Now of course this condition can be affected by the policy of the particular officials; but when the Colorado figures are compared with the whole of Nebraska, it appears that under the felony provisions of the latter, officials in 30 counties collected only 1.1 per cent of short checks, which is still only two-thirds of the Colorado ratio. So if in spite of the legal ethics, criminal penalties are necessary to aid the collection of checks, there is no evidence that a misdemeanor charge is not sufficient. There is further substantiation of this fact in Vermont, where tort is the remedy but legal imprison-

[14] Supra p. 292.

ment for debt in absence of payment is available; there the sheriff collects 4.1 per cent of the apparent number of bad checks in the county, almost four times the Nebraska rate and nearly three times the rate of Colorado. Nearby New Hampshire, with an enforcement system like the provisions of the Nebraska statute, has a 1.4 per cent ratio, standing between Nebraska and Colorado.

TABLE 63

Ratio of Collection by Officials in Four States:
Nebraska, Colorado, Vermont and New Hampshire, 1953

	Total Bad Checks in Area	Bad Checks Given Officials		Collections by Officials	
		Number	Per Cent of Bad Checks in Area	Number	Per Cent of Bad Checks in Area
NEBRASKA	282,907*	6,175*	2.2*	1,623†	1.1 †
Four Counties	64,593	707	1.1	247	.38
1	5,500	60	1.1	42	.76
5	27,744	80	.3	26	.09
18	10,447	167	1.6	118	1.13
26	20,902	400	1.9	61	.29
COLORADO					
Four Counties	41,400	773‡	1.9‡	607	1.50
1	11,400	120	1.1	115	1.01
2	9,600	253	2.6	192	2.00
3	14,500	200‡	1.4	200	1.37
4	5,900	200	3.6	100	1.69
VERMONT					
One County	6,500	300	4.6	270	4.1
NEW HAMPSHIRE					
One County	5,500	125	2.3	77	1.4

* 30 Counties
† 21 Counties
‡ Understatement; only a record of the total number of collections was available for one Colorado county.

There is, then, no evidence that the felony penalties are any aid to the officials in collecting checks. On the contrary, it seems that they do better without them, especially in Vermont, where a collection process, using the legal threat of imprisonment in jail until payment, is the most efficient of all.

CARELESSNESS OF BUSINESSMEN IN TAKING CHECKS AS
AFFECTED BY HARSH PENALTIES

The argument commonly heard in the legislature and among law enforcement officials that the businessman is more careless about tak-

ing checks when the penalties are higher or when the officials are effective in collecting checks also seems to be without substantiation. Table
62 shows the estimated per cent of checks which were originally turned
back by the banks as bad in ten like cities of the four states studied.
Here again Nebraska, with the strictest laws, has the most bad checks
originally taken by the business units. This would seem to support
the theory that the businessmen are more careless when the laws are
strict, except for the fact that in New Hampshire, which has an enforcement system almost identical to Nebraska's, there is next to the smallest
proportion of bad checks and the lowest rate of bad checks per capita.
Further, Nebraska Cities 5 and 26, with the highest rate of bad checks
returned, were the ones where the felony penalties were most strictly
enforced; and although the businessmen complained the loudest that
the county attorneys would not collect checks, they went right on cashing them at a rate which made the two cities together the highest takers
of bad checks and, as shown by Tables 62 and 63, the biggest losers
of any two of the ten cities in four states. On the other hand, Vermont,
with the smallest area of penalties and the most effective collection
system of all, had the lowest percentage of bad checks dishonored by
the banks.

Strange to say, although the bad-check rate differs widely in the
four states, the questionnaires returned by the businessmen show no
discernible difference in precautions taken in cashing checks, which
leads one to the conclusion that few businessmen outside of bankers
know the state of the penalties imposed by the law; but even if they do,
the precautions they take in cashing checks probably will be determined
by their evaluation of the size of their losses in proportion to the good
will built up by honoring checks. So, with losses as small as they are,
businessmen do not worry about the possible effect of the legal system
on a few bad checks when good will can be purchased so cheaply by
cashing them freely.

If the businessman has any discernible interest in the enforcement
of the criminal law, it seems to be chiefly as an aid in collecting bad
checks after he has cashed them. Here the evidence is clear that he both
wants and demands collection. This is especially true in the case of
small checks, where the court costs, lawyers' fees and collection charges,
all part of the civil collection process, are too expensive to make it
possible for collections to yield any appreciable returns on a check for
less than $25. This is why checks in this range and below appear so
often in the criminal processes.[15] The businessman wants collection,

[15] See Table 41, p. 314.

being interested in prosecution only as a secondary matter; but even the demand for collection in this area of small checks is not as strong as one might believe because, as shown above,[16] about three-fourths of the business losses on bad checks were not even taken to the law enforcement officials either because, as in the case of about ten per cent, they would not collect,[17] or because, with the large majority, the losses were too small to bother with the expensive, slow, cumbersome and extra-legal collection process. Once he gets his money by any process, the businessman usually seems to lose all interest in penalties.

HOW COLLECTION BY OFFICIALS AFFECTS THE NUMBER OF CHECKS

Now it should be clear that the number of bad checks in circulation is due primarily to two factors: (1) the carelessness of the businessman in taking checks and (2) the negligence or diabolical skill of the writers in putting them into circulation. As indicated above, the stiffness of the criminal penalties, insofar as their attitudes are discernible from the statistics, seems to have no appreciable effect on the businessmen or the writers. It might be well, then, to examine how prompt collection, either legal or extra-legal, under the threat of criminal action affects the statistics. Here there is remarkable correlation between the number of bad checks and the vigor of collection activities by the officials. In Table 59 the counties of Nebraska are arranged in five groups in the second column in the order of the number of bad checks per capita calculated for the county. The next column shows the per cent of bad checks collected by the officials. Although there is the expected variation among individual counties, it is significant that, on the whole, as collection activities decline, the number of bad checks per capita increases.

This inverse ratio between collection and the number of bad checks is shown even more strikingly by the Nebraska-Colorado figures in Table 64. Here in three groups are the six most alike county-seat cites. In the first and last groups, the cities were in like territory less than 100 miles apart. The first two were oil boom towns, and the last two, border cities with many transients and a heavy Mexican population. The middle two were centrally located agricultural centers in less-alike territory, and were over 300 miles apart. The third column shows the collection activities of the officials; and in every case where the collection activity was substantially greater, the bad checks per capita, the business losses from bad checks and the number charged back by

---

[16] Supra p. 315.
[17] See Table 28, p. 288, and supra p. 290 ff.

TABLE 64

Collection by Officials Related to Check Losses in Six Like County-Seat Cities, Colorado and Nebraska, 1953

City and State	Population 1950 Census	Retail, Etc., Sales Volume (Thousands of Dollars)*	Per Cent of Bad Checks Collected by Officials†	Bad Checks per Capita‡	Per Cent Loss Uncollected Checks**	Per Cent Checks Charged Back by Banks‡
Neb. 5	5,000	14,623	.09	3.51	.061	.89
Colo. 2	5,300	20,069	2.6	1.26	.026	.69
Neb. 18	22,700	40,061	1.13	.40	.018	.40
Colo. 3	20,400	62,528	1.37	.44	.007††	.43
Neb. 26	12,900	44,896	.29	1.21	.016	.68
Colo. 1	14,900	44,773	1.01	.45	.013	.45

* U. S. Census of Business 1948.
** Business questionnaires.
† Interviews with officials.
‡ Banking questionnaires 1954.
†† These losses are probably reduced by the fact that there were two active private civil collection agencies in this city but none in the others.

the banks were less. It is particularly significant that in the middle group, Nebraska 18 and Colorado 3, where the collection activity by officials was almost the same, the other indices were also very close together. Furthermore, it should be noted, as shown in Tables 62 and 63, that in Vermont, where collection by the officials is legalized and is at the highest rate, the estimated ratio of bad checks to total checks is less than one-half of the Nebraska and Colorado rate. However, this ratio cannot be attributed entirely to the increased collection, because New Hampshire, which appears to have less than half the collection activity, has about the same bad-check ratio, so there are other non-legal factors at work. But at any rate, the correlation between collection under the threat of punishment by officials and a reduced bad-check rate is sufficiently clear to suggest that it is one of the important causes of the lower bad-check ratio.

This makes better sense when it is considered, as indicated by the reports above from a typical Nebraska county,[18] that less than one per cent of the bad checks returned by banks and less than 12 per cent of the checks brought to officials for prosecution are written by transients who are not apprehended. Thus the great bulk of bad checks are drawn by local people, so, as the statistics indicate, the presence of immediate and forceful collection by the officials may be an excellent deterrent.

[18] Supra p. 336 ff.

361

HOW THE STATE OF THE LAW AFFECTS THE SIZE OF BAD CHECKS

Where the law provides a division between felonies and misdemeanors depending upon the size of the checks, as, in Nebraska, writing an insufficient-fund check for an amount below $35 is a misdemeanor and above that amount a felony, officials and bankers will be heard to assert confidently that raising or abolishing the felony limit will cause bad checks to be larger. Thus it is argued that in Nebraska, because of the $35 limit, the great majority of bad checks will be below that amount; while in Colorado, for example, where there is no such division, all short checks being misdemeanors, the amount will be larger.

Table 65 shows the average relative size of good and bad checks in the banks visited in Nebraska, Colorado, New Hampshire and Vermont.

TABLE 65

Average Size of Good and Bad Checks in Nebraska, Colorado, New Hampshire and Vermont, Banking Questionnaires, 1954

State	All Checks Average Size	Bad Checks Average Size
Nebraska*		
Sample	$125	$54
Non-Sample	114	64
Colorado†	115	60
New Hampshire‡	133	106
Vermont‡	136	160

* Outside of Douglas County; see Table 14, p. 261.
† Six banks in four counties.
‡ One city bank each.

Since only a small per cent of bad checks are in the criminal class, one would not expect the law to have any appreciable effect on the size of bad checks, and such is the case as shown by the figures. The estimated average size of good and bad checks in Nebraska, where short checks, except for insufficient-funds below $35, are felonies, and in Colorado, where all short checks are misdemeanors, turn out to be so close that there is no statistical difference. Likewise, the figures for Vermont and New Hampshire are also similar. It is interesting that in one Vermont bank the average bad check is larger than the average good one, while in New Hampshire bad checks, though smaller, are still almost twice as big as they are in Nebraska. To disclose why this is so, or whether or not it is a statewide phenomenon, would require a much more extensive study, but it cannot be caused by the state of the law because, as indicated above,[19] the enforcement of the law in New Hampshire is about the same as in Nebraska, but in Vermont it is totally different. Nevertheless, the bad-check picture, so far as average amounts are concerned, is quite different in Nebraska and New Hampshire and very similar in New Hampshire and in Vermont.

Turning to checks tinged with criminality, three sets of figures are available. Table 66 shows the distribution of the amounts of checks brought to the local authorities in County 18 in Nebraska (to the county attorney) and County 2 in Colorado (to the sheriff). Although these two county seats are quite different economically, the Colorado one being an oil boom town and the Nebraska one a farming center, it is interesting to note that the Colorado sheriff, though he is in a much smaller town, got larger checks. This, of course, was partly due to the fact that his reputation as a good collector caused more businessmen to entrust him with very large checks, which incidentally he collected, so no professional criminal was involved there. It seems significant that in the Colorado figures in Table 66 there is a break in the third quartile size of checks at or about the $35 point, which is where the felony penalty begins to apply to insufficient-fund checks in Nebraska, and this would tend to support the theory that the law affects the size and the amount of checks.

A better picture of the effect, if any, of the penalties upon the size of checks can be had from the figures showing the size of checks upon which prosecutions were brought. As indicated by Table 69, over 80

TABLE 66

Size of Checks Given Officials for Collection in Nebraska and Colorado Cities, 1953

	Nebraska City (County 18)	Colorado City (County 2)
Number of Checks	346	326
Total Dollar Value of Checks	$12,098	$18,852
Average Size of Checks		
Arithmetic Average	35	58
Median	15	20
Mode	10	10
Quartile 1	8	10
Quartile 3	25	49
Spread	1-1,075	2-3,500

[19] Supra p. 356.

TABLE 67

Size of Short Checks for Which Court Charges Were Made, Nebraska Counties and Colorado Counties, 1952-1953

	Thirty-one Nebraska Counties	Four Nebraska Counties	Four Colorado Counties
Number of Check Cases*	1,020	390	72
Total Dollar Value of Checks	$86,235	$19,707	$2,222
Average Size of Checks			
Arithmetic Average	85	51	31
Median	18	15	24
Mode	10	10	....
Quartile 1	10	10	10
Quartile 3	40	30	30
Spread	1-12,040	1-1,627	3-203

* Number of cases for which the record of the size of check was available.

per cent of the Colorado cases were in the misdemeanor class because short checks are misdemeanors only, while, as shown by Table 36,[20] 57 per cent of the Nebraska cases were felonies. But Table 67 shows that the dollar amounts of checks upon which prosecutions were brought were larger in Nebraska than in Colorado, and the Colorado figures show no break at the $35 point. In fact, quite the contrary. Table 67 shows that even in the four comparable counties, the checks upon which criminal charges were brought were larger and more numerous in Nebraska than in Colorado, with many more and larger checks in the area above $35.

Even more persuasive are the figures relating to professional check-writers. Table 32[21] shows the convictions in County 18 in Nebraska over a two-year period. Well over half of the sentences fell into the felony class, but well over two-thirds of the checks upon which these charges were brought were for amounts less than $23. These, of course, were no-fund checks, and if the criminals had known that the felony limit applied only to insufficient-fund checks, they probably would have written them in larger amounts. So there is probably no relation between the amounts of the checks and the felony limit in the statute.

Where professional check writers are concerned, the results are the same. Turning to Table 55,[22] which shows the distribution of the size of checks written by professionals in Nebraska County 18, it immediately becomes apparent on these figures that there is no relationship

[20] Supra p. 308.
[21] Supra p. 302.
[22] Supra p. 337.

between the felonious criminal punishment and the size of the checks. Of the 18, only four were written near the $35 limit, three were well above it and the other 11 were far below.

So again the statistics show almost conclusively that the fact that the charge against a bad-check writer may be a tort, a misdemeanor or a felony will have no appreciable effect upon the size of the check he writes. He is going to get all that he thinks he can for his immediate purpose, and even the professional seems to pay no attention to the state of the penal law.

INFLUENCE OF FELONY PROVISIONS ON OFFICIAL ACTIONS

It is hard to estimate the influence of the felony provisions of the law upon the actions of the officials. By the nature of their work, the duties of the county attorney, the sheriff and the courts are very closely interwoven, and the attitude of each in any county affects the actions of all the others. So the influence of the law upon a particular individual or county can never be actually ascertained; but perhaps by comparison of the statistics on official actions in a number of jurisdictions where the law differs, some facts as to its influence may be revealed. There is, of course, some difficulty in making such comparisons due to the difference in duties placed upon the official by laws governing jurisdiction and procedures. This is further complicated by the fact that 31 counties in Nebraska were visited, while only four in Colorado and one each in New Hampshire and Vermont were studied. If the samples in the other three states were larger, thus spreading the base of the statistics, firmer conclusions might be possible; but with the limitations of finances, staff and time, only a few inferences are indicated.

ACTION OF LAW ENFORCEMENT OFFICIALS

As already pointed out, the literal provisions of the bad-check laws of Nebraska, being too strict, have proven unenforceable, and the variations of action and policy of county attorneys and sheriffs in the various counties have been indicated. Figures 5 and 6[23] show that there is no enforcement of the felony provisions in about one-third of the counties. Table 28[24] shows the tremendous variations in collection activities of sheriffs and county attorneys, and Table 29[25] points up the diversity of practices in bringing misdemeanor and felony charges in

[23] Supra pp. 294, 320.
[24] Supra p. 288.
[25] Supra p. 299.

the courts. In all, the Nebraska picture is one of spotty performance by law enforcement officials, varying all the way from those who are frustrated by the enormity of enforcing the laws as written and consequently do nothing or as little as possible to those who try to enforce the statute literally but usually fail at re-election. In between are the officials who attempt as best they can to get along with their ideals of professional ethics and the demands of the businessmen for collection. Now the question might be asked if this would be different, if there would be more uniformity and stability in the action of the law enforcement officials, if the law were less strict. The answer to this question can perhaps be found in examining the activities of law enforcement officials where the law is less strict.

Turning to Colorado, and keeping in mind that because of the lack of further study the results are tentative, one is immediately struck by the fact that in the four counties studied, there was much more regularity and uniformity than in Nebraska. No county attorney was found who devoted any large amount of his time to collecting checks under the threat of criminal process. On the other hand, Table 63 shows that all the sheriffs did collect checks, and they did a much better job of it than their Nebraska counterparts and thus rendered more uniform service to businessmen, and without felony threats. Whether this is a proper sample of the whole state, of course, is not known, but reference to the four Nebraska counties which were chosen as geographic counterparts of the four Colorado counties reveals a similar discrepancy in enforcement, shown by Figures 5 and 6,[26] for the whole state. For example, estimated collections of checks in Nebraska, as shown by Table 63, vary from .09 per cent to 1.13 per cent, while in Colorado the spread is from 1.01 to 2 per cent.

Turning to Table 68 and comparing it with Tables 63 and 61, it appears that the Colorado area, with a slightly larger population and bank deposits, not only has fewer bad checks and better collection but, as shown in Table 68, it has less checks cases per capita but a larger ratio of check cases per thousand bad checks than Nebraska. Though, like Nebraska, it too has county variations, Colorado on the whole has fewer sentences per capita but more per thousand bad checks, showing a comparatively more efficient enforcement system.

Since the Nebraska four-county sample is a pretty good clue as to the disparity of enforcement throughout the state, it is perhaps not too great an assumption to expect that if the Colorado sample were expanded, it might show the same statewide efficiency of enforcement

[26] Supra pp. 294, 320.

TABLE 68

Comparison: Nebraska and Colorado
Number of Court Cases, Sentences and Imprisonments Per Year,*
Four Colorado and Four Nebraska Counties

County	Number of Cases In All Courts			Number of Sentences			Number of Imprisonment Sentences (Misdemeanor and Felony)		
	Total One Year*	Per 1000 People	Per 1000 Bad Checks	Total One Year*	Per 1000 People	Per 1000 Bad Checks	Total One Year*	Per 1000 People	Per 1000 Bad Checks
Nebraska									
1	13.0	.450	2.364	7.0	.243	1.434	6.0	.208	1.091
5	23.5	1.945	.847	10.0	.829	.360	5.5	.456	.198
18	84.5	2.626	8.089	35.0	1.087	3.350	15.5	.482	1.483
26	126.5	3,728	6.052	71.0	2,092	3.397	22.5	.665	1.071
Total	247.5	2.313	3.831	123.0	1.150	1.904	49.5	.461	.766
Colorado									
1	17.5	.402	1.558	9.5	.218	.846	4.5	.103	.401
2	26.5	1.472	2.732	11.0	.611	1.134	3.0	.167	.309
3	99.5	1.474	6.932	48.0	.711	3.340	16.5	.244	1.146
4	30.0	1.744	5.085	18.5	1.076	3.136	11.0	.645	1.864
Total	173.5	1.188	4.232	87.0	.596	2.122	35.0	.240	.854

* Annual number of court cases and sentences are one-half the 1952-1953 totals.

as found in the sample. Thus all statistics available point to the fact that Colorado gets better law enforcement and better collections on a statute which omits felony provisions for short checks. There are a large number of facts in support of this conclusion, and there is certainly no evidence whatsoever to sustain the popular supposition that strict penalties in Nebraska result in better law enforcement.

ACTIONS OF THE COURTS

There is a widespread popular belief found in both official and lay circles that when the law is strict in its penalties, the criminals will be frightened away from the proscribed action (a theory already shown to be untrue in the case of bad checks), and that the courts, having terrible punishment available, will be more effective, thus having less cases. This second belief, a sort of corollary of the first, is also shown to be highly questionable when applied to the bad-check laws as enforced in the courts of Nebraska and Colorado.

Tables 69, 70 and 71 show the Colorado court statistics for the four sample counties set out on total cases, lower court and district court cases in the same fashion as were the Nebraska court records for 31

TABLE 69

Four Colorado Counties
Disposition of Bad-Check Cases
All Courts, 1952 and 1953
(Check Cases Classified by Type of Crime)

Disposition	Total		Forgery		Confidence Game		Short-Check	
	Number	Per Cent	Number	Per Cent	Number	Per Cent	Number	Per Cent
Total	347	100.0	46	100.0	10	100.0	291	100.0
Without Sentence	173	49.8	11	23.9	1	10.0	161	55.3
No Warrant Ret.	94	27.1	4	8.7			90	30.9
Dismissed	65	18.7	7	15.2			58	19.9
Paid	7	2.0					7	2.4
Acquitted								
No Record	1*	.3			1*	10.0		
Bailed to County	6	1.7					6	2.1
With Sentence	174	50.2	35	76.1	9	90.0	130	44.7
Penitentiary	26	7.5	22	47.8	4	40.0		
Reformatory	8	2.3	7	15.2	1	10.0		
Probation or Parole	12	3.5	6	13.1	3	30.0	3	1.0
Suspended Sentence								
Jail	36	10.4					36	12.4
Fine	91	26.2					91	31.3
Other Sentence or No Record of Type	1	.3			1	10.0		

* Escaped.

counties in Tables 36, 37 and 38.[27] Tables 72, 73 and 74 show the same data for the four Nebraska counties which were chosen as a sample most like the four Colorado counties.

A comparison of Tables 36, 37 and 38 with Tables 72, 73 and 74 will show that in all the main outlines of the total statistics, the four Nebraska counties contain a good replica of the check cases found in the total of the 31 counties in the entire Nebraska sample. Now, when the figures for the four Nebraska counties are compared with the totals for the four Colorado counties shown in Tables 69, 70 and 71, certain statistical features emerge, revealing the manner in which the two systems of law affect the administration of the courts.

The first outstanding feature of the figures is the relation of the number of cases to the population and business done in the two areas. Although, as shown in earlier tables, the Colorado area has 40 per cent

[27] Supra pp. 308, 309 and 310.

TABLE 70

Four Colorado Counties
Disposition of Bad-Check Cases
Lower Courts, 1952 and 1953
(Check Cases Classified by Type of Crime)

Disposition	Total		Forgery		Confidence Game		Short-Check	
	Num-ber	Per Cent	Num-ber	Per Cent	Num-ber	Per Cent	Num-ber	Per Cent
Total	319	100.0	25	100.0	3	100.0	291	100.0
Without Sentence	168	52.7	7	28.0	0	0	161	55.3
No Warrant Ret.	94	29.5	4	16.0			90	30.9
Dismissed	61	19.1	3	12.0			58	19.9
Paid	7	2.2					7	2.4
Acquitted								
Warrant Collected, No Other Record								
No Record								
Bailed to County	6	1.9					6	2.1
Bound Over	21	6.6	18	72.0	3	100.0	0	0
With Sentence	130	40.7	0	0	0	0	130	44.7
Jail	36	11.3					36	12.4
Fine	91	28.5					91	31.3
State School								
Probation or Parole	3	.9					3	1.0
Suspended Sentence								
Other Sentence								

more population,[28] about 20 per cent more bank deposits[29] and with only 18 per cent less total sales volume[30] than the corresponding four Nebraska counties, the four Colorado counties, Table 69, had only 347 bad-check cases in all their courts, while the four Nebraska counties, Table 72, had 495 cases. Thus, under the more lenient laws and in an area with more population, more bank deposits and almost as great a volume of retail sales, Colorado had 30 per cent less bad-check cases in court. The greater strictness of the law covering the same area of activity does not seem to decrease the number of cases but actually to increase them.

Of course it might be argued that the Colorado officials are more lax under the more lenient statutes; but as already shown, they collect

[28] Table 61, supra p. 355.
[29] Table 60, supra p. 354.
[30] Table 61, supra p. 355.

TABLE 71

Four Colorado Counties
Disposition of Bad-Check Cases
District Courts, 1952 and 1953
(Check Cases Classified by Type of Crime)

Disposition	Total		Forgery		Confidence Game		Short-Check	
	Num-ber	Per Cent	Num-ber	Per Cent	Num-ber	Per Cent	Num-ber	Per Cent
Total	49	100.0	39	100.0	10	100.0	0	0
Without Sentence	5	10.2	4	10.3	1	10.0	0	0
No Warrant Ret.								
Dismissed	4	8.2	4	10.3				
Paid								
Acquitted								
Warrant Collected, No Other Record								
No Record	1	2.0			1*	10.0		
With Sentence	44	89.8	35	89.7	9	90.0	0	0
Penitentiary	26	53.1	22	56.4	4	40.0		
Reformatory	8	16.3	7	17.9	1	10.0		
Women's Reformatory								
Mental Hospital								
State School								
Probation or Parole	9	18.4	6	15.4	3	30.0		
Suspended Sentence								
Jail								
Fine								
Other Sentence or No Rec. of Type	1	2.0			1	10.0		

* Escaped.

a greater proportion of bad checks than do the officials in Nebraska.[31] The court figures also show that in all the courts in Colorado, Table 69, 49.8 per cent of the check defendants went without sentencing; while in Nebraska, Table 72, 50.3 per cent were in this class. In the lower courts in Colorado, Table 70, 52.7 per cent went without sentencing; while in Nebraska, Table 73, 46.4 per cent were without sentence.[32] But in the district courts of Colorado, Table 71, only 10.2 per cent were not sentenced; while in Nebraska, Table 74, this figure was

[31] Table 63, supra p. 358.
[32] This figure is smaller for Nebraska because, as shown in Table 78 infra, 32 per cent of the cases were bound over to the district court for disposal under their felony jurisdiction.

TABLE 72

Four Nebraska Counties
Disposition of Bad-Check Cases
All Courts, 1952 and 1953
(Check Cases Classified by Type of Crime)

Disposition	Total		Forgery		No-Account		Insufficient-Fund	
	Num-ber	Per Cent	Num-ber	Per Cent	Num-ber	Per Cent	Num-ber	Per Cent
Total	495	100.0	97	100.0	195	100.0	203	100.0
Without Sentence	249	50.3	46	47.4	110	56.4	93	45.8
No Warrant Ret.	130	26.3	35	36.1	66	33.9	29	14.3
Dismissed	107	21.6	10	10.3	40	20.5	57	28.1
Paid	9	1.8			4	2.0	5	2.4
Acquitted								
Warrant Collected, No Other Record	1	.2					1	.5
No Record	2	.4	1	1.0			1	.5
With Sentence	246	49.7	51	52.6	85	43.6	110	54.2
Penitentiary	60	12.1	23	23.7	37	19.0		
Reformatory	13	2.6	5	5.1	7	3.6	1	.5
Women's Reform.	1	.2			1	.5		
Mental Hospital	3	.6	2	2.1	1	.5		
State School	3	.6	2	2.1	1	.5		
Probation or Parole	39	7.9	13	13.4	21	10.8	5	2.4
Suspended Sentence	2	.4			1	.5	1	.5
Jail	19	3.8			10	5.1	9	4.4
Fine	100	20.3			6	3.1	94	46.4
Other Sentence	6	1.2	6	6.2				

13 per cent. So over all, the Colorado area sentenced 50.2 per cent of its bad-check writer defendants, while the similar Nebraska counties sentenced a few less, 49.7 per cent.

Turning to the area of short checks alone (insufficient- and no-fund in Nebraska) where the laws of the two states show the greatest variations, Table 75 indicates that in this segment, as in the entire field, the Colorado courts studied have less cases per capita, but more cases per thousand bad checks issued than do Nebraska courts. There are also more sentences per thousand bad checks but fewer imprisonments, due largely to the fact that the Colorado courts used fine and restitution more extensively than their Nebraska counterparts.[33] The

[33] In the Colorado courts, fines were assessed in 26.2 per cent of all cases filed. In Nebraska courts in the similar counties, 20.3 per cent were fined. Ordering restitution was a common practice of the Colorado courts, but it occurred only in spots in Nebraska.

TABLE 73

Four Nebraska Counties
Disposition of Bad-Check Cases
Lower Courts, 1952 and 1953
(Check Cases Classified by Type of Crime)

Disposition	Total		Forgery		No-Account		Insufficient-Fund		No Record of Type	
	Number	Per Cent	Number	Per Cent	Number	Per Cent	Number	Per Cent	Number	Per Cent
Total	492	100.0	98	100.0	148	100.0	193	100.0	53	100.0
Without Sentence	228	46.4	37	37.8	98	66.2	89	46.1	0	0
No Warrant Returned	130	26.5	35	35.7	62	41.9	29	15.0		
Dismissed	87	17.7	2	2.1	32	21.6	53	27.5		
Paid	9	1.8			4	2.7	5	2.6		
Acquitted										
Warrant Collected, No Other Record	1	.2					1	.5		
No Record	1	.2					1	.5		
Bound Over	159	32.3	61	62.2	42	28.4	3	1.6	53	100.0
With Sentence	105	21.3	0	0	8	5.4	101	52.3	0	0
Jail	9	1.8			4	2.7	9	4.7		
Fine	95	19.3			4	2.7	91	47.1		
State School										
Probation or Parole										
Suspended Sentence	1	.2					1	.5		
Other Sentence										

imprisonment figures in Colorado are necessarily almost entirely confined to jail sentences, because a short check as such cannot be a felony in Colorado.[34] It is only when such a check is used as part of a larger confidence game that its issue is subject to felony sentences.[35] On the whole, however, it should be noted that, taking together all imprisonments, both jail and penitentiary, for bad checks, the Colorado courts, under the more lenient laws, commit practically as many per thousand bad checks issued as do the Nebraska courts.

If anything, then, the Colorado courts, as a whole, were as strict or stricter in enforcing the more lenient laws than the Nebraska courts

[34] Colo. Rev. Stat. 40-14-10 (1953), cf. id. 40-10-1; People v. Lindsay, 202 P. (2d) 951 (Colo. 1949); cf. People v. Dist. Court, 119 Colo. 451, 208 P. (2d) 79 (1949).
[35] Munsell v. People, 222 P. (2d) 615 (Colo. 1951); McBride v. People, 248 P. (2d) 725 (Colo. 1952).

TABLE 74

Four Nebraska Counties
Disposition of Bad-Check Cases
District Courts, 1952 and 1953
(Check Cases Classified by Type of Crime)

Disposition	Total		Forgery		No-Account		Insufficient-Fund	
	Number	Per Cent	Number	Per Cent	Number	Per Cent	Number	Per Cent
Total	162	100.0	60	100.0	89	100.0	13	100.0
Without Sentence	21	13.0	9	15.0	8	9.0	4	30.8
No Warrant Ret.								
Dismissed	20	12.4	8	13.3	8	9.0	4	30.8
Paid								
Acquitted								
Warrant Collected, No Other Record								
No Record	1*	.6	1*	1.7				
With Sentence	141	87.0	51	85.0	81	91.0	9	69.2
Penitentiary	60	37.1	23	38.3	37	41.6		
Reformatory	13	8.0	5	8.3	7	7.9	1	7.7
Women's Reform.	1	.6			1	1.1		
Mental Hospital	3	1.8	1	1.7	2	2.3		
State School	3	1.8	3	5.0				
Probation or Parole	39	24.1	13	21.7	21	23.6	5	38.4
Suspended Sentence	1	.6			1	1.1		
Jail	10	6.2			10	11.2		
Fine	5	3.1			2	2.3	3	23.1
Other Sentence or No Rec. of Type	6	3.7	6	10.0				

* "Transferred."

were with the stricter statutes. The smaller number of cases in the Colorado courts may be accounted for by the efficiency of collection of checks by the sheriffs,[36] and the fact that there were fewer criminal checks in Colorado.[37]

In the area of forgery, where the law in Colorado is as strict as in Nebraska, it is interesting to note that all the Colorado courts, Table 69, sentenced 76 per cent of these defendants; while in the Nebraska area, Table 72, only 53 per cent of the forgers were sentenced. In the field of short checks (insufficient- and no-account in Nebraska),

[36] See Table 63, supra p. 358.
[37] See Table 60, supra p. 354.

TABLE 75

Short-Check Cases, Sentences, Imprisonments, Misdemeanors and Felonies—Four Colorado Counties Compared with Four Nebraska Counties, Annual Average

County	Number of Cases			Number of Sentences			Number of Imprisonment Sentences			Misdemeanors Jail Sentences			Felony Sentences Penitentiary and Reformatory		
	Annual Total	Per 1000 People	Per 1000 Checks	Annual Total	Per 1000 People	Per 1000 Checks	Annual Total	Per 1000 People	Per 1000 Checks	Annual Total	Per 1000 People	Per 1000 Checks	Annual Total	Per 1000 People	Per 1000 Checks
Nebraska															
1	7.0	.243	1.273	3.5	.121	.636	2.5*	0.87	.455	0	0	0	2.0	.069	.364
5	14.5	1.200	.523	6.5	.538	.234	5.5	.455	.198	2.0	.166	.072	3.5	.290	.126
18	71.0	2.206	6.796	29.0	.901	2.776	11.5	.357	1.101	5.5	.171	.526	6.0	.186	.574
26	106.5	3.138	5.095	58.5	1.724	2.799	14.0*	.413	.670	2.0	.059	.096	11.5	.339	.550
Total	199.0	1.859	3.081	97.5	.911	1.509	33.5	.313	.519	9.5	.089	.147	23.0	.215	.356
Colorado															
1	10.5	.241	.935	5.0	.114	.445	.5	.011	.045	0	0	0	.5	.011	.045
2	25.0	1.389	2.577	10.0	.555	1.031	2.0	.111	.206	1.0	.056	.103	1.0	.056	.103
3	89.0	1.317	6.192	40.0	.592	2.783	11.0	.163	.765	10.0	.148	.696	1.0	.015	.696
4	26.0	1.511	4.407	14.5	.843	2.458	7.0	.407	1.186	7.0	.407	1.186	0	0	0
Total	150.5	1.029	3.653	74.5	.509	1.808	20.5	.140	.498	18.0	.123	.437	2.5	.017	.061

* Nebraska County 1—5 in State Hospital
Nebraska County 26—5 in State Hospital

49 per cent of the Nebraska defendants were sentenced, and 45 per cent of the Colorado short-check writers were convicted. In light of these figures, it is impossible to say that the courts of either area were more lenient in the handling of bad-check writers. If any conclusion is warranted, it may be that in Colorado, where the law is more lenient for short checks and strict for forgeries, the forgery law gets more literal interpretation than it does in Nebraska, where forgeries are only part of a widespread felony system covering a much larger area of bad checks than in **Colorado**.

TABLE 76

New Hampshire One County, Disposition of Bad-Check Cases, 1953, All Courts (Checks Classified by Type of Crime)

Disposition	Total		Forgery		Larceny by Check	
	Number	Per Cent	Number	Per Cent	Number	Per Cent
Total	13	100.0	3	100.0	10	100.0
Without Sentence	2	15.4	2	66.7	0	0
Dismissed	2	15.4	2	66.7		
With Sentence	11	84.6	1	33.3	10	100.0
Penitentiary	2	15.4	1	33.3	1	10.0
Probation or Parole	2	15.4			2	20.0
Jail	7	53.8			7	70.0

TABLE 77

Vermont One County, Disposition of Bad-Check Cases, 1953, City Court* (County Court Had No Check Cases, 1953)

Disposition	Total		Forgery		Uttering No-Fund Check		Obtaining Money under False Pretenses		Obtaining Money by False Token	
	No.	Per Cent	No.	Per Cent	No.	Per Cent	No.	Per Cent	No.	Per Cent
Total	9	100.0	4	100.0	1	100.0	1	100.0	3	100.0
Without Sentence	2	22.2	2	50.0	0	0	0	0	0	0
Dismissed	1	11.1	1	25.0						
Acquitted	1	11.1	1	25.0						
With Sentence	7	77.8	2	50.0	1	100.0	1	100.0	3	100.0
Penitentiary	3	33.3	1	25.0	1	100.0	1	100.0		
Jail	4	44.4	1	25.0					3	100.0

* This court was only court in county with check cases. Checks classified by type of crime; but the records of the other courts disclosed no check cases.

The total figures from New Hampshire and Vermont, set out in Tables 76 and 77,[38] do not cover a sufficiently large number of counties to offer a useful statistical comparison.

DOCKET AND WORK-LOAD OF THE COURTS

When the dockets and work-loads of the courts in Colorado and Nebraska are compared, it will be seen that the Colorado courts are doing a much more efficient job of law enforcement under the Colorado statutes than are the Nebraska courts under their law. Tables 78 and 79 show the comparative output of the courts in the two states so far as bad checks are concerned.

Table 78 shows that in the four Colorado counties, only the justice of the peace and district courts have check cases and none appear in the county courts, while in Nebraska, these cases are scattered over all three court systems. Further, 32.1 per cent of the check cases in Nebraska are tried in the lower courts, either county or justice of the

TABLE 78

*Distribution of Check Cases, Four Nebraska Counties
Compared with Four Colorado Counties, 1952 and 1953*

	All Courts Number of Cases			
	Four Nebraska Counties		Four Colorado Counties	
	Number	Per Cent	Number	Per Cent
Cases Filed				
All Courts Total (Net)	495	100.0	347	100.0
District Courts	162	32.7	49	14.1
Lower Courts	492	99.4	319	92.2
Bound over,				
Lower to District Courts	159	32.1	21	6.0
Cases Terminated				
District Courts	162	32.7	49	14.1
Lower Courts	333	67.3	298	85.9
Lower Courts Total Cases	492	100.0	319	100.0
Justice of the Peace Courts	154*	31.3*	319	100.0
County Courts	338*	68.7*	0	0

* One Nebraska county filed the bulk of its lower court cases (154 out of 162) in the justice of the peace courts. The other three counties used only the county courts for check cases.

[38] It is interesting to note that in the Vermont courts, which were operating after a very effective legalized collection system, there were practically no short-check cases, and that among those that were brought, convictions were much higher than in Colorado and Nebraska; but compare also the high rate of convictions in New Hampshire.

376

TABLE 79

Comparison of Four Nebraska Counties with Four Colorado Counties, 1952 and 1953
(Check Cases Classified by Type of Crime)

Courts	Four Nebraska Counties				Four Colorado Counties	
	Number	Per Cent			Number	Per Cent
Total All Courts						
Total	495	100.0		Total	347	100.0
Forgery	97	19.6		Forgery	46	13.3
No-Account }				Confidence Game*	10	2.9
Insufficient-Fund }	398	80.4		Short-Check	291	83.8
Lower Courts						
Total	492	100.0		Total	319	100.0
Forgery	98	20.0		Forgery	25	7.9
No-Account				Confidence Game*	3	.9
Insufficient-Fund				Short-Check	291	91.2
No Record of Type	394	80.0				
District Courts						
Total	162	100.0		Total	49	100.0
Forgery	60	37.0		Forgery	39	79.6
No-Account }				Confidence Game*	10	20.4
Insufficient-Fund }	102	63.0		Short-Check	0	0

* Only confidence game cases involving checks are listed here.

peace, and then bound over to be tried again in the district courts; while in Colorado, only six per cent of the check cases are so handled. Since the typical check case is simple in its facts and over 95 per cent of the defendants plead guilty,[39] there is no administrative necessity for this duplication, which involves a waste of the time of the courts and a delay in justice while the defendant waits in jail to be bound over to the district court; but the optional felony penalties for no-account checks and the mandatory felony sentences for insufficient-fund checks over $35 make this procedure necessary in Nebraska. For this same reason, it should be noted that the justice of the peace courts in Colorado handled 93.4 per cent of all their check cases and 85.9 per cent of the whole of the check cases to a conclusion, while in Nebraska, the lower courts, both justice of the peace and county, finally disposed of only 67.7 per cent of the cases. This state of the law also caused 32.7 per cent of all the check cases to terminate in the district court in Ne-

[39] See Table 39, supra p. 312.

braska, while only 14.1 per cent were so terminated in Colorado. It should also be noted that 63 per cent of the check cases in the district courts of Nebraska were of the short-check classification group which never reached the district courts in Colorado.

Since the bad-check cases are all simple and susceptible of easy proof, since there is no necessity and no demand for jury trial and little need for the services of legal counsel,[40] the great majority of these cases can be disposed of administratively. Only forgery cases require any complicated trial procedures. These, of course, receive equal service in each state; so it appears that the Colorado law results in a much more efficient court procedure than do the Nebraska statutes. The businessmen get better collection and the criminal is brought to swifter and more effective justice under the more lenient laws of Colorado than under the heavy-handed felony system of Nebraska.

V. SUGGESTIONS FOR FURTHER STUDY OF THE BAD-CHECK PROBLEM

The fields of possible further fruitful study of the bad-check problem indicated here are numerous and should be obvious to the thoughtful reader. It seems wise at this time only to discuss a few.

The need for a psychiatric study of bad-check offenders seems to be indicated. The statistical material taken from the files of the Penitentiary and Reformatory show that bad-check writers are a different class of criminals from other felons. They seem to be more intelligent, in fact as intelligent as a representative cross-section of society; but there also appears to be a strong tendency among them to develop into habitual criminals. It would be important to discover whether or not this tendency is greater among bad-check writers than in other classes of inmates of the Penitentiary. The question is also raised whether or not there are psychiatric deviations in bad-check writers which differ from those found among the other criminals. Finding the answer to this question might make it possible to prescribe treatment to prevent criminal tendencies toward bad-check writing early in life. These and many other bits of evidence indicate that a study by a team of psychiatrists, criminologists and lawyers at not too great expense might yield valuable information on the criminals in this class.

The variation in the bad-check rate in various states which appears in the meager studies of New Hampshire and Vermont as compared

[40] Supra p. 312.

with Nebraska and Colorado indicates a fertile field for further study. There must be factors in these states other than the condition of the laws and enforcement practices which may account for this apparent difference in the number of bad checks as related to total population and total business. If an investigation in this area were carried forward and perhaps extended to other states, it seems that much useful data could be easily disclosed. In the absence of a careful study of factors involved, it seems that few techniques or methods other than those developed in the current study would be needed to effectuate a further investigation in this area.

The legalizing of the collection practice by public officials also needs further study. Vermont, where the body attachment is still used, is the only state where this practice is now legally recognized. It therefore offers a unique opportunity to study further the possibilities of refining this method of social control of the bad-check phenomena. If the proposed statute set out in the Appendix were adopted, it would then be possible to carry forward such a study in any such jurisdiction on a more complete experimental basis than has been possible here.

Comparative enforcement policies based both on the state of the statutes and upon the administration practices thereunder in the various states also offer a fruitful field for further investigation. Here the application of more elegant statistical methods, more careful sampling and greater refinement in interviewing techniques would go a long way toward substantiating or changing the jural laws and hypotheses suggested in Chapter XII.

These are only a few possibilities of further study which obviously suggest themselves. The thoughtful reader can add many more.

The suggestion of fields or types of laws which might yield useful results or further study does not appear to be wise at this time. Although some slight effort in this direction was attempted in Chapter VIII and may appear to be suggested from the pilot studies set out in Chapters VIII and IX, the variation in the facts of the social situations surrounding laws, the detailed provisions of the statutes themselves, and their impact upon administration are so various that a careful examination of each statute proposed for study seems necessary. Here the technique of pilot studies and preliminary investigation will prove very useful. With the meager information available at this time, it would be rash to attempt to classify either civil or criminal laws in an effort to decide at best what might be most fruitfully subjected to the methods of study indicated by Experimental Jurisprudence. Here again long and careful experimentation itself may prove a necessary prerequisite to useful knowledge.

CHAPTER XII

Suggested Hypotheses, Jural Laws, and Further Application of Experimental Jurisprudence

It might be useful to review the various steps in the process of Experimental Jurisprudence in light of the material discussed throughout this book to see what concrete results may be expected from application of the suggested methods.

The materials in Chapter VIII and in Part II, although taken from brief pilot studies and incomplete results, show great possibilities for a broader application of the technique of Experimental Jurisprudence. Even though the evidence set out there covers only partial studies and indicates that the support of a permanent organization is best calculated to produce conclusive results, still many interesting suggestions emerge. The following discussion, except where it is noted to the contrary, will be limited almost entirely to subjects arising from the materials exposed in the five pilot studies, the study of bad checks and other matters mentioned in preceding chapters. In the interests of accuracy, it should also be noted that where this material and the tentative conclusions from the bad-check studies are used as evidence to support the statement of conclusions and jural laws, they are used as they theoretically would be only if they were proven to be true. In most cases it is realized that the facts herein assumed rest on something less than tenuous inferences, so the conclusions and jural laws herein set out, resting as they do upon such speculative evidence, are not offered as ultimate findings but only as indications of the manner in which jural laws evolve and the kind of material which would emerge if and when like sound results were produced. In spite of this limited factual basis, it will be useful to summarize what the various steps in the process of Experimental Jurisprudence, as set out in Chapter II, might be expected to yield, relying only on our present information and techniques.

NATURE OF THE PHENOMENA REGULATED

The nature of the phenomena the law attempts to regulate is entirely within the reach of the experimental jurist and his team of experts. The pilot studies illustrate that one can, in most cases, start from a particular statute and reason back to the problem which it intends to solve. Although the historical reasons for passing the statute are often missing, they can be reconstructed, as in the case of the cigarette law regarding smoking by minors, rules requiring sterilization of barber's instruments and the other statutes regulating various types of activities, so that the purpose of the law is sufficiently clear for a basis of study. In the case of the bad-check statutes, the reasons are self-evident.

The facts surrounding the activities which the law seeks to regulate, if care is used in delimiting the field of inquiry as shown by the examples set out, are entirely within the reach of known methods of sociological research or of such devices as the investigators may be able to contrive. More complicated statutes will of course disclose a more difficult social background with the necessity for more extensive sociological research to reach the problems which they encompass. But as studies progress from the simple to the complex, more research techniques and measuring devices are certain to appear.

STATEMENT OF THE LAW

Accurate statements of the rule of law and the administrative methods for enforcement which are also regulated by law are entirely within the grasp of any good lawyer as now trained. These include, of course, statutes, ordinances and regulations, and to some extent judicial actions, decisions and administrative variations in the form of rules and established practices. Here the claim of the realist school of jurisprudence that what the officers do is the law is easily shown to be an impossibility by the results of the bad-check study. These actions, even in the single state of Nebraska, as indicated there are completely conflicting;[1] thus they obviously could not be the law, but they do throw important light upon its effect through more or less authoritative interpretations placed thereon by the officials involved.

As shown by the preliminary studies on tree-planting[2] and weights and measures,[3] the law on even simple subjects is far more intricate

---

[1] For the conflicting action of sheriff's and county attorneys, see supra pp. 289, 290 ff, and for the variation in court behavior, see supra pp. 306 ff.

[2] Supra pp. 174 ff.

[3] Supra p. 209, N. 22.

than is ordinarily supposed. This fact has long been known to the legal profession, but it is almost wholly overlooked by layman and social scientists. These complications seem to take three forms: (1) Although the states are no longer isolated, and transactions under one may affect many others, the laws of the several states are in wide variation on the same subjects. (2) Statutes within a single state on the same topic when enforcement is attempted may be found to be vague, conflicting and contradictory. (3) Solution of the same problem may be authorized by law to be undertaken simultaneously by state, county, city, and federal statutes or regulations having the force of law. Reconciliation of this maze of overlapping and often contradictory laws in itself offers a field of serious analytical research for the lawyer to determine just what is the law governing the particular problem at hand.

Although it is clear that the law on any subject is far more complicated than is usually assumed in law schools or by legal philosophers, there is nothing here beyond the ability of a good research lawyer to uncover, correlate and expose to analysis. When this is thoroughly done, many recommendations for improvement or further research will be self-evident.

EFFECT OF THE LAWS

The effects of the laws which can be stated even as shown by these simple studies are multifarious. In the case of the bad-check study, Chapter XI on results indicates in detail how these laws affected the communities visited. The following are simply a few generalizations deduced from all of these studies.

The complications in the statement of laws such as are noted above have caused much confusion in their administration. Examples of this may be found in the mistakes of the officials in changing the age of persons to whom tobacco could be sold from 21 to 18 on the licenses issued to tobacco dealers.[4] Thus the resulting chaos or lack of action in enforcement can to some extent be traced directly to the confusing statutes themselves. An even more striking example is the situation under the plumbing code where the variations in administrative rules have become so numerous that the building and plumbing inspectors stand practically in the position of dictators.[5] This result, of course, is contrary to the constitutional demand that there be standards in the delegation of power by legislation, but it is a clear outgrowth of the defects of set rules of law in a field where there should be broad delegation to effectuate adequate administration.

[4] Supra p. 205.
[5] Supra p. 217.

Enforcement of law is found to range all the way from zero up toward 100 per cent. In the case of statutes prescribing the size of bricks, the law had no influence whatsoever.[6] Regulations for planting trees commanded very little, if any, attention;[7] but when smoking by minors was involved, enforcement, though almost complete on the matter of issuing of and payment for licenses, was entirely lacking when it came to punishment for illegal sales or use of tobacco.[8] The influence of the barbers' tools sterilization statute was perhaps less than 50 per cent effective,[9] and the plumbing statute, which most closely affected the occupation and livelihood of a particular class of people, seemed to be most effectively enforced against the licensed plumbers, even though the administrative agents were taking the law into their own hands.[10] On the other hand, the enforcement of the bad-check laws was shown to vary all the way from zero to a high percentage of efficiency, with sporadic variations.[11] Thus official discretion and business pressure created a collection type of enforcement.[12] This was not only not contemplated by the statute but was contrary to accepted legal ethics and theory.[13]

Among other things, this failure of officials to act clearly, decisively and effectively may be followed by lack of knowledge of the law in the public, which, to a large degree, is ignorantly or wilfully ignoring its provisions. Here again the variation is wide, ranging from complete ignorance of the law in the case of the brick statute through wide disregard in tree-planting and smoking by minors to some attempt at compliance in the case of barbers sterilizing their instruments and plumbers obeying the dictates of administrators who had assumed arbitrary power to vitally affect their livelihood. In the case of checks where the public seemed conscious of the law, its purposes were nevertheless diverted by transferring law enforcement agencies into a commercial collection service.

Many of the laws when enforced require actions and results which are out of line with the known requirements of contemporary science or run counter to established and useful trade practices or harmless mores. Here the laws seem to be based on little more than prejudices,

---

[6] Supra p. 210.
[7] Supra pp. 176 ff.
[8] Supra p. 205.
[9] Supra pp. 198, 199 ff.
[10] Supra pp. 217 ff.
[11] See Figure 5, supra p. 294.
[12] Supra pp. 293 ff.
[13] Supra p. 289.

old wives' tales or outworn social customs. The intervals required in planting trees,[14] the liquids specified for sterilization of barbers' instruments,[15] and the specifications of the size of bricks clearly run contrary to the dictates of science.[16] The rules for smoking by minors are perhaps unscientific and are obviously based on prejudices and outworn social customs. The specifications for plumbing seem to be an example which is somewhat affected by all three of these defects. The check laws are the best example of the statutes being out of line with the trade practices they seek to support.[17]

HYPOTHESES FROM OBSERVED REACTIONS

Possible hypotheses on observed reactions to the laws are, of course, legion, and at this stage are limited only by the imagination of the observers, hardly held in check by a few of the observed facts. As the collection of data increases and the facts are carefully compiled and ordered, the number of apparently tentative hypotheses will, of course, diminish. It is not possible in the present state of research to offer with any confidence suggestions that are hoped to be conclusive, but a few random and exceedingly tentative hypotheses might be mentioned to indicate the type of thing which further scientific research would be expected to develop and establish. Some of the suggested hypotheses will seem to be almost self-evident, while others will appear fantastic and perhaps beyond present means of confirmation.

ADMINISTRATIVE DISCRETION

These studies indicate that the old slogan, "Ours is a government of laws and not of men," is an expression of a hope rather than a statement of fact. The administrative discretion which is exercised by the officials of American governmental units is far beyond that which appears on the face of the Constitution or statutes. Figure 5[18] shows that, in spite of the fact that legal duties, ethics and words of the law require criminal prosecutions, the enforcement of the bad-check laws in Nebraska varies from almost nothing at all to a conscientious attempt to incarcerate most of the violators. Courts, attorneys, sheriffs and judges were found in abundance who substituted their own system of collection for the plain meaning of the statutes,[19] just as the plumbing in-

[14] Supra p. 175.
[15] Supra p. 195.
[16] Supra p. 211 ff.
[17] Supra p. 278 ff.
[18] Supra p. 294.
[19] Supra p. 291 ff., 314 ff.

spector allowed his own judgment and not the rules of law to determine the type of pipe used in constructing new houses.[20]

In the exercise of these administrative prerogatives, for reasons of their own, officials may also entirely ignore the easily duducible intent of the statutes and refuse to enforce the laws against smoking or those requiring clear rules for dimensions of bricks. Even among conscientious judges who purported more than others to be bound by the law, there is a marked tendency to stretch discretion to achieve extra-legal results.[20] This tendency seems to increase as one leaves the area of life or long terms for officials with broad jurisdiction and few local contacts and approaches those officials who serve local governments "close to the people."[21] These variations, of course, are partly determined by the personality, honesty and integrity of the particular official, but the information at hand indicates that there are other underlying causes of deviations in official actions which will be found to affect policy. The reasons for these variations appear in inertia, public pressure, quality of officials and the nature of compensation in the form of good will, re-election, salaries, etc., which they receive for their services. Careful statistical studies averaging out the personal elements should disclose these factors, which in turn may prove to be so uniformly present that hypotheses can be devised to plot the nature and course of the variations from the expected legal norm.[22]

CONFUSION RESULTING FROM VAGUE LAWS

Among the first hypotheses that may be advanced is the explanation that confusion in the laws results in confusion in administration. Self-evident reasons are many. Under our present form of government, key public officials charged with law enforcement are elected, and as a rule, their tenure of office is short-lived. Lesser officials who are on a lower level usually owe their positions to appointment. Even under civil service, they are at the mercy of elected officials. The terms of these "policy directors" are short, and the ever-present task of seeking re-election presses hard upon them. They do not therefore have the time to devote to the reconciliation of conflicting laws. Their assistants being, by and large, political hangers-on, they are likely not to be fitted to solve such problems. Insofar as they have expert legal advice, it will be found to

[20] Supra p. 221 ff. For this same tendency even in the Supreme Court of the United States see, Rodell, Nine Old Men (1955).

[21] Note especially this yielding to pressure among the sheriffs and county attorneys, supra p. 292 ff.

[22] See this tendency in Tables 28, 29, 59 and in the materials comparing enforcement in Nebraska and Colorado, supra p. 253 ff.

be temporary or of short duration, the attorneys being underpaid and usually more interested in establishing outside connections than in working out difficult conflicts in the law. Similar deficiencies are likely to be encountered with other professional help. There is also the ever-present necessity of keeping public relations on a cordial plane; otherwise the very basis of the power of public office may be threatened. Therefore the effect will be to resolve any conflicts in the law along the lines of least resistance. So the solution which adversely affects the interest of the most people is certain to be avoided, regardless of the verbiage and purposes of the vague laws. This hypothesis may explain the fact that the age at which customers could buy cigarettes was reduced from 21 to 18 on a slight pretext of ambiguity because it removed the area of conflict with dealers and customers in three age brackets of the potential purchasers.[23] In like fashion it may reveal the reason why the machinery of the criminal laws against bad checks is turned into a commercial collection agency contrary to, and beyond the authority of, the law.[24]

LAWS BASED UPON OUTWORN OR DISCARDED MORAL CONCEPTS

Laws based upon outworn or discarded moral concepts will be found to meet with resistance for a number of reasons. Individual moral standards will be found to be exceedingly various and conflicting upon any question in any stage of society. If a test were taken on such a basic subject as the validity of the Ten Commandments, it would be found that a large portion of society in the case of each, and a majority in many, did not believe in or practice the admonitions there set out. When this is applied to admittedly outworn beliefs like the idea that it is wrong to smoke cigarettes or play ball on Sunday, although the rules can still find supporters, the great majority of the public will be opposed to the beliefs. So any statute enacting into law any moral code whatsoever, being an attempt to force upon some of the population the morals of others, will not be popular in many quarters.

The fact that one or another of the numerous degrees of moral codes available has been enacted into law will affect only slightly the beliefs and perhaps will change even less the interests of the people it affects. Thus it will become apparent that the success of an attempt to enforce morals by law will be dependent upon the amount of imbalance of the pressures on both sides. The greater the preponderance of pressure behind enforcement, the less effort will have to be ex-

---

[23] Supra p. 205.
[24] Supra p. 289 ff.

pended by the law enforcement officials. If the law is to be effective as pressure behind the law diminishes, efforts to enforce must be increased, and as resistance, either passive or active, to the law increases, still more power must go into enforcement. Under these circumstances there comes a point where the effort to enforce outworn moral concepts by law is not worth the price. Theoretically at this point the law should be repealed, but since our legislatures do not have the time, knowledge or research staff to determine this repeal point for each of the myriad laws on the books, the enforcement officials are called upon to make the decisions themselves.

This decision usually appears in the form of laxity of enforcement, because strict complience costs too much in popularity or other discomforts. Where the law loses popular support and gains opposition, as in the case of smoking cigarettes by minors or applying felony penalties to bad-check writers, the enforcement begins to disappear.

In like fashion, laws affecting commercial interests will tend to lose enforcement as they lose interest behind them and there is built up economic opposition. The dealer who sees a large and profitable market for cigarettes among minors, little chance of public indignation and no sign of harm in selling becomes an habitual lawbreaker and enforcement officials see no use in stopping him. So likewise when a merchant has been paid for the bad check, he no longer is interested in criminal prosecution of the bad-check writer.[25]

This is even clearer in the case where selling bricks contrary to the statute creates no opposition among the public, the manufacturers or in any customer, and the law is nullified collectively by the dealer, the citizen and the law enforcement official.[26]

LAW CONTRARY TO SCIENCE

In cases where legally required courses of action are found to run contrary to the discoveries of science, similar forces are at work. Where, as in the building codes, the law requires the use of certain pipes which have been proved to be inadequate for the purpose for which they are being installed, the purchaser will resist enforcement of the code, the plumber does not want to lose the good will of the customer, and the inspector, knowing that the legally required pipe is no better or not as good as the illegal substitute, sees no purpose in enforcing, against mounting opposition, a line of conduct which is certain to fail

[25] Supra p. 293.
[26] Supra p. 213.

to accomplish the purpose for which it was prescribed.[27] The tendency is to follow the line of least resistance and vary the code provisions.

In cases where the scientific usefulness of the prescribed action is doubtful or negligible and the resulting discomfort or loss of business is great, the pressure against law enforcement is likely to be too strong for the officials, who will find it expedient not to enforce the useless laws and to await legislative action. The failure to enforce the use of some of the unpleasant statutory liquids to sterilize barbers' instruments is a good example of the working of this hypothesis.[28] Where, as in the case of bricks, enforcement of a law in changed business conditions would be at complete variance with the scientific purpose for which it was created, the statute becomes a nullity.[29]

REGULATORY LAWS IN GREAT DETAIL

A corollary to those same principles is the fact that laws specifying in detail a line of action are likely to run into opposition and disuse.[30] In a rapidly changing society like ours where science and inventions are constantly creating new and better ways of supplying human needs, laws specifying a particular detailed line of conduct are likely to become obsolete through variations from approved and useful methods. Thus, fixed details of the interval between trees fail to take into account the variation in species, soil, road conditions and private taste;[31] rigid speed limits ignore improvements in roads and in safety devices for automobiles,[32] likewise prescription of particular antiseptics denies the progress of science and is attempting to freeze a state of social activity in a changing society.[33] Such rules seem to develop types of friction and lose social support in the same manner as fixed rules of law seeking to freeze morals or commercial practices. The result, like the others, is a tendency toward breakdown of enforcement.

THE TREND TO OVERLAPPING LAWS

One of the most interesting phenomena observed in all the studies of the administration of various laws was the tendency toward duplication. Almost every investigation showed that where the law attempted

---

[27] Supra p. 220 ff.

[28] Supra p. 199.

[29] Supra pp. 210.

[30] For an example of this principle appearing after exhaustive study, see Dahlberg, Adams and Held, Sanitary Milk Control, Nat. R. Com. 104 ff. (1953).

[31] Supra p. 177 ff.

[32] Supra p. 126 ff.

[33] Supra p. 199.

to reach a solution of a general problem which existed within the geographic jurisdiction of any governmental unit, there was an effort to cope with the problem on a number of levels of government covering the area. Although the legal solutions were found to vary, it was notable that, in spite of theoretical constitutional limitations, some solution was available under national, state and local laws. If this tendency is confirmed by broader studies, which casual observation indicates it is almost certain to be,[34] its existence is subject to interesting hypotheses which are likely to throw grave doubts upon the theories back of the distribution of powers in our present governmental system.

In the first place, it should be noted that most of the clashes of interest between human beings which result in problems requiring legal solutions are universal, in the sense that they are found wherever there are people. Most needs and demands do not follow geographical boundaries; neither do they fall into the arbitrary and historical classifications which are the basis of the divisions of sovereignty between governmental units or the separation of powers between the various branches of a single governmental unit. It would be a rare case indeed where a human problem seeking legal solution would fall wholly within the jurisdictional powers of a single city, county, state or national government. Human clashes of interest requiring legal resolution will be found to cross jurisdictional lines much as molasses poured upon a checkerboard soon covers the squares, runs onto the table and then over the floor. Each of the governmental units as now constituted is likely to get a contact with part of the problem.

When this phenomenon is approached from the point of view of pressure upon lawmaking bodies, it may be expected that people seeking remedies will approach the most convenient legislative or administrative body. Pressure groups, not being experts in constitutional structure, and looking for legal rules to solve their problems, will go after any official who seems to promise a remedy.

Looked at from the point of view of the official, courts alone are the most nearly completely sophisticated about the limits of their jurisdiction, administrators less so, and legislators are the most subject to pressure for laws. In these circumstances, legislators in all branches of government are most likely to respond to pressure by creating a law,

---

[34] This tendency has been evident in every law studied in this text; for example, the traffic study in Chapter VI, the milk regulations in Chapter VII, the bad-check study in Part II, where city, county, state and national officials take part in apprehending writers. In addition to the materials published in this text, this has been the state of the law in over 30 pilot studies conducted on other laws by the writer and his students.

and administrators may be found to yield to similar pressure to stretch their delegated powers to solve the problem. Even courts have been known to go outside the law to grant popularly demanded relief.[35]

So far as administrators are concerned, there is also the phenomenon of grasping for power by many bureau chiefs and subordinates which is well known to every budget officer. This human frailty often causes them to reach out and to take in the solution of problems which lie on the borders of their little empires.

The net result of it all is the creation of overlapping legal devices of federal, state and local units and further conflict in the exercise of the powers within particular branches of the three classes of units. Just as there is a constant pressure toward overlapping powers, there is also a tendency, once the power is established and the legal remedy set up, to allow the exercise of the power to atrophy through slackening of the pressures which created it, inertia in the personnel or frustration caused by more efficient exercise of the problem-solving technique by rival agencies.[36]

The study of this phenomenon of overlapping government is one of the most important phases of Experimental Jurisprudence, and the understanding of the jural laws governing its operation will be one of the most necessary achievements of legal science if governmental organization is to be kept efficiently abreast of the task which it faces in the future.

FAILURE TO ENFORCE PENALTY PROVISIONS

The failure to enforce penalty provisions as required by law was quite obvious in the case of bad checks.[37] The reasons for this may be many, but it is rather clear that the public as a whole is relatively careless about its check writing. The felony requirements for no-account checks of any amount and for insufficient-fund checks beginning at $35 is much more severe than the larceny statutes and for many financial derelictions.[38] The idea that a man should be sentenced for ten to

[35] See the decision of Dennis v. U. S., 71 S. Ct. 857 (1951) which Mr. Justice Black states in his dissent, at 903, was dictated by public passion; and see Rodell, Nine Men (1955).

[36] This tendency was shown all through the bad-check study where in some counties the county attorney collected checks, in others it was the sheriff, and in some both, see supra p. 290 ff. In like manner the justice of peace courts handled checks in some counties, in others the county courts, and in still others the district courts. In many this was to the exclusion of one or more of the others.

[37] See Figure 1, p. 237.

[38] The line between misdemeanors and felonies for other property is $100, see Neb. Rev. Stat. §§ 28-506 to 28-513 (1953 Supp.).

twenty years imprisonment on conviction for the third time of writing a $10 no-fund check is revolting to most people, yet this is the law.[39] It is not surprising then that prosecutors and judges who are dependent upon popularity to hold their positions in the community refuse, whenever possible, to do the bidding of a legislature apparently driven by a small group of credit men and bankers to make such minor derelictions a felony. The amount of loss involved in these cases simply will not inflame sufficient public opinion to support the tough felony sentences required by law.[40]

MORE EFFICIENT LAW ENFORCEMENT UNDER LESSER PENALTIES

More efficient law enforcement under lesser penalties seems to be the result of this feeling. When the law enforcement official finds it necessary or useful to refuse to enforce a statute, it is easy for this laxity to become habitual. On the other hand, where the penalties are smaller the official may find it more rewarding to do his duty. The over-all result, then, is that the lesser penalty gets tighter law enforcement policy, stronger public support and better achieves the social purpose of the statute.[41]

FAILURE OF HEAVY PENALTIES TO DETER CRIMES

The reasons for failure of heavy criminal penalties to deter the crimes of bad-check writing probably lie in the field of abnormal psychology and will not be completely explained until there has been much more research in this area.[42] It should be noted that the bad-check writers in the Penitentiary, though the most numerous, were a class of criminals by themselves.[43] The opportunity for psychological research here is tremendous and should be attempted. Pending such investigation, however, it might be noted that the lax enforcement of the too-strict penalties tends to let the prohibited crime go on unpunished; so even among that class of persons to whom punishment is a deterrent, if such a class exists, there is encouragement of the effervescent hope that the law will not catch up with the wrongdoer. In fact, it developed that most of the offenders had become habitual bad-check writers, caught and released many times before they received the first

[39] See supra p. 325 and authorities there cited.
[40] See supra p. 329 ff.
[41] See the comparative record of Nebraska and Colorado officials in enforcing the bad-check statutes of their respective states, supra p. 356ff.
[42] See Menninger, The Human Mind 446 ff. (1937); Andenaes, General Prevention—Illusion or Reality, 43 Jour. Cr. Law 178, 197 (1952).
[43] Supra p. 335 ff.

felony sentence for a series of crimes which the law classified as felonies.[44]

VERIFICATION

The hypotheses here mentioned are not advanced with any hope that they are a final or a sound explanation of the current phenomena surrounding even those few laws which were subjects of the studies outlined in Chapters VIII, IX and XI. They are at best only meager samples to illustrate what might be the product of more complete investigation. It should be noted, however, that each of the explanations here offered is capable of verification by further studies and experiments which are within the grasp of fact-finding techniques now available or capable of being created. In this way the scientific method can be set to work solving current social problems.

JURAL LAWS

Jural laws, like hypotheses, to be sound must be the product of thorough research and the checking and rechecking of the hypotheses. This, of course, is a process which will never be completed. Thus it is impossible here to state with accuracy or confidence any final or immutable jural law; but for the sake of illustration, it might be interesting to postulate five such jural laws as examples of what a more refined end-product might be. As indicated above, assuming that the illustrations in the pilot studies and the material there cited can be proved by proper statistical research, but realizing that at present such is usually not the case, the following jural laws are offered simply as illustrations of what might be expected on the basis of further research in the fields noted. As research widens and as their application to concrete situations is tested by adopting and enforcing new laws drafted with their tenets in mind, the jural laws will, of course, assume both different form and content, each change approaching a more complete explanation of the phenomena surrounding laws, their enactment and enforcement. Many more jural laws should also appear with further study.

It is clear, of course, that these jural laws are meant to apply only in a system of government where officials are elected. This was the sole source of the data upon which they are based. They might also be relevant in varying degrees in a dictatorship, but no such claims are made for them at this time. It is also possible that none of the five offered here will survive research and criticism; but if only one sur-

[44] Supra 345.

vives, or if they point the way to the discovery of others, they will have served their purpose.

The generalizations stated as jural laws might also be limited more accurately only to the material which was subject to the studies covered in this text. If this were done, each statement should be preceded by the limitation, "In the case of bad-check laws, traffic regulations, milk statutes, laws governing trees, cigarettes for minors, barbers, plumbing, etc., the following are the pertinent generalizations which observations seem to have disclosed." Accuracy then would require that each proposition in the form of a jural law be limited to the operation of those fields of positive law which are given as examples supporting it. If the reader cares to so limit them, there is no valid objection to his doing so; but long experience with and observation of the operation of other laws causes the writer to believe that the propositions stated as jural laws will be found to be much broader and to be present in the operation of many laws other than those given as illustrations. Just as the physical laws of conservation of energy and matter, though based upon a few observations, were stated generally and were useful in solving many engineering problems before they were proved by atomic experiment to be limited and inaccurate, so here the writer has chosen to state the jural laws more broadly than the experimental base would seem to warrant. This is done consciously in hope that others may test them in more diverse fields and may eventually prove the areas of their application and the nature of their inherent inaccuracies. Keeping in mind that they are intended as general statements of statistical results, which should be true on the average but not necessarily binding on individuals, some of these highly tentative jural laws might be like the following set out in italics. They are given here with a minimum of illustration and explanation.

Jural Law I: Laws will seldom be enforced literally either as they were written or intended.

This jural law is not intended to be limited only to obvious facts. It is truism from the psychological factors that the intent behind a law, except in a simple one-man dictatorship, is a composite thing and therefore not accurately ascertainable. Likewise there is the semantic difficulty that a gross intent, if discovered, cannot be reduced to words with minute delicacy. Assuming workable intelligence on these points where no certainty exists, it can be said with confidence that lawmakers never have before them the complete social facts surrounding problems which they seek to solve by creating a law. It is clear that there is at least one[45] optimum legal solution for each difficulty which is attempted to be resolved by lawmaking. A regulation in such perfect form could be said to supply the maximum of enforcement at least cost, giving the most useful result with a minimum of social friction in the form of interference with the needs and demands of members of the group regulated. Lawmakers will usually seek such a solution.

If draftsmanship were perfect, still the laws which are supposed to have universal application are predicated upon a partial knowledge of the social situation which they seek to remedy. *Ab initio,* they are therefore somewhat out of line with the requirements of an optimum regulation of the status quo; but since rules of law are timeless and intended to be effective until repealed, this condition of maladjustment with the facts of life which the law intends to control varies with the lapse of time. In a dynamic society the facts upon which a law is based are changing even as the law is being enacted, and these changes continue throughout its administration. This tendency to some extent is augmented or retarded by the effect of the law itself on society.

If lawmakers have acted wisely on complete information, the maladjustment at enactment between the law and immediate social conditions which it attempts to control may be slight; but more often lawmakers are neither wise nor well informed. They simply yield to the most insistent demands for a law which may not and usually does not fit the needs of those absent from the lobby or the polls. So pressure against enforcement and latent obsolescence may start with or before enactment.

Beyond the obvious divergencies mentioned above there are three major factors which influence the variation between the law as written and the law as enforced. The first is the relevance of the devices intended to be created by the words of the law to the wants of the society, the second is the interpretation put upon the written law by the officials and the third the relationship between the law as enforced and the pressures from needs and demands in the society affected.

The more the devices set up by the words of law vary from those needed to control the situation the law attempts to regulate, the less will they be enforced. Thus a law which fulfills no demands or needs is a dead letter,[46] and by like test, a law which satisfies many needs

[45] It is entirely possible that there may be a multiple number of possible legal solutions to the same problem which under the same conditions might get equally good results, but the principle here stated will apply with equal force to a variation from any perfect solution.

[46] For example, the brick statute, supra p. 210 ff.

without depriving anybody of anything is easily administered.[47] These needs and demands as indicated in Chapter III must, of course, be taken to be the ones objectively discernible by social research; and it is clear that for a law to be successful, there must be an overwhelming preponderance of active needs and demands on the side of the law enforcement.

Since laws do not enforce themselves, a second proposition under this jural law might be: The variations available through official interpretations are legion, and are likely to appear in direct proportion as the law fails to meet the needs of the situation or runs afoul of the pressure from demands of persons affected. Even before he starts to enforce the law, the official in charge will attempt to apply it to the situation where enforcement is needed. This application, as everyone knows, gives the law additional meaning and the official a rationalization to explain his actions. The needs of the situation will impinge heavily upon the meaning he will give the statute. When this occurs, administrative officials may come up with interpretations not intended or considered by the lawmakers. An example of this is found in the county attorney's letter turning the presumption of fraudulent intent on failure to pay five days after protest, found in the Nebraska insufficient-funds statute,[48] into a means of collecting for all bad checks.[49] Many other such variations by administrative action appear throughout these studies.[50]

This laxness of enforcement leads to a third corollary to the jural law. There is an optimum point at which a rule of law can be most effectively enforced. The location of this point depends upon how the means used to enforce the end sought affects the needs and demands of the persons regulated. Laws that seek ends out of line with the needs or strongly asserted demands of many individuals in the society are difficult of enforcement. There will be resistance to such laws when the objectives which they accomplish fail to meet the express needs and demands of individuals and organized social units. This resist-

[47] For example, the so-called G. I. Bill of Rights.

[48] 28-1214.

[49] See county attorney's form letter supra p. 290.

[50] For example, see the instances in which justices of the peace with the approval of the county attorney extended their jurisdiction to collect large checks, supra p. 298; where the courts allowed themselves to become part of a process for collecting checks, supra p. 311; where the courts sentenced the defendants to pay the checks and ordered them released when they did, supra p. 311; the police treated bad-check offenders as vagrants, supra p. 305; how the licensing officials changed the age at which minors could purchase cigarettes, supra p. 205; and where the plumbing inspector changed the law to suit his purposes, supra p. 217.

ance will vary as the intensity of such wants. In like fashion, support for laws will come from the needs and demands which their enforcement satisfies. The optimum point at which these forces can be brought into balance may be determined experimentally by examining the results of the enforcement of different rules of law attempting to solve the same problem. If the regulation is one which can be changed easily and quickly by administrative action, then, as shown in Chapter VI dealing with traffic control, the adjustment of the rule can be based on observed results of each change.[51] On the other hand, if the variations in the law require the slower legislative action, then similar conclusions can be reached by examining diverse legal solutions of the same problems in different jurisdictions or legal units, as in the case of the Nebraska, Colorado, New Hampshire and Vermont handling of the felony penalties.[52] In a society where conditions change rapidly, this comparative technique is less accurate but still useful. Here another jural law may be said to come into play.

Jural Law II: In a changing society, inflexibility is likely to be the death of a law.

Laws which specify without variation details to be enforced to the letter are most likely to fall into the type of obsolescence and non-enforceability illustrated in this jural law. The failures of the statutes fixing the distance between shade trees,[53] the regulation requiring the use of a particular strength solution to sterilize barbers' instruments[54] and the prescription of exact dimensions for bricks[55] are all illustrations of the validity of this principle.

This jural law might lead to a corollary for lawmaking which might be: Details of required actions within changing fields should not be put into statutes but should be left to administrative regulation and enforcement. Thus those portions of statutes on tree-planting, barbers' tool sterilization, the plumbing code and speed regulations discussed in Chapters VI and IX which are laid down as iron-clad rules in the statutes themselves[56] fail of enforcement. These rules to be workable must be flexible and within the power of administrative officers to meet changing needs in particular standard situations.[57]

[51] See especially Chapter VI, figure 8.
[52] Supra p. 353 ff.
[53] Supra p. 175 ff.
[54] Supra p. 199 ff.
[55] Supra p. 299 ff.
[56] See notes 49, 52, 53 and 54.
[57] Here again the facts of the studies show results that are contrary to popular beliefs. Again and again the idea is repeated that bureaucracy is a dangerous thing

Corollaries of this jural law are also found in the operation of those statutes which attempt to reach results contrary to known scientific knowledge or those which seek to enforce moral concepts.

Since scientific knowledge changes much faster than law, a second corollary to this jural law might be: The greater the variation of legal requirements from the known predictions of science on the utility of the required subject matter, the stronger is likely to be the pressure for laxity in enforcement. The apparent failure of enforcement of the rules on sterilization of barbers' instruments and the rigid prescription of intervals for tree-planting discussed above are illustrations tending to support this corollary.[58] In a case where the scientific usefulness of the prescribed action is doubtful or negligible and the resulting discomfort or loss of business is great, the pressure against law enforcement in this situation is likely to be too strong for the officials, who will find it expedient not to enforce the useless laws but to await legislative action. Where, as in the case of the brick statute, due to the advancement of science, the enforcement of the law in changed conditions would be at complete variance with the purpose for which it was created, it becomes a nullity.

Another proposition following from Jural Law II might be: Laws based on moral concepts out of line with social practices cannot be enforced without unnecessary and useless expense. The enforcement of rules of law based on such moral concepts is impossible when the practical results of such legal action run contrary to the needs and demands of that part of the public against whom the enforcement is sought and where there is no great demand or need behind the law.[59] Resistance to any regulation, even that against murder, will be found

and that public officials should be limited in their power and discretion by laws which make them subject to judicial review and to legislative checks. While this may be a justifiable fear of despotism remaining as a sort of aftermath of misrule by certain incompetent, corrupt or hereditary autocrats, there is every indication that successful operation of government in a complicated modern society will require that public officials have great latitude to change the rules in the spheres in which they operate so that by proper experimentation they may reach the optimum results in carrying out the purposes for which their offices were created. The ultimate limits upon such discretion may not flow from any theory of checks and balances but rather from the restraints inherent in the scientific method itself.

[58] For an example of this principle appearing after exhaustive study of the milk statutes, see Dahlberg, Adams and Held, Sanitary Milk Control, Nat. Research Coun. (1953) 104 ff.

[59] The failure of enforcement of the cigarette laws, supra Ch. IX, is a good example of this principle, and the failure of the Eighteenth Amendment and similar prohibition laws is known to all.

397

to exist. The force of this pressure will vary as the rule of law tends to interfere with the intensity of the beliefs, the demands and the needs of a greater or lesser number of persons. Opposition will also be found in proportion to the size of the personal and financial interests and desires which are frustrated by the law. There are probably other factors not pertinent at the moment. Support for enforcement will also tend to fluctuate, dependent upon like factors in like proportion and for the same reason.

Thus laws passed to enforce a type of moral concept no longer held by most individuals in a changing society will tend to fall into disuse.[60] Laws which have reached a type of obsolescence through the fact that they require results contrary to new social practices are likely to be ignored alike by both officials and the public. The statutes setting out the exact dimensions of bricks and the attempt to prohibit smoking or buying of tobacco by minors are good examples.

Observation of this opposition to outmoded laws and the resulting laxity of enforcement may have far-reaching effects in testing the validity (efficiency, goodness, etc.) of the laws whose operation is being studied. The extent to which the officials' action in enforcing the law varies from its plain written intent is a workable index of the usefulness of the law; and the nearer the enforcement practices approximate the requirements of the legal standard, the greater is its effectiveness in the society to which it is being applied.

In like fashion it can be said that the general direction in which the officials vary from the statutory requirements may be a good indication of the type of amendments needed. Thus in the bad-check study, the fact that the great majority of sheriffs and county attorneys engaged in collection of checks[61] shows that the law needs to be amended to legalize this practice.

There is also a second test which can be applied here, that of cost. Even when the law appears to be literally enforced as written, the "cost" of such operation in terms of money, time, sacrifice of other needs and the suppression of desires and demands when measured against the benefits in the same areas may prove to be too great. If such is the case, change in the law will be indicated. Thus in the bad-check study, again, when it develops that the enforcement of the present felony penalties alone on bad-check writers costs about as much as

[60] See the Kinsey Report on the sex habits of the human male and female and comments thereon, supra Chapter II, p. 35.

[61] Supra p. 292 ff.

398

the total loss from bad checks in the entire state of Nebraska,[62] and when it develops further that these provisions seem not to deter the writing nor to aid the collection of checks,[63] then it is clear that these felony penalties should be replaced by less costly devices.[64]

It should be noted that no resort to predetermined "values" is necessary when these tests of effectiveness of a law are applied.

Not only is there a variation existing between the rules of law set down in the books and the ultimate action of officials, but there is also a wider divergence between the rules of law on the books and the manner in which they impinge upon the actions of the persons subject to the law. When the subject learns that laws interfering with his liberties are not enforced, another jural law comes into play.

Jural Law III: Obsolete and unenforced or unenforceable laws left on the books are likely to cause a spread of the breakdown of law enforcement into related areas.

The tendencies toward law violations are of two classes, the unconscious violation of the rule of law and the conscious violation. As to the first, all persons carrying out their impulses and desires are likely to transgress laws of which they have no notice. This predilection is present and will not be affected very much by the nonenforcement of laws in related fields, except as it may fail to bring general notice of the existence of legal sanctions to the prospective actor, and to this extent it may fail a little to make the transgressor currently conscious of the existence of law. It is in the second class of cases, where the law violator is conscious of the existence of the law he is violating and also has knowledge of the nonenforcement of the related laws, that this jural law comes into play. Here the known fact that one law is not being enforced acts as encouragement to violate a related one.

For example, one of the main causes of juvenile delinquency may be the fact that we have so many laws regulating the acts of youth which are not based upon the natural requirements of healthy young people. When a young person is confronted with the knowledge of the fact that he can violate one law with impunity, this cannot help but encourage other violations in areas where the law thwarts the fulfillment of his desires. Preliminary studies indicate that about 50 per cent of the young people of the ages of 16 and over were violating

[62] Supra p. 349.
[63] Supra p. 352 ff; 356 ff.
[64] In the case of the bad-check laws, both of these tests indicate that a change is advisable.

the law in regard to buying and smoking cigarettes,[65] and a large percentage of them knew that they were doing so. In like fashion, if they successfully ignore obsolete laws on speeding, it is only one step from these to breaking the laxly enforced laws governing drinking, gambling and sex. The progressive violation of laws which adults seem to think need more strict enforcement follows in course.[66] Of the ten most common measures of juvenile delinquency chosen by the Gluecks in one of their studies of this subject, over 60 per cent involve breaches of laws which are out of line with current social practices where juveniles and adults alike openly violate the law without penalty.[67] Bad laws thus may be one of the principal causes of juvenile delinquency. In fact, laws and law enforcement are in such an unrealistic state that it is a mark of maturity to be able to discern which laws can be violated with impunity, a problem which also occupies much of the time of the organized Bar.

There is another important jural law growing out of this gap between law and its enforcement.

Jural Law IV: Severe punishment prescribed by law does not seem to deter crime any more than mild penalties.

It should be observed here that there is a wide divergence between the punishment prescribed in the statute and that enforced by the officials. Following Jural Law I, it is clear that statutes prescribing too-strict penalties cause enforcement to atrophy. The theory that increasing the penalty on the books will increase actual enforcement tends to fail; but even where the officials gave stricter enforcement to the penalty provisions of the bad-check law, there was no evidence of corresponding decrease in the crime.

These studies indicate that when law enforcement tends to fail to accomplish its ends, there is no correlation between increasing the penalty and improving administration of a law or preventing the proscribed crime. Thus, in the case of bad checks, there is no relation between the enforcement of the felony penalties and the incidence of the crime.[68] In fact, felony provisions on the books and their sub-

[65] Supra p. 207.

[66] The bad-check study revealed that, due to lax enforcement, most of the inmates of penal institutions had become habitual bad-check-writers before they were ever sentenced. See supra p. 345 ff.

[67] The tests are: Stealing rides or truck-hopping, keeping late hours, smoking at an early age, sneaking into theaters, destroying property, running away from home, bunking out, gambling, drinking at an early age, setting fires, Glueck, Unraveling Juvenile Delinquency 161 (1950); cf., id. Delinquents in the Making 89 (1951); id., 500 Criminal Careers 127-128 (1939).

[68] Supra p. 353 ff and Table 34, p. 306 and Table 59.

sequent enforcement in the areas studied are not as effective in increasing collection as misdemeanor penalties, and collection and enforcement were both more effective in Colorado under the misdemeanor provisions than in Nebraska where there were strict felony provisions.[69] Thus, making the penalties on the books more severe not only does not seem to decrease incidence of the crime but may actually be a factor in increasing it.

It is too soon to state it as a corollary to this jural law, but evidence is rapidly accumulating which indicates that punishment prescribed by statutes does not deter criminals at all in the commission of crime.[70] The exact statement of this jural law will have to await more research in the fields of criminology and abnormal psychology.

There also seems to be emerging a jural law touching the administration of public law.

Jural Law V: Where there is competition between governmental units in law enforcement, that unit which most effectively meets the actual wants of the people governed tends to replace the less efficient, in spite of constitutional or legal limits to the contrary.

As indicated above, where there is a pressing social problem which is believed capable of solution by law, all levels of government existing within geographical units, such as national, state, city or county, will have rules of law affecting the problem. These laws or regulations seem to exist in spite of constitutional theories of distribution of powers, and their administrations are likely to conflict with or nullify each other. This overlapping of laws seems to be found in every study.

Where many overlapping levels of government try to solve the same problems without the closest integration, which does not now exist, there is certain to be a breakdown in enforcement on one or more levels. There may be in this jural law a principle contrary to Gresham's Law that in the circulation of currency bad money pushes out the good. Here government which most effectively gives the people what they want, whether it be strict law enforcement, no enforcement or extra-legal activity, replaces the inefficient, whether legal or not.

---

[69] Supra p. 367.

[70] See, for example, Menninger, The Human Mind 447 ff. (1937); Glueck, After Conduct of Discharged Offenders 95 ff. (1945); Caldwell, Red Hannah 78 (1947); Phelps, Frequency of Crime and Punishment, 19 Jour. Cr. L. 165 (1928); Coates, Punishment for Crime in North Carolina, 17 N. Car. L. Rev. 205, 223 (1938); Caldwell, The Deterrent Influence of Corporal Punishment Upon Prisoners Who Have Been Whipped, 9 Am. Sociological Rev. 171 (1944); Grazia, Crime without Punishment: A Psychiatric Conundrum, 52 Col. L. Rev. 746 (1952); Andenaes, General Prevention—Illusion or Reality, 43 Jour. Cr. L. 176 (1952).

"The wants of the people" as used here means that combination of needs and demands which is most effectively brought to bear as pressure on the officials. (See Chapter III.) This principle was found to run through almost every problem studied.[71]

These attempted statements of general jural laws are most tentative and incomplete. It may be and probably is true that they are not accurately deduced from the material at hand or that they may not exhaust the possibilities of developing such principles from the data here set out, but they indicate the type of material which further research might develop. Under the searching examination of further study, they might be greatly expanded, contracted or even discredited. They are stated here because they seem to run through all the data examined; but jural laws, like chemical laws, are not limited only to the material in the test tube. This statement illustrates the possibility of experimental juridical methods, and it is submitted that they can be disproved or altered only by further application of such techniques. Illustrations of detailed jural laws in a single field like traffic are set out at length in Chapter VI.

SUGGESTED REFORMS

Suggested reforms, as in the case of jural laws, should be offered only after comparatively complete results are in, but meager as are the returns from the studies here listed, certain reforms are already indicated.

---

[71] In the case of the brick statutes, the regulations of the federal government and the trade associations completely replaced the state law which has the constitutional jurisdiction, supra 214 ff. In like fashion, federal pamphlets tended to replace the specific state law on the subject of tree-planting, supra pp. 177 ff. The federal government, with no constitutional power over the subject matter, has come to dominate completely the laws governing the purity of milk, see Ch. VII, p. 152 ff. The same thing is occurring in the area of automobile safety, see Ch. VI, p. 127 ff. and the bad-check study as set out in Ch. XI shows how the most efficient officials take over in all fields where there is overlapping jurisdiction.

It might also be noted in passing that, in spite of the commonly held belief that the federal government is likely to be more inefficient and corrupt than are governments close to the people, the meager evidence which has been collected here seems to indicate to the contrary. In almost every instance examined, it has appeared that the best work of all the governmental agencies attempting to solve a particular problem has been done by the larger units of government. If this trend continues to appear in future studies, it may cast serious doubts upon the commonly held tenet of political theory that the preservation of local government is one of the important ends of politics.

The amendments to the Nebraska law which appear to be necessary as a result of the bad-check study are discussed beginning in Chapter XIII, page 409, and there is also printed in the Appendix a tentative draft of a bad-check statute which might replace those now on the books. The reasons for these changes are also discussed in detail in Chapter XIII and need not be repeated here, but as a whole they indicate the possibilities which can develop from a proper factual study of the operation of laws.

The more meager pilot studies also seem to indicate that certain changes in the laws there examined are desirable.

The study on tree-planting[72] indicates clearly that fixed details prescribed by statutes, like the intervals between trees, should be eliminated. Also the tax feature of this law should be strengthened or repealed, and since the amounts involved are so small and do not recur at reasonable intervals, they are not worth the expense involved in collection of such taxes; therefore, repeal would seem to be proper. Power over planting, if used at all, should be clearly delegated to city and county groups. Perhaps entire repeal of the statute would be indicated by further study.

In the case of the statute requiring sterilization of barbers' instruments,[73] correlation of the overlapping state laws and city ordinances is definitely needed. Details of sterilizing agents will have to be removed from the statute and probably set up within the powers of the inspector's office or the Board of Health to prescribe proper formulas. Complete renovation of the law and its administration awaits only a further factual study.

The statutes governing smoking by minors and their administrative setup[74] clearly need changing, but the details of such reorganization will have to await further study.

The brick standard statute[75] surely needs to be repealed, as it now serves no purpose. After further study, detailed uniform state or federal statutes governing weights and measures seem desirable.

The plumbing code,[76] in regard to pipes in particular, needs revision to bring it in line with modern science, and the administration in general needs overhauling; but here, also, detailed suggestions must await further study.

[72] Chapter VIII, p. 175.
[73] Chapter IX, p. 194.
[74] Chapter IX, p. 203.
[75] Chapter IX, p. 209.
[76] Chapter IX, p. 216 ff.

Taking the statutes all together, there is revealed a portion of what appears to be a wasteful and useless overlapping of laws on various levels of the government structure which needs to be studied and eliminated. Here is a tremendous demand for long-range experiment and reform which should be continuous and drastic. The obsolescence and overlapping in our government machinery revealed by these casual pilot studies is so shocking as to indicate that further study would suggest a crying need for far-reaching constitutional alterations which would greatly reduce the cost of government and add to the efficiency of law enforcement. Here is a field for continuous and fruitful application of Experimental Jurisprudence. Where it will lead only time and study will tell, but preliminary investigations indicate that changes not yet dreamed of are needed to bring legal devices into line with the social developments coming out of progress caused by scientific discoveries in other fields.

ENACTMENT OF NEW LAWS AND TESTS OF THEIR VALIDITY

The enactment of new laws and their testing lies too far in the future for present comment. However it is hoped that, if the legislatures see fit to make changes in the bad-check law along the lines indicated below,[77] it will be possible to study future results of these changes. When this is done, the whole cycle of experimental juridical methods in this one field will have been completed.

Even in instances where the legislatures do not act, as already indicated, properly chosen studies of laws in other jurisdictions can be used to carry forward checks of hypotheses and jural laws under statistical controls which may get results similar to those produced by true experiments.

---

[77] Chapter XIII, p. 409 ff.

CHAPTER XIII

Summary of Results and Possible Amendments to the Nebraska Bad-Check Laws

Returning to the bad-check study and carrying that experiment forward, it will be seen that certain of the hypotheses and jural laws mentioned in Chapter XII have a direct bearing on the efficiency of the present bad-check laws of Nebraska, and their application would seem to suggest that amendments to these statutes may be in order.

SUMMARY OF THE FACTS AND CONDITIONS

As has been shown, bad checks are a common phenomenon not only in Nebraska but all over the country. Although the figures collected in this study indicate that there are approximately one-half million bad checks written yearly in the state of Nebraska alone, totaling over $30,000,000, they constitute less than one-half of one per cent of all checks so cleared by the banks. About 45/100ths of one per cent of all the checks so cleared, or 90 per cent of all bad checks, are for insufficient funds, nine-tenths of the rest are no-fund checks and less than 4/1000ths of one per cent of the checks are forgeries. Most of these bad checks are immediately paid or collected. The total loss from all will run less than $500,000, or about 30 cents per capita per year.

In terms of volume, this is less than 7/1000ths of one per cent of the gross sales in the state.[1] In fact, 40 per cent of the businesses seem to have no loss at all from checks. Of the remainder, the average appears to be about one bad check, or $10, a year. Gasoline stations, liquor dispensers and restaurants have the highest per cent of loss, followed by apparel, jewelry and general merchandise stores. The first three account for over half of the state's losses from bad checks, but in no classification is the loss over 9/100ths of one per cent of the yearly volume of business.

[1] See Table 21, supra p. 268.

405

The bad checks themselves are also small. The average size of checks in the state is about $200, but the average bad check is less than $70. In fact, over half of them are $10 or less, and three-fourths of the bad checks are less than $30.

In light of these facts, businessmen freely cash checks with little or no requirement of identification. It seems that the good will engendered by this policy far offsets any trivial loss from uncollected checks, so both the customers and businessmen are careless in the writing and handling of checks.

Forgeries and no-fund checks are felonies, and writing insufficient-fund checks above $35 is also a felony, but below $35 the unpaid insufficient-fund check becomes a misdemeanor punishable by a fine up to $100 and 90 days in jail.

Although the law on the books is strict, it is not being uniformly enforced. On the average, only about two per cent of the bad checks returned by the bankers get to the officials; and instead of prosecuting as required by law, the officials are chiefly engaged in collecting the checks under threat of criminal prosecution. Over 75 per cent of the county attorneys and 50 per cent of the sheriffs are engaged in collecting. City police also have a hand in this practice. Sometimes both prosecuting and police officers in the county collect checks, and in only two out of 31 counties was there no collection activity by officers of the law. In like fashion, two-thirds of all court cases involving checks were part of a collection process aimed at getting his money for the businessman.

In spite of this laxity of enforcement and the fact that three-fourths of all the checks in criminal cases involved less than $40, about one-third of the prisoners in the Penitentary and one-fourth of those in the Reformatory and over 40 per cent in the Women's Reformatory were sentenced for bad-check writing. One-half of those at the Penitentiary were incarcerated for writing checks of $20 or less, and at the reformatories, of $40 or less. Thus three-fourths of the "felons" were sentenced for wrongs below $100, the low felony limit for other property offense statutes.

It also appeared that these "felons" were nonviolent criminals and above the average in intelligence, in other words, not the type of person usually considered as a felon. The professional check writers who attract so much attention in fiction and news items were not very important, writing about 17 per cent of the money value lost in bad checks. On the other hand, it was indicated that the over-all cost to the state of handling all "bad-check felons" was over one-half million dollars, or more than the total loss to business from all bad checks in the state.

The statistics here collected also indicate that the felony sentences were no deterrent to writing bad checks, and that most of the inmates of the penal institutions were habitual bad-check writers. In the Colorado counties studied which had no felony penalties for short checks, the law was much more efficiently administered, and there were proportionally fewer bad checks. The same facts also are indicated in Vermont and New Hampshire. Under these circumstances, it seems that the Nebraska laws are too strict and are not being efficiently administered.

JURAL LAWS COMING INTO PLAY IN THE OPERATION OF NEBRASKA BAD-CHECK LAWS

This brief recapitulation of the facts indicated by the bad-check study recalls certain jural laws which seem to be applicable to the present enforcement of these statutes. There are also evident a number of narrower hypotheses which seem to bear upon facts here developed and which might merit much further and fruitful discussion; but since the purpose of Part II is to demonstrate available methods, the bearing of the jural laws will be touched upon only lightly before turning directly to the task of drafting needed amendments.

In formulating Jural Law I, it was pointed out that laws are seldom enforced literally.[2] The more a law varies from the needs of the situation, the less will it be effective, and the degrees of variation in enforcement may indicate the need of revision.

In the case of the bad-check laws, this jural law is seen to be at work. There is extremely spotty administration, and it is clear that prosecutors and judges are not enforcing the felony provisions literally but in many instances are busily engaged in collecting the checks to meet the demands of the business world. This indicates strongly that the felony provisions should be removed and collections legalized.

It also appears that the check laws of Nebraska are far from the optimum point for enforcing penalties. The comparative Colorado statistics[3] show that mere misdemeanor sanctions are as good a deterrent and a better means of collecting, thus more effectively meeting the needs of businessmen.

[2] See supra p. 393.
[3] See supra p. 378.

Jural Law II,[4] dealing with inflexibility of the law, also plays a part here. The strictness of the penalties, making every writing of a no-fund check a presumption of a crime, with optional heavy felony penalties in all no-fund cases and for insufficient-fund checks above $35, is completely out of line with the public attitude toward bad checks.[5] As shown in the study, the businessmen do not regard writing of checks with no immediate funds to pay them as a serious offense, and if they eventually get their money, they refuse to testify in felony prosecutions.[6] This means that rigid criminal penalties are not enforceable as written. It also indicates that a law ameliorating criminal penalties upon restitution might be more efficacious.

Even though the law is only partially enforced, the current cost of administering the felony provisions is as great or greater than the total loss from bad checks in the state. This being so, it seems clear that, as indicated above, felony provisions should be replaced with less costly enforcement devices, provided they can carry out as effectively the purposes of the statutes. Here again the Colorado experience shows that misdemeanor deterrents are sufficient in the overwhelming majority of the cases. The Vermont figures,[7] meager as they are, seem to indicate clearly that in over 90 per cent of the incidents of bad checks, a legalized collection routine is a more effective deterrent as well as a surer means for giving the businessman what he wants, recoupment of his losses. The experience of these two states offers experimental evidence that predicts a better operational record for a milder and a less rigid statute in Nebraska.

Jural Law III[8] indicates that obsolete laws may cause breakdown of law enforcement. The working of this phenomenon is far advanced in the case of bad-check laws, where failure of the felony clauses seems complete in one-third of the counties,[9] and in the balance, enforcement is in various states of decay. Modernization of the statute is therefore strongly indicated.

Jural Law IV,[10] stating that severe punishment prescribed by law does not seem to deter criminals, is clearly evident here. The severe penalties are shown by comparative county figures[11] and by the state

---

[4] Supra p. 396.
[5] Supra p. 278.
[6] Supra p. 360.
[7] Supra p. 358.
[8] Supra p. 399.
[9] See Figure 5 supra p. 294.
[10] Supra p. 400.
[11] Table 59, p. 351.

results from Colorado[12] to have no correlation with the percentages of bad checks in the areas studied. On the other hand, collection practices seem to affect the number of bad checks.[13] It is apparent that this jural law and the data collected would seem to predict that reduction of penalties would serve a salutory purpose.

Jural Law V[14] indicates that in the competition between various law enforcement groups, the most efficient seems to replace the less effective. Here, in the area of collecting, although the practice may be extra-legal and contrary to legal ethics in the present state of the law, the sheriffs have a slight edge in complying with the merchants' demands for collection.[15] This would seem to show that if collection were legalized to meet the needs of the business communities, the sheriff would be the official best fitted to undertake these duties.

It appears then that all five of the tentative jural laws set out in Chapter XII indicate that revision of the Nebraska bad-check statutes and changes of administration are in order, and that success of such an experiment along the lines suggested may be predicted.

SUGGESTIONS FOR CHANGE

Suggestions for amendments to the law based upon this study, of course, might be legion. Some good can be accomplished by a change in enforcement policies under the present law; but fundamentally there is a necessity for revision of the statutes.

SUGGESTIONS FOR CHANGE IN ADMINISTRATION

The first thing that strikes the eye of one interested in enforcement policies is that the penalties for bad-check writers are far above what the situation requires. It should be noted that over two-thirds of the check inmates of the penal institutes were under the influence of liquor at the time they cashed the criminal checks. It is also apparent that 13 per cent of the total state losses from bad checks are suffered by taverns and liquor dealers, who have less than two per cent of the business. Now the present state statutes make it illegal to sell liquor at retail for credit.[16] A check is a form of credit, and by a fair interpretation of that statute it is illegal to accept checks for liquor. For this reason many county attorneys properly refuse to collect checks for liquor dealers; but the proprietors would be glad to suffer the loss

---

[12] Tables 60 to 63, pp. 354 to 358.
[13] Supra p. 360 ff.
[14] Supra p. 401.
[15] Supra p. 292.
[16] Neb. Rev. Stat. § 53-183 (1952).

from bad checks rather than lose business from cashing them. The Liquor Commission, however, has rule-making powers[17] and can revoke licenses for violation of the law; so if they would do so, they could stop the cashing of checks at taverns, liquor stores and bars. This, of course, would not prevent bad-check writers from cashing checks elsewhere and then taking the money to the liquor dealers; but it would make it harder and would strike at two-thirds of the situations which ultimately result in felony sentences.

Various types of protective devices, like photographing, fingerprinting and stricter means of identification, have been invented and suggested; but as long as the losses are as small as they are, businessmen will not inconvenience themselves and their customers by adopting cumbersome and sometimes costly protections. Insurance or detective services are likewise to no avail because the business losses are too small to justify these precautions. Major improvement, therefore, will have to come from amendments to the present statutes.

SUGGESTED AMENDMENTS

The felony provisions of the bad-check law[18] are the first to strike the eye as being out of line with social conditions in Nebraska. The great majority of the people do not regard the writing and handling of bad checks as a serious matter, so these severe penalties are not being enforced, causing a breakdown of the law in this area. The enforcement of these provisions, spotty and unsatisfactory as it is, is filling our penal institutions with a type of nondangerous criminals who should not be there. As a result, it is costing the state more than the total losses which the law seeks to prevent, and, finally, the Colorado figures as compared with the Nebraska statistics indicate that the felony provisions of the Nebraska law are not an additional deterrent to the crime. For these reasons, as already indicated, the felony provisions should be repealed. The tentative draft of a Model Bad-Check Statute set out in the Appendix repeals *in toto* all the felony sections of the law on insufficient- and no-fund checks.

Such a repeal would involve also changing the present statutes on forgeries. Since they are a part of a larger system of statutes which penalize forgeries of all kinds in addition to checks, it might be wise not to change the forgery statute without further study; but if the felony penalty for forgery is left, it ought to be raised to cover only cases totaling over $100, thus bringing it into line with the other

[17] Id. §§ 53-117, 118.
[18] Id. §§ 28-1212, 28-1213, 28-1214.

statutes on property offenses.[19] If a man breaks into a merchant's cash register and takes $50, he is guilty of a misdemeanor only. It does not make sense to provide that it is a felony when the merchant hands him the same amount of money for a forged check. Such a change in the law would eventually save the state the cost of incarcerating in the penal institutions well over 25 per cent of its present felons and also the expense to the county of numerous trips by peace officers to extradite such check writers from other states. The amount saved by the county on extradiction would go a long way toward financing additional costs, if any, of enforcing misdemeanor penalties for acts which are now felonies. The Colorado results indicate that the misdemeanor penalties get better all-around enforcement and collection than do the felony sentences.[20]

Based upon these considerations, the felony provisions have been entirely removed from the suggested model bad-check statute set out in the Appendix. This does not mean that all felony provisions would be out of the law. Felony sentences for serious forgeries would still remain,[21] and also obtaining money under false pretenses would continue to be a felony[22] as provided in the statutes governing those two activities. Although it has not been necessary to use these statutes in Nebraska to cover offenses based on checks, the overwhelming weight of authority from other states shows that they cover such crimes.[23] The professional bad-check writer who attracts so much attention in fiction, in the news items and from the businessmen's lobby, but who, in fact, writes less than one-fourth of one per cent of the bad checks, can still be prosecuted under both of these statutes. The more lenient law suggested here is directed at catching and collecting from the great bulk of the other bad-check writers, the financially careless, the petty criminals and the drunkards who together write over 99 per cent of all bad checks. It adopts the wording of the Colorado statute on short checks which covers both insufficient-fund and no-

---

[19] Id. §§ 28-506 to 28-513. Such a change could be accomplished by adding the words "of an amount above one hundred dollars" after the word "check" in Section 28-601 (c) of the Nebraska Revised Statutes of 1943.

[20] See supra p. 272 ff.

[21] Neb. Rev. Stat. § 28-601 (1948).

[22] Id. § 28-1207.

[23] People v. State of Illinois, 309 Ill. 207, 140 N.E. 820, 35 A.L.R. 339 (1923) with exhaustive note; cf. State of Oregon v. Hammelsy, 52 Or. 156, 96 Pac. 865. 17 L.R.A. (N.S.) 244 (1948) with note; Hagerty, False Pretenses, Confidence Game and Short Check in Colordao, 25 Rocky Mountain L. Rev. 325 (1953); Note 14 Va. L. Rev. 135 (1927); see note, 34 W. Va. L. Rev. 207, 208 (1928); and authorities there cited.

fund checks,[24] and also adds forged checks so that they too may be included in the process.

Collection of bad checks is shown in this study to be the chief occupation of officials in administering this law. At the present time this activity is carried on extra-legally under pressure from the businessmen. It could be and in some instances is subject to abuse and corruption and, at its best, is rendering business a free illegal service. There is no doubt that, socially, the demand for collection seeks a desirable end; and that, where vigorously pursued, it tends to reduce the number of bad checks.[25] Under these circumstances, it should be regularized and made part of the legal processes.

There may be some objections to having peace officers engaging in the collection of checks under a threat of criminal prosecution. These objectives may be made on grounds both of ethics and policy. The argument on an ethical basis, which does not seem to prevail even now, entirely disappears when the process is regularized and made legal. On the side of policy, this is an ancient practice rooted deep in the common law itself,[26] and, as shown below, the threat of penal action by peace officers to enforce legal obligations has never disappeared from our law but remains extremely potent today.

The process also should be constituted so as to carry its fair share of the cost of administration. With these considerations in mind, an amendment to the law should provide, as does the Vermont system,[27] that payment of the checks and the costs absolves the crime; but the businessman also should bear some of the cost of this legal service, which is often made necessary in the first place by his careless acceptance of bad checks. The suggested statute provides, therefore, that when a businessman requests the sheriff to take action, he is required to put up a bond to cover part of the costs, not more than one-third of the check nor less than one dollar. It is further stipulated that in case the check and costs are collected from the wrongdoer, the bond is to be returned to the complainant. If not, it should go to pay all or part of the cost of attempted collection.

FITTING CHANGES INTO PRESENT LEGAL STRUCTURES

It is clear that the projected changes must also be so devised as to fit readily into the current legal structure. The discussion has already

---

[24] See People v. Lindsay, 119 Colo. 248, 202 P.2d 951, 952 (1949).

[25] See supra p. 360 ff.

[26] See Ford, Imprisonment for Debt, 25 Mich. L. Rev. 24 (1926).

[27] See supra p. 356.

touched on some of these considerations, and others are legion, but a few of the more important ones need to be examined here. The first under our current system of government always is: does the statute meet the requirements of the state and federal constitutions?

The constitutionality of the proposed statute raises a number of questions. The Nebraska Constitution, like that of many states, contains a provision against imprisonment for debt;[28] but both in Nebraska[29] and in the rest of the country it has been held that where the statute is based upon criminal intent, it does not run counter to the prohibition of imprisonment for debt.[30] The essence of the old as well as the proposed new statutes is that fraud is the basis of the criminal prosecution,[31] and imprisonment for fraud is specifically excepted in the Nebraska Constitution, Article I, Section 20.

The fact that the fraud may be based upon a rebuttable statutory presumption arising from dishonor has also been held not to violate any constitutional or procedural rights.[32] In these respects, the suggested statute merely continues the well established provisions of previous acts.

The new statute also contains two features that are not in the present laws of Nebraska: (1) that payment of the check and costs at any time wipes out the crime, and (2) that peace officers are empowered to make collections and payment to the holders of the checks. As has already been shown, these two provisions simply legalize the practices current in the great majority of the counties of Nebraska and in many of the other states.

There has been objection in some states that where payment wipes out the crime, the statute is an unconstitutional attempt to use imprisonment for debt; but in the instances where this was the holding, the statute required no fraudulent intent at the time of issue.[33] As

[28] Art. I, Sec. 20, 2 Rev. Stats. (1943).

[29] White v. State, 135 Neb. 154, 280 N.W. 433 (1938).

[30] Ford, Imprisonment for Debt, 25 Mich. L. Rev. 24 (1926); Note 23 A.L.R. 495.

[31] See numerous cases collected in Notes L.R.A. 1918 F 982; 35 A.L.R. 375 (1925) 43 id. 49 (1926); 95 id. 486 (1935).

[32] Lahners v. State, 118 Neb. 184, 223 N.W. 951 (1929); Notes 35 A.L.R. 375, 380 (1925); 95 id. 486, 490 (1935) and cases there cited. See also Morgan, Constitutional Limitations on Presumptions Created by State Legislatures, Har. Legal Essays (1934) 323; McCormick, Validity of Statutory Presumptions, 22 Tex. L. Rev. 75 (1942).

[33] State v. Johnson, 163 Miss. 521, 141 So. 338 (1932) interpreting, Laws of Miss. Ch. 172, p. 223 (1924), Miss. Code (1930) sec. 924. This act was amended to cover fraud. Laws of Miss. Ch. 299, p. 635 (1932); Starr v. Baldwin Piano Co., 59 N.D. 174, 238 N.W. 877 (1931) interpreting, N.D. Laws c. 121 p. 104 (1923) which requires no criminal intent; Burnam v. Commonwealth, 228 Ky. 410, 15 S.W. (2d) 256 (1929)

413

shown above, in the old Nebraska statute and also in the suggested new one the basis of the crime is fraudulent intent; so these cases have no application here. In those instances where payment abates the crime or criminal intent, the cases from other states are overwhelmingly to the effect that such provisions are valid.[34] In like manner, the fact that payment forgives the crime or abates punishment does not interfere with the pardoning power. There are many instances in Nebraska law where officials other than the executive can pardon crime or mitigate sentences.[35]

It should be clear also that there is no change in the law in regard to "hold" checks, postdated checks, and those given for pre-existing debts. Where there is no intent to defraud, such checks are usually held not to support criminal action;[36] but if they are part of a fraudulent transaction, the result is, of course, contrary, and the drawer can be held under the old or the suggested statutes.[37]

The use of the threat of imprisonment to force payment of obligations as it appears in the proposed statute is neither new nor harsh. As indicated above, since the beginning of the common law, such processes have been known and widely enforced. The terrible interferences with liberty involved in imprisonment for debt have properly caused this practice to be outlawed in that area; but there remain many instances in which obligations civil in nature are properly enforced, both under statutes and court decision, by threat of imprisonment, or where a person can purge himself of the liability to criminal or quasi-criminal punishment only by paying his just obligations. Among these are cases involving the duty to pay alimony,[38] wife and

Kentucky Acts, Ch. 41, p. 175 (1928); Ward v. Commonwealth, 288 Ky. 468, 15 S.W. (2d) 276 (1929); contra even where the statute required no fraud, State v. Avery, 111 Kan. 588, 207 Pac. 838, 23 A.L.R. 453 (1922).

[34] State v. Avery, supra, and see cases collected, Notes 35 A.L.R. 375, 391 (1925), 43 id. 49, 51 (1926), 95 id. 486, 501 (1935); see also Pleuler v. State, 11 Neb. 547, 10 N.W. 481, 489 (1881) holding valid Ch. 61 § 28, Laws of Neb. (1881).

[35] Welfare Boards, 14-126 (3); Mayors, 15-315, 16-316, 17-117; Superintendent of Industrial School, 83-472, Board of Pardons and Legislature, Constitution Art. IV § 13 28-2604, 29-2630, 2634; Judges, 28-447.

[36] Neidlinger v. State, 88 S.C. 687 (Ga. App. 1916); State v. Nelson, 58 S.D. 562, 237 N.W. 766, 76 A.L.R. 1226 (1931) with note; Note 24 Rocky Mt. L. Rev. 123 (1951).

[37] White v. State, 135 Neb. 154, 280 N.W. 433 (1938); State v. Eikelberger, 72 Ida. 245, 239 P. (2d) 1069, 29 A.L.R. (2d) 1176 (1951) with note.

[38] 42-323, Cain v. Miller, 109 Neb. 441, 191 N.W. 704, 30 A.L.R. 125 (1922) with exhaustive note; see also notes 136 A.L.R. 689 (1942), 154 id. 443, 464 (1945), where numerous statutes and decisions to this effect are cited.

child support[39] and bastardy proceedings where the natural father is required to support the child.[40] In all of these cases, the obligation to pay is supported by criminal sanctions which are removed by payment.[41] In like fashion, one who takes mortgaged property out of the state or disposes of it improperly may be subject to criminal sanctions which are abated by payment.[42] So also there have been many statutes where payment of certain types of debts were enforced by criminal statutes[43] and the penalty removed by payment.[44] Most of these latter have been repealed because they involved a system of peonage by which agricultural workers were held on the farm.[45] No such danger is involved in requiring payment of bad checks, and the suggested statute specifically provides that where the defendant, at the discretion of the judge, may be remanded to the custody of a probation officer, the supervision shall not last longer than two years.[46] This is a common practice for a much longer period of time in dealing with other criminal offenders and generally has the approval of modern criminologists.[47] Any danger that these provisions may result in some kind of endless imprisonment for debt or failure to pay the fine is taken care of by the present provisions of the Nebraska statute that the county judge may release prisoners unable to pay after they have served the term and an amount equal to three dollars a day for the unpaid fine.[48]

Using the criminal law to collect obligations may raise further objections in some quarters, but it should be kept in mind that this does not involve imprisonment for a debt. The defendant in these

---

[39] Neb. Rev. Stat. §§ 28-446, 446.01, 449, 449.01, 450.01 (1948); Ala. Code Tit. 34 § 90 (1940); Calif. Penal Code §§ 270 a and b (1949).

[40] Ariz. Code § 27-410 (1939); id. § 40-204 (Supp. 1953).

[41] Code of Ala. Tit. 34 §§ 98 to 100 (1940); Ariz. Code 27-411 (1939); Ariz. Stat. 1947 41-213 (Supp. 1953); Calif. Penal Code § 270 b (1949).

[42] S.C. Code § 45-157 (1952); State v. Campbell, 159 S.C. 128, 155 S.E. 750 (1930); La. Stat. Ann. §§ 5358, 5359 (West 1951), id. § 5359 (Supp. 1954).

[43] For example see New Mexico Stats. § 40-21-12 (1953).

[44] Id. § 40-21-12.

[45] See New Mexico Stats. § 40-21-12 repealed (Supp. 1955).

[46] See proposed Model Statute, Appendix I.

[47] See Neb. Rev. Stats. 29-2219 (1948). Attorney General's Survey of Release Procedures, 29 ff., 513 ff. (1939); Orfield, Improving Parole in Nebraska, 19 Neb. L. Rev. 354 (1940); 26 id. 69 (1946); Gandet, Differences between Judges in Granting Sentences of Probation, 19 Tem. L.Q. 471 (1946); Chandler, Probation, 12 Fed. Probation 11 (1948); Printzlien, Deferred Probation, 12 id. 17 (1948); cf. Cosalich, Adult Probation Laws of the United States (1940).

[48] Neb. Rev. Stat. 29-2412 (1948); see also id. § 18-206 giving police magistrates a similar power.

cases has written a bad check, an action which is recognized as a crime in every state in the Union. Experience has shown that in many states the officials of the criminal law, under the pressure of business, are now collecting from the wrongdoers. Statistics also show that severe penalties do not deter this kind of crime but that immediate collection does. The facts also show that the business community is not interested in further punishment if the checks are paid. Under these circumstances, it seems entirely proper to adopt the type of practice which is now current in many other statutes, that of making reparation expiate the crime.

It is also quite clear that in this area the usual processes of the civil law are of no help. Most of the bad-check writers are judgment-proof; and their checks are for such small amounts that, even if judgments could be obtained from them and collected, the costs would be prohibitive.

If there were some type of summary small claims procedure available, it might be conceivable that it could handle bad checks on the civil side, but the experience in Colorado, where there is such a statute,[49] indicates that the courts do not use it at all for this purpose, probably due to the fact that the bad-check writer is likely to be an indigent and a ne'er-do-well, and, without the sanction of the criminal law, civil processes have no effect upon him. Apparently he is the sort of fellow who would irresponsibly write checks in circumstances where he could not or would not otherwise pay and can be deterred or made to pay only by the threat of immediate and sustained action which will make him work out the wrong he has done.

Central control and supervision of procedures, since the bad checks are small, is also a desirable quality of a model statute. Therefore the tentative draft law, except in large cities, places responsibility for collection in the hands of peace officers. Experience has shown that in the smaller counties the sheriff is best equipped to do this work. He represents the force of the law and is sufficiently mobile in his activities immediately to apprehend delinquent check writers. In the larger cities and in some of the non-county-seat towns, this work may be done by the metropolitan police, and the model statute so provides.

In cases where the culprit does not or cannot pay the bad check, it will, of course, be necessary to take him to court. In this instance, the statute, in the interest of simplicity and efficiency, should give the jurisdiction to one court. The county courts in the small counties and the city courts in the larger metropolitan areas, where the police have

---

[49] Colo. Rev. Stats. §§ 127-1-1 to 9 (1953).

collection powers, seem to be the best fitted for this work. They are not courts of record, and since 98 per cent of the defendants plead guilty, they can summarily administer the penalties. In this respect, the statute also legalizes the practice of remanding the culprit to the sheriff or probation officer to work out the debt and make retitution. This is shown by all the studies to be the most desired feature of the present system. In this case, as law enforcement is now organized, the sheriff in most of the small counties is the jailor and probation officer; but where, as in the more populous areas, separate probation officers are available, the court is given the discretion to turn supervision of working out the sentences and the payments over to them. As in other cases of misdemeanors, the defendant, of course, has the protection of appeal to higher courts if he so desires.[50]

If the legislature sees fit to adopt the proposed Model Bad-Check Statute, it should go a long way toward controlling the issue of bad checks, reducing the cost to the state of incarcerating the wrongdoers, simplifying the administration of the law and increasing the efficiency of check-collecting service for the business community.

CONCLUSION

Throughout these few pages, there has been offered a theory under which Experimental Jurisprudence may become a more important part of social science and a demonstration of the manner in which such an experimental science could be applied to new laws. If the legislature of Nebraska, or any other state, sees fit to adopt the Model Bad-Check Statute set out in the Appendix, the experiment begun in this field will be further accelerated, and an additional research will then be indicated.

Whether or not conditions are propitious for continuing this particular project, as indicated in Part I, many partial or complete experiments of like manner are in various stages of execution. The problems are difficult, the field of research wide and tedious and the methods are still in the formulative stage; but progress in many directions is an established fact.

As a consequence of all these factors, it appears that lawmaking for a modern society is rapidly advancing beyond the capacity of the organizations available to the people who are now being elected to our legislative bodies. There is an immediate need for skilled assistants to aid in scientific research to develop the facts surrounding present and future laws. Without such expert staff, the legislative product

---

[50] Nebraska Constitution, Art. V, Sec. 17, Neb. Rev. Stat. §§ 24-302, 24-204 (1948).

will be in danger of increasing the practice of violation of law and causing lower effectiveness of regulations.

Once the process of Experimental Jurisprudence is adopted and perfected in this and other fields, it is foreseeable that its results can be as startling and useful to human welfare as have been the fruits of scientific method in other areas.

Model Bad-Check Statute

Tentative Draft

A BILL[1]

FOR AN ACT to repeal and re-enact sections 28-1212, 28-1213, and 28-1214 of the Revised Statutes of Nebraska as amended; relating to the issue of insufficient-, no-fund and forged checks; to change the penalties therefor; to create an alternate criminal procedure thereon; to provide means for the collection of such checks; for abating the penalties on payment thereof; and to define the powers of the city and county courts, sheriffs and probation officers with reference thereto.

Be it enacted by the people of the State of Nebraska.

Sec. 1. That section 28-1212 of the Revised Statutes of Nebraska be re-enacted to read as follows:

28-1212. *Passing Short Check or Forgery—Penalty Payment.* Any person who, with intent to defraud, shall make, draw, utter, forge or deliver any check, draft, assignment of funds or order for the payment of money upon any bank, credit association or other depositary, knowing, at the time of making, drawing or delivery that there are not sufficient funds or credit for the payment of the same, shall be guilty of a misdemeanor, and upon conviction thereof shall be fined not to exceed $500 or imprisoned in the county jail not to exceed six months, or shall suffer both such fine or imprisonment. The fact that such check when presented in the usual course of business shall be dishonored by such bank or credit association because of lack of sufficient funds to the credit of the maker or drawer with which to pay the same, or for forged signature, shall be prima facie evidence of the fraudulent intent herein mentioned, *provided, however,* that

---

[1] For convenience, the Nebraska legislative forms are used here. If any other state desires to adopt the bill, it is obvious that the format should be changed.

payment of such check, the legal penalties and costs accrued to the time of payment, shall discharge any further criminal liability thereon.

Sec. 2. That section 28-1213 of the Revised Statutes of Nebraska be re-enacted to read as follows:

28-1213. *Collection of Checks, Abating Crime,—Bond.* Any person holding any check unpaid for the reasons mentioned in the next preceding section may present such check to the sheriff or chief of police of the city with a copy of a letter demanding payment from the maker or drawer. If the check remains unpaid ten days after receipt of the letter and the unpaid holder shall have posted a bond for costs which shall be not more than one-third of the amount of the check or not less than $1, the sheriff or chief of police shall proceed to collect the check and costs either directly or by swearing and serving a warrant for the maker or drawer. The officer's mileage and the court and other costs for this process shall be the same as now provided by law. If the maker or drawer pays the check, penalties, fines, if any, and costs accrued at the time of payment, the sheriff or chief of police shall return the amount due on the check together with the bond to the unpaid holder, and the officer's receipt to the maker or drawer shall be evidence to abate the crime mentioned in the next preceding section even if paid after conviction, and shall authorize the ending of imprisonment, if any, to which the maker or drawer may have been sentenced therefor. But if the check be not paid by the drawer, the holder's bond shall be forfeited and applied to the payment of the usual costs, but any balance remaining thereafter shall be returned to the unpaid holder of the check. This process shall be supplementary to and not in lieu of the usual criminal procedure.

Sec. 3. That section 28-1214 of the Revised Statutes of Nebraska be re-enacted to read as follows:

28-1214. *Payment, Bench Paroles, Probation and Collection.* If the maker fails to make good the check and costs as provided in section 28-1213, the city or county courts on conviction of the misdemeanor provided in section 28-1212 may, at their discretion, exercise all the powers now prescribed by law in section 29-2219, including the power to place the accused on probation under the charge of the sheriff or probation officer to work out under his supervision the principal of the check and costs in such manner as the court may prescribe, provided, however, that such period shall not be longer than two years.

Sec. 4. Original and amended sections 28-1212, 28-1213 and 28-1214 of the Revised Statutes of Nebraska are hereby repealed.

Sample County Memoranda

The following memoranda are a reproduction of the original notes on three of the 31 Nebraska, four Colorado and two New England counties which were visited by the investigators who interviewed the officials, bankers and businessmen for the purpose of gathering the data contained in the various tables throughout the bad-check report. In order to meet the promise of anonymity, facts or factors which identify the particular county have been removed from the memoranda, and the counties are simply numbered. The memoranda have also been rewritten and abbreviated in interest of conserving space. They are set out here only to illustrate the type of information upon which the compiled data about law enforcement conditions in the counties rest.

COUNTY 7

Population: 10,000-12,000
White County.[1]
This is a farming community with corn, wheat and some grains.
There is no industry other than a grain elevator.
It is on the main line of a railroad and just off of a U. S. highway.
It has saloons and liquor stores, lots of them.
The county seat has about 30 per cent of the entire county population.
There were 11 business questionnaires.

Banks

There was no bank in the sample, but we called on one bank which had deposits of about $4,000,000. The bank had 88 bad checks in June of 1954, 7.5 per cent of the yearly estimated total of 1,173 for this bank, which had 65 per cent of the city business and 43 per cent

---

[1] Color refers to the number of pentientiary convictions for no-account and insufficient-fund checks per 1,000 population from Nebraska counties, 1942-1953. White indicates no convictions, Grey .20 to .41 per 1000 population for the period and Black the highest—1.05 to 2.77 per 1000. See Figure 1, p. 237 supra.

421

of the county business, making an estimated total of 1,800 bad checks for the town and 2,703 for the county, or .27 per capita bad checks for the year. About 13 per cent of these or 350 were no-account checks.

County Attorney

The county attorney was away. I received the information from his secretary. He is paid only $1,200 a year. He has been in office about three and a half years, has no deputy, spends about three-fourths of his time for the county and about an hour a week on checks. The secretary spends half her time for the county and about one-twentieth of the county time on checks.

The businessmen bring in checks, asking for collection. The county attorney writes a form letter, asking the drawers to come in. There were about 40 to 45 such letters in 1953. Three-fourths of them paid up. The county attorney gets the money, pays the holders and keeps no records. For those who do not pay, he swears out a warrant in the county court. If they pay at any stage, the case is just forgotten. The secretary doesn't know who gets the money after warrants are issued from the court.

Sheriff

There is a full-time sheriff and deputy. He thinks they spend about one-third of their time on checks. (I doubt it. The county attorney's estimate seems better.) They collect checks by personal contact and turn the money over to the merchants. Some people pay the county attorney, and some pay the sheriff. There are no records kept, and the county attorney handles most of the money. The sheriff and his deputy estimate they get about 50 checks a year for collection and get about one-third collected. All the rest go to the county attorney. The sheriff and his deputy get no fees for collecting checks and no mileage. It is just a courtesy on the part of the sheriff. On warrants they often get the money and turn it over to the merchants or the county attorney, usually the latter. When serving a warrant, the sheriff collects mileage, and the defendant pays it. Then the case is forgotten. He also enforces warrants for neighboring counties, and vice versa.

County Court

There were 88 criminal cases in 1952, 74 cases in 1953. There were no forgeries and none bound over to the district court. There were 11 check cases in 1952, ten insufficient-funds and one no-account. There was not a single conviction, and in most of these no warrant was returned. On four the sheriff still has the warrant, but the rest appear to be settled.

Eight check cases in 1953. All were insufficient-funds and all no warrants returned. The sheriff has only one. All the rest were probably settled.

District Court

There were four criminal and 34 civil cases in 1952. There were six criminal and 19 civil cases in 1953. Not a single check case. Not a penitentiary or reformatory conviction for checks in the county for 12 years.

Summary

Out of an estimated 2,703 bad checks in the county a year, not over 100 get to the law enforcement officials, who are running a collection agency and no more. There was not a single conviction in the county court or district court in two years. There is no criminal law enforcement here other than possible threats for the purpose of collecting the checks. This is perhaps an example of what would happen if the public officials were a collection agency only. Note also the low per-capita rate of bad checks in the county.

COUNTY 25

Population: 12,500-15,000.
The county seat has less than ten per cent of the county population.
Grey county—.21[1]
This is a local-option county. Liquor by the drink is served in two of the towns. The taverns seem to get most of the bad checks.

Bank

There were three banks in the county seat. The one examined had deposits just under $1,000,000. The total for the town was over $3,000,-000 deposited. During one week the examined bank had six bad checks. The town estimate for one year is 1,059 bad checks.

The bank has seven per cent of the county deposits. There are 4,657 bad checks a year for the county. One hundred thirty-four no-account, with .33 bad checks per capita.

County Attorney

The county attorney devotes about half his time to his public office and half to private practice. He has no regular deputies, and the secretary in his office spends about half her time working on public cases. He estimates that about one-sixth of the time of his office on the public side is devoted to bad-check cases.

---

[1] For the meaning of the color, see F.N. 1, p. 421.

The county attorney says that he refuses to act as a collection agency for the businessmen, but his files for the years 1952-53 show the following: He had a total of 34 complaints from businessmen on bad checks during the two years, 17 in each year. His policy on receipt of the complaint was to write the drawer of the check a letter, pointing out that failure to pay an insufficient-fund or a no-fund check was a criminal action. After writing such letters to each drawer, he received the following results: 16 were immediately collected, and 11 gave no response. Of these 11, three were directed to persons convicted in other jurisdictions, and on the remaining, the payees made no formal complaints. Five were carried to court proceedings, three in the County Court and two in the Justice of the Peace Court. Two checks were passed in other counties, and the county attorney had no jurisdiction.

Court Records

The District Court had four cases, one in 1952 and three in 1953. The one in 1952 was dismissed for lack of sufficient evidence. Of the three in 1953, one defendant was sentenced and paroled. He broke parole, and the sheriff is in Colorado looking for him now. One defendant was sentenced to the Reformatory for one year, and one was sentenced to 30 days in jail.

County Court

There were five cases over the two years, for four of which the county attorney had records. For one of them he did not. The county attorney also recorded two cases wherein he swore out warrants, but these did not appear in the County Court records. Two of the County Court cases were bound over to the District Court. The judges seemed to be of the impression that no-fund checks are all felonies and must be tried by the District Court. There were no convictions in the County Court. In all of the remaining cases, the sheriff failed to serve the warrant, and the defendant was never produced.

General Remarks

There is some evidence that the businessmen take insufficient-fund checks like promissory notes, and when they are not paid, they attempt to collect them by enforcing the criminal law against the drawer. The county attorney discourages this practice, and in one of the cases mentioned above he refused to prosecute, in spite of the presumption of guilt, because he felt that the drawer and payee were conniving in this practice.

Bad checks show up in the District Court, the County Court and the Justice of the Peace Court outside of the county seat. The justice of the peace in the county seat does not handle bad-check cases, but the justices of the peace in outlying cities apparently do. In one town the county attorney reported two cases tried in the Justice of the Peace Court, and the justice of the peace himself, in addition, reported that he collected one insufficient-fund check and three no-fund checks in 1952 and three insufficient-fund checks in 1953. He says that he uses both civil and the threat of criminal action in these collections. The businessmen also say that the sheriff collects bad checks for them.

Eighteen questionnaires were collected from businessmen. This information and the discussion with the county attorney and judges reveal that the taverns are the chief recipients of bad checks in this county. The county attorney discourages collecting such checks, but his records show a large number of complaints from tavern owners. One private attorney in the county seat, where there are only two attorneys, indicated that he had 28 bad checks in his office for collection, all of them from tavern owners.

COUNTY 26

Population: Over 25,000.
Black county—2.77[1]
The highest conviction rate per capita in the state.
It is a ranching area, irrigated land, with sugar beets, some small grain and a good deal of cattle.
There is a lot of transient labor working on the crops, including a large Mexican and Indian population.
The county has open saloons, taverns and liquor stores.
There is a large amount of migrant labor on the transcontinental railway and the highways running into five states.
There is some industry, mostly for processing agricultural products.
Sixteen business questionnaires.
The county seat has over ten per cent of the county population.

Banks

Banks from three different towns were examined, one with $5,000,-000 in deposits, the second with under $500,000 in deposits and the third with over $5,000,000 in deposits. The first town's bank shows 2,064 bad checks per year, .5 plus per capita; the second 572 per year, .83 per capita; the third 16,000 or 1.0 plus per capita. The total de-

---

[1] For the meaning of the color, see F.N. 1, p. 421.

posits in the three banks sampled is $10,500,000. The total deposits for all banks in the county is over $31,000,000. The total bad checks per year for the three sampled was 7,065, making the total estimated bad checks for the county 20,902, or .62 per capita per year. It should be noted also that by actual count in the third town, the no-account checks run 13 per cent of all bad checks. The figures for the other banks were only estimates and are not reliable. This is one of the highest ratios of no-account checks. The cashier of this bank says one reason why they have so many no-account checks is that three banks in the area use the same color counter checks. These are distributed among the merchants, who often write the checks to be signed by the drawers who ask for the checks by the color of the pad rather than the name of the bank. There seems to be extreme carelessness in writing checks and keeping check stubs all over the county. This habit among the people is verified by reports from other nearby counties, especially in the ranching area.

It should be noted also that this carelessness in keeping accounts occurs in an area where there is the highest rate of prosecution and conviction, indicating that prosecution is no deterrent to the carelessness in banking habits of the community.

County Attorney

There is a new county attorney, who has been in office only one year, but the records show that he is more rigorous in the prosecution of bad checks than his predecessors. In 1953 alone he sent 16 men to the Penitentiary on this charge. He spends half his time for the county and has one assistant who spends three-fourths of his time for the county. Both devote about one-half of the county time to collecting bad checks. His secretary spends about one-fourth of her time on checks and is entirely paid by the county. The county attorney collects no checks civilly. He claims that he sends no collection letters but only prosecutes. However, his files show that in 1953 he wrote 32 letters to people about bad checks, of which 11 resulted in collections. His predecessor in 1952, according to the files, wrote 28 such letters, 17 of which resulted in collection. The sheriff also collected 16 payments by means of 24 letters written in 1952, but in 1953 on the advice of the new county attorney the sheriff stopped writing collection letters. His files show only eight letters for the year 1953, three of which resulted in collections. The county attorney demands that the holders of checks sign a written complaint. He then prosecutes in the County Court. His report for 1953 shows that he brought 206 check cases in the County Court in 1953, resulting in restitution to the holders of about $5,000. For the results of this policy, see the County Court report below.

Sheriff

The sheriff is full time and has three full-time deputies. They estimate that they spend about one-fourth to one-third of their time on checks. They accumulate about 80 no-account checks or forgeries in their dead file each year. About 40 insufficient-fund checks a year are collected by the sheriff and his deputies by personal contact without writing any letters or entering complaints. The sheriff used to collect checks (see above), but he has now quit. The sheriff says it should be illegal for liquor dealers to take checks but would like to leave the felony penalty in its present condition so that check writers can be extradited.

County Court

The new county attorney in 1953 made the county court into a collection agency by throwing all complaints on bad checks into cases in that court. (See the difference between 1952 and 1953, below.)

The county judge says all no-account checks and all insufficient-fund checks above $35 can be felonies, so he has no jurisdiction except to bind over the case to the District Court. (Note the split on this by the various county courts.) The cases in court totaled as follows:

Three hundred seventy-five cases in 1952 and 655 cases in 1953.

In 1952, 64 cases were on checks. Eleven were forgeries, five were bound over to the District Court, six had no warrant returned, 17 were insufficient-fund and no-account cases, bound over to the District Court. Most were no-account cases. Thirty-six cases were disposed of by County Court. Twenty-two were for insufficient funds, on seven no warrant was returned, five defendants paid or were dismissed, nine defendants were fined and the cases were settled and one defendant got a suspended sentence. In 1953 there were 191 check cases. Twenty-nine were for forgery, 21 were bound over to the District Court and eight had no warrants returned. Thirty-six bad-check cases were bound over to the District Court; mostly they were no-account cases. One hundred twenty-six check cases were disposed of. One hundred were for insufficient funds. Four defendants were jailed, 15 cases had no warrants returned, 22 cases were dismissed or paid and dismissed, 59 defendants were fined or the check was paid in court or both, and many times other checks were paid both to the complaining witness and even to others. Twenty-six were no-account cases in which there were 19 with no warrants returned, and seven were dismissed or **settled.**

Apparently we missed 16 cases in the court records, or they had been settled before they got there. (See the county attorney's report quoted above.)

It is clear that the court is being used as a collection agency as well as a means of binding over felony cases to the District Court. In all cases the complaint seems to be sworn out by the county attorney, though he has an informal complaint which is signed by the holders of the check before he takes action.

In 1953 under the new county attorney, there were 280 more cases in the County Court. One hundred twenty-nine of these were on checks. In 1952 only 15 cases were collected through the court, but in 1953, 88 cases ended in collection, and in addition many of them resulted in payment of other outstanding checks. Thus it is clear that the increase in cases in the County Court is all out of proportion to the number of bad checks normally involved. The court became a collection agency in 1953 when fines, costs and mileage for the sheriff were added in most cases to the cost of collection.

District Court

Total cases in District Court in 1952 was 329, and in 1953, 421. (Note also the increase here.) Of these cases, there were 26 forgeries covering both years. In 1952 there were 14 no-account cases. Six defendants were sent to the Penitentiary, six were put on probation, one went to the Reformatory, and two cases were dismissed. (There is an overlapping of one case first put on probation and then sent to the Penitentiary.) In 1953 there were 38 other check cases. Eleven were for insufficient funds. Four defendants were put on probation, three cases were dismissed, and three defendants were fined. There were 26 no-account cases. Sixteen defendants went to the Penitentiary, one went to the mental hospital, and nine went on probation. (Most of these were repeaters.) In addition, two cases were dismissed. (There was also one here who appears both on probation and the Penitentiary list.)

On May 21, 1954, an audit of probation officer's records shows 96 adult cases on probation, including four women, and 39 juvenile cases on probation, including five girls. Forty of these cases were for bad checks and nine for forgeries.

Summary

Of 20,900 estimated bad checks written in a year in the county, only about 400 get into the hands of the legal authorities. The county attorney and sheriff have quit being free collection agencies, but the

County Court has definitely taken over the duty, so now the drawer pays court costs and mileage as well as a fine, whereas formerly the collection by letter was largely free. In addition to the highest rates of prison convictions per capita, the court also shows a heavy proportion of fines and probations.

The long history of hard-fisted law enforcement does not seem to affect the number of bad checks per capita.

The high percentage of bad checks in no way seems to be due to the Mexican or Indian population. Mexican and Indian names do not appear on the court records involving the writing of bad checks, but there are a few of them involved in forgery cases, probably not out of proportion to their numbers in the population.

INDEX

A

Accidents, location in traffic, 119

Acheson, Dean, 161

Administration: cigarette law, 204; law enforcement, 383; suggestions for change, 409; variation from plain meaning of law, 398

Administrative agencies, research to determine policy of, 157

Administrative experiments, 145

Administrative law, variation of statutes in, 217

Administrative procedures, 169

Administrative records, 184

Administrators, 172; condoning by, of law violation, 221; discretion of, 384

Age: of bad-check writers, 329; distribution of bad-check writers, 332

Agricultural Adjustment Act, 156

Agronomist, 167

Agronomy, 7

Air traffic, regulation of, 137

American Bar Association, 58

American Dental Association, relation to fluoridation laws, 85

American Law Institute, 21, 58; and Code of Criminal Procedure, 102; and Commercial Code, 102; and Federal Income Tax Statute, 103; lag behind science of, 99; and Model Code of Evidence, 102; and Model Penal Code, 103; and Restatement of the Common Law, 101; and Youth Correction Authority Act, 102

American Medical Association, 58

American Revolution, 33

American Society for Testing Materials, 213

American Water Works Association, 83

Anthropologists, 10, 36, 168

Anthropology, 41

Applied science: jurisprudence as, 67; Medicine as, 67

Arbitration, 169

Architects, 171

Aristotle, 11

Army enginers, 147

Art of government, 46

Astronomers, 6

Astronomy, 7

Atomic energy, 142, 165

Atomic Energy Commission, 141

Attorneys (see also Lawyers), private collection of checks by, 287

Automobile law (see Traffic)

B

Bacon, Roger, 8

Bacon, Sir Francis, 69

Bad-check laws, suggested amendments of, 405, 410

Bad checks: amount of, 302; average size of, 300; business losses due to, 263; city police and, 304; claims on, size of, 301; collection activities on, 351; collection affecting numbers of, 360; collection of, 287; cost of law enforcement on, 345; court activity and, 305; court procedure on, 312; criminal law on, 278; experimental design for study of, 224; failure of felony penalties for, 400; felonies, distribution of conviction for, 295; financial significance of, 260; habitual criminal and, 325; incidence of, felony, 353; incidence of, per capita, 260; jural laws affecting, 407; laws, interest involved in, 349; losses related to collection, 361; nature of, 256; Nebraska and Colorado compared, 354; Nebraska and New Hampshire compared, 356; Nebraska and Vermont compared, 356; number of, accepted by business, 267; number of businesses affected by, 265; number of, uncollected, 267; number of, written by defendants, 300; pre-trial procedures for, 293; ratio of, to total circulation, 261; relation of, to total business, 258; retail trade and, 268; sentences on, 302, size of, affected by law, 362; size of, given officials for collection, 363; size of, in court, 314; size of, 260, 362; size of, written by professionals, 337; social effect of law on, 286; social problems of, 226;